CAMBRIDGE TEXTS IN THE
HISTORY OF PHILOSOPHY

GEORGE BERKELEY
*Philosophical Writings*

# CAMBRIDGE TEXTS IN THE HISTORY OF PHILOSOPHY

*Series Editor*
## KARL AMERIKS
*Professor of Philosophy at the University of Notre Dame*

## DESMOND M. CLARKE
*Emeritus Professor of Philosophy at University College Cork*

The main objective of Cambridge Texts in the History of Philosophy is to expand the range, variety and quality of texts in the history of philosophy which are available in English. The series includes texts by familiar names (such as Descartes and Kant) and also by less well-known authors. Wherever possible, texts are published in complete and unabridged form, and translations are specially commissioned for the series. Each volume contains a critical introduction together with a guide to further reading and any necessary glossaries and textual apparatus. The volumes are designed for student use at undergraduate and postgraduate level and will be of interest not only to students of philosophy, but also to a wider audience of readers in the history of science, the history of theology and the history of ideas.

*For a list of titles published in the series, please see end of book.*

# GEORGE BERKELEY

# *Philosophical Writings*

EDITED BY

## DESMOND M. CLARKE

*Emeritus, University College, Cork*

# CAMBRIDGE
## UNIVERSITY PRESS

University Printing House, Cambridge CB2 8BS, United Kingdom

Cambridge University Press is part of the University of Cambridge.

It furthers the University's mission by disseminating knowledge in the pursuit of education, learning and research at the highest international levels of excellence.

www.cambridge.org
Information on this title: www.cambridge.org/9780521707626

© Desmond M. Clarke 2008

First published 2008
Reprinted 2012

A catalogue record for this publication is available from the British Library

Library of Congress Cataloguing in Publication data
Berkeley, George, 1685–1753.
Philosophical writings / George Berkeley;
edited by Desmond M. Clarke.
p. cm.
(Cambridge texts in the history of philosophy) Includes bibliographical references and index.
ISBN 978-0-521-88135-7 (alk. paper)
1. Philosophy. I. Clarke, Desmond M. II. Title. III. Series.
B1303 2009
192–dc22
2008040945

ISBN 978-0-521-88135-7 Hardback
ISBN 978-0-521-70762-6 Paperback

# Contents

# Acknowledgments

I have checked these texts against editions that were published during Berkeley's lifetime. I am grateful to the British Library and to the library of Trinity College, Dublin for providing access to original editions. Karl Ameriks, David Berman, Dolores Dooley, Connell Fanning, and David Tomkin read a draft of the Introduction, and provided helpful comments and corrections. Ernan McMullin suggested that I include some excerpts from *Siris*, as an example of Berkeley's explanatory strategies in later life; I was happy to accept his advice, and to borrow from his publications concerning scientific method in the seventeenth century. The library research for this edition was supported financially by a Research Award from the Arts Faculty, University College, Cork.

# Abbreviations

## Works by Berkeley

| | |
|---|---|
| *Works* (vol. and page) | *The Works of George Berkeley Bishop of Cloyne*, ed. A. A. Luce and T. E. Jessop (Edinburgh, 1948–57) |
| *ALC* | *Alciphron: or, the Minute Philosopher* |
| *D* | *Three Dialogues between Hylas and Philonous* |
| *DM* | *Essay on Motion* |
| *NTV* | *An Essay towards a New Theory of Vision* |
| *PHK* | *A Treatise Concerning the Principles of Human Knowledge (Part I)* |
| *S* | *Siris: A Chain of Philosophical Reflexions and Inquiries Concerning the Virtues of Tar-Water* |

## Works by other authors

| | |
|---|---|
| *Essay* | John Locke, *An Essay Concerning Human Understanding*, ed. Peter H. Nidditch (Oxford: Clarendon Press, 1975) |
| *Principles* | Isaac Newton, *Mathematical Principles of Natural Philosophy*, trans. A. Motte, rev. F. Cajori (1962) |
| *Oeuvres* | *Oeuvres de Descartes*, ed. C. Adam and P. Tannery, revised edn. (Paris: Vrin and CNRS, 1964–76) |

# Introduction

> 'There are men who say there are insensible extensions, there are others who say the wall is not white, the fire is not hot &c. We Irish men cannot attain to these truths.'[1]

George Berkeley may have been echoing Swift's irony when he linked his nationality, as an Irishman, with the limited scope of his ideas. However, his apparent diffidence about the metaphysical excursions of others did not prevent him from proposing, in his relative youth, a form of idealism that many of his contemporaries considered counter-intuitive and possibly irrational. The so-called immaterialism of the *Principles* and the *Dialogues* may still strike some readers today as bizarre, or even as symptomatic of psychiatric illness, because it appears to deny the reality of familiar objects of everyday experience. There is, therefore, a paradox at the core of what Berkeley presents as a 'revolt from metaphysical notions to the plain dictates of nature and common sense' (*D*, 172). On the one hand, he claims to defend common sense, not to speculate beyond the limits of sensory experience, and to provide a bulwark against scepticism. On the other hand, he seems to deny the reality of the familiar physical world, of houses, mountains and rivers, and even of the people with whom we discuss the merits of philosophical theories. The paradox

---

[1] *Notebooks*, # 392, *Works*, I, 47. Cf. # 398: 'I Publish not this so much for anything else as to know whether other men have the same ideas as we Irishmen' (ibid.). For references to the more familiar works of Berkeley I use the abbreviations listed on p. vii. In the case of *D*, I provide the page numbers to the edition in *Works* (which are also provided below in this text); and in the case of *ALC*, I provide the Dialogue number and the paragraph number.

is acutely illustrated by Berkeley's discussion of God. While apparently denying the reality of bodies or matter, he argued that God communicates with us in a 'visual language' (*ALC*, iv, 16) and that 'the existence of God is far more evidently perceived than the existence of men' (*PHK*, 147).

These apparently dissonant elements in Berkeley's thought make it difficult to construct a coherent interpretation of his philosophy. If such an interpretation is possible, it is likely to emerge from a close reading of the historical context in which he wrote and of the philosophical views that he rejected as inimical to his religious beliefs.

## Life

Berkeley was born on 12 March 1685 in or near Kilkenny, a relatively small city within the eastern region of Ireland that had been anglicized most successfully during the seventeenth century 'plantations'. He was educated at Kilkenny College, a residential school for Church of Ireland boys, and subsequently matriculated in 1700 at Dublin University, to which he remained attached until 1724. Following graduation in 1704, he was appointed a Fellow of Trinity College in 1707, and began work on his early philosophical publications. Some initial thoughts or reactions to what he read in other philosophers are recorded in notebooks that were published posthumously as the *Philosophical Commentaries*. These included often very brief, discrete notes and suggestions, some of which were subsequently expanded and defended in his published work. Berkeley published *A New Theory of Vision* and *The Principles of Human Knowledge (Part I)* in Dublin, in 1709 and 1710 respectively, but neither one attracted much critical attention. Although the *Principles* had been scheduled to appear in at least two parts, Berkeley seems to have deferred publication of Part II in favour of reworking his central philosophical theses in dialogue form, which he published in London, following his arrival there in 1713, as *Three Dialogues between Hylas and Philonous*.

Berkeley remained in London for a number of years, where he was acquainted with many prominent writers, including Steele, Addison, Pope, and Swift. While in London he contributed to the *Guardian*, which was edited by Steele, and undertook two extensive trips to continental Europe in 1713–14 and 1716–20. He met Malebranche in Paris in 1713 and, during the second of these journeys, the Académie royale des sciences (Paris) invited submissions for a competition on the topic of motion. Berkeley submitted, unsuccessfully, an essay in Latin entitled *De Motu*, and subsequently published it on his return to London. This is translated below as *An Essay on Motion*.

In 1722, at the age of thirty-three, Berkeley began to consider a missionary career among indigenous peoples in America, which he later described as a plan 'to spend the residue of my days in the Island of Bermuda' (*Works*, VIII, 127). The main objective was to found a college in Bermuda in which local students could be trained as Church of England priests to evangelize their own people or, in the words of the proposal, to convert 'the savage Americans to Christianity'. These ambitions were facilitated by Berkeley's appointment as Dean of Derry in 1724, which provided a salary without the inconvenience of moving to Derry, and by an unexpected inheritance from Swift's friend, Vanessa. He was further encouraged when the British Parliament provided a charter for his projected college, and a promise of £20,000 towards the cost of its establishment. Berkeley married Anne Forster in 1728 and set sail for the New World. He settled initially in Rhode Island, in the eastern United States, to await payment of the monies promised by Parliament in London. However, following a delay of three years, he received a clear indication that the monies would not be paid as promised, and he returned to London in 1731 without ever having reached Bermuda.

Berkeley published *Alciphron* in London soon after his return there, which confirms that he had been working while in Rhode Island on ways to accommodate, within philosophy, the theological beliefs that inspired his missionary enterprise. He remained in London until 1734, when he was appointed Bishop of Cloyne (in County Cork, Ireland); he was consecrated bishop in Dublin, before travelling south to his diocese. Apart from a few brief interludes, Berkeley remained in the village of Cloyne for the following seventeen years. During this period, he published various pamphlets which addressed some of the economic, political, and religious issues that were relevant to Ireland at the time. He also became familiar with the miseries caused by famine and the lack of medical care among the poor, and wrote *Siris* in response to those experiences. This book, about the therapeutic benefits of tar-water, appeared in six editions in 1744. In contrast with his early publications, this unusual work was widely read and sections were translated the following year into Dutch, French, and German. Berkeley left Cloyne in rather poor health, in August 1752, and moved to Oxford, where his son George was a student. He died in Oxford, on 14 January 1753.

Berkeley was one of a number of mostly Anglo-Irish thinkers and essayists in the early eighteenth century, whose members expressed their ambivalent relationship with the political, religious, and literary influences of England. These included William Molyneux (1656–98), whose work in optics significantly influenced Berkeley's theory of vision; John Toland (1670–1722), whose objections to traditional Christian accounts of mystery, in *Christianity not Mysterious* (1696), challenged Berkeley to discuss the meaning of theological language; and Francis Hutcheson (1694–1746), who was almost an exact contemporary of Berkeley, although he belonged to a dissenting Christian church, rather than the Church of Ireland, and later pursued an academic career in Scotland. This group also included the dramatist William Congreve (1670–1729), and Jonathan Swift (1667–1745), who had attended the same school and university as Berkeley and was described by him as 'one of the best natured and agreeable men in the world' (*Works*, VIII, 63). Thus the immediate context of Berkeley's writings was provided by literary, religious, and philosophical authors, who were based in or associated with Dublin, and who discussed publicly the issues that confronted a reformed church and colonial power that were attempting to consolidate their influence – both political and theological – on a reluctant native population that remained predominantly Roman Catholic. Some of those involved were also prominent theologians and bishops in the Church of Ireland, whose names have since lapsed into relative obscurity: William King (1650–1729), who was Archbishop of Dublin; Peter Browne (1666–1735), who was professor of theology and provost at Trinity College, and later Bishop of Cork and Ross; Robert Clayton (1695–1758), and Edward Synge (1659–1741), both of whom also became Church of Ireland bishops.

While these Anglo-Irish authors were the immediate inspiration for much of Berkeley's work, especially in philosophy of religion, the primary source of their common interests was the philosophy that had been developed in Britain and elsewhere in Europe in response to the scientific revolution of the seventeenth century. Robert Boyle and Isaac Newton were pre-eminent representatives of the new natural philosophy. Various well-known philosophers who had adapted their theories to accommodate the new sciences – such as Descartes, Malebranche, Hobbes,

Leibniz, and especially Locke – provided the philosophical background with which Berkeley and his Irish contemporaries engaged.

One understands Berkeley best, then, by considering both the local and international contexts in which he wrote. He was associated, in Ireland, with theologians and philosophers who constituted a community of Anglo-Irish, colonial, Protestant thinkers. These, in turn, were conscious of the wider intellectual context that had been dominated by the scientific revolution in the seventeenth century, and by philosophical and theological reactions to that revolution by authors from Descartes to Locke. George Berkeley was actively engaged with both contexts. Their combined influence meant that, as a committed member of the Church of Ireland in the eighteenth century, he attempted to defend his theological beliefs against what he understood as heterodox interpretations of Christianity. These included deism, socinianism, and atheism – terms which were used almost interchangeably to denote deviations from a strict understanding of Trinitarian Christianity – and, at the other extreme, Roman Catholicism, which was associated following the so-called 'Glorious Revolution' of 1688 with international enemies of the restored English monarchy. One of the central themes in Berkeley's philosophy, then, was the defence of his religious faith against both philosophical and theological critics.

## Empiricism and certainty

For empiricists such as Locke, experience was the exclusive source of human knowledge.

> Whence has it [the mind] all the materials of Reason and Knowledge? To this I answer, in one word, From *Experience*: In that, all our Knowledge is founded; and from that it ultimately derives it self.[2]

Locke's understanding of experience was wider in scope than might initially appear. It included both external and internal sources, so that the content of the mind (what Locke called 'ideas') may originate from either sensory observation or from reflection on the mind's own operations. Although Berkeley adopted a more restrictive version of Locke's theory (which is discussed below), their common reliance

[2] *Essay*, II, i. 2.

exclusively on experience highlighted an issue that had emerged in the early seventeenth century, about the extent to which our perceptions are accurate representations – almost like mental pictures – of the realities of which they are perceptions.

Galileo argued in 1623 that if we tickle someone's foot – for example, by using a feather – and then repeat the same action on the foot of a marble statue, the objective events are similar in both cases; there is a slow movement of a feather in glancing contact with two bodies (one living, the other made of marble). Although a living person (normally) experiences the sensation of tickling, it would be absurd to believe that there is some characteristic 'tickling quality' in the feather that matches the subjective feel or phenomenological quality of the sensation. Galileo concluded that the objective events are the same in the case of the statue and the foot of a living person, and that a tickling feeling results only in the latter because of the physiology and perceptual faculties of the perceiver. 'Anyone would make a serious error if he said that the hand, in addition to the properties of moving and touching, possessed another faculty of "tickling," as if tickling were a phenomenon that resides in the hand that tickled.'[3]

Once it is accepted that there is no resemblance, in the case of a tickling sensation, between the qualities of the objective events that trigger the sensation and the sensation that is experienced, there is reason to raise a more general question: have we any reason to believe that other sensations correspond qualitatively to the external stimuli that cause them? If not, our view of the objective world would be misguided if we projected onto external reality the qualities of the sensations that we experience. This concern was further motivated by Descartes who argued that words, as purely conventional signs, succeed in triggering appropriate thoughts in our minds without any resemblance between the words and the realities that we think about.[4] The word 'horse', for example, either when written or spoken, has none of the features of a horse, and yet it succeeds in triggering the thought of a horse in the minds of those who speak English. If conventional signs consistently evoke appropriate ideas without resembling them, why would it not be possible for sensations to

---

[3] Galileo Galilei, *The Assayer*, in *Discoveries and Opinions of Galileo*, ed. Stillman Drake (New York: Doubleday, 1957), p. 275.
[4] *The World*, in *Oeuvres*, XI, 4.

trigger appropriate ideas in the human mind without resembling the realities that we think about?

The solution adopted by Galileo, Descartes, and the subsequent tradition of natural philosophy was to distinguish between two kinds of properties in external (i.e. mind-independent) realities, which were called primary and secondary qualities. Both were thought to be genuine properties of the external world. Secondary qualities were defined as those qualities of things, whatever they turn out to be, which cause us to have sensations *without* resembling them. For example, it was assumed that there is something about red things that causes us to perceive them as red; it may be some property of the surface of objects by which they reflect or absorb rays of light, but certainly not a 'quality of redness' that resembles the sensation we experience. A similar account was assumed in the case of sound, taste, etc. – that is, for all sensory perceptions. In contrast, primary properties were defined as those features of bodies that correspond to our conceptions of them. For example, if we think of a piece of matter as a cube, we think it has six faces, that its sides are equal in length, and that these features of the object thus correspond to our conception of what a cube is like. There is no suggestion, of course, that our *ideas* have qualities which are similar to the qualities of the corresponding realities – for example, that our *idea* of a cube has a cubic shape (as if it were even meaningful to speak literally about the shape of an idea). The suggestion is, rather, that a primary quality has those features that are implied by the relevant idea of that quality.

Locke provided, in his *Essay*, what came to be recognized as the standard account of this distinction.[5] He defined primary qualities as those that are 'utterly inseparable from the body, in what estate soever it be'; and he defined secondary qualities as 'powers to produce various sensations in us by their primary qualities, i.e. by the bulk, figure, texture, and motion of their insensible parts'.[6] In contemporary theory,

---

[5] It is more accurate to say that Locke made a number of distinctions and combined them ambiguously under the same rubric. See Michael Jacovides, 'Locke's Distinctions between Primary and Secondary Qualities', in L. Newman, ed., *The Cambridge Companion to Locke's 'Essay Concerning Human Understanding'* (Cambridge: Cambridge University Press, 2007), 101–29. The only distinctions that are relevant here are (a) between qualities that do, and those that do not, 'resemble' the ideas of such qualities (where 'resemble' is understood appropriately); (b) between qualities that are, or are not, reducible to more elementary qualities.
[6] *Essay*, II, viii, 9.

that corresponds to a distinction between (a) the ultimate particles and/or properties that are used in a scientific explanation of physical phenomena, and (b) other properties of bodies that are reducible to (a).

Although Locke emphasized a number of times that *qualities* are in *objects* (or events), and *ideas* are in the *mind* of someone who thinks about or has sensations of qualities, he anticipated the possibility of confusion between qualities and ideas, even in his own book. Accordingly, he warned readers concerning 'ideas, if I speak of sometimes, as in the things themselves, I would be understood to mean those qualities in the objects which produce them in us'.[7] For Locke, then, it made no sense to talk about ideas as if they were extra-mental realities, independent of someone's thinking or sensing. Ideas are mental states of some kind; properties are features of extra-mental realities that somehow cause us to have ideas.

Galileo and Descartes drew a distinction between primary and secondary qualities for a number of reasons. One reason was to challenge the naïve assumption that the realities that cause our sensations have similar qualities to the sensations themselves. Without that assumption, there is no justification for projecting the latter onto the former, and natural philosophers must instead *speculate* about the kinds of objective qualities that are likely to cause our sensations. A second, related, reason was to reject the assumption that there are as many fundamental properties in matter as there are distinct types of human sensory perception. For example, an explanation of the almost indefinitely large number of colours that we can distinguish visually does not require the same number of corresponding properties in matter. Variations in the size of one parameter, namely the length of a wavelength, could explain variations in colour perception.

This fundamental insight, which was widely shared in the period immediately prior to Berkeley, may be summarized as follows:
1. we have no reason to believe that any sensory perception provides an accurate resemblance or picture of the external stimulus that causes it;
2. the only way to discover the natural phenomena that trigger our sensory perceptions is by hypothesis, and by other strategies that were developed in the scientific methods of the seventeenth century;

---

[7] *Essay*, II, viii, 8.

3. the results of these speculative excursions can never realize the degree of certainty that was traditionally associated with intuition and demonstration.

In a word, we can make progress in understanding nature only by taking epistemological risks.

Berkeley's philosophy represents a rejection of this interpretation of sensations, which developed within natural philosophy. He limited the foundations of knowledge to the data of immediate experience, rejected the hypothetical methods of science, and required of all knowledge-claims a degree of certainty that was impossible to achieve outside of logic and mathematics. He also accused of scepticism those who speculated about natural phenomena in a manner that implied uncertainty. This comprehensive rejection of the new sciences was worked out in several ways, one of which was by denying the distinction between primary and secondary qualities.

Berkeley's argument against the validity of this distinction in the First Dialogue systematically confuses the reader by failing to observe Locke's warning about the difference between qualities and ideas. Hylas attempts to explain the distinction, but Berkeley makes him misdescribe secondary qualities as 'only so many sensations or ideas existing nowhere but in the mind' (*D*, 188). This contrived concession collapses Locke's distinction between (a) sensations and (b) the powers or qualities in bodies that cause those sensations in us, and it fails to acknowledge that terms such as 'colour' or 'sound' may refer to either one. It thus invites the reader to believe that, at least in the case of secondary qualities, the relevant *quality* is nothing more than the perceptual experience of seeing something coloured or hearing some sound. It was impossible to argue against Boyle's or Locke's distinction in that way, because the argument was based on a misunderstanding. Since Berkeley's analysis fails in respect of secondary qualities, *a fortiori* it fails in the case of primary qualities.

Locke had surprisingly combined his thesis about experience as the exclusive source of knowledge with a traditional demand that beliefs may be deemed knowledge only if they realize the degree of certainty achieved by intuition or demonstration. 'These two, (*viz.*) Intuition and Demonstration, are the degrees of our Knowledge; whatever comes short of one of these, with what assurance soever embraced, is but Faith, or Opinion, but not Knowledge, at least in all general

Truths.'[8] Thus while (for example) mathematics and morality both satisfied this criterion for Locke – he thought they were immune from empirical disconfirmation because they describe only an ideal or constructed world and do not claim to correspond to some independent reality – the speculative hypotheses of natural philosophers fall far short of such certainty. They were therefore excluded from the scope of knowledge by the restrictive limits of Locke's stipulative definition.

> And therefore I am apt to doubt that, how far soever humane Industry may advance useful and *experimental* Philosophy *in physical Things*, *scientifical* will still be out of our reach; because we want perfect and adequate *Ideas* of those very Bodies, which are nearest to us, and most under our Command.
> ... we are under an absolute ignorance. ...
> But as to a perfect *Science* of natural Bodies ... we are, I think, so far from being capable of any such thing, that I conclude it lost labour to seek after it.[9]

Berkeley seems to have endorsed, in his early works, the same demand for certainty in any belief that counts as genuine knowledge. He had Philonous say on his behalf, in the *Dialogues*: 'I assure you, Hylas, I do not pretend to frame any hypothesis at all. I am of a vulgar cast, simple enough to believe my senses, and leave things as I find them' (*D*, 229). He thought it was a 'jest for a philosopher to question the existence of sensible things ... or to pretend our knowledge in this point falls short of intuition and demonstration' (*D*, 230), thereby implicitly endorsing Locke. The combined effect of both claims – (i) of limiting knowledge-claims to what is given in experience, and (ii) limiting the scope of knowledge to what is established by intuition or demonstration – was to devalue precisely the novel methods that began to emerge in the new sciences, methods that inevitably involved speculating about the hidden causes of observable natural phenomena.

Rather than fear that such speculations would lead to scepticism, there was another alternative available, *viz.* to challenge the traditional definition of knowledge, and to accept that explanations of natural phenomena are unavoidably hypothetical. That solution was adopted by Christiaan Huygens, in the same year (1690) in which Locke's *Essay*

---

[8] *Essay*, IV, ii, 14. Cf. *Essay*, IV, iii, 14: 'Probability, amounts not to Certainty; without which, there can be no true Knowledge.'
[9] *Essay*, IV, iii, 26, 27, 29.

appeared. In the Preface to his *Treatise on Light*, Huygens described the kind of knowledge that could be realized in natural philosophy:

> There will be seen in it demonstrations of those kinds which do not produce as great a certitude as those of Geometry, and which even differ much therefrom, since whereas the geometers prove their propositions by fixed and incontestable principles, here the principles are verified by the conclusions to be drawn from them; the nature of these things not allowing of this being done otherwise. It is always possible to attain thereby to a degree of probability which very often is scarcely less than complete proof. To wit, when things which have been demonstrated by the principles that have been assumed correspond perfectly to the phenomena which experiment has brought under observation; especially when there are a great number of them, and further, principally, when one can imagine and foresee new phenomena which ought to follow from the hypotheses which one employs, and when one finds that therein the fact corresponds to our prevision.[10]

There were evident dangers for natural philosophers if they accepted as true mere speculations that were not confirmed by experiment or observation. However, there was even greater danger to the development of modern science in a refusal to speculate about the hidden causes of the phenomena we observe. Berkeley chose the second option, by imposing on natural philosophy a traditional definition of knowledge that it could satisfy only at the cost of obstructing its most creative developments.

## Matter and bodies

Berkeley's critique of matter may be read narrowly as a technical discussion among philosophers of how best to define matter or, more specifically, as a critical analysis of Locke's concept of material substance. This interpretation is suggested by Philonous in the *Dialogues*: 'that there is no such thing as what philosophers call "material substance", I am seriously persuaded' (*D*, 172).[11] Alternatively, it may be seen as a radical idealism that denies the reality of physical bodies, which are understood as external things that exist independently of any thought or idea of

---

[10] C. Huygens, *Treatise on Light*, trans. S. P. Thompson (New York: Dover, 1912), vi–vii.

[11] Cf. *PHK*, 35: 'The only thing whose existence we deny is that which philosophers call matter or corporeal substance.'

them. A third option combines both interpretations; Berkeley may have offered apparently plausible arguments for the former, while presenting the conclusions as supportive of the latter.

Locke famously argued that our *idea* of a particular material thing or body is a *complex idea* composed of specific ideas of the various qualities of the body in question. For example, in the case of a silver coin, we have ideas of its shape, size, colour, hardness, its chemical reactions with various acids, etc. Our idea of a silver coin is a combination of these ideas; we have no other idea of some underlying reality that is independent of all these qualities, because (according to Locke) it would be impossible to acquire such an idea from sensory experience. A similar analysis applies to our ideas of thinking, willing, etc., which are known by reflection. The latter comprise the complex idea of a human mind, and we have no independent notion of (what Locke assumes is) an immaterial substance – of something that is distinct from the activities of thinking, etc. Since both kinds of substance, material and immaterial, are equally known (as complex ideas of qualities) or unknown (as independent *substrata*), Locke argued:

> From our not having any notion of the *Substance* of Spirit, we can no more conclude its non-Existence, than we can, for the same reason, deny the Existence of Body; It being as rational to affirm, there is no Body, because we have no clear and distinct *Idea* of the *Substance* of Matter; as to say, there is no Spirit, because we have no clear and distinct *Idea* of the *Substance* of a Spirit.[12]

Despite this apparent parity, Locke left his readers with ambivalent cues about substances. He needed the concept of a spiritual substance to talk about God, whose existence he claimed was known by demonstration. In contrast, he found no similar use for the concept of a material substance because our knowledge of material substances was limited to ideas of their properties. He could thus make the theological doctrine of transubstantiation appear silly, because it invited people to believe that, underlying all the qualities that are perceived in bread or wine, there is

---

[12] *Essay*, II, xxiii, 5. Newton argued for a similar conclusion in the *Principles* (2nd edn. 1713), General Scholium (II, 546): 'what the real substance of anything is we know not. In bodies, we see only their figures and colours ... much less, then, have we any idea of the substance of God. We know him only by his most wise and excellent contrivances of things, and final causes.'

some unobservable substance that changes without a corresponding change in the observable qualities.

> Take an intelligent *Romanist* ... How is he prepared easily to swallow, not only against all Probability, but even the clear Evidence of his Senses, the Doctrine of *Transubstantiation*. This Principle has such an influence on his Mind that he will believe that to be Flesh, which he sees to be Bread.[13]

Berkeley was as critical as Locke of the doctrine of transubstantiation (*ALC*, VII, 15; *PHK*, 124), and of the concept of an underlying substance on which it relied. However, as will be seen below, he retained the concept of an immaterial substance to describe human minds and God. His critical comments, therefore, were exclusively focused on the concept of a 'material substance'.

For many natural philosophers, from Descartes to Newton, the concept of matter did not necessarily imply motion, and matter was defined as passive with respect both to motion and rest. If a piece of matter moves, it remains in motion unless impeded by something else; and if it is not in motion, it remains in that condition unless some external agent intervenes to move it. Berkeley exploited this analysis by including passivity as a defining feature of material substances. He also accepted Locke's argument that, when we perceive a body, we perceive its observable qualities and we have no experience of some distinct underlying reality called a substance. Since for Berkeley it was 'a sufficient reason not to believe the existence of anything, if I see no reason for believing it' (*D*, 218), he shifted the burden of defending material substances onto those who wished to introduce them. According to Berkeley's interpretation, proponents of material substance talked about a completely passive reality, 'an unthinking, unperceiving, inactive substance'; more seriously, substances were realities of which they had no distinct ideas, 'unknown quiddities ... or *substratums*' (*D*, 233, 256).

If Berkeley had merely rejected an abstruse metaphysical account of material substance, it would hardly have caused his readers, either in the eighteenth century or now, to believe that he denied the reality of familiar physical bodies. However, it was also part of Locke's account of ideas that physical bodies, and their qualities, cause us to have ideas 'manifestly *by*

---

[13] *Essay*, IV, xx, 10.

*impulse*, the only way which we can conceive Bodies operate in'.[14] Even Locke had to admit that he had not *explained* how the impact of a physical body on an eye or ear could cause an idea to arise in a human mind. Berkeley identified the gaps in this account as a reason for rejecting it, and offered instead what he proposed as a more plausible explanation of how ideas arise in our minds. This choice, between bodies as causes of our ideas and some alternative cause, presupposed a number of independent theses for which Berkeley needed other arguments.

One of those theses, widely shared at the time, was that ideas or thoughts are mental events, and that mental events are immaterial. If someone wished to hold that immaterial events are caused by the physical impact of bodies on our sense organs, they could claim, as Descartes had done, that we are certain that this occurs but are unable to explain it. However, Berkeley noticed that the Cartesians and, in fact, nearly all those whose philosophy he read, had also assumed that God is in some sense the ultimate or primary cause of everything that happens in the universe, and that other so-called secondary causes, such as bodies in motion, derive their limited efficacy from God. This raised a question about the possible redundancy of secondary causes.

Berkeley's reflections on this issue were influenced by the French Cartesian, Nicolas Malebranche, who argued that God is the only genuine efficient cause of everything that occurs in the universe. According to Malebranche, what appear to be secondary causes, such as the impact of one moving body on another, are merely the occasions on which God exercises his omnipotent efficient causality. These considerations led Berkeley to reduce the options available to two rival accounts of what happens when we passively receive ideas, apparently from some external source: (i) God directly causes ideas to arise in our minds; or (ii) God causes some physical phenomenon to cause an idea in our minds. There were a number of reasons for rejecting the latter. One was that it presumes a causal link that is not explained, *viz.* between the natural phenomenon (which is physical) and our minds (which are immaterial). Secondly, it introduces a redundant cause because, given God's involvement in both accounts, it is unnecessary to introduce any further cause as if God could not achieve the desired result alone. When combined with the alleged passivity of material substances, Berkeley could argue that the

---

[14] *Essay*, II, viii, 11.

accepted account of how ideas arise in the mind suffers from three serious
defects. It postulates unobserved causes that, by definition, are inactive;
it compromises the radical distinction between mind and matter; and it
describes God's agency as if it required assistance from natural phenomena. It would be a simpler and more coherent theory to assume that God
directly causes us to have ideas, without any intermediary. However, this
argument ignores another alternative: that physical phenomena are the
causes of ideas, which in turn are understood as events in human bodies
rather than as 'immaterial' events in the mind. Berkeley anticipated that
this view could be used to support atheism, because it undermines the
notion of an immaterial mind on which the notion of God depends. That
alone was a sufficient reason for him to avoid it.

Berkeley concludes his discussion of matter with denials of the reality
of physical bodies (as this word is normally understood). This might
appear to have the same status as the claim that there were no tigers in
Dublin in 1713. However, it is completely different from the latter, and
therefore requires a different kind of evidence. The claim about tigers
presupposes the reality of physical objects in an extra-mental world, and
simply denies that those objects include tigers. In contrast, Berkeley's
claim was not made within the framework of physical objects; it was a
claim about that whole framework, to the effect that it is redundant or
otherwise dispensable. For that reason, it seems to result from his theory
of perception and ideas (which is discussed below) rather than from
anything he says about material substance, or from the associated claim
that all our language about the world, including the biblical account of
creation, can be translated into language about perceptions.

It remains an open question, then, whether the Bishop of Cloyne
travelled to Oxford while denying the reality of the boat in which he
sailed, or whether he merely claimed that his travel experiences could be
described adequately in the language of phenomenalism.

## Explanation

When Berkeley began to reflect on what counts as an explanation of
natural phenomena, there were at least two models available, one deeply
traditional and the other relatively novel. They differed in the relative
uncertainty of the explanations that each one tolerated, and in the extent
to which they required all claims to be based directly or indirectly on

experience. Berkeley's stand on these two issues left him little choice between the two models. He was supported in this by his reading of Newton, who was widely acknowledged at the time as the pre-eminent scientist of the age.

Natural philosophers of the seventeenth century had begun to notice many patterns in natural phenomena which, when described, were called laws of nature. For example, the correlation between pressure, volume, and absolute temperature that is expressed in Boyle's Law is based on observation, and it describes a general pattern that applies (within limits) to all gases. In one sense, therefore, one can 'explain' changes in the volume or temperature of a given gas by showing how it conforms to the general rule expressed by Boyle's Law. Since the law in question is known by induction and based on numerous observations, there is little doubt about the certainty or experiential basis of the resulting explanation.[15]

Such an explanation still leaves unanswered the question: why do gases expand when heated? The corpuscularians of the seventeenth century initiated a revolutionary approach in response to that question. They speculated that observable bodies are composed of unobservable parts or corpuscles, and that the properties and interactions of those underlying parts produce the effects that we observe. One corollary of this, of course, is that we cannot discover anything about such unobservable corpuscles by direct observation or experiment. We are forced to speculate about them, to construct hypotheses, and then to devise strategies by which the hypotheses may be confirmed indirectly. However, no confirmatory argument can ever cure hypotheses completely of their initial uncertainty. Therefore, in this second sense, we can 'explain' natural phenomena only at the expense of tolerating hypotheses that are more or less confirmed by their success in explaining the phenomena. There is an unavoidable appearance of circularity here, as Descartes famously acknowledged in his *Discourse on Method*.[16]

When Newton published the *Mathematical Principles of Natural Philosophy* in 1687, he relied very much on the concept of gravitational attraction between bodies at a distance, and on the forces inherent in moving bodies. He presented his results as if he had merely observed

---

[15] This understanding of scientific explanation became almost canonical in philosophy of science in the twentieth century, and was known as deductive-nomological explanation.

[16] Discourse VI, in *Oeuvres*, VI, 76.

natural phenomena and had generalized, by induction, the results of his observations. In that way, he claimed, he stayed within the limits of the first model of explanation, and avoided the speculative and uncertain hypotheses that characterize the second model. Despite his claims, however, many of his early readers were convinced that gravity was either a speculative, hidden cause of observable effects or, even worse, an occult quality disguised as an observed property. In response to critics, Newton added a famous response in the second edition of the *Principles* (1713):

> But hitherto I have not been able to deduce the cause of these properties of gravity from phenomena and I feign no hypotheses; for whatever is not deduced from the phenomena is to be called an *hypothesis*; and hypotheses, whether metaphysical or physical, whether of occult qualities or mechanical, have no place in experimental philosophy. In this philosophy propositions are deduced from the phenomena and rendered general by induction.[17]

Newton was evidently claiming that the laws of motion on which his whole physics depended were based on observation and made general by induction, just like Boyle's Law. He could then 'explain' a wide range of natural phenomena that fell within the scope of the *Principles* by applying the laws of motion to specific phenomena. Despite the implausibility of Newton's interpretation of what he was actually doing in the *Principles*, it provided Berkeley with a launching pad for his own defence of instrumentalism.

Berkeley's empiricism made it impossible for him to accept the concept of force or gravity as referring to something that is both real and distinct from observable properties. He argued in the *Essay on Motion*:

> This word ['force'] is used ... as if it signified a quality that is known and is distinct from motion, shape, and every other sensible thing and from every affection of living things. In fact, anyone who examines the matter more closely will find that it is nothing other than an occult quality. (*DM*, 5)

Berkeley also accepted that the science of mechanics had made great progress, especially following Newton, even though the principal contributors to the science could not agree on what they meant by 'force'. He thought he could accommodate both the development of mechanics and

---

[17] Newton, *Principles*, General Scholium, II, 547.

the unresolved nature of forces in dynamics by endorsing Newton's account of the methodology used in the *Principles*. Accordingly, he offered the following analysis of mechanical explanation:

> Accordingly, something can be said to be explained mechanically when it is reduced to such very simple and universal principles and is shown by careful reasoning to be consistent with and related to them. For, once the laws of nature have been discovered, it is the philosopher's task to show how any phenomenon necessarily follows by the consistent observance of those laws, that is, from those principles. That is what is meant by explaining and solving a phenomenon and assigning its cause, that is, the reason why it occurs. (*DM*, 37)

This kind of instrumentalism was consistent with Berkeley's conceptual empiricism, according to which explanatory concepts are acceptable in a theory only if they can be acquired by sensory experience. It was also compatible with his unwillingness to accept hypotheses, because of the uncertainty that they entailed. Finally, this interpretation of scientific explanation had some initial plausibility when applied to Newtonian mechanics, and it had the obvious advantage of having been endorsed by Newton himself.

However, instrumentalism was much less plausible when applied to other scientific fields. Even in Berkeley's day, chemists understood their task as an attempt to identify combinations of particles, which exist below the threshold of observability and whose interactions at a micro-level explain the chemical interactions that are observable. Likewise in medicine, as illustrated in *Siris*, the alleged therapeutic effects of tar-water are explained by hypothesizing interactions between the chemical ingredients of tar-water and the unobservable bodily fluids with which they interact. It was clear that the Boyle's Law model of explanation did not apply to many of the explanatory investigations that were being undertaken by Berkeley's contemporaries. To defend instrumentalism, he had to reject such developments as not being genuinely scientific, or reinterpret them as if they conformed to his instrumentalist limitations.

In a wider context, however, the kind of conceptual empiricism imposed on mechanics and, by extension, on all scientific explanations contrasted markedly with Berkeley's willingness to introduce God as the most plausible explanation of the consistency and apparent independence of our sensory experiences.

# God

Berkeley's philosophy should not be read as a purely intellectual exercise that was unrelated to his religious faith and the doctrinal orthodoxy that made possible his appointment as a Church of Ireland bishop. He had signalled, from the beginning of his writing career, that one of his objectives was to inquire into 'the chief causes ... of atheism and irreligion' (*PHK*, title), and 'to demonstrate ... the immediate providence of a deity' (*D*, title). He also linked these objectives with a critique of the new sciences, and with philosophical implications of those sciences which he thought were inimical to Christian belief. In addressing the assumed tension between religious faith and scientific explanation, Berkeley followed a tradition that was already well established. It involved reducing scientific theories to calculating instruments, in which theoretical terms have no ontological reference, and defending a special role for religious theories as veridical accounts of reality[18] – in other words, instrumentalism for scientific theories and realism for theological theories.

Berkeley's radical empiricism made it particularly difficult to provide a satisfactory theory of the meaning of religious language. His default account of meaningful terms, which was borrowed from Locke, was that a word is meaningful if and only if it corresponds to a specific idea and that ideas, in turn, denote corresponding realities. Without ideas that are sufficiently determinate, words would be meaningless. Thus, in order to speak meaningfully about God, one must have an idea of God, and to believe in the Trinity, one must have ideas of three persons in one nature. John Toland relied on that theory to argue that it is impossible to believe in religious mysteries because, by definition, it is impossible to have an idea of something that is genuinely mysterious. Toland's critique attracted a predictable outcry from Church of Ireland theologians; however, even those theologians were not united in their defence of Christianity. Archbishop William King and Bishop Peter Browne both

---

[18] See, for example, Pierre Duhem, *To Save the Phenomena: An Essay on the Idea of Physical Theory from Plato to Galileo*, trans. E. Doland and C. Maschler (Chicago: University of Chicago Press, 1969).

relied on analogy to bridge the gap between the concepts that apply literally to human experience and those that apply to an incomprehensible God. For example, Browne argued, against the *Alciphron*: 'That of the real *Intrinsic* Properties and Perfections of God we cannot have the least *Direct* and *Immediate* Conception or Idea: And can therefore have no other way of conceiving them but by Resemblance or Similitude with those that are human.'[19]

Berkeley rejected both Toland's critique of mysteries and Browne's recourse to analogy. He wished to defend a literal application of some concepts to God – concepts that are known initially in their natural or human application – and to defend the meaningfulness of religious language about mysteries, such as the Trinity or the Incarnation, by recourse to an emotive theory of language. The first part of this strategy, following Descartes, claimed that we can conceive of God indirectly by amending our conception of our own minds. However, in contrast with Descartes and Locke, Berkeley did not accept that we have an idea of our own mind, because he defined ideas as 'passive' and the mind as 'active'. He claimed instead that we have a 'notion' of our minds insofar as we have an experience, by reflection, of what the activity of thinking is like. With this adjustment of terminology, he could argue that we have a notion of God that is derived from our notion of ourselves as active thinking beings. 'For all the notion I have of God is obtained by reflecting on my own soul, heightening its powers, and removing its imperfections' (*D*, 231). Without a notion that could be applied literally to God, Berkeley feared that we could not prove God's existence and thereby establish a basis for belief in revealed truths.

However, in addition to this amended Lockean view that each meaningful term is linked with a specific idea or notion, Berkeley also developed in *Alciphron* another interpretation of religious language that had been intimated in his earlier writing. According to this account, one can use religious language meaningfully without having ideas or notions that correspond to the words used, if one's purpose is to evoke appropriate

---

[19] *Things Divine and Supernatural Conceived by Analogy with Things Natural and Human* (London, 1733), 405. King had argued similarly in *Divine Predestination and Fore-Knowledge* (Dublin, 1709), section xiii: 'This analogical knowledge of God's nature and attributes is all we are capable of at present, and we must either be contented to know him thus, or sit down with an intire ignorance and neglect of God.'

responses or actions in listeners – for example, that they accept misfortune, or act morally in the hope of future reward or punishment.

> Thus much ... may be said of all signs: that they do not always
> suggest ideas signified to the mind; ... that they have other uses
> besides barely standing for and exhibiting ideas, such as raising
> proper emotions, producing certain dispositions or habits of mind,
> and directing our actions in pursuit of that happiness, which is the
> ultimate end and design, the primary spring and motive that sets
> rational agents at work. (*ALC*, VII, 14)[20]

This supplement to a purely referring theory of terms was intended to provide Berkeley with a buffer against Toland's objections, by denying that all the words used in Christianity must satisfy a Lockean account of meaning. However, this emotive theory presupposes that a literal interpretation of some God-talk is both necessary and available. Otherwise, it is not clear why Christians should fear God, if there is no reality corresponding to the term 'God', nor why they should modify their behaviour in anticipation of future reward or punishment if there is literally no afterlife in which these threats or promises are fulfilled.

In contrast with Berkeley, King and Browne had defended a traditional position to the effect that 'the nature of God considered in it self is ... agreed by all hands to be incomprehensible by human understanding',[21] and that any meaningful talk about God is possible only by using human concepts analogically. To hold otherwise, they thought, implied reducing God to the limitations of our understanding or, equally unacceptably, conceding the conclusions of Toland's rationalism. Berkeley's starting point was the relatively feeble 'notion' of the human mind that was derived from, and identical with, our awareness of the activity of thinking or perceiving. From this minimalist starting point, and without relying on metaphors or analogy, he claimed to acquire an idea of God that could be applied literally to God. It was not surprising that his critics within the Church of Ireland episcopate thought he had conceded the main point of Toland's critique, a concession summarized by Peter Browne as follows: that, for Berkeley, 'believing a God ... may be no more than Faith in a Monosyllable'.[22]

---

[20] Berkeley appealed to this use of language in *PHK*, Introduction, §20.
[21] *Divine Predestination and Fore-Knowledge*, section III.
[22] *Things Divine and Supernatural*, 539.

However, even if a secure reference to God could be secured in a charitable reading of Berkeley's theory of language, the question would re-emerge about his dissimilar treatment of the theoretical terms used in scientific explanations. It seems arbitrary to concede the ontological reference of metaphysical terms such as 'God' while denying a realist interpretation to scientific terms such as 'force'. In each case, the terms in question fail to describe an immediate experience; they are introduced, both by analogy with realities that are experienced and by reasoning, because the realities to which they refer, if they existed, would provide a plausible explanation of natural phenomena. The source of the problem seems to have been Berkeley's empiricism, which prevented him from developing a plausible account of theoretical terms in science and from accepting an analogical account of talk about God. Browne summarized the issue in the comment that Berkeley 'every where confounds the general word *Intelligible*, with *Perceptible* which is of a more particular signification'.[23] The extent to which this objection is valid is best seen from Berkeley's theory of ideas.

## Ideas

By the early decades of the eighteenth century, the term 'idea' had lost many of its Platonic connotations. With the exception of Malebranche, who attempted to recover elements of the Platonic account by describing ideas as '*êtres représentatives*' – as if they were free-standing entities that represent the realities of which they are ideas – the emerging consensus was to understand ideas as acts of thought or perception that occur in the mind of a thinker or perceiver.[24] This view was endorsed by Locke, who rejected the possibility that any idea could exist apart from the activity of a mind that is involved in perceiving or thinking. It therefore made no sense, for Locke, to say that ideas could be innate, that they could be stored in a mind which is not actually thinking, or even that they could be present unconsciously in the mind. According to the *Essay*, to have an idea, and to be in the process of perceiving or thinking about something, consciously, are identical.

---

[23] *Things Divine and Supernatural*, 422.

[24] One defence of this position, as a Cartesian response to Malebranche, is found in Antoine Arnauld, *On True and False Ideas*, trans. S. Gaukroger (Manchester: Manchester University Press, 1990).

It is difficult to see how this account was transformed so radically into Berkeley's theory of ideas. Even a sympathetic reader may feel that the subtlety and relative brevity of the arguments deployed disguise the implausibility of the conclusions. Standard locutions about thinking or perceiving suggest a distinction between a subject, in whom these activities are occurring, and the content of their thought or the object of their perceptual experience. Berkeley asked readers to apply the term 'idea' to the content or object of a perceptual act. He summarized this suggestion in the famous epigram, that, in the case of an idea, its '*esse* is *percipi*', that is, the reality of an idea is its being perceived. A very significant further linguistic adjustment was required in order to describe ideas as 'sensible things' (*D*, 174). Once ideas were identified with sensible things, however, nothing more was required to transform sensible things into ideas and to claim that the words normally used in English to refer to external physical objects, such as 'cherry' or 'carriage', should be reinterpreted as referring to our ideas of such objects. The reaction of Hylas in the *Dialogues* acknowledges the magnitude of the leap involved: how does one get from talking about perception to the conclusion that we perceive only ideas?

One subsidiary argument, a lemma against scepticism, is Berkeley's claim that we 'immediately' perceive only our own ideas, and that those who try to infer some correlation between ideas and extra-mental realities (a correlation that, in principle, is inaccessible to our experience) have already embarked on the road to scepticism. Rather than explore that path, he radicalized his empiricist starting-point by a double limitation: we perceive only our own ideas, and the term 'ideas' applies only to what is perceived through the senses (rather than what originates from any other source).

Without an extensive survey of the literature on this topic, Berkeley may be read as alternating between the two competing attitudes to natural philosophy that were mentioned above. On one reading, he was trying simply to *describe* accurately perceptual experiences and the patterns in which they occur, rather than to *explain* them in any manner that would involve theories or hypotheses. On the second reading, he was unwittingly engaged in the kind of explanatory enterprise that he officially rejected by postulating intermediaries in the relationship between active minds and the objects of their perceptions.

If Berkeley was involved in a purely descriptive project, he could choose the language in which to present his results. The alacrity with which he identified 'objects of perception' and 'ideas' was not tempered by the obvious objection, acknowledged in the *Dialogues*, that 'common custom is the standard of propriety in language' (*D*, 216). The word 'idea' was certainly not used in Berkeley's time, no more than it is today, to refer to the objects of perception. He even concedes this point in the *Dialogues*: 'In common talk, the objects of our senses are not termed "ideas" but "things"' (*D*, 251). Berkeley evaded this objection by an implicit appeal to Bacon, who recommended that we should 'think with the learned, and speak with the vulgar' (*PHK*, 51). Accordingly, he invited readers to speak like their ordinary-language contemporaries, about eating cherries and hearing carriages passing on the cobbled streets of Dublin. But he also argued that, when using those phrases in a philosophical discussion, they should mean nothing more than that they had perceptions of cherries – of their colour, taste, and smell – and that they had aural or visual perceptions of horse-drawn carriages. This would amount, in effect, to understanding Berkeley as speaking non-standardly about perceptions, but still in Hiberno-English – a kind of Swiftian subversion of the language of his contemporaries. However, if ordinary language is rejected as authoritative for describing perceptions, one's philosophy of perception cannot subsequently be presented as a descriptive metaphysics, as uncovering the metaphysical presuppositions of that language. Besides, the veracity or plausibility of the novel descriptions would still be tested by the experiences of each perceiver, who would apply to Berkeley the criterion that he often invoked: 'Everyone is himself the best judge of what he perceives, and what not' (*NTV*, 12). If we combine this principle with the counsel that we focus not on language but on the realities involved (*NTV*, 120; *PHK*, Introd. 21), Berkeley seems open to the objection that he simply misdescribes our experiences.

The alternative is that Berkeley was not describing perceptual experiences, but speculating about what we must assume about the mechanisms by which such experiences occur if we are to explain the relevant facts. The latter would include misperceptions, and the apparent similarity – from the perspective of the perceiver – of veridical and illusory perceptual experiences. Macbeth's experience of seeing a dagger seemed indistinguishable to him, at the time, from other occasions on which there were real daggers in his perceptual field. On this reading, Berkeley may be saying that, whenever he perceives a cherry as red, his perceptual experience presupposes the presence of a 'red sense content'.[25] Having a sensation, in the sense of being affected by a red sense content, is not a conceptual fact, and the 'idea' involved is of the same type as the various brain-states that Descartes assumed, as intermediaries, in perceptual experiences.[26] Being affected by an idea (understood as a 'sense-content') cannot be transformed into a cognitive state without introducing, as Kant later argued, a framework of concepts with which to express such claims. Berkeley does not explain how sensory states can produce a conceptual framework; for example, he does not explain how our experience of thinking gets described as an *immaterial* activity. *A fortiori*, he does not explain why a conceptual framework must be limited to describing the sensory states on which his empiricism is based. He might have agreed that our concepts are acquired only by learning a language, in a context that assumes the existence of physical objects in space and time. Once acquired in this way, however, the language cannot be translated, without remainder, into a language that describes only actual and possible sense-contents.

The transition from perceiving cherries to 'immediately perceiving' the ideas of cherries, and then to the reduction of cherries to complexes of mind-dependent ideas, is much more complex than this brief summary suggests. While it seemed to support Berkeley's theological enterprise in the short term, he found another way of achieving the same objective in his final work, in which echoes of his earlier immaterialism reappear without occupying a central role.

## Siris and the material world

In his final work, *Siris*, Berkeley returned to the language of physical objects that he had used in his first book, *A New Theory of Vision*, in

---

[25] Berkeley writes sometimes as if there are internal bodily states that mediate visual perceptions. See for example, *NTV*, 88: 'no one [is] ignorant that the pictures of external objects are painted on the retina or fund of the eye'; and *NTV*, 114: 'Let us suppose pictures in the fund of the eye to be the immediate objects of the sight.' However, since no one perceives these retinal paintings in the process of perceiving external objects, they seem open to the objection made against a similar theoretical entity in *NTV*, 90: 'for the mind to judge of the situation of objects by those things without perceiving them, or to perceive them without knowing it, is equally beyond my comprehension'.

[26] I borrow here from the detailed analysis of various kinds of phenomenalism in Wilfrid Sellars, *Science, Perception, and Reality* (London: Routledge & Kegan Paul, 1963), 105–60. Descartes' use of the term 'idea' in reference to mere brain-states is found in the *Traité de l'Homme, Oeuvres*, XI, 177.

which he discussed the transmission and refraction of light through real eyes rather than ideas or perceptions of such events. The extensive discussion of tar-water presupposed the interaction of mind and body, so that anything that would benefit the latter would also assist the former: 'the operations of the mind so far depend on the right tone or good condition of its instrument, that anything which greatly contributes to preserve or recover the health of the body is well worth the attention of the mind' (*S*, Introduction). Once the human body was readmitted as a significant factor in our mental health, Berkeley had to speculate about the mechanisms by which tar-water could improve the body's condition. This led him into at least speaking the language of his corpuscularian contemporaries, without officially abandoning the instrumentalism and phenomenalism of the *Principles* and the *Dialogues*.

Berkeley speculated about the micro-features of the human body, about the nerves as the 'inner garment' of the soul and the 'instruments of sensation' (*S*, 86, 102), about the 'latent causes' of diseases (*S*, 87), and about 'animal spirit' as the 'physical or instrumental cause of sense and motion' in human beings (*S*, 153). It no longer seemed objectionable that this 'animal spirit' was unobservable, and that no sense could perceive it 'otherwise than from its effects' (*S*, 159). He even engaged with the objection, mentioned above, that 'if the explaining a phenomenon be to assign its proper efficient and final cause, it should seem the mechanical philosophers never explained anything' (*S*, 231). However, while relying on unobservable 'minute corpuscles' (*S*, 235) to explain the efficacy of tar-water, he continued to repeat the theory of explanation that had been developed in the *Essay on Motion*. By doing so, he left readers in the same dilemma as those of Newton's *Principles* – that he seemed to use a method that was officially rejected in the very work in which it was effectively deployed.

This language of the micro-world was now adapted to support the fundamental objective of Berkeley's entire *oeuvre*, which was to demonstrate the existence of God and 'the natural immortality of the soul' (*D*, 167). One sign of this pervasive objective is that references to 'nature' in some of Berkeley's earlier works were quietly amended, in later editions, to references to the 'Author of nature'. In *Siris*, he attributed a secondary causality to animal spirits (which were understood, in the seventeenth century, as a very fluid or ethereal matter); but this was integrated into an account, inspired by the *Theaetetus*, of a world-fire endowed with force, a 'diffused and active principle' which operates under the influence of the divine Mind and is ultimately the only genuine cause in the universe. As long as God's existence and causality were secure, it seemed, bodies could also be accepted in *Siris* as exercising a residual or secondary causality, and Berkeley could remain true to his favourite biblical quotation about God, in whom 'we live, and move, and have our being' (*Acts* 17:28).

## Conclusion

Berkeley's political and cultural isolation in Ireland seems to have contributed to the regressive character of his work. He was educated and lived, for much of his life, among what may be described in Swift's phrase as 'an idolatrous and barbarous people',[27] whose condition Berkeley described as 'indolence in dirt' (*Works*, VI, 242). The political situation in Ireland was so consistently unstable that, at least on one occasion, he organized a defensive unit of thirty horsemen from among the 'Protestants of Cloyne' to protect themselves against local 'rapparees' and 'rogues' (*Works*, VIII, 277). The Bishop of Cloyne perceived the Church of Ireland as permanently under threat from so-called 'free-thinkers', Presbyterians, and Roman Catholics, and from followers of Hobbes and Spinoza who were deemed atheists. Politically, philosophically, and even theologically, Berkeley represented a minority view in an island where civil war and the threat of civil unrest were more permanent than peace.

Swift's *Modest Proposal* – in which satirical suggestions for 'preventing the children of poor people from being a burthen to their parents' were used to highlight plausible policies that fell on deaf ears – suggests one way of understanding Berkeley's immaterialism. On that reading, the primary targets of the *Principles* and the *Dialogues* were philosophical views, including those of Locke, which Berkeley understood as supporting atheism and religious unorthodoxy. He argued that those philosophies were less plausible, even on their own assumptions, than the immaterialist alternative that he outlined. The structure of this critique reappeared in many of Berkeley's other writings. For example, those who

---

[27] Jonathan Swift, *Gulliver's Travels*, ed. C. Rawson and I. Higgins (Oxford: Oxford University Press, 2005), 275.

objected to the Christian account of grace should have noticed that the concept of force, in dynamics, was no more secure than that of grace.

In addition to systematic critiques of so-called atheists and free-thinkers, Berkeley proposed a criterion by reference to which all philosophical issues should be adjudicated. Without apology, he consistently rejected concepts or theories that exceeded the scope of his sensory experience. 'This I am sure of as to myself: how far the faculties of other men may reach they best can tell' (*NTV*, 123). The shadows of that empiricist turn were visible for centuries in the efforts made by subsequent philosophers, from Hume to Mill and beyond, to acknowledge the incontrovertible advances of science while limiting their conceptual repertoire to what can be gleaned from sensory experience.

While Berkeley's writing was motivated initially by theological concerns that were specific to early eighteenth-century Ireland, it represents a philosophical position about a wide range of interrelated issues – about perception, theoretical concepts, causality, instrumentalism, the foundations of knowledge, and the concept of God – at a crucial juncture in the history of ideas, when the aspirations of natural science to deliver genuine knowledge still remained unfulfilled. The significance of his contribution is confirmed by the frequency with which his empiricist theory of knowledge continues to be defended, almost three centuries later, when the natural sciences are widely accepted almost as the defining standard of what counts as genuine knowledge. Thus the spirit of Berkeley's empiricism survives without the theological context in which it was originally developed.

# Chronology

| | |
|---|---|
| 1711 | Shaftesbury (Anthony Ashley Cooper): *Characteristics of Men, Manners, Opinions, and Times* |
| 1712 | Berkeley: *Passive Obedience* |
| 1713 | Moves to London; publishes *Three Dialogues between Hylas and Philonous*; Anthony Collins: *A Discourse on Free-Thinking* |
| 1713–14 | Berkeley travels in France and Italy |
| 1714 | Bernard Mandeville: *The Fable of the Bees* |
| 1716–20 | Further travels in France and Italy |
| 1721 | Berkeley: *De Motu; sive de Motus Principio & Natura, et de Causa Communicationis Motuum* |
| 1724 | Appointed Dean of Derry, and resigned from Trinity College, Dublin |
| 1725 | Francis Hutcheson: *Inquiry into the Original of our Ideas of Beauty and Virtue* |
| 1726 | Jonathan Swift: *Gulliver's Travels* |
| 1728 | Peter Browne: *The Procedure, Extent, and Limits of Human Understanding*; Berkeley marries Anne Forster (1 August); travels to Rhode Island, where he remains until 1731 |
| 1729 | Jonathan Swift: *A Modest Proposal* |
| 1731 | Berkeley returns to London, remaining there until 1734 |
| 1732 | *Alciphron: or, the Minute Philosopher* |
| 1733 | *The Theory of Vision or Visual Language showing the immediate Presence and Providence of a Deity Vindicated and Explained*; Peter Browne: *Things Divine and Supernatural Conceived by Analogy with Things Natural and Human* |
| 1734 | *The Analyst; or a Discourse addressed to an Infidel Mathematician*; Berkeley consecrated Bishop of Cloyne (in County Cork) |
| 1739/40 | David Hume: *A Treatise of Human Nature* |
| 1744 | *Siris: A Chain of Philosophical Reflexions and Inquiries Concerning the Virtues of Tar-Water, and Divers Other Subjects Connected Together and Arising One from Another* |
| 1749 | *A Word to the Wise, or an Exhortation to the Roman Catholic Clergy of Ireland* |
| 1752 | Leaves Cloyne for Oxford |
| 1753 | Dies in Oxford, 14 January |

# Further reading

The standard edition of Berkeley's works is A. A. Luce and T. E. Jessop, eds., *The Works of George Berkeley Bishop of Cloyne*, 9 vols. (London: Nelson, 1948–57). For Berkeley's biography, see A. A. Luce, *The Life of George Berkeley Bishop of Cloyne* (Edinburgh and London: Nelson, 1949).

Some early reactions to Berkeley are reproduced in David Berman, ed., *George Berkeley: Eighteenth-Century Responses*, 2 vols. (New York and London: Garland, 1989). These appear in a nine-volume reprint of studies of Berkeley: George Pitcher, ed., *The Philosophy of George Berkeley* (London and New York: Garland, 1988–9). Walter E. Creery has edited a complementary collection of journal articles: *George Berkeley: Critical Assessments*, 3 vols. (London and New York: Routledge, 1991), while David Berman, *Berkeley and Irish Philosophy* (London and New York: Continuum, 2005) reviews the Irish context of Berkeley's work.

Other authors whose work influenced Berkeley include Isaac Newton, *Mathematical Principles of Natural Philosophy* [2nd edn. 1713], trans. A. Motte, rev. F. Cajori, 2 vols. (Berkeley and Los Angeles: University of California Press, 1962), and *Opticks* [1st edn. 1704] (New York: Dover, 1952); and Nicolas Malebranche, *The Search after Truth* [1st edn. 1674/5], trans. T. M. Lennon and P. J. Olscamp (Cambridge: Cambridge University Press, 1997). For the composition of the *New Theory of Vision*, Berkeley borrowed significantly from William Molyneux, *Dioptrica Nova: A Treatise of Dioptricks, in Two Parts* (London: Benjamin Tooke, 1692), and from Isaac Barrow, *Lectiones XVIII*,

*Cantabrigiae in Scholis publicis habitae* (London, 1669). His most evident intellectual debts, however, were to John Locke, *An Essay concerning Human Understanding* [1st edn. 1689], ed. Peter H. Nidditch (Oxford: Clarendon Press, 1975), while the most critical objections to the intelligibility of religious language came from John Toland, *Christianity not Mysterious* (London, 1696). There is a representative selection of the texts that influenced Berkeley's two main works in C. J. McCracken and I. C. Tipton, eds., *Berkeley's Principles and Dialogues: Background Source Materials* (Cambridge: Cambridge University Press, 2000).

The instrumentalist tradition from which Berkeley borrowed is summarized by Pierre Duhem, *To Save the Phenomena: An Essay on the Idea of Physical Theory from Plato to Galileo*, trans. E. Doland and C. Maschler (Chicago and London: University of Chicago Press, 1969). Berkeley's philosophy of science and his account of explanation are discussed by Gabriel Moked, *Particles and Ideas: Bishop Berkeley's Corpuscularian Philosophy* (Oxford: Clarendon Press, 1988). Recent work on the extent to which Berkeley deviates from instrumentalism in *Siris* is found in Catherine Wilson, 'Berkeley and the Microworld', *Archiv für Geschichte der Philosophie*, 76 (1994), 37–64, and Lisa J. Downing, '*Siris* and the Scope of Berkeley's Instrumentalism', *British Journal for the History of Philosophy*, 3 (1995), 279–300, while the significance of Newton as a source of Berkeley's philosophy of science is discussed in Ernan McMullin, 'The Impact of Newton's *Principia* on the Philosophy of Science', *Philosophy of Science*, 68 (2001), 279–310. The contest between 'occult' powers and hypotheses is discussed in Desmond M. Clarke, *Occult Powers and Hypotheses* (Oxford: Clarendon Press, 1989).

The theory of vision is examined in Robert Schwartz, *Vision: Variations on Some Berkeleian Themes* (Oxford: Blackwell, 1994) and Margaret Atherton, *Berkeley's Revolution in Vision* (Ithaca and New York: Cornell University Press, 1990). *George Berkeley: De Motu and the Analyst*, ed. and trans. Douglas M. Jesseph (Dordrecht: Kluwer, 1992) includes his dynamics and reflections on mathematics.

Some of Berkeley's principal philosophical arguments are analysed in Jonathan Bennett, *Locke, Berkeley, Hume: Central Themes* (Oxford: Clarendon Press, 1971). Recent general studies of Berkeley include George Pitcher, *Berkeley* (London: Routledge & Kegan Paul, 1977); A. C. Grayling, *Berkeley: The Central Arguments* (London: Duckworth,

1986); Jonathan Dancy, *Berkeley: An Introduction* (Oxford: Blackwell, 1987); Kenneth P. Winkler, *Berkeley: An Interpretation* (Oxford: Clarendon Press, 1989); David Berman, *George Berkeley: Idealism and the Man* (Oxford: Clarendon Press, 1994); and Robert G. Muehlmann, ed., *Berkeley's Metaphysics: Structural, Interpretive, and Critical Essays* (University Park, PA: Pennsylvania State University Press, 1995). There is a general assessment of Berkeley's contribution to philosophy in Kenneth P. Winkler, ed., *The Cambridge Companion to Berkeley* (Cambridge: Cambridge University Press, 2005).

# Note on the texts

Apart from the *Essay on Motion*, which Berkeley published only in Latin, the texts published here are modernized versions of the original texts that appeared during the author's lifetime. I have adopted some general principles in modernizing. Berkeley's spelling of various words was not consistent even between different editions. I have therefore substituted consistent and familiar modern spelling for all words, such as 'entire' rather than 'intire' and 'system' rather than 'systeme'. Eighteenth-century punctuation also differed from current standards, especially in its frequent use of commas. I have omitted many commas where a smooth reading of the text results, without compromising the sense of the original. Thirdly, Berkeley used italics both frequently and inconsistently. In particular, he used italics to indicate quoted words or phrases, and I have substituted quotation marks instead. Italics were also used in some cases, not to identify a genuine quotation from another source, but to attribute an opinion to another author or school (often anonymously). I have likewise used quotation marks in those cases, to indicate that they are views attributed by Berkeley to someone else. Apart from its use for foreign words, and a few cases in which we would still use italics for emphasis, I have removed all italics from the texts. In addition, I have not reproduced Berkeley's use of capital letters; in the case of words such as 'nature', a capital letter is likely to mislead readers today into thinking that Berkeley believed in some reality called 'Nature' which was independent of its appearances or its divine author. Finally, I have replaced Berkeley's use of 'hath' by its contemporary equivalents, 'has' or 'have' (singular or plural), and I have also modernized his use of 'doth' – as in phrases such as: he doth perceive – by substituting the contemporary equivalents of such verb forms (e.g. 'perceives' in place of 'doth perceive'). In negative uses of 'doth' – such as: he doth not perceive – I have substituted 'does not'. In a few sentences, I have inserted in square brackets a definite or indefinite article, where their addition seems to make the text read more smoothly.

The *New Theory of Vision* appeared in 1709, 1710 (although 1709 was given as the date of this edition), and twice in 1732, as additions to the two editions of the *Alciphron* published in that year. The second edition included a short Appendix, in which the author replied to some published criticisms of his work. However, both this Appendix and the Dedication were omitted in the 1732 editions. I have reproduced the 1732 edition here, and indicated (in footnotes) some significant changes from the first two editions.

There were two editions of the *Principles* during the author's lifetime, in 1710 and 1734. The text used here is the latter, in which Berkeley made a number of changes, including deletions and additions. I have indicated all significant changes in the editor's footnotes.

Three editions of the *Dialogues* were published during Berkeley's lifetime, in 1713, 1725, and 1734 (the last one jointly with the *Principles*). I have followed the 1734 edition here, and have indicated significant changes between that and earlier editions. The *Dialogues* are not divided into short sections, as were all of Berkeley's other texts. To facilitate finding references, therefore, I have provided on the margins the pagination of the text that appeared in the Luce and Jessop edition of Berkeley's *Works*, vol. II (1949).

When Berkeley was travelling in France in 1720, the Académie royale des sciences (Paris) announced a prize for an essay on the nature of motion, and the cause of the communication of motion. Berkeley wrote this text in Latin and published it in London in 1721. The translation published here was made from the first edition.

Berkeley drafted *Alciphron* during his stay in Newport, and published it on his return to London in 1732. He also published a similar edition in the same year in Dublin, and a further London edition, also in the same year. Each of these 1732 editions appeared in two volumes, which included *A New Theory of Vision*. There was a further edition, called the 'third edition', which appeared in 1752 and omitted the *Theory of Vision*. *Alciphron* included seven dialogues, each of which was sub-divided into sections in the usual style of Berkeley's publications. I have included only

Dialogues IV and VII here, from the 1752 edition, and in each case have omitted the concluding sections. As usual, significant changes from earlier editions are noted.

Finally, *Siris* was published in Dublin in 1744, and was so popular that six editions seem to have appeared in the same year, two in Dublin and four in London, although the order in which they appeared remains unclear. There was only one other edition during Berkeley's lifetime, in 1747, and I have followed Luce and Jessop in republishing a modernized version of the 1747 text (as it appears in *Works*, vol. V [1953], pp. 25–164). However, I have included only an abridged version of the text for reasons of space. Since Berkeley adopted his usual pattern of numbering sections of the text, I have included his paragraph numbers for easy reference to the original. The excerpted sections illustrate Berkeley's adoption of a form of corpuscularianism to explain diseases and the effectiveness of medicines, and some further clarifications of what he meant by a scientific explanation.

*Footnotes*: With some exceptions, Berkeley provided references within the body of his text and highlighted them by using italics. I have moved all his references to footnotes, and have used letters to identify them. Where his references are incomplete, I have added further relevant information in square brackets. Editor's notes are identified throughout by Arabic numerals.

*Glossary*: Berkeley used many words that are now obsolete, and he used others in ways that are likely to seem unfamiliar to readers today. I have provided a glossary of such words at the end of the text.

# An Essay towards a New Theory of Vision

## 3rd edition 1732

### The Contents

Section

---

[1] The final section was omitted in the 1732 editions.

## An Essay towards a New Theory of Vision

1   My design is to show the manner wherein we perceive by sight the distance, magnitude, and situation of objects. Also to consider the difference there is betwixt the ideas of sight and touch, and whether there be any idea common to both senses.

2   It is, I think, agreed by all that distance, of itself and immediately, cannot be seen. For distance being a line directed end-wise to the eye, it projects only one point in the fund of the eye, which point remains invariably the same, whether the distance be longer or shorter.[2]

3   I find it also acknowledged that the estimate we make of the distance of objects considerably remote is rather an act of judgment grounded on experience than of sense. For example, when I perceive a great number of intermediate objects, such as houses, fields, rivers, and the like, which I have experienced to take up a considerable space, I thence form a judgment or conclusion that the object I see beyond them is at a great distance. Again, when an object appears faint and small, which at a near distance I have experienced to make a vigorous and large appearance, I instantly conclude it to be far off. And this, it is evident, is the result of experience; without which, from the faintness and littleness, I should not have inferred anything concerning the distance of objects.

4   But when an object is placed at so near a distance as that the interval between the eyes bears any sensible proportion to it, the opinion of speculative men is that the two optic axes (the fancy that we see only with one eye at once being exploded) concurring at the object do there make an angle, by means of which, according as it is greater or lesser, the object is perceived to be nearer or farther off.[a]

5   Betwixt which and the foregoing manner of estimating distance there is this remarkable difference: that whereas there was no apparent, necessary connexion between small distance and a large and strong appearance, or between great distance and a little and faint appearance, there appears a very necessary connexion between an obtuse angle and

[a]   See what Descartes and others have written on this subject [Descartes, *Dioptrics*, Sixth Discourse, in *Oeuvres*, VI, 130–47; N. Malebranche, *The Search after Truth*, trans. T. M. Lennon and P. J. Olscamp (Cambridge: Cambridge University Press, 1997), Book I, Chs. vi–ix, pp. 25–47].

[2]   Cf. William Molyneux, *Dioptrica Nova: A Treatise of Dioptricks, in Two Parts* (London: Tooke, 1692), p. 113: 'For *Distance* of it self, is not to be perceived; for 'tis a Line (or a Length) presented to our Eye with its End towards us, which must therefore be only a *Point*, and that is *Invisible*.'

near distance, and an acute angle and farther distance. It does not in the least depend upon experience, but may be evidently known by anyone before he had experienced it, that the nearer the concurrence of the optic axes, the greater the angle, and the remoter their concurrence is, the lesser will be the angle comprehended by them.

6   There is another way mentioned by optic writers, whereby they will have us judge of those distances, in respect of which the breadth of the pupil has any sensible bigness. And that is the greater or lesser divergency of the rays, which issuing from the visible point do fall on the pupil, that point being judged nearest which is seen by most diverging rays, and that remoter which is seen by less diverging rays. And so on, the apparent distance still increasing as the divergency of the rays decreases, till at length it becomes infinite when the rays that fall on the pupil are to sense parallel. And after this manner it is said we perceive distance when we look only with one eye.

7   In this case also it is plain we are not beholding to experience: it being a certain, necessary truth that the nearer the direct rays falling on the eye approach to a parallelism, the farther off is the point of their intersection, or the visible point from whence they flow.

8   [Now though the accounts here given of perceiving near distance by sight are received for true, and accordingly made use of][3] in determining the apparent places of objects, they do nevertheless seem very unsatisfactory, and that for these following reasons.

9   It is evident that when the mind perceives any idea, not immediately and of itself, it must be by the means of some other idea. Thus, for instance, the passions which are in the mind of another are of themselves to me invisible. I may nevertheless perceive them by sight, though not immediately, yet by means of the colours they produce in the countenance. We often see shame or fear in the looks of a man, by perceiving the changes of his countenance to red or pale.

10   Moreover it is evident that no idea which is not itself perceived can be the means of perceiving any other idea. If I do not perceive the redness or paleness of a man's face themselves, it is impossible I should perceive by them the passions which are in his mind.

[3] The phrase in parentheses was given as follows in the 1709 edition: 'I have here set down the common, current accounts that are given of our perceiving near distances by sight, which though they are unquestionably received for true by mathematicians, and accordingly made use of by them ...'

11   Now from section 2 it is plain that distance is in its own nature imperceptible, and yet it is perceived by sight. It remains, therefore, that it be brought into view by means of some other idea that is itself immediately perceived in the act of vision.

12   But those lines and angles, by means whereof some men pretend to explain the perception of distance, are themselves not at all perceived, nor are they in truth ever thought of by those unskilful in optics. I appeal to anyone's experience whether, upon sight of an object, he computes its distance by the bigness of the angle made by the meeting of the two optic axes? Or whether he ever thinks of the greater or lesser divergency of the rays, which arrive at any point to his pupil?[4] Everyone is himself the best judge of what he perceives, and what not. In vain shall any man tell me that I perceive certain lines and angles which introduce into my mind the various ideas of distance, so long as I myself am conscious of no such thing.

13   Since, therefore, those angles and lines are not themselves perceived by sight, it follows from section 10 that the mind does not by them judge of the distance of objects.

14   The truth of this assertion will be yet farther evident to anyone that considers those lines and angles have no real existence in nature, being only an hypothesis framed by the mathematicians, and by them introduced into optics, that they might treat of that science in a geometrical way.

15   The last reason I shall give for rejecting that doctrine is, that though we should grant the real existence of those optic angles, *etc.*, and that it was possible for the mind to perceive them, yet these principles would not be found sufficient to explain the phenomena of distance, as shall be shown hereafter.

16   Now, it being already shown that distance is suggested to the mind by the mediation of some other idea which is itself perceived in the act of seeing, it remains that we inquire what ideas or sensations there be that attend vision, unto which we may suppose the ideas of distance are connected, and by which they are introduced into the mind. And *first*, it is certain by experience that when we look at a near object with both eyes, according as it approaches or recedes from us, we alter the disposition of our eyes by lessening or widening the distance between the pupils. This disposition or turn of the eyes is attended with a sensation, which seems

---

[4] The 1709 edition included the following extra phrase here: 'Nay, whether it be not perfectly impossible for him to perceive by sense, the various angles wherewith the rays according to their greater or lesser divergence do fall on his eye.'

to me to be that which in this case brings the ideas of greater or lesser distance into the mind.

17   Not that there is any natural or necessary connexion between the sensation we perceive by the turn of the eyes and greater or lesser distance, but because the mind has by constant experience found the different sensations corresponding to the different dispositions of the eyes to be attended each with a different degree of distance in the object, there has grown an habitual or customary connexion between these two sorts of ideas, so that the mind no sooner perceives the sensation arising from the different turn it gives the eyes, in order to bring the pupils nearer or farther asunder, but it withal perceives the different idea of distance which was wont to be connected with that sensation; just as upon hearing a certain sound, the idea is immediately suggested to the understanding which custom had united with it.

18   Nor do I see how I can easily be mistaken in this matter. I know evidently that distance is not perceived of itself. That by consequence it must be perceived by means of some other idea, which is immediately perceived and varies with the different degrees of distance. I know also that the sensation arising from the turn of the eyes is of itself immediately perceived, and various degrees thereof are connected with different distances, which never fail to accompany them into the mind, when I view an object distinctly with both eyes, whose distance is so small that in respect of it the interval between the eyes has any considerable magnitude.

19   I know it is a received opinion that, by altering the disposition of the eyes, the mind perceives whether the angle of the optic axes or the lateral angles comprehended between the interval of the eyes and the optic axes are made greater or lesser; and that accordingly, by a kind of natural geometry, it judges the point of their intersection to be nearer or farther off. But that this is not true I am convinced by my own experience, since I am not conscious that I make any such use of the perception I have by the turn of my eyes. And for me to make those judgments, and draw those conclusions from it, without knowing that I do so, seems altogether incomprehensible.

20   From all which it follows that the judgment we make of the distance of an object, viewed with both eyes, is entirely the result of experience. If we had not constantly found certain sensations, arising from the various disposition of the eyes, attended with certain degrees of distance, we should never make those sudden judgments from them concerning the distance of

objects, no more than we would pretend to judge of a man's thoughts by his pronouncing words we had never heard before.

**21** *Secondly,* an object placed at a certain distance from the eye, to which the breadth of the pupil bears a considerable proportion, being made to approach, is seen more confusedly; and the nearer it is brought, the more confused appearance it makes. And this being found constantly to be so, there arises in the mind an habitual connexion between the several degrees of confusion and distance: the greater confusion still implying the lesser distance, and the lesser confusion the greater distance of the object.

**22** This confused appearance of the object, therefore, seems to be the medium whereby the mind judges of distance in those cases wherein the most approved writers of optics will have it judge by the different divergency with which the rays flowing from the radiating point fall on the pupil. No man, I believe, will pretend to see or feel those imaginary angles that the rays are supposed to form according to their various inclinations on his eye. But he cannot choose seeing whether the object appear more or less confused. It is therefore a manifest consequence from what has been demonstrated that, instead of the greater or lesser divergency of the rays, the mind makes use of the greater or lesser confusedness of the appearance, thereby to determine the apparent place of an object.

**23** Nor does it avail to say there is not any necessary connexion between confused vision and distance, great or small. For I ask any man what necessary connexion he sees between the redness of a flush and shame? And yet no sooner shall he behold that colour to arise in the face of another, but it brings into his mind the idea of that passion which has been observed to accompany it.

**24** What seems to have misled the writers of optics in this matter is that they imagine men judge of distance as they do of a conclusion in mathematics, betwixt which and the premises it is indeed absolutely requisite there be an apparent, necessary connexion. But it is far otherwise in the sudden judgments men make of distance. We are not to think that brutes and children, or even grown reasonable men, whenever they perceive an object to approach or depart from them, do it by virtue of geometry and demonstration.

**25** That one idea may suggest another to the mind it will suffice that they have been observed to go together, without any demonstration of the necessity of their coexistence, or without so much as knowing what it is that makes them so to coexist. Of this there are innumerable instances of which no one can be ignorant.

26    Thus, greater confusion having been constantly attended with nearer distance, no sooner is the former idea perceived but it suggests the latter to our thoughts. And if it had been the ordinary course of nature that the farther off an object were placed, the more confused it should appear, it is certain the very same perception that now makes us think an object approaches would then have made us to imagine it went farther off. That perception, abstracting from custom and experience, being equally fitted to produce the idea of great distance, or small distance, or no distance at all.

27    *Thirdly*, an object being placed at the distance above specified and brought nearer to the eye, we may nevertheless prevent, at least for some time, the appearances growing more confused by straining the eye. In which case that sensation supplies the place of confused vision in aiding the mind to judge of the distance of the object; it being esteemed so much the nearer by how much the effort or straining of the eye in order to distinct vision is greater.

28    I have here set down those sensations or ideas that seem to be the constant and general occasions of introducing into the mind the different ideas of near distance. It is true in most cases that divers other circumstances contribute to frame our idea of distance, to wit, the particular number, size, kind, *etc.*, of the things seen. Concerning which, as well as all other the forementioned occasions which suggest distance, I shall only observe they have none of them, in their own nature, any relation or connexion with it. Nor is it possible they should ever signify the various degrees thereof, otherwise than as by experience they have been found to be connected with them.

29    I shall proceed upon these principles to account for a phenomenon which has hitherto strangely puzzled the writers of optics, and is so far from being accounted for by any of their theories of vision that it is, by their own confession, plainly repugnant to them; and of consequence, if nothing else could be objected, were alone sufficient to bring their credit in question. The whole difficulty I shall lay before you in the words of the learned Dr. Barrow, with which he concludes his optic lectures.[5]

---

[5] Isaac Barrow, *Lectiones XVIII, Cantabrigiae in Scholis publicis habitae; in quibus Opticorum PhenomenΩn genuinae rationes investigantur, ac exponuntur* (London, 1669), pp. 125–6. Berkeley quotes the Latin text and then provides an English translation. The Latin is omitted in this edition. For a recent English translation, see *Isaac Barrow's Optical Lectures*, trans. H. C. Fay (London: The Worshipful Company of Spectacle Makers, 1987), pp. 224–6.

*In English as follows:*
I have here delivered what my thoughts have suggested to me concerning that part of optics which is more properly mathematical. As for the other parts of that science (which being rather physical, do consequently abound with plausible conjectures instead of certain principles), there has in them scarce anything occurred to my observation different from what has been already said by Kepler, Scheinerus, Descartes, and others.[6] And methinks, I had better say nothing at all than repeat that which has been so often said by others. I think it therefore high time to take my leave of this subject. But before I quit it for good and all, the fair and ingenuous dealing that I owe both to you and to truth obliges me to acquaint you with a certain untoward difficulty, which seems directly opposite to the doctrine I have been hitherto inculcating, at least, admits of no solution from it. In short it is this.

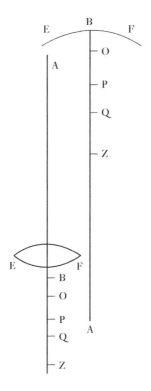

---

[6] Johannes Kepler (1571–1630) and Christoph Scheiner (1573–1650).

Before the double convex glass or concave speculum EBF, let the point A be placed at such a distance that the rays proceeding from A, after refraction or reflexion, be brought to unite somewhere in the Ax [i.e. axis] AB. And suppose the point of union (*i.e.* the image of the point A, as has been already set forth) to be Z; between which and B, the vertex of the glass or speculum, conceive the eye to be anywhere placed. The question now is: where the point A ought to appear? Experience shows that it does not appear behind at the point Z, and it were contrary to nature that it should, since all the impression which affects the sense comes from towards A. But from our tenets it should seem to follow that it would appear before the eye at a vast distance off, so great as should in some sort surpass all sensible distance. For since if we exclude all anticipations and prejudices, every object appears by so much the farther off, by how much the rays it sends to the eye are less diverging. And that object is thought to be most remote from which parallel rays proceed unto the eye. Reason would make one think that object should appear at yet a greater distance which is seen by converging rays.

Moreover it may in general be asked concerning this case what it is that determines the apparent place of the point A, and makes it to appear after a constant manner sometimes nearer, at other times farther off? To which doubt I see nothing that can be answered agreeable to the principles we have laid down, except only that the point A ought always to appear extremely remote. But on the contrary we are assured by experience that the point A appears variously distant, according to the different situations of the eye between the points B and Z. And that it almost never (if at all) seems farther off, than it would if it were beheld by the naked eye, but on the contrary it sometimes appears much nearer. Nay, it is even certain that by how much the rays falling on the eye do more converge, by so much the nearer does the object seem to approach. For the eye being placed close to the point B, the object A appears nearly in its own natural place, if the point B is taken in the glass, or at the same distance, if in the speculum. The eye being brought back to O, the object seems to draw near: and being come to P it beholds it still nearer. And so on by little and little, till at length the eye being placed somewhere, suppose at Q, the object appearing extremely near, begins to vanish into mere confusion.

All which seems repugnant to our principles, at least not rightly to agree with them. Nor is our tenet alone struck at by this experiment, but likewise all others that ever came to my knowledge are, every whit as much, endangered by it. The ancient one especially (which is most commonly received, and comes nearest to mine) seems to be so effectually overthrown thereby that the most learned Tacquet has been forced to reject that principle, as false and uncertain, on which alone he had built almost his whole *Catoptrics*; and consequently by taking away the foundation, has himself pulled down the superstructure he had raised on it.[7] Which, nevertheless, I do not believe he would have done had he but considered the whole matter more thoroughly, and examined the difficulty to the bottom. But as for me, neither this nor any other difficulty shall have so great an influence on me as to make me renounce that which I know to be manifestly agreeable to reason: especially when, as it here falls out, the difficulty is founded in the peculiar nature of a certain odd and particular case. For in the present case something peculiar lies hid, which being involved in the subtlety of nature will, perhaps, hardly be discovered till such time as the manner of vision is more perfectly made known. Concerning which, I must own, I have hitherto been able to find out nothing that has the least show of probability, not to mention certainty. I shall, therefore, leave this knot to be untied by you, wishing you may have better success in it than I have had.

**30**   The ancient and received principle, which Dr. Barrow here mentions as the main foundations of Tacquet's *Catoptrics*, is that 'every visible point seen by reflexion from a speculum shall appear placed at the intersection of the reflected ray and the perpendicular of incidence.' Which intersection in the present case, happening to be behind the eye, it greatly shakes the authority of that principle, whereon the aforementioned author proceeds throughout his whole *Catoptrics* in determining the apparent place of objects seen by reflexion from any kind of speculum.

**31**   Let us now see how this phenomenon agrees with our tenets. The eye, the nearer it is placed to the point B in the foregoing figures, the more distinct is the appearance of the object. But as it recedes to O the appearance grows more confused; and at P it sees the object yet more

---

[7] André Tacquet (1612–1660), Jesuit mathematician and astronomer, whose posthumously published *Opera Mathematica* (Antwerp, 1669), Part II, contains sections on optics and catoptrics. Barrow was probably familiar with him from William Whiston's English translation of *The Elements of Euclid with select Theorems out of Archimedes* (London: Roberts, 1714).

confused; and so on till the eye, being brought back to Z, sees the object in the greatest confusion of all. Wherefore by section 21 the object should seem to approach the eye gradually as it recedes from the point B, that is, at O it should (in consequence of the principle I have laid down in the aforesaid section) seem nearer than it did at B, and at P nearer than at O, and at Q nearer than at P; and so on, till it quite vanishes at Z. Which is the very matter of fact, as anyone that pleases may easily satisfy himself by experiment.

32    This case is much the same as if we should suppose an Englishman to meet a foreigner who used the same words with the English, but in a direct contrary signification. The Englishman would not fail to make a wrong judgment of the ideas annexed to those sounds in the mind of him that used them. Just so, in the present case the object speaks (if I may so say) with words that the eye is well acquainted with, that is, confusions of appearance. But whereas heretofore the greater confusions were always wont to signify nearer distances, they have in this case a direct, contrary signification, being connected with the greater distances. Whence it follows that the eye must unavoidably be mistaken, since it will take the confusions in the sense it has been used to, which is directly opposed to the true.

33    This phenomenon, as it entirely subverts the opinion of those who will have us judge of distance by lines and angles, on which supposition it is altogether inexplicable, so it seems to me no small confirmation of the truth of that principle whereby it is explained. But in order to a more full explication of this point, and to show how far the hypothesis of the mind's judging by the various divergency of rays may be of use in determining the apparent place of an object, it will be necessary to premise some few things, which are already well known to those who have any skill in dioptrics.

34    *First*, any radiating point is then distinctly seen when the rays proceeding from it are, by the refractive power of the crystalline, accurately reunited in the retina or fund of the eye. But if they are reunited, either before they arrive at the retina or after they have passed it, then there is confused vision.

35    *Secondly*, suppose in the adjacent figures NP represent an eye duly framed and retaining its natural figure. In Figure 1 the rays falling nearly parallel on the eye, are by the crystalline AB refracted, so as their focus or point of union F falls exactly on the retina. But if the rays fall

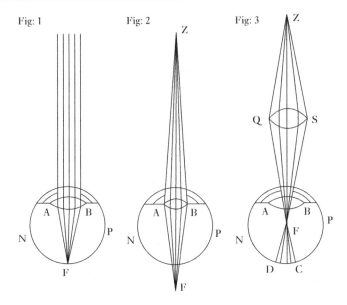

sensibly diverging on the eye, as in Figure 2, then their focus falls beyond the retina. Or if the rays are made to converge by the lens QS before they come at the eye, as in Figure 3, their focus F will fall before the retina. In which two last cases it is evident from the foregoing section that the appearance of the point Z is confused. And by how much the greater is the convergency or divergency of the rays falling on the pupil, by so much the farther will the point of their reunion be from the retina, either before or behind it, and consequently the point Z will appear by so much the more confused. And this, by the bye, may show us the difference between confused and faint vision. Confused vision is when the rays proceeding from each distinct point of the object are not accurately recollected in one corresponding point on the retina, but take up some space thereon, so that rays from different points become mixed and confused together. This is opposed to a distinct vision, and attends near objects. Faint vision is when, by reason of the distance of the object or grossness of the interjacent medium, few rays arrive from the object to the eye. This is opposed to vigorous or clear vision, and attends remote objects. But to return.

**36** The eye, or (to speak truly) the mind, perceiving only the confusion itself, without ever considering the cause from which it proceeds, constantly annexes the same degree of distance to the same degree of confusion. Whether that confusion be occasioned by converging or by diverging rays, it matters not. Whence it follows that the eye, viewing the object Z through the glass QS (which by refraction causes the rays ZQ, ZS, *etc.*, to converge) should judge it to be at such a nearness at which, if it were placed, it would radiate on the eye with rays diverging to that degree as would produce the same confusion which is now produced by converging rays, *i.e.* would cover a portion of the retina equal to DC (*vid.* Figure 3 *supra*). But then this must be understood (to use Dr. Barrow's phrase) '*seclusis praenotionibus et praejudiciis*',[8] in case we abstract from all other circumstances of vision, such as the figure, size, faintness, *etc.* of the visible objects, all which do ordinarily concur to form our idea of distance, the mind having by frequent experience observed their several sorts or degrees to be connected with various distances.

**37** It plainly follows from what has been said that a person perfectly purblind (*i.e.* that could not see an object distinct but when placed close to his eye) would not make the same wrong judgment that others do in the forementioned case. For to him greater confusions constantly suggesting greater distances, he must, as he recedes from the glass and the object grows more confused, judge it to be at a farther distance, contrary to what they do who have had the perception of the objects growing more confused connected with the idea of approach.

**38** Hence also it appears there may be good use of computation by lines and angles in optics; not that the mind judges of distance immediately by them, but because it judges by somewhat which is connected with them, and to the determination whereof they may be subservient. Thus the mind judging of the distance of an object by the confusedness of its appearance, and this confusedness being greater or lesser to the naked eye, according as the object is seen by rays more or less diverging, it follows that a man may make use of the divergency of the rays in computing the apparent distance, though not for its own sake, yet on account of the confusion with which it is connected. But, so it is, the confusion itself is entirely neglected by mathematicians as having no necessary relation with distance, such as the greater or lesser angles of

---

[8] 'If we exclude all anticipations and prejudices.'

divergency are conceived to have. And these (especially for that they fall under mathematical computation) are alone regarded in determining the apparent places of objects, as though they were the sole and immediate cause of the judgments the mind makes of distance. Whereas, in truth, they should not at all be regarded in themselves, or any otherwise, than as they are supposed to be the cause of confused vision.

**39** The not considering of this has been a fundamental and perplexing oversight. For proof whereof we need go no farther than the case before us. It having been observed that the most diverging rays brought into the mind the idea of nearest distance, and that still, as the divergency decreased, the distance increased; and it being thought the connexion between the various degrees of divergency and distance was immediate, this naturally leads one to conclude, from an ill-grounded analogy, that converging rays shall make an object appear at an immense distance, and that, as the convergency increased, the distance (if it were possible) should do so likewise. That this was the cause of Dr. Barrow's mistake is evident from his own words which we have quoted. Whereas had the learned doctor observed that diverging and converging rays, how opposite soever they may seem, do nevertheless agree in producing the same effect, to wit, confusedness of visions, greater degrees whereof are produced indifferently, either as the divergency or convergency of the rays increases; and that it is by this effect, which is the same in both, that either the divergency or convergency is perceived by the eye. I say, had he but considered this, it is certain he would have made a quite contrary judgment, and rightly concluded that those rays which fall on the eye with greater degrees of convergency should make the object from whence they proceed appear by so much the nearer. But it is plain it was impossible for any man to attain to a right notion of this matter so long as he had regard only to lines and angles, and did not apprehend the true nature of vision, and how far it was of mathematical consideration.

**40** Before we dismiss this subject, it is fit we take notice of a query relating thereto, proposed by the ingenious Mr. Molyneux, in his *Treatise of Dioptrics*,[b] where speaking of this difficulty, he has these words:

> And so he (*i.e.* Dr. Barrow) leaves this difficulty to the solution of others, which I (after so great an example) shall do likewise; but with

[b] Par. I, Prop. 31, Section 9 [*Dioptrica Nova*, pp. 118–19. I have restored Molyneux's punctuation, and the word 'the' that was omitted in Berkeley's quotation].

the resolution of the same admirable author of not quitting the evident doctrine, which we have before laid down, for determining the *locus objecti*,[9] on [the] account of being pressed by one difficulty, which seems inexplicable, till a more intimate knowledge of the visive faculty be obtained by mortals. In the mean time, I propose it to the consideration of the ingenious, whether the *locus apparens*[10] of an object placed as in this 9th section, be not as much before the eye, as the distinct base is behind the eye?

To which query we may venture to answer in the negative. For in the present case the rule for determining the distance of the distinct base, or respective focus from the glass, is this. 'As the difference between the distance of the object and focus: is to the focus or focal length:: so the distance of the object from the glass: is to the distance of the respective focus or distinct base from the glass.'[c] Let us now suppose the object to be placed at the distance of the focal length, and one half of the focal length from the glass, and the eye close to the glass. Hence it will follow by the rule that the distance of the distinct base behind the eye is double the true distance of the object before the eye. If therefore Mr. Molyneux's conjecture held good, it would follow that the eye should see the object twice as far off as it really is, and in other cases at three or four times its due distance, or more. But this manifestly contradicts experience, the object never appearing, at farthest, beyond its due distance. Whatever, therefore, is built on this supposition[d] comes to the ground along with it.

**41** From what has been premised it is a manifest consequence that a man born blind, being made to see, would at first have no idea of distance by sight. The sun and stars, the remotest objects as well as the nearer, would all seem to be in his eye, or rather in his mind. The objects intromitted by sight would seem to him (as in truth they are) no other than a new set of thoughts or sensations, each whereof is as near to him as the perceptions of pain or pleasure, or the most inward passions of his soul. For our judging objects perceived by sight to be at any distance, or

---

[c] Molyneux, *Dioptrics*, Par. I, Prop. 5 [*Dioptrica Nova*, Proposition V, p. 42].

[d] *Vid. Corol. 1, Prop. 57, ibid.* [*Dioptrica Nova*, Proposition LVII, Corollary 1, p. 179].

[9] The location of an object.  [10] The apparent location of an object.

without the mind, is[e] entirely the effect of experience, which one in those circumstances could not yet have attained to.

**42** It is indeed otherwise upon the common supposition that men judge of distance by the angle of the optic axes, just as one in the dark, or a blind man by the angle comprehended by two sticks, one whereof he held in each hand.[11] For if this were true, it would follow that one blind from his birth, being made to see, should stand in need of no new experience in order to perceive distance by sight. But that this is false has, I think, been sufficiently demonstrated.

**43** And perhaps upon a strict inquiry we shall not find that even those who from their birth have grown up in a continued habit of seeing are irrecoverably prejudiced on the other side, to wit, in thinking what they see to be at a distance from them. For at this time it seems agreed on all hands, by those who have had any thoughts of that matter, that colours, which are the proper and immediate object of sight, are not without the mind. But then it will be said, by sight we have also the ideas of extension, and figure, and motion, all which may well be thought without, and at some distance from the mind, though colour should not. In answer to this I appeal to any man's experience, whether the visible extension of any object does not appear as near to him as the colour of that object; nay, whether they do not both seem to be in the very same place. Is not the extension we see coloured, and is it possible for us, so much as in thought, to separate and abstract colour from extension? Now, where the extension is, there surely is the figure, and there the motion too. I speak of those which are perceived by sight.

**44** But for a fuller explication of this point, and to show that the immediate objects of sight are not so much as the ideas or resemblances of things placed at a distance, it is requisite that we look nearer into the matter and carefully observe what is meant in common discourse, when one says that which he sees is at a distance from him. Suppose, for example, that looking at the moon I should say it were fifty or sixty semidiameters of the earth distant from me. Let us see what moon this is spoken of. It is plain it cannot be the visible moon, or anything like the visible moon, or that which I see, which is only a round, luminous plane of about thirty visible points in diameter. For in case I am carried from

---

[e] *Vide* section 28.

[11] See for example Descartes, *Dioptrics*, Sixth Discourse, *Oeuvres*, VI, 134–6.

the place where I stand directly towards the moon, it is manifest the object varies, still as I go on. And by the time that I am advanced fifty or sixty semidiameters of the earth, I shall be so far from being near a small, round, luminous flat that I shall perceive nothing like it; this object having long since disappeared, and if I would recover it, it must be by going back to the earth from whence I set out. Again, suppose I perceive by sight the faint and obscure idea of something which I doubt whether it be a man, or a tree, or a tower, but judge it to be at the distance of about a mile. It is plain I cannot mean that what I see is a mile off, or that it is the image or likeness of anything which is a mile off, since that every step I take towards it the appearance alters, and from being obscure, small, and faint, grows clear, large, and vigorous. And when I come to the mile's end, that which I saw first is quite lost, neither do I find anything in the likeness of it.

**45** In these and the like instances the truth of the matter stands thus. Having of a long time experienced certain ideas, perceivable by touch – as distance, tangible figure, and solidity – to have been connected with certain ideas of sight, I do upon perceiving these ideas of sight forthwith conclude what tangible ideas are, by the wonted ordinary course of nature, like to follow. Looking at an object I perceive a certain visible figure and colour, with some degree of faintness and other circumstances, which from what I have formerly observed, determine me to think that if I advance forward so many paces or miles, I shall be affected with such and such ideas of touch. So that in truth and strictness of speech I neither see distance itself, nor anything that I take to be at a distance. I say, neither distance nor things placed at a distance are themselves, or their ideas, truly perceived by sight. This I am persuaded of, as to what concerns myself; and I believe whoever will look narrowly into his own thoughts and examine what he means by saying he sees this or that thing at a distance, will agree with me that what he sees only suggests to his understanding that, after having passed a certain distance, to be meas-ured by the motion of his body, which is perceivable by touch, he shall come to perceive such and such tangible ideas which have been usually connected with such and such visible ideas. But that one might be deceived by these suggestions of sense, and that there is no necessary connexion between visible and tangible ideas suggested by them, we need go no farther than the next looking-glass or picture to be convinced. Note that when I speak of tangible ideas, I take the word 'idea' for any the immediate object of sense or understanding, in which large signification it is commonly used by the moderns.

**46** From what we have shown it is a manifest consequence that the ideas of space, outness, and things placed at a distance are not, strictly speaking, the object of sight. They are not otherwise perceived by the eye than by the ear. Sitting in my study I hear a coach drive along the street; I look through the casement and see it; I walk out and enter into it. Thus common speech would incline one to think I heard, saw, and touched the same thing, to wit, the coach. It is nevertheless certain, the ideas intromitted by each sense are widely different and distinct from each other; but having been observed constantly to go together, they are spoken of as one and the same thing. By the variation of the noise I perceive the different distances of the coach, and know that it approaches before I look out. Thus by the ear I perceive distance, just after the same manner as I do by the eye.

**47** I do not nevertheless say I hear distance in like manner as I say that I see it, the ideas perceived by hearing not being so apt to be confounded with the ideas of touch as those of sight are. So likewise a man is easily convinced that bodies and external things are not properly the object of hearing, but only sounds, by the mediation whereof the idea of this or that body or distance is suggested to his thoughts. But then one is with more difficulty brought to discern the difference there is betwixt the ideas of sight and touch, though it be certain a man no more sees and feels the same thing than he hears and feels the same thing.

**48** One reason of which seems to be this. It is thought a great absurdity to imagine that one and the same thing should have any more than one extension and one figure. But the extension and figure of a body, being let into the mind two ways, and that indifferently either by sight or touch, it seems to follow that we see the same extension and the same figure which we feel.

**49** But if we take a close and accurate view of things, it must be acknowledged that we never see and feel one and the same object. That which is seen is one thing, and that which is felt is another. If the visible figure and extension be not the same with the tangible figure and extension, we are not to infer that one and the same thing has divers extensions. The true consequence is that the objects of sight and touch are two distinct things. It may perhaps require some thought rightly to conceive this distinction. And the difficulty seems not a little increased, because the combination of visible ideas has constantly the same name as the combination of tangible ideas wherewith it is connected, which of necessity arises from the use and end of language.

**50** In order therefore to treat accurately and unconfusedly of vision, we must bear in mind that there are two sorts of objects apprehended by the eye, the one primarily and immediately, the other secondarily and by intervention of the former. Those of the first sort neither are, nor appear to be, without the mind or at any distance off. They may indeed grow greater or smaller, more confused or more clear, or more faint, but they do not, cannot, approach or recede from us. Whenever we say an object is at a distance, whenever we say it draws near or goes farther off, we must always mean it of the latter sort, which properly belong to the touch, and are not so truly perceived as suggested by the eye in like manner as thoughts by the ear.

**51** No sooner do we hear the words of a familiar language pronounced in our ears, but the ideas corresponding thereto present themselves to our minds. In the very same instant the sound and the meaning enter the understanding; so closely are they united that it is not in our power to keep out the one, except we exclude the other also. We even act in all respects as if we heard the very thoughts themselves. So likewise the secondary objects, or those which are only suggested by sight, do often more strongly affect us, and are more regarded than the proper objects of that sense, along with which they enter into the mind and with which they have a far more strict connexion than ideas have with words. Hence it is we find it so difficult to discriminate between the immediate and mediate objects of sight, and are so prone to attribute to the former what belongs only to the latter. They are, as it were, most closely twisted, blended, and incorporated together. And the prejudice is confirmed and riveted in our thoughts by a long tract of time, by the use of language, and want of reflexion. However, I believe anyone that shall attentively consider what we have already said and shall say, upon this subject, before we have done (especially if he pursue it in his own thoughts), may be able to deliver himself from that prejudice. Sure I am it is worth some attention, to whoever would understand the true nature of vision.

**52** I have now done with distance, and proceed to show how it is that we perceive by sight the magnitude of objects. It is the opinion of some that we do it by angles, or by angles in conjunction with distance. But neither angles nor distance being perceivable by sight, and the things we see being in truth at no distance from us, it follows that, as we have shown lines and angles not to be the medium the mind makes use of in apprehending the apparent place, so neither are they the medium whereby it apprehends the apparent magnitude of objects.

**53** It is well known that the same extension at a near distance shall subtend a greater angle, and at a farther distance a lesser angle. And by this principle (we are told) the mind estimates the magnitude of an object, comparing the angle under which it is seen with its distance and thence inferring the magnitude thereof. What inclines men to this mistake (beside the humour of making one see by geometry) is that the same perceptions or ideas which suggest distance do also suggest magnitude. But if we examine it, we shall find they suggest the latter as immediately as the former. I say, they do not first suggest distance, and then leave it to the judgment to use that as a medium whereby to collect the magnitude. But they have as close and immediate a connexion with the magnitude as with the distance, and suggest magnitude as independently of distance as they do distance independently of magnitude. All which will be evident to whoever considers what has been already said, and what follows.

**54** It has been shown there are two sorts of objects apprehended by sight, each whereof has its distinct magnitude or extension. The one, properly tangible, *i.e.* to be perceived and measured by touch, and not immediately falling under the sense of seeing; the other, properly and immediately visible, by mediation of which the former is brought in view. Each of these magnitudes are greater or lesser, according as they contain in them more or fewer points, they being made up of points or minimums. For, whatever may be said of extension in abstract, it is certain sensible extension is not infinitely divisible. There is a *minimum tangibile* and a *minimum visibile*,[12] beyond which sense cannot perceive. This everyone's experience will inform him.

**55** The magnitude of the object which exists without the mind, and is at a distance, continues always invariably the same. But the visible object still changing as you approach to, or recede from, the tangible object, it has no fixed and determinate greatness. Whenever, therefore, we speak of the magnitude of anything, for instance a tree or a house, we must mean the tangible magnitude; otherwise there can be nothing

---

[12] The Latin phrases refer, respectively, to the smallest thing that can be perceived by touch or sight.

steady and free from ambiguity spoken of it. But though the tangible and visible magnitude in truth belong to two distinct objects, I shall nevertheless (especially since those objects are called by the same name, and are observed to coexist), to avoid tediousness and singularity of speech, sometimes speak of them as belonging to one and the same thing.

**56** Now in order to discover by what means the magnitude of tangible objects is perceived by sight, I need only reflect on what passes in my own mind, and observe what those things be which introduce the ideas of greater or lesser into my thoughts, when I look on any object. And these I find to be, *first*, the magnitude or extension of the visible object, which being immediately perceived by sight, is connected with that other which is tangible and placed at a distance. *Secondly*, the confusion or distinctness. And *thirdly*, the vigorousness or faintness of the aforesaid visible appearance. *Ceteris paribus*, by how much the greater or lesser the visible object is, by so much the greater or lesser do I conclude the tangible object to be. But, be the idea immediately perceived by sight never so large, yet if it be withal confused, I judge the magnitude of the thing to be but small. If it be distinct and clear, I judge it greater. And if it be faint, I apprehend it to be yet greater. What is here meant by confusion and faintness has been explained in section 35.

**57** Moreover the judgments we make of greatness do, in like manner as those of distance, depend on the disposition of the eye, also on the figure, number, and situation of objects and other circumstances that have been observed to attend great or small tangible magnitudes. Thus, for instance, the very same quantity of visible extension, which in the figure of a tower suggests the idea of great magnitude, shall in the figure of a man suggest the idea of much smaller magnitude. That this is owing to the experience we have had of the usual bigness of a tower and a man no one, I suppose, need be told.

**58** It is also evident that confusion or faintness have no more a necessary connexion with little or great magnitude than they have with little or great distance. As they suggest the latter, so they suggest the former to our minds. And by consequence, if it were not for experience, we should no more judge a faint or confused appearance to be connected with great or little magnitude, than we should that it was connected with great or little distance.

**59** Nor will it be found that great or small visible magnitude has any necessary relation to great or small tangible magnitude, so that the one may certainly be inferred from the other. But before we come to the proof of this, it is fit we consider the difference there is betwixt the extension and figure which is the proper object of touch, and that other which is termed visible; and how the former is principally, though not immediately, taken notice of when we look at any object. This has been before mentioned, but we shall here inquire into the cause thereof. We regard the objects that environ us in proportion as they are adapted to benefit or injure our own bodies, and thereby produce in our minds the sensations of pleasure or pain. Now bodies operating on our organs by an immediate application, and the hurt or advantage arising therefrom depending altogether on the tangible, and not at all on the visible qualities of any object: this is a plain reason why those should be regarded by us much more than these. And for this end the visive sense seems to have been bestowed on animals, to wit, that by the perception of visible ideas (which in themselves are not capable of affecting or any wise altering the frame of their bodies) they may be able to foresee (from the experience they have had what tangible ideas are connected with such and such visible ideas) the damage or benefit which is like to ensue, upon the application of their own bodies to this or that body which is at a distance. Which foresight, how necessary it is to the preservation of an animal, everyone's experience can inform him. Hence it is that when we look at an object, the tangible figure and extension thereof are principally attended to, whilst there is small heed taken of the visible figure and magnitude, which, though more immediately perceived, do less concern us, and are not fitted to produce any alteration in our bodies.

**60**   That the matter of fact is true will be evident to anyone who considers that a man placed at ten foot distance is thought as great as if he were placed at a distance only of five foot: which is true not with relation to the visible, but tangible greatness of the object, the visible magnitude being far greater at one station than it is at the other.

**61**   Inches, feet, *etc.*, are settled stated lengths whereby we measure objects and estimate their magnitude. We say, for example, an object appears to be six inches or six foot long. Now, that this cannot be meant of visible inches, *etc.*, is evident because a visible inch is itself no constant, determinate magnitude, and cannot therefore serve to mark out and determine the magnitude of any other thing. Take an inch marked upon a ruler. View it, successively, at the distance of half a foot, a foot, a foot and a half, *etc.*, from the eye; at each of which, and at all the intermediate distances, the inch shall have a different visible extension, *i.e.* there shall be more or fewer points discerned in it. Now I ask which of all these various extensions is that stated, determinate one that is agreed on for a common measure of other magnitudes? No reason can be assigned why we should pitch on one more than another. And except there be some invariable, determinate extension fixed on to be marked by the word 'inch', it is plain it can be used to little purpose; and to say a thing contains this or that number of inches shall imply no more than that it is extended, without bringing any particular idea of that extension into the mind. Farther, an inch and a foot, from different distances, shall both exhibit the same visible magnitude, and yet at the same time you shall say that one seems several times greater than the other. From all which it is manifest that the judgments we make of the magnitude of objects by sight are altogether in reference to their tangible extension. Whenever we say an object is great or small, of this or that determinate measure, I say it must be meant of the tangible, and not the visible extension, which, though immediately perceived, is nevertheless little taken notice of.

62    Now, that there is no necessary connexion between these two distinct extensions is evident from hence: because our eyes might have been framed in such a manner as to be able to see nothing but what were less than the *minimum tangibile*. In which case it is not impossible we might have perceived all the immediate objects of sight, the very same that we do now. But, unto those visible appearances, there would not be connected those different tangible magnitudes that are now. Which shows the judgments we make of the magnitude of things placed at a distance from the various greatness of the immediate objects of sight do not arise from any essential or necessary but only a customary tie, which has been observed between them.

63    Moreover, it is not only certain that any idea of sight might not have been connected with this or that idea of touch, which we now observe to accompany it. But also that the greater visible magnitudes might have been connected with, and introduced into our minds, lesser tangible magnitudes, and the lesser visible magnitudes greater tangible magnitudes. Nay, that it actually is so we have daily experience, that object which makes a strong and large appearance, not seeming near so great as another, the visible magnitude whereof is much less but more faint [and the appearance upper, or which is the same thing, painted

lower on the retina, which faintness and situation suggest both greater magnitude and greater distance.][13]

**64** From which, and from sections 57 and 58, it is manifest that as we do not perceive the magnitudes of objects immediately by sight, so neither do we perceive them by the mediation of anything which has a necessary connexion with them. Those ideas that now suggest unto us the various magnitudes of external objects before we touch them, might possibly have suggested no such thing. Or they might have signified them in a direct contrary manner, so that the very same ideas, on the perception whereof we judge an object to be small, might as well have served to make us conclude it great. Those ideas being in their own nature equally fitted to bring into our minds the idea of small or great, or no size at all, of outward objects, just as the words of any language are in their own nature indifferent to signify this or that thing, or nothing at all.

**65** As we see distance, so we see magnitude. And we see both in the same way that we see shame or anger in the looks of a man. Those passions are themselves invisible; they are nevertheless let in by the eye along with colours and alterations of countenance, which are the immediate object of vision, and which signify them for no other reason than barely because they have been observed to accompany them. Without which experience we should no more have taken blushing for a sign of shame than of gladness.

**66** We are nevertheless exceeding prone to imagine those things which are perceived only by the mediation of others to be themselves the immediate objects of sight; or, at least, to have in their own nature a fitness to be suggested by them, before ever they had been experienced to coexist with them. From which prejudice everyone, perhaps, will not find it easy to emancipate himself, by any the clearest convictions of reason. And there are some grounds to think that if there was one only invariable and universal language in the world, and that men were born with the faculty of speaking it, it would be the opinion of many that the ideas of other men's minds were properly perceived by the ear, or had at least a necessary and inseparable tie with the sounds that were affixed to them. All which seems to arise from want of a due application of our discerning faculty, thereby to discriminate between the ideas that are in our understandings, and consider them apart from each other; which

---

[13] The phrase in parentheses was added in the 1732 editions.

would preserve us from confounding those that are different, and make us see what ideas do, and what do not, include or imply this or that other idea.

**67** There is a celebrated phenomenon, the solution whereof I shall attempt to give by the principles that have been laid down, in reference to the manner wherein we apprehend by sight the magnitude of objects. The apparent magnitude of the moon when placed in the horizon is much greater than when it is in the meridian, though the angle under which the diameter of the moon is seen be not observed greater in the former case than in the latter; and the horizontal moon does not constantly appear of the same bigness, but at some times seems far greater than at others.

**68** Now in order to explain the reason of the moon's appearing greater than ordinary in the horizon, it must be observed that the particles which compose our atmosphere intercept the rays of light proceeding from any object to the eye. And by how much the greater is the portion of atmosphere interjacent between the object and the eye, by so much the more are the rays intercepted, and by consequence the appearance of the object rendered more faint, every object appearing more vigorous or more faint in proportion as it sends more or fewer rays into the eye. Now between the eye and the moon, when situated in the horizon, there lies a far greater quantity of atmosphere than there does when the moon is in the meridian. Whence it comes to pass that the appearance of the horizontal moon is fainter, and therefore by section 56 it should be thought bigger, in that situation than in the meridian or in any other elevation above the horizon.

**69** Farther, the air being variously impregnated, sometimes more and sometimes less, with vapours and exhalations fitted to retund and intercept the rays of light, it follows that the appearance of the horizontal moon has not always an equal faintness, and by consequence that luminary, though in the very same situation, is at one time judged greater than at another.

**70** That we have here given the true account of the phenomena of the horizontal moon will, I suppose, be farther evident to anyone from the following considerations. *First*, it is plain that which in this case suggests the idea of greater magnitude must be something which is itself perceived; for that which is unperceived cannot suggest to our perception any other thing. *Secondly*, it must be something that does not constantly remain the same, but is subject to some change or variation, since the appearance of the horizontal moon varies, being at one time greater than at another. And yet, *thirdly*,[14] it cannot be the visible figure or magnitude, since that remains the same or is rather lesser, by how much the moon is nearer to the horizon. It remains therefore that the true cause is that affection or alteration of the visible appearance which proceeds from the greater paucity of rays arriving at the eye, and which I term faintness, since this answers all the forementioned conditions, and I am not conscious of any other perception that does.

71   Add to this that, in misty weather, it is a common observation that the appearance of the horizontal moon is far larger than usual, which greatly conspires with and strengthens our opinion. Neither would it prove in the least irreconcilable with what we have said if the horizontal moon should chance sometimes to seem enlarged beyond its usual extent, even in more serene weather. For we must not only have regard to the mist which happens to be in the place where we stand; we ought also to take into our thoughts the whole sum of vapours and exhalations which lie betwixt the eye and the moon. All which co-operating to render the appearance of the moon more faint, and thereby increase its magnitude, it may chance to appear greater than it usually does, even in the horizontal position, at a time when, though there be no extraordinary fog or haziness just in the place where we stand, yet the air between the eye and the moon, taken all together, may be loaded with a greater quantity of interspersed vapours and exhalations than at other times.

72   It may be objected that in consequence of our principles the interposition of a body in some degree opaque, which may intercept a great part of the rays of light, should render the appearance of the moon in the meridian as large as when it is viewed in the horizon. To which I answer, it is not faintness anyhow applied that suggests greater magnitude, there being no necessary but only an experimental connexion between those two things. It follows that the faintness which enlarges the appearance must be applied in such sort, and with such circumstances, as have been observed to attend the vision of great magnitudes.

[14]   The first two editions gave alternative versions of the third reason, both of which were omitted in 1732. The first edition was as follows: 'Thirdly, it must not lie in the external circumjacent or intermediate objects, but be an affection of the very visible moon itself since, by looking through a tube, when all other objects are excluded from sight, the appearance is as great as ever. And yet, *fourthly* ...' The second edition read as follows: 'Thirdly, it must not lie in the circumjacent or intermediate objects, such as mountains, houses, fields, *etc.* because, that when all those objects are excluded from sight, the appearance is as great as ever. And yet, *fourthly* ...'

When from a distance we behold great objects, the particles of the intermediate air and vapours, which are themselves unperceivable, do interrupt the rays of light and thereby render the appearance less strong and vivid. Now, faintness of appearance caused in this sort has been experienced to coexist with great magnitude. But when it is caused by the interposition of an opaque sensible body, this circumstance alters the case, so that a faint appearance this way caused does not suggest greater magnitude, because it has not been experienced to coexist with it.

73   Faintness, as well as all other ideas or perceptions which suggest magnitude or distance, does it in the same way that words suggest the notions to which they are annexed. Now, it is known a word pronounced with certain circumstances, or in a certain context with other words, has not always the same import and signification that it has when pronounced in some other circumstances or different context of words.[15]

[The very same visible appearance as to faintness and all other respects, if placed on high, shall not suggest the same magnitude that it would if it were seen at an equal distance on a level with the eye. The reason whereof is that we are rarely accustomed to view objects at a great height. Our concerns lie among things situated rather before than above us, and accordingly our eyes are not placed on the top our heads, but in such a position as is most convenient for us to see distant objects standing in our way. And this situation of them being a circumstance which usually attends the vision of distant objects, we may from hence account for (what is commonly observed) an object's appearing of different magnitude, even with respect to its horizontal extension, on the top of a steeple, for example, an hundred feet high to one standing below, from what it would if placed at an hundred feet distance on a level with his eye. For it has been shown that the judgment we make on the magnitude of a thing depends not on the visible appearance alone, but also on divers other circumstances, any one of which being omitted or varied may suffice to make some alteration in our judgment. Hence, the circumstance of viewing a distant object in such a situation as is usual, and sits with the ordinary posture of the head and eyes being omitted, and instead thereof a different situation of the object, which requires a different

---

[15] The lengthy section in parentheses that follows replaced, in the second (1709) and subsequent editions, the following conclusion in the first edition. 'This well considered may, perhaps, prevent some objections that might otherwise be made, against what we have offered as the true explication of the appearances of the horizontal moon.'

posture of the head taking place, it is not to be wondered at if the magnitude be judged different.

But it will be demanded why an high object should constantly appear less than an equidistant low object of the same dimensions, for so it is observed to be. It may indeed be granted that the variation of some circumstances may vary the judgment made on the magnitude of high objects, which we are less used to look at. But it does not hence appear why they should be judged less rather than greater? I answer that in case the magnitude of distant objects was suggested by the extent of their visible appearance alone, and thought proportional thereto, it is certain they would then be judged much less than now they seem to be.[f] But several circumstances concurring to form the judgment we make on the magnitude of distant objects, by means of which they appear far larger than others, whose visible appearance has an equal or even greater extension, it follows that upon the change or omission of any of those circumstances, which are wont to attend the vision of distant objects and so come to influence the judgments made on their magnitude, they shall proportionably appear less than otherwise they would. For any of those things that caused an object to be thought greater than in proportion to its visible extension being either omitted or applied without the usual circumstances, the judgment depends more entirely on the visible extension, and consequently the object must be judged less. Thus in the present case the situation of the thing seen being different from what it usually is in those objects we have occasion to view, and whose magnitude we observe, it follows that the very same object, being an hundred feet high, should seem less than if it was an hundred feet off on (or nearly on) a level with the eye. What has been here set forth seems to me to have no small share in contributing to magnify the appearance of the horizontal moon, and deserves not to be passed over in the explication of it.]

**74** If we attentively consider the phenomenon before us, we shall find the not discerning between the mediate and immediate objects of sight to be the chief cause of the difficulty that occurs in the explication of it. The magnitude of the visible moon, or that which is the proper and immediate object of vision, is no greater when the moon is in the horizon than when it is in the meridian. How comes it, therefore, to seem greater in one situation than the other? What is it can put this cheat on the

---

[f] *Vide* section 79.

understanding? It has no other perception of the moon than what it gets by sight: and that which is seen is of the same extent, I say, the visible appearance has the same, or rather a less, magnitude when the moon is viewed in the horizontal than when in the meridional position; and yet it is esteemed greater in the former than in the latter. Herein consists the difficulty, which vanishes and admits of a most easy solution if we consider that, as the visible moon is not greater in the horizon than in the meridian, so neither is it thought to be so. It has been already shown that in any act of vision the visible object absolutely, or in itself, is little taken notice of, the mind still carrying its view from that to some tangible ideas which have been observed to be connected with it, and by that means come to be suggested by it. So that when a thing is said to appear great or small, or whatever estimate be made of the magnitude of any thing, this is meant not of the visible but of the tangible object. This duly considered, it will be no hard matter to reconcile the seeming contradiction there is, that the moon should appear of a different bigness, the visible magnitude thereof remaining still the same. For by section 56 the very same visible extension, with a different faintness, shall suggest a different tangible extension. When therefore the horizontal moon is said to appear greater than the meridional moon, this must be understood not of a greater visible extension, but of a greater tangible or real extension, which by reason of the more than ordinary fitness of the visible appearance, is suggested to the mind along with it.

75   Many attempts have been made by learned men to account for this appearance. Gassendus, Descartes, Hobbes, and several others have employed their thoughts on that subject. But how fruitless and unsatisfactory their endeavours have been is sufficiently shown in *The Philosophical Transactions*[g] [by Mr. Molyneux],[16] where you may see their several opinions at large set forth and confuted, not without some surprise at the gross blunders that ingenious men have been forced into by endeavouring to reconcile this appearance with the ordinary principles of optics. Since the writing of which there has been published in the *Transactions*[h] another paper relating to the same affair by the celebrated Dr. Wallis, wherein he attempts to account for that phenomenon which,

[g] *Philosophical Transactions*, number 187, p. 314 [vol. 16, 1692, 314–23].
[h] Number 187, p. 323.

[16] This phrase was in the first two editions only.

though it seems not to contain anything new or different from what had been said before by others, I shall nevertheless consider in this place.[17]

**76** His opinion, in short, is this: we judge not of the magnitude of an object by the visual angle alone, but by the visual angle in conjunction with the distance. Hence, though the angle remain the same or even become less, yet if withal the distance seem to have been increased, the object shall appear greater. Now, one way whereby we estimate the distance of anything is by the number and extent of the intermediate objects. When therefore the moon is seen in the horizon, the variety of fields, houses, *etc.*, together with the large prospect of the wide extended land or sea that lies between the eye and the utmost limb of the horizon, suggest unto the mind the idea of greater distance and consequently magnify the appearance. And this, according to Dr. Wallis, is the true account of the extraordinary largeness attributed by the mind to the horizontal moon at a time when the angle subtended by its diameter is not one jot greater than it used to be.

**77** With reference to this opinion, not to repeat what has been already said concerning distance, I shall only observe, *first*, that if the prospect of interjacent objects be that which suggests the idea of farther distance, and this idea of farther distance be the cause that brings into the mind the idea of greater magnitude, it should hence follow that if one looked at the horizontal moon from behind a wall, it would appear no bigger than ordinary. For in that case the wall interposing cuts off all that prospect of sea and land, *etc.*, which might otherwise increase the apparent distance and thereby the apparent magnitude of the moon. Nor will it suffice to say the memory even then suggests all that extent of land, *etc.*, which lies within the horizon – which suggestion occasions a sudden judgment of sense that the moon is farther off and larger than usual. For ask any man who, from such a station beholding the horizontal moon, shall think her greater than usual, whether he has at that time in his mind any idea of the intermediate objects, or long tract of land that lies between his eye and the extreme edge of the horizon? And whether it be that idea which is the cause of his making the aforementioned judgment? He will, I suppose, reply in the negative, and declare the horizontal moon shall appear greater than the meridional, though he never thinks of all or any of those things that lie between him and it.

[17] John Wallis (1616–1703).

*Secondly*, it seems impossible by this hypothesis to account for the moon's appearance in the very same situation at one time greater than at another; which nevertheless has been shown to be very agreeable to the principles we have laid down, and received a most easy and natural explication from them. [For the further clearing up of this point it is to be observed that what we immediately and properly see are only lights and colours in sundry situations and shades and degrees of faintness and clearness, confusion and distinctness. All which visible objects are only in the mind, nor do they suggest aught external, whether distance or magnitude, otherwise than by habitual connexion as words do things. We are also to remark that, beside the straining of the eyes, and beside the vivid and faint, the distinct and confused appearances (which, bearing some proportion to lines and angles, have been substituted instead of them in the foregoing part of this treatise), there are other means which suggest both distance and magnitude: particularly the situation of visible points or objects, as upper or lower, the one suggesting a farther distance and greater magnitude, the other a nearer distance and lesser magnitude. All which is an effect only of custom and experience, there being really nothing intermediate in the line of distance between the uppermost and lowermost, which are both equidistant, or rather at no distance from the eye, as there is also nothing in upper or lower, which by necessary connexion would suggest greater or lesser magnitude. Now, as these customary, experimental means of suggesting distance do likewise suggest magnitude, so they suggest the one as immediately as the other. I say they do not[i] first suggest distance, and then leave the mind from thence to infer or compute magnitude, but suggest magnitude as immediately and directly as they suggest distance.][18]

78    This phenomenon of the horizontal moon is a clear instance of the insufficiency of lines and angles for explaining the way wherein the mind perceives and estimates the magnitude of outward objects. There is nevertheless a use of computation by them in order to determine the apparent magnitude of things, so far as they have a connexion with, and are proportional to, those other ideas or perceptions which are the true and immediate occasions that suggest to the mind the apparent

---

[i] *Vide* section 53.

[18] The material in parentheses was added in the 1732 editions.

magnitude of things. But this, in general, may I think be observed concerning mathematical computation in optics: that it can never be very precise and exact, since the judgments we make of the magnitude of external things do often depend on several circumstances, which are not proportionable to, or capable of being defined by, lines and angles.

79   From what has been said we may safely deduce this consequence; to wit, that a man born blind and made to see would, at first opening of his eyes, make a very different judgment of the magnitude of objects intromitted by them from what others do. He would not consider the ideas of sight with reference to, or as having any connexion with, the ideas of touch. His view of them being entirely terminated within themselves, he can no otherwise judge them great or small than as they contain a greater or lesser number of visible points. Now, it being certain that any visible point can cover or exclude from view only one other visible point, it follows that whatever object intercepts the view of another has an equal number of visible points with it; and consequently they shall both be thought by him to have the same magnitude. Hence it is evident [that] one in those circumstances would judge his thumb, with which he might hide a tower or hinder its being seen, equal to that tower, or his hand, the interposition whereof might conceal the firmament from his view, equal to the firmament. How great an inequality soever there may in our apprehensions seem to be betwixt those two things, because of the customary and close connexion that has grown up in our minds between the objects of sight and touch; whereby the very different and distinct ideas of those two senses are so blended and confounded together as to be mistaken for one and the same thing; out of which prejudice we cannot easily extricate ourselves.

80   For the better explaining the nature of vision, and setting the manner wherein we perceive magnitudes in a due light, I shall proceed to make some observations concerning matters relating thereto, whereof the want of reflexion, and duly separating between tangible and visible ideas, is apt to create in us mistaken and confused notions. And *first*, I shall observe that the *minimum visibile* is exactly equal in all beings whatsoever that are endowed with the visive faculty. No exquisite formation of the eye, no peculiar sharpness of sight, can make it less in one creature than in other; for it not being distinguishable into parts, nor in any wise consisting of them, it must necessarily be the same to all. For suppose it otherwise, and that the *minimum visibile* of a mite, for instance, be less

than the *minimum visibile* of a man; the latter therefore may by detraction of some part be made equal to the former. It therefore consists of parts, which is inconsistent with the notion of a *mimimum visibile* or point.

81   It will perhaps be objected that the *minimum visibile* of a man really and in itself contains parts whereby it surpasses that of a mite, though they are not perceivable by the man. To which I answer, the *minimum visibile* having (in like manner as all other the proper and immediate objects of sight) been shown not to have any existence without the mind of him who sees it, it follows there cannot be any part of it that is not actually perceived, and therefore visible. Now for any object to contain several distinct visible parts, and at the same time to be a *minimum visibile*, is a manifest contradiction.

82   Of these visible points we see at all times an equal number. It is every whit as great when our view is contracted and bounded by near objects as when it is extended to larger and remoter. For it being impossible that one *minimum visibile* should obscure or keep out of sight more than one other, it is a plain consequence that when my view is on all sides bounded by the walls of my study, I see just as many visible points as I could, in case that by the removal of the study-walls and all other obstructions, I had a full prospect of the circumjacent fields, mountains, sea, and open firmament. For so long as I am shut up within the walls, by their interposition every point of the external objects is covered from my view. But each point that is seen being able to cover or exclude from sight one only other corresponding point, it follows that whilst my sight is confined to those narrow walls I see as many points, or *minima visibilia*, as I should were those walls away, by looking on all the external objects whose prospect is intercepted by them. Whenever therefore we are said to have a greater prospect at one time than another, this must be understood with relation, not to the proper and immediate, but the secondary and mediate objects of vision, which, as has been shown, properly belong to the touch.

83   The visive faculty considered with reference to its immediate objects may be found to labour of two defects. *First*, in respect of the extent or number of visible points that are at once perceivable by it, which is narrow and limited to a certain degree: it can take in at one view but a certain determinate number of *minima visibilia*, beyond which it cannot extend its prospect. *Secondly*, our sight is defective in that its view is not only narrow, but also for the most part confused. Of those things

that we take in at one prospect, we can see but a few at once clearly and unconfusedly; and the more we fix our sight on any one object, by so much the darker and more indistinct shall the rest appear.

**84**   Corresponding to these two defects of sight, we may imagine as many perfections, to wit: $1^{st}$, that of comprehending in one view a greater number of visible points; 2dly, of being able to view them all equally and at once with the utmost clearness and distinction. That those perfections are not actually in some intelligences of a different order and capacity from ours, it is impossible for us to know.

**85**   In neither of those two ways do microscopes contribute to the improvement of sight. For when we look through a microscope we neither see more visible points, nor are the collateral points more distinct than when we look with the naked eye at objects placed in a due distance. A microscope brings us, as it were, into a new world. It presents us with a new scene of visible objects quite different from what we behold with the naked eye. But herein consists the most remarkable difference, to wit, that whereas the objects perceived by the eye alone have a certain connexion with tangible objects, whereby we are taught to foresee what will ensue upon the approach or application of distant objects to the parts of our own body, which much conduces to its preservation, there is not the like connexion between things tangible and those visible objects that are perceived by help of a fine microscope.

**86**   Hence it is evident that were our eyes turned into the nature of microscopes, we should not be much benefited by the change. We should be deprived of the forementioned advantage we at present receive by the visive faculty, and have left us only the empty amusement of seeing, without any other benefit arising from it. But in that case, it will perhaps be said, our sight would be endued with a far greater sharpness and penetration than it now has. But it is certain from what we have already shown that the *minimum visibile* is never greater or lesser, but in all cases constantly the same. And in the case of microscopical eyes I see only this difference, to wit, that upon the ceasing of a certain observable connexion betwixt the divers perceptions of sight and touch, which before enabled us to regulate our actions by the eye, it would now be rendered utterly unserviceable to that purpose.

**87**   Upon the whole it seems that if we consider the use and end of sight, together with the present state and circumstances of our being, we shall not find any great cause to complain of any defect or imperfection in it, or easily conceive how it could be mended. With such admirable wisdom is that faculty contrived, both for the pleasure and convenience of life.

**88**   Having finished what I intended to say concerning the distance and magnitude of objects, I come now to treat of the manner wherein the mind perceives by sight their situation. Among the discoveries of the last age, it is reputed none of the least that the manner of vision has been more clearly explained than ever it had been before. There is at this day no one ignorant that the pictures of external objects are painted on the retina or fund of the eye; that we can see nothing which is not so painted; and that, according as the picture is more distinct or confused, so also is the perception we have of the object. But then, in this explication of vision, there occurs one mighty difficulty. The objects are painted in an inverted order on the bottom of the eye, the upper part of any object being painted on the lower part of the eye, and the lower part of the object on the upper part of the eye; and so also as to right and left. Since therefore the pictures are thus inverted, it is demanded how it comes to pass that we see the objects erect and in their natural posture?

**89**   In answer to this difficulty we are told that the mind, perceiving an impulse of a ray of light on the upper part of the eye, considers this ray as coming in a direct line from the lower part of the object; and in like manner tracing the ray that strikes on the lower part of the eye, it is directed to the upper part of the object. Thus in the adjacent figure, C, the lower point of the object ABC, is projected on *c*, the upper part of the eye. So likewise the highest point A is projected on *a*, the lowest part of the eye, which makes the representation *cba* inverted. But the mind considering the stroke that is made on *c* as coming in the straight line C*c* from the lower end of the object, and the stroke or impulse on *a* as coming in the line A*a* from the upper end of the object, is directed to make a right judgment of the situation of the object ABC, notwithstanding the picture of it is inverted. This is illustrated by conceiving a blind man who, holding in his hands two sticks that cross each other, with them touches the extremities of an object placed in a perpendicular situation. It is certain this man will judge that to be the upper part of the object, which he touches with the stick held in the undermost hand, and that to be the lower part of the object, which he touches with the stick in his uppermost hand. This is the common explication of the erect appearance of objects,

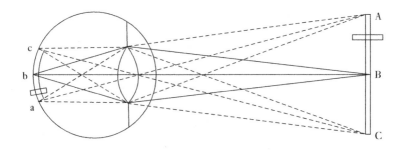

which is generally received and acquiesced in, being (as Mr. Molyneux tells us[i]) 'allowed by all men as satisfactory.'

**90** But this account to me does not seem in any degree true. Did I perceive those impulses, decussations, and directions of the rays of light in like manner as has been set forth, then indeed it would not be altogether void of probability, and there might be some pretence for the comparison of the blind man and his cross sticks. But the case is far otherwise. I know very well that I perceive no such thing. And of consequence I cannot thereby make an estimate of the situation of objects. I appeal to anyone's experience, whether he be conscious to himself that he thinks on the intersection made by the radious pencils, or pursues the impulses they give in right lines, whenever he perceives by sight the position of any object? To me it seems evident that crossing and tracing of the rays is never thought on by children, idiots, or in truth by any other, save only those who have applied themselves to the study of optics. And for the mind to judge of the situation of objects by those things without perceiving them, or to perceive them without knowing it, is equally beyond my comprehension. Add to this that the explaining the manner of vision by the example of cross sticks, and hunting for the object along the axes of the radious pencils, supposes the proper objects of sight to be perceived at a distance from us, contrary to what has been demonstrated.[19]

---

[i] *Dioptrics*, par. 2, chap. 7, p. 289 [*Dioptrica Nova*, Part 2, Chapter 7].

[19] The first two editions concluded the section with the following sentence, which was omitted in the 1732 editions: 'We may, therefore, venture to pronounce this opinion concerning the way wherein the mind perceives the erect appearance of objects, to be of a piece with those other tenets of writers in optics, which in the foregoing parts of this treatise we have had occasion to examine and refute.'

91   It remains, therefore, that we look for some other explication of this difficulty. And I believe it not impossible to find one, provided we examine it to the bottom, and carefully distinguish between the ideas of sight and touch, which cannot be too oft inculcated in treating of vision. But more especially throughout the consideration of this affair we ought to carry that distinction in our thoughts, for that from want of a right understanding thereof the difficulty of explaining erect vision seems chiefly to arise.

92   In order to disentangle our minds from whatever prejudices we may entertain with relation to the subject in hand, nothing seems more apposite than the taking into our thoughts the case of one born blind, and afterwards, when grown up, made to see. And though, perhaps, it may not be an easy task to divest ourselves entirely of the experience received from sight, so as to be able to put our thoughts exactly in the posture of such a one's, we must nevertheless, as far as possible, endeavour to frame true conceptions of what might reasonably be supposed to pass in his mind.

93   It is certain that a man actually blind, and who had continued so from his birth, would by the sense of feeling attain to have ideas of upper and lower. By the motion of his hands he might discern the situation of any tangible object placed within his reach. That part on which he felt himself supported, or towards which he perceived his body to gravitate, he would term lower, and the contrary to this upper, and accordingly denominate whatsoever objects he touched.

94   But then, whatever judgments he makes concerning the situation of objects are confined to those only that are perceivable by touch. All those things that are intangible and of a spiritual nature, his thoughts and desires, his passions, and in general all the modifications of the soul, to these he would never apply the terms 'upper' and 'lower', except only in a metaphorical sense. He may, perhaps, by way of allusion, speak of high or low thoughts; but those terms in their proper signification would never be applied to anything that was not conceived to exist without the mind. For a man born blind, and remaining in the same state, could mean nothing else by the words 'higher' and 'lower' than a greater or lesser distance from the earth, which distance he would measure by the motion or application of his hand or some other part of his body. It is therefore evident that all those things which, in respect of each other, would by him be thought higher or lower, must be such as were conceived to exist without his mind in the ambient space.

**95**  Whence it plainly follows that such a one, if we suppose him made to see, would not at first sight think that anything he saw was high or low, erect or inverted. For it has been already demonstrated in section 41 that he would not think the things he perceived by sight to be at any distance from him, or without his mind. The objects to which he had hitherto been used to apply the terms 'up' and 'down', 'high' and 'low', were such only as affected or were some way perceived by his touch. But the proper objects of vision make a new set of ideas, perfectly distinct and different from the former, and which can in no sort make themselves perceived by touch. There is, therefore, nothing at all that could induce him to think those terms applicable to them. Nor would he ever think it till such time as he had observed their connexion with tangible objects, and the same prejudice began to insinuate itself into his understanding, which from their infancy had grown up in the understandings of other men.

**96**  To set this matter in a clearer light I shall make use of an example. Suppose the above-mentioned blind person by his touch perceives a man to stand erect. Let us inquire into the manner of this. By the application of his hand to the several parts of a human body he had perceived different tangible ideas, which being collected into sundry complex ones, have distinct names annexed to them. Thus one combination of a certain tangible figure, bulk, and consistency of parts is called the head, another the hand, a third the foot, and so of the rest. All which complex ideas could, in his understanding, be made up only of ideas perceivable by touch. He had also by his touch obtained an idea of earth or ground, towards which he perceives the parts of his body to have a natural tendency. Now, by 'erect' nothing more being meant than that perpendicular position of a man wherein his feet are nearest to the earth, if the blind person by moving his hand over the parts of the man who stands before him perceives the tangible ideas that compose the head to be farthest from, and those that compose the feet to be nearest to, that other combination of tangible ideas which he calls earth, he will denominate that man erect. But if we suppose him on a sudden to receive his sight and that he behold a man standing before him, it is evident in that case he would neither judge the man he sees to be erect nor inverted. For he never having known those terms applied to any other save tangible things, or which existed in the space without him, and what he sees neither being tangible nor perceived as existing without, he could not know that in propriety of language they were applicable to it.

97  Afterwards, when upon turning his head or eyes up and down, to the right and left, he shall observe the visible objects to change, and shall also attain to know that they are called by the same names and connected with the objects perceived by touch, then indeed he will come to speak of them and their situation, in the same terms that he has been used to apply to tangible things. And those that he perceives by turning up his eyes he will call upper, and those that by turning down his eyes he will call lower.

98  All this seems to me the true reason why he should think those objects uppermost that are painted on the lower part of his eye. For by turning the eye up they shall be distinctly seen; as likewise those that are painted on the highest part of the eye shall be distinctly seen by turning the eye down, and are for that reason esteemed lowest. For we have shown that to the immediate objects of sight, considered in themselves, he would not attribute the terms 'high' and 'low'. It must therefore be on account of some circumstances which are observed to attend them. And these, it is plain, are the actions of turning the eye up and down, which suggest a very obvious reason why the mind should denominate the objects of sight accordingly high or low. And without this motion of the eye, this turning it up and down in order to discern different objects, doubtless 'erect', 'inverse', and other the like terms relating to the position of tangible objects would never have been transferred, or in any degree apprehended to belong to, the ideas of sight, the mere act of seeing including nothing in it to that purpose. Whereas the different situations of the eye naturally direct the mind to make a suitable judgment of the situation of objects intromitted by it.

99  Farther, when he has by experience learned the connexion there is between the several ideas of sight and touch, he will be able, by the perception he has of the situation of visible things in respect of one another, to make a sudden and true estimate of the situation of outward tangible things corresponding to them. And thus it is he shall perceive by sight the situation of external objects which do not properly fall under that sense.

100  I know we are very prone to think that, if just made to see, we should judge of the situation of visible things as we do now. But we are also as prone to think that, at first sight, we should in the same way apprehend the distance and magnitude of objects as we do now, which has been shown to be a false and groundless persuasion. And for the like

reasons the same censure may be passed on the positive assurance that most men, before they have thought sufficiently of the matter, might have of their being able to determine by the eye, at first view, whether objects were erect or inverse.

**101**  It will, perhaps, be objected to our opinion that a man, for instance, being thought erect when his feet are next the earth and inverted when his head is next the earth, it hence follows that by the mere act of vision, without any experience or altering the situation of the eye, we should have determined whether he were erect or inverted. For both the earth itself, and the limbs of the man who stands thereon, being equally perceived by sight, one cannot choose seeing what part of the man is nearest the earth, what part farthest from it, *i.e.*, whether he be erect or inverted.

**102**  To which I answer, the ideas which constitute the tangible earth and man are entirely different from those which constitute the visible earth and man. Nor was it possible, by virtue of the visive faculty alone, without superadding any experience of touch or altering the position of the eye, ever to have known, or so much as suspected, there had been any relation or connexion between them. Hence a man at first view would not denominate anything he saw earth, or head, or foot; and consequently he could not tell by the mere act of vision whether the head or feet were nearest the earth. Nor, indeed, would we have thereby any thought of earth or man, erect or inverse, at all: which will be made yet more evident if we nicely observe, and make a particular comparison between, the ideas of both senses.

**103**  That which I see is only variety of light and colours. That which I feel is hard or soft, hot or cold, rough or smooth. What similitude, what connexion have those ideas with these? Or how is it possible that anyone should see reason to give one and the same name to combinations of ideas so very different, before he had experienced their coexistence? We do not find there is any necessary connexion betwixt this or that tangible quality and any colour whatsoever. And we may sometimes perceive colours where there is nothing to be felt. All which makes it manifest that no man, at first receiving of his sight, would know there was any agreement between this or that particular object of his sight and any object of touch he had been already acquainted with. The colours, therefore, of the head would to him no more suggest the idea of head than they would the idea of foot.

**104**   Farther, we have at large shown[k] there is no discoverable necessary connexion between any given visible magnitude and any one particular tangible magnitude, but that it is entirely the result of custom and experience, and depends on foreign and accidental circumstances, that we can by the perception of visible extension inform ourselves what may be the extension of any tangible object connected with it. Hence it is certain that neither the visible magnitude of head or foot would bring along with them into the mind, at first opening of his eyes, the respective tangible magnitudes of those parts.

**105**   By the foregoing section it is plain the visible figure of any part of the body has no necessary connexion with the tangible figure thereof, so as at first sight to suggest it to the mind. For figure is the termination of magnitude; whence it follows that no visible magnitude having in its own nature an aptness to suggest any one particular tangible magnitude, so neither can any visible figure be inseparably connected with its corresponding tangible figure, so as of itself, and in a way prior to experience, it might suggest it to the understanding. This will be farther evident if we consider that what seems smooth and round to the touch may to sight, if viewed through a microscope, seem quite otherwise.

**106**   From all which laid together and duly considered, we may clearly deduce this inference. In the first act of vision no idea entering by the eye would have a perceivable connexion with the ideas to which the names 'earth', 'man', 'head', 'foot', *etc.*, were annexed in the understanding of a person blind from his birth, so as in any sort to introduce them into his mind, or make themselves be called by the same names, and reputed the same things with them, as afterwards they come to be.

**107**   There nevertheless remains one difficulty, which perhaps may seem to press hard on our opinion and deserve not to be passed over. For though it be granted that neither the colour, size, nor figure of the visible feet have any necessary connexion with the ideas that compose the tangible feet, so as to bring them at first sight into my mind, or make me in danger of confounding them before I had been used to, and for some time experienced, their connexion; yet thus much seems undeniable, namely, that the number of the visible feet being the same with that of the tangible feet, I may from hence without any experience of sight reasonably conclude that they represent or are connected with the feet

---

[k]   *Vide* sections 63 and 64.

rather than the head. I say, it seems the idea of two visible feet will sooner suggest to the mind the idea of two tangible feet than of one head; so that the blind man, upon first reception of the visive faculty, might know which were the feet or two, and which the head or one.

**108** In order to get clear of this seeming difficulty, we need only observe that diversity of visible objects does not necessarily infer diversity of tangible objects corresponding to them. A picture painted with great variety of colours affects the touch in one uniform manner; it is therefore evident that I do not by any necessary consecution, independent of experience, judge of the number of things tangible from the number of things visible. I should not, therefore, at first opening my eyes conclude that, because I see two, I shall feel two. How therefore can I, before experience teaches me, know that the visible legs, because two, are connected with the tangible legs, or the visible head, because one, is connected with the tangible head? The truth is, the things I see are so very different and heterogeneous from the things I feel, that the perception of the one would never have suggested the other to my thoughts or enabled me to pass the least judgment thereon, until I had experienced their connexion.

**109** But for a fuller illustration of this matter it ought to be considered that number (however some may reckon it amongst the primary qualities) is nothing fixed and settled, really existing in things themselves. It is entirely the creature of the mind, considering either an idea by itself, or in any combination of ideas to which it gives one name, and so makes it pass for an unit. According as the mind variously combines its ideas, the unit varies, and as the unit, so the number, which is only a collection of units, also varies. We call a window one, a chimney one, and yet a house in which there are many windows and many chimneys has an equal right to be called one, and many houses go to the making of one city. In these and the like instances it is evident the unit constantly relates to the particular draughts the mind makes of its ideas, to which it affixes names, and wherein it concludes more or less as best suits its own ends and purposes. Whatever, therefore, the mind considers as one, that is an unit. Every combination of ideas is considered as one thing by the mind, and in token thereof is marked by one name. Now, this naming and combining together of ideas is perfectly arbitrary, and done by the mind in such sort as experience shows it to be most convenient: without which our ideas had never been collected into such sundry distinct combinations as they now are.

110 Hence it follows that a man born blind and afterwards, when grown up, made to see, would not in the first act of vision parcel out the ideas of sight into the same distinct collections that others do, who have experienced which do regularly coexist and are proper to be bundled up together under one name. He would not, for example, make into one complex idea, and thereby esteem an unit, all those particular ideas which constitute the visible head or foot. For there can be no reason assigned why he should do so, barely upon his seeing a man stand upright before him. There crowd into his mind the ideas which compose the visible man, in company with all the other ideas of sight perceived at the same time. But all these ideas offered at once to his view, he would not distribute into sundry distinct combinations till such time as, by observing the motion of the parts of the man and other experiences, he comes to know which are to be separated and which to be collected together.

111 From what has been premised it is plain the objects of sight and touch make, if I may so say, two sets of ideas which are widely different from each other. To objects of either kind we indifferently attribute the terms 'high' and 'low', 'right' and 'left' and suchlike, denoting the position or situation of things. But then we must well observe that the position of any object is determined with respect only to objects of the same sense. We say any object of touch is high or low, according as it is more or less distant from the tangible earth; and in like manner we denominate any object of sight high or low, in proportion as it is more or less distant from the visible earth. But to define the situation of visible things with relation to the distance they bear from any tangible thing, or *vice versa*, this were absurd and perfectly unintelligible. For all visible things are equally in the mind and take up no part of the external space and, consequently, are equidistant from any tangible thing which exists without the mind.

112 Or rather, to speak truly, the proper objects of sight are at no distance, neither near nor far, from any tangible thing. For if we inquire narrowly into the matter, we shall find that those things only are compared together in respect of distance which exist after the same manner or appertain unto the same sense. For by the distance between any two points nothing more is meant than the number of intermediate points. If the given points are visible, the distance between them is marked out by the number of the interjacent visible points; if they are tangible, the distance between them is a line consisting of tangible points. But if they are one tangible and the other observable, the distance between them

does neither consist of points perceivable by sight nor by touch, *i.e.* it is utterly inconceivable. This, perhaps, will not find an easy admission into all men's understanding. However, I should gladly be informed whether it be not true by anyone who will be at the pains to reflect a little and apply it home to his thoughts.

113    The not observing what has been delivered in the two last sections seems to have occasioned no small part of the difficulty that occurs in the business of erect appearances. The head, which is painted nearest the earth, seems to be farthest from it; and on the other hand the feet, which are painted farthest from the earth, are thought nearest to it. Herein lies the difficulty, which vanishes if we express the thing more clearly and free from ambiguity, thus: how comes it that, to the eye, the visible head which is nearest the tangible earth seems farthest from the earth, and the visible feet, which are farthest from the tangible earth, seem nearest the earth? The question being thus proposed, who sees not the difficulty is founded on a supposition that the eye or visive faculty, or rather the soul by means thereof, should judge of the situation of visible objects with reference to their distance from the tangible earth? Whereas it is evident the tangible earth is not perceived by sight, and it has been shown in the two last preceding sections that the location of visible objects is determined only by the distance they bear from one another, and that it is nonsense to talk of distance, far or near, between a visible and tangible thing.

114    If we confine our thoughts to the proper objects of sight, the whole is plain and easy. The head is painted farthest from, and the feet nearest to, the visible earth; and so they appear to be. What is there strange or unaccountable in this? Let us suppose the pictures in the fund of the eye to be the immediate objects of the sight. The consequence is that things should appear in the same posture they are painted in; and is it not so? The head which is seen seems farthest from the earth which is seen, and the feet which are seen seem nearest to the earth, which is seen; and just so they are painted.

115    But, say you, the picture of the man is inverted, and yet the appearance is erect. I ask, what mean you by the picture of the man or, which is the same thing, the visible man's being inverted? You tell me it is inverted, because the heels are uppermost and the head undermost? Explain me this. You say that by the head's being undermost you mean that it is nearest to the earth, and by the heels being uppermost that they

are farthest from the earth. I ask again what earth you mean? You cannot mean the earth that is painted on the eye, or the visible earth. For the picture of the head is farthest from the picture of the earth, and the picture of the feet nearest to the picture of the earth; and accordingly the visible head is farthest from the visible earth, and the visible feet nearest to it. It remains, therefore, that you mean the tangible earth, and so determine the situation of visible things with respect to tangible things, contrary to what has been demonstrated in sections 111 and 112. The two distinct provinces of sight and touch should be considered apart, and as if their objects had no intercourse, no manner of relation one to another, in point of distance or position.

116    Farther, what greatly contributes to make us mistake in this matter is that, when we think of the pictures in the fund of the eye, we imagine ourselves looking on the fund of another's eye, or another looking on the fund of our own eye, and beholding the pictures painted thereon. Suppose two eyes A and B. A from some distance looking on the pictures in B sees them inverted, and for that reason concludes they are inverted in B; but this is wrong. There are projected in little on the bottom of A the images of the pictures of, suppose, man, earth, *etc.*, which are painted on B. And besides these the eye B itself, and the objects which environ it, together with another earth, are projected in a larger size on A. Now, by the eye A these larger images are deemed the true objects, and the lesser only pictures in miniature. And it is with respect to those greater images that it determines the situation of the smaller images. So that comparing the little man with the great earth, A judges him inverted, or that the feet are farthest from and the head nearest to the great earth. Whereas, if A compare the little man with the little earth, then he will appear erect, *i.e.* his head shall seem farthest from, and his feet nearest to, the little earth. But we must consider that B does not see two earths, as A does. It sees only what is represented by the little pictures in A, and consequently shall judge the man erect. For, in truth, the man in B is not inverted, for there the feet are next the earth; but it is the representation of it in A which is inverted, for there the head of the representation of the picture of the man in B is next the earth, and the feet farthest from the earth, meaning the earth which is without the representation of the pictures in B. For if you take the little images of the pictures in B, and consider them by themselves, and with respect only to one another, they are all erect and in their natural posture.

**117**   Farther, there lies a mistake in our imagining that the pictures of external objects are painted on the bottom of the eye. It has been shown there is no resemblance between the ideas of sight and things tangible. It has likewise been demonstrated that the proper objects of sight do not exist without the mind. Whence it clearly follows that the pictures painted on the bottom of the eye are not the pictures of external objects. Let anyone consult his own thoughts and then say what affinity, what likeness, there is between that certain variety and disposition of colours which constitute the visible man or picture of a man, and that other combination of far different ideas, sensible by touch, which compose the tangible man. But if this be the case, how come they to be accounted pictures or images, since that supposes them to copy or represent some originals or other?

**118**   To which I answer: in the forementioned instance the eye A takes the little images, included within the representation of the other eye B, to be pictures or copies, whereof the archetypes are not things existing without, but the larger pictures projected on its own fund and which by A are not thought pictures, but the originals or true things themselves. Though if we suppose a third eye C from a due distance to behold the fund of A, then indeed the things projected thereon shall, to C, seem pictures or images in the same sense that those projected on B do to A.

**119**   Rightly to conceive this point we must carefully distinguish between the ideas of sight and touch, between the visible and tangible eye; for certainly, on the tangible eye, nothing either is or seems to be painted. Again, the visible eye, as well as all other visible objects, have been shown to exist only in the mind which, perceiving its own ideas and comparing them together, calls some 'pictures' in respect of others. What has been said, being rightly comprehended and laid together, does, I think, afford a full and genuine explication of the erect appearance of objects; which phenomenon, I must confess, I do not see how it can be explained by any theories of vision hitherto made public.

**120**   In treating of these things the use of language is apt to occasion some obscurity and confusion, and create in us wrong ideas. For language being accommodated to the common notions and prejudices of men, it is scarce possible to deliver the naked and precise truth without great circumlocution, impropriety, and (to an unwary reader) seeming contradictions. I do therefore once for all desire whoever shall think it worth his while to understand what I have written concerning vision, that he would not stick in this or that phrase or manner of expression, but candidly collect my meaning from the whole sum and tenor of my discourse, and laying aside the words as much as possible, consider the bare notions themselves, and then judge whether they are agreeable to truth and his own experience, or no.

121   We have shown the way wherein the mind by mediation of visible ideas perceives or apprehends the distance, magnitude, and situation of tangible objects. We come now to inquire more particularly concerning the difference between the ideas of sight and touch, which are called by the same names, and see whether there be any idea common to both senses. From what we have at large set forth and demonstrated in the foregoing parts of this treatise, it is plain there is no one selfsame numerical extension perceived both by sight and touch; but that the particular figures and extensions perceived by sight, however they may be called by the same names and reputed the same things with those perceived by touch, are nevertheless different, and have an existence distinct and separate from them. So that the question is not now concerning the same numerical ideas, but whether there be any one and the same sort or species of ideas equally perceivable to both senses; or, in other words, whether extension, figure, and motion perceived by sight are not specifically distinct from extension, figure, and motion perceived by touch.

122   But before I come more particularly to discuss this matter, I find it proper to consider extension in abstract. For of this there is much talk, and I am apt to think that when men speak of extension as being an idea common to two senses, it is with a secret supposition that we can single out extension from other tangible and visible qualities, and form thereof an abstract idea, which idea they will have common both to sight and touch. We are therefore to understand by 'extension in abstract' an idea of extension, for instance, a line or surface entirely stripped of all other sensible qualities and circumstances that might determine it to any particular existence. It is neither black nor white nor red, nor has it any colour at all or any tangible quality whatsoever, and consequently it is of no finite determinate magnitude, for that which bounds or distinguishes one extension from another is some quality of circumstance wherein they disagree.

123   Now I do not find that I can perceive, imagine, or any wise frame in my mind such an abstract idea as is here spoken of. A line or surface

which is neither black, nor white, nor blue, nor yellow, *etc.*, nor long, nor short, nor rough, nor smooth, nor square, nor round, *etc.*, is perfectly incomprehensible. This I am sure of as to myself; how far the faculties of other men may reach they best can tell.

**124** It is commonly said that the object of geometry is abstract extension. But geometry contemplates figures. Now, figure is the termination of magnitude; but we have shown that extension in abstract has no finite determinate magnitude. Whence it clearly follows that it can have no figure, and consequently is not the object of geometry. It is indeed a tenet as well of the modern as of the ancient philosophers that all general truths are concerning universal abstract ideas; without which, we are told, there could be no science, no demonstration of any general proposition in geometry. But it were no hard matter, did I think it necessary to my present purpose, to show that propositions and demonstrations in geometry might be universal, though they who make them never think of abstract general ideas of triangles or circles.

**125** After reiterated endeavours to apprehend the general idea of a triangle, I have found it altogether incomprehensible. And surely if anyone were able to introduce that idea into my mind, it must be the author of the *Essay concerning Human Understanding*,[20] he who has so far distinguished himself from the generality of writers by the clearness and significancy of what he says. Let us therefore see how this celebrated author describes the general or abstract idea of a triangle.

> It must be (says he) neither oblique nor rectangular, neither equi-lateral, equicrural, nor scalenum; but all and none of these at once. In effect, it is somewhat[21] imperfect that cannot exist; an idea, wherein some parts of several different and inconsistent ideas are put together.[1]

This is the idea which he thinks needful for the enlargement of knowledge which is the subject of mathematical demonstration, and without which we could never come to know any general proposition concerning triangles.[22] That author acknowledges it does 'require some pains and

---

[1] *Essay on Human Understanding*, IV, vii, 9.

[20] John Locke.    [21] A slight misquotation from Locke, who has the term 'something' here.

[22] The following sentence, in the first two editions, was omitted in 1732. 'Sure I am, if this be the case, it is impossible for me to attain to know even the first elements of geometry; since I have not the faculty to frame in my mind such an idea as is here described.'

skill to form this general idea of a triangle.'[m] But had he called to mind what he says in another place, to wit, 'that ideas of mixed modes wherein any inconsistent ideas are put together cannot so much as exist in the mind, *i.e.* be conceived.'[n] I say, had this occurred to his thoughts, it is not improbable he would have owned it above all the pains and skill he was master of to form the above-mentioned idea of a triangle, which is made up of manifest, staring contradictions. That a man who laid so great a stress on clear and determinate ideas should nevertheless talk at this rate seems very surprising. But the wonder will lessen if it be considered that the source whence this opinion flows is the prolific womb which has brought forth innumerable errors and difficulties in all parts of philosophy and in all the sciences. But this matter, taken in its full extent, were a subject too comprehensive to be insisted on in this place. And so much for extension in abstract.

**126**  Some, perhaps, may think pure space, vacuum, or trine dimension to be equally the object of sight and touch. But though we have a very great propension to think the ideas of outness and space to be the immediate object of sight, yet, if I mistake not, in the foregoing parts of this essay that have been clearly demonstrated to be a mere delusion, arising from the quick and sudden suggestion of fancy, which so closely connects the ideas of distance with those of sight, that we are apt to think it is itself a proper and immediate object of that sense till reason corrects the mistake.

**127**  It having been shown that there are no abstract ideas of figure, and that it is impossible for us by any precision of thought to frame an idea of extension separate from all other visible and tangible qualities which shall be common both to sight and touch, the question now remaining is: whether the particular extensions, figures, and motions perceived by sight be of the same kind with the particular extensions, figures, and motions perceived by touch? In answer to which I shall venture to lay down the following proposition: *The extension, figures, and motions perceived by sight are specifically distinct from the ideas of touch called by the same names, nor is there any such thing as one idea or kind of idea*

---

[m]  *Ibid.*

[n]  *Ibid.*, III, x, 33 [What Locke wrote was as follows: 'Only if I put in my ideas of mixed modes or relations, any inconsistent ideas together, I fill my head also with *chimeras*; since such ideas, if well examined, cannot so much as exist in the mind, much less any real being be ever denominated from them.'].

*common to both senses.* This proposition may without much difficulty be collected from what has been said in several places in this essay. But because it seems so remote from, and contrary to, the received notions and settled opinion of mankind, I shall attempt to demonstrate it more particularly and at large by the following arguments.

**128**  When upon perception of an idea I range it under this or that sort, it is because it is perceived after the same manner, or because it has likeness or conformity with, or affects me in the same way as, the ideas of the sort I rank it under. In short, it must not be entirely new, but have something in it old and already perceived by me. It must, I say, have so much at least in common with the ideas I have before known and named as to make me give it the same name with them. But it has been, if I mistake not, clearly made out that a man born blind would not at first reception of his sight think the things he saw were of the same nature with the objects of touch, or had anything in common with them, but that they were a new set of ideas, perceived in a new manner, and entirely different from all he had ever perceived before. So that he would not call them by the same name, nor repute them to be of the same sort with anything he had hitherto known.[23]

**129**  *Secondly*, light and colours are allowed by all to constitute a sort or species entirely different from the ideas of touch. Nor will any man, I presume, say they can make themselves perceived by that sense. But there is no other immediate object of sight besides light and colours. It is therefore a direct consequence that there is no idea common to both senses.

**130**  It is a prevailing opinion, even amongst those who have thought and writ most accurately concerning our ideas and the ways whereby they enter into the understanding, that something more is perceived by sight than barely light and colours with their variations. Mr. Locke terms sight 'the most comprehensive of all our senses, conveying to our minds the ideas of light and colours, which are peculiar only to that sense; and also the far different ideas of space, figure, and motion.'[o] Space or distance, we have shown, is not otherwise the object of sight than of hearing.[p] And as for figure and extension, I leave it to anyone that shall calmly attend to

---

[o] *Essay on Human Understanding*, II, ix, 9.    [p] *Vide* section 46.

[23]  This final sentence from the first edition was omitted in subsequent editions. 'And surely, the judgment of such an unprejudiced person is more to be relied on in this case, than the sentiments of the generality of men: who in this, as in almost everything else, suffer themselves to be guided by custom, and the erroneous suggestions of prejudice, rather than reason and sedate reflexion.'

his own clear and distinct ideas to decide whether he has any idea intromitted immediately and properly by sight save only light and colours, or whether it be possible for him to frame in his mind a distinct abstract idea of visible extension or figure exclusive of all colour; and on the other hand, whether he can conceive colour without visible extension? For my own part, I must confess I am not able to attain so great a nicety of abstraction. In a strict sense, I see nothing but light and colours, with their several shades and variations. He who beside these also perceives by sight ideas far different and distinct from them has that faculty in a degree more perfect and comprehensive than I can pretend to. It must be owned that by the mediation of light and colours other far different ideas are suggested to my mind; but so they are by hearing, which beside sounds, which are peculiar to that sense, by their mediation suggests not only space, figure, and motion, but also all other ideas whatsoever that can be signified by words.

131 *Thirdly*, it is, I think, an axiom universally received that quantities of the same kind may be added together and make one entire sum. Mathematicians add lines together; but they do not add a line to a solid or conceive it as making one sum with a surface. These three kinds of quantity being thought incapable of any such mutual addition, and consequently of being compared together in the several ways of proportion, are by them esteemed entirely disparate and heterogeneous. Now let anyone try in his thoughts to add a visible line or surface to a tangible line or surface, so as to conceive them making one continued sum or whole. He that can do this may think them homogeneous; but he that cannot, must by the foregoing axiom think them heterogeneous. A blue and a red line I can conceive added together into one sum and making one continued line. But to make in my thoughts one continued line of a visible and tangible line added together is, I find, a task far more difficult and even insurmountable, and I leave it to the reflexion and experience of every particular person to determine for himself.

132 A farther confirmation of our tenet may be drawn from the solution of Mr. Molyneux's problem, published by Mr. Locke in his *Essay*,[24] which I shall set down as it there lies, together with Mr. Locke's opinion of it.

---

[24] Molyneux sent the problem to Locke on 2 March 1693, and he inserted it in the second edition of the *Essay* (II, ix, 8). Leibniz also discussed it in the *New Essays on Human Understanding*, trans. and ed. P. Remnant and J. Bennett (Cambridge: Cambridge University Press, 1996), II, ix, 8 (pp. 136–8).

'Suppose a man born blind, and now adult, and taught by his touch to distinguish between a cube and a sphere of the same metal, and nighly of the same bigness, so as to tell, when he felt one and t'other, which is the cube and which the sphere. Suppose then the cube and sphere placed on a table, and the blind man to be made to see. *Quaere*, Whether by his sight, before he touched them, he could now distinguish and tell which is the globe, which the cube?' To which the acute and judicious proposer answers: 'Not. For though he has obtained the experience of how a globe, how a cube, affects his touch, yet he has not yet attained the experience, that what affects his touch so or so, must affect his sight so or so; or that a protuberant angle in the cube that pressed his hand unequally, shall appear to his eye as it does in the cube.' I agree with this thinking gentleman, whom I am proud to call my friend, in his answer to this his problem; and am of opinion that the blind man at first sight would not be able with certainty to say which was the globe, which the cube, whilst he only saw them.[q]

**133** Now, if a square surface perceived by touch be of the same sort with a square surface perceived by sight, it is certain the blind man here mentioned might know a square surface as soon as he saw it. It is no more but introducing into his mind by a new inlet an idea he has been already well acquainted with. Since, therefore, he is supposed to have known by his touch that a cube is a body terminated by square surfaces, and that a sphere is not terminated by square surfaces; upon the supposition that a visible and tangible square differ only *in numero* it follows that he might know, by the unerring mark of the square surfaces, which was the cube, and which not, while he only saw them. We must therefore allow either that visible extension and figures are specifically distinct from tangible extension and figures, or else that the solution of this problem given by those two thoughtful and ingenious men is wrong.

**134** Much more might be laid together in proof of the proposition I have advanced. But what has been said is, if I mistake not, sufficient to convince anyone that shall yield a reasonable attention. And as for those that will not be at the pains of a little thought, no multiplication of words will ever suffice to make them understand the truth, or rightly conceive my meaning.

---

[q] *Essay on Human Understanding*, II, ix, 8.

**135** I cannot let go the above-mentioned problem without some reflexion on it. It has been made evident that a man blind from his birth would not, at first sight, denominate anything he saw by the names he had been used to appropriate to ideas of touch.[r] 'Cube', 'sphere', 'table' are words he has known applied to things perceivable by touch, but to things perfectly intangible he never knew them applied. Those words in their wonted application always marked out to his mind bodies or solid things which were perceived by the resistance they gave. But there is no solidity, no resistance or protrusion, perceived by sight. In short, the ideas of sight are all new perceptions to which there be no names annexed in his mind; he cannot therefore understand what is said to him concerning them. And to ask of the two bodies he saw placed on the table: which was the sphere, which the cube? were to him a question downright bantering and unintelligible; nothing he sees being able to suggest to his thoughts the idea of body, distance, or in general of anything he had already known.

**136** It is a mistake to think the same thing affects both sight and touch. If the same angle or square which is the object of touch be also the object of vision, what should hinder the blind man at first sight from knowing it? For though the manner wherein it affects the sight be different from that wherein it affected his touch, yet, there being beside this manner or circumstance, which is new and unknown, the angle or figure, which is old and known, he cannot choose but discern it.

**137** Visible figure and extension having been demonstrated to be of a nature entirely different and heterogeneous from tangible figure and extension, it remains that we inquire concerning motion. Now that visible motion is not of the same sort with tangible motion seems to need not farther proof, it being an evident corollary from what we have shown concerning the difference there is between visible and tangible extension. But for a more full and express proof hereof, we need only observe that one who had not yet experienced vision would not at first sight know motion. Whence it clearly follows that motion perceivable by sight is of a sort distinct from motion perceivable by touch. The antecedent I prove thus: by touch he could not perceive any motion but what was up or down, to the right or left, nearer or farther from him. Besides these and their several varieties or complications, it is impossible he

---

[r] *Vide* section 106.

should have any idea of motion. He would not therefore think anything to be motion, or give the name 'motion' to any idea which he could not range under some or other of those particular kinds thereof. But from section 95 it is plain that, by the mere act of vision, he could not know motion upwards or downwards, to the right or left, or in any other possible direction. From which I conclude he would not know motion at all at first sight. As for the idea of motion in abstract, I shall not waste paper about it, but leave it to my reader to make the best he can of it. To me it is perfectly unintelligible.

**138** The consideration of motion may furnish a new field for inquiry.[25] But since the manner wherein the mind apprehends by sight the motion of tangible objects, with the various degrees thereof, may be easily collected from what has been said concerning the manner wherein that sense suggests their various distances, magnitudes, and situations, I shall not enlarge any farther on this subject, but proceed to consider what may be alleged, with greatest appearance of reason, against the proposition we have shown to be true. For where there is so much prejudice to been countered, a bare and naked demonstration of the truth will scarce suffice. We must also satisfy the scruples that men may raise in favour of their preconceived notions, show whence the mistake arises, how it came to spread, and carefully disclose and root out those false persuasions that an early prejudice might have implanted in the mind.

**139** *First*, therefore, it will be demanded how visible extension and figures come to be called by the same name with tangible extension and figures, if they are not of the same kind with them? It must be something more than humour or accident that could occasion a custom so constant and universal as this, which has obtained in all ages and nations of the world, and amongst all ranks of men, the learned as well as the illiterate.

**140** To which I answer, we can no more argue a visible and tangible square to be of the same species from their being called by the same name, than we can that a tangible square, and the monosyllable consisting of six letters whereby it is marked, are of the same species because they are both called by the same name. It is customary to call written words and the things they signify by the same name. For words not being regarded in their own nature, or otherwise than as they are marks of things, it had been superfluous and beside the design of language to have given them

---

[25] Berkeley later undertook this study in his *Essay on Motion*, 1721.

names distinct from those of the things marked by them. The same reason holds here also. Visible figures are the marks of tangible figures, and from section 59 it is plain that in themselves they are little regarded, or upon any other score than for their connexion with tangible figures, which by nature they are ordained to signify. And because this language of nature does not vary in different ages or nations, hence it is that in all times and places visible figures are called by the same names as the respective tangible figures suggested by them, and not because they are alike or of the same sort with them.

**141** But, say you, surely a tangible square is liker to a visible square than to a visible circle. It has four angles and as many sides; so also has the visible square. But the visible circle has no such thing, being bounded by one uniform curve without right lines or angles, which makes it unfit to represent the tangible square but very fit to represent the tangible circle. Whence it clearly follows that visible figures are patterns of, or of the same species with, the respective tangible figures represented by them; that they are like unto them, and of their own nature fitted to represent them, as being of the same sort: and that they are in no respect arbitrary signs, as words.

**142** I answer, it must be acknowledged the visible square is fitter than the visible circle to represent the tangible square, but then it is not because it is liker or more of a species with it, but because the visible square contains in it several distinct parts, whereby to mark the several distinct corresponding parts of a tangible square, whereas the visible circle does not. The square perceived by touch has four distinct, equal sides; so also has it four distinct equal angles. It is therefore necessary that the visible figure which shall be most proper to mark it contain four distinct equal parts corresponding to the four sides of the tangible square, as likewise four other distinct and equal parts whereby to denote the four equal angles of the tangible square. And accordingly we see the visible figures contain in them distinct visible parts, answering to the distinct tangible parts of the figures signified or suggested by them.

**143** But it will not hence follow that any visible figure is like unto, or of the same species with, its corresponding tangible figure, unless it be also shown that not only the number but also the kind of the parts be the same in both. To illustrate this, I observe that visible figures represent tangible figures much after the same manner that written words do sounds. Now, in this respect words are not arbitrary, it not being indifferent what written word stands for any sound. But it is requisite that each word contain in it so many distinct characters as there are variations in the sound it stands for. Thus the single letter 'a' is proper to mark one simple uniform sound; and the word 'adultery' is accommodated to represent the sound annexed to it, in the formation whereof there being eight different collisions or modifications of the air by the organs of speech, each of which produces a different sound, it was fit the word representing it should consist of as many distinct characters, thereby to make each particular difference or part of the whole sound. And yet nobody, I presume, will say the single letter 'a' or the word 'adultery' are like unto, or of the same species with, the respective sound by them represented. It is indeed arbitrary that, in general, letters of any language represent sounds at all. But when that is once agreed, it is not arbitrary what combination of letters shall represent this or that particular sound. I leave this with the reader to pursue, and apply it in his own thoughts.

**144** It must be confessed that we are not so apt to confound other signs with the things signified, or to think them of the same species, as we are visible and tangible ideas. But a little consideration will show us how this may be, without our supposing them of a like nature. These signs are constant and universal, their connexion with tangible ideas has been learnt at our first entrance into the world; and ever since, almost every moment of our lives, it has been occurring to our thoughts, and fastening and striking deeper on our minds. When we observe that signs are variable, and of human institution; when we remember there was a time they were not connected in our minds with those things they now so readily suggest, but that their signification was learned by the slow steps of experience, this preserves us from confounding them. But when we find the same signs suggest the same things all over the world; when we know they are not of human institution, and cannot remember that we ever learned their signification, but think that at first sight they would have suggested to us the same things they do now: all this persuades us they are of the same species as the things respectively represented by them, and that it is by a natural resemblance they suggest them to our minds.

**145** Add to this that whenever we make a nice survey of any object, successively directing the optic axis to each point thereof, there are certain lines and figures described by the motion of the head or eye, which being in truth perceived by feeling, do nevertheless so mix themselves, as it were, with the ideas of sight, that we can scarce think but they appertain to that sense. Again, the ideas of sight enter into the mind several at once, more distinct and unmingled than is usual in the other senses beside the touch. Sounds, for example, perceived at the same instant, are apt to coalesce, if I may so say, into one sound; but we can perceive at the same time great variety of visible objects, very separate and distinct from each other. Now tangible extension being made up of several distinct coexistent parts, we may hence gather another reason that may dispose us to imagine a likeness or analogy between the immediate objects of sight and touch. But nothing, certainly, more contributes to blend and confound them together than the strict and close connexion they have with each other. We cannot open our eyes but the ideas of distance, bodies, and tangible figures are suggested by them. So swift and sudden and unperceived is the transition from visible to tangible ideas, that we can scarce forbear thinking them equally the immediate object of vision.

**146** The prejudice which is grounded on these, and whatever other causes may be assigned thereof, sticks so fast that it is impossible without obstinate striving and labour of the mind to get entirely clear of it. But the reluctancy we find in rejecting any opinion can be no argument of its truth to whoever considers what has been already shown with regard to the prejudices we entertain concerning the distance, magnitude, and situation of objects, prejudices so familiar to our minds, so confirmed and inveterate, as they will hardly give way to the clearest demonstration.

**147** Upon the whole, I think we may fairly conclude that the proper objects of vision constitute an universal language of the Author of nature,[26] whereby we are instructed how to regulate our actions in order to attain those things that are necessary to the preservation and well-being of our bodies, as also to avoid whatever may be hurtful and destructive of them. It is by their information that we are principally guided in all the transactions and concerns of life. And the manner wherein they signify and mark unto us the objects which are at a distance is the same with that of languages and signs of human appointment, which do not suggest the things signified by any likeness or identity of nature, but only by an habitual connexion that experience has made us to observe between them.

---

[26] The first edition had the phrase 'the universal language of Nature'.

**148**  Suppose one who had always continued blind to be told by his guide that, after he has advanced so many steps, he shall come to the brink of a precipice, or be stopped by a wall; must not this to him seem very admirable and surprising? He cannot conceive how it is possible for mortals to frame such predictions as these, which to him would seem as strange and unaccountable as prophesy does to others. Even they who are blessed with the visive faculty may (though familiarity make it less observed) find therein sufficient cause of admiration. The wonderful art and contrivance wherewith it is adjusted to those ends and purposes for what it was apparently designed, the vast extent, number, and variety of objects that are at once with so much ease and quickness and pleasure suggested by it: all these afford subject for much and pleasing speculation and may, if anything, give us some glimmering, analogous praenotion of things which are placed beyond the certain discovery and comprehension of our present state.

**149**  I do not design to trouble myself with drawing corollaries from the doctrine I have hitherto laid down. If it bears the test others may, so long as they shall think convenient, employ their thoughts in extending it farther and applying it to whatever purposes it may be subservient to. Only, I cannot forbear making some inquiry concerning the object of geometry, which the subject we have been upon naturally leads one to. We have shown there is no such idea as that of extension in abstract, and that there are two kinds of sensible extension and figures, which are entirely distinct and heterogeneous from each other. Now, it is natural to inquire which of these is the object of geometry.

**150**  Some things there are which at first sight incline one to think geometry conversant about visible extension. The constant use of the eyes, both in the practical and speculative arts of that science, very much induces us thereto. It would, without doubt, seem odd to a mathematician to go about to convince him the diagrams he saw upon paper were not the figures, or even the likeness of the figures, which make the subject of the demonstration; the contrary being held an unquestionable truth, not only by mathematicians, but also by those who apply themselves more particularly to the study of logic – I mean, who consider the nature of science, certainty, and demonstration – it being by them assigned as one reason of the extraordinary clearness and evidence of geometry that in this science the reasonings are free from those inconveniences which attend the use of arbitrary signs, the very ideas themselves being copied out and exposed to view upon paper. But, by the bye, how well this agrees with what they likewise assert of abstract ideas being the object of geometrical demonstration, I leave to be considered.

**151** To come to a resolution in this point we need only observe what has been said in sections 59, 60, 61, where it is shown that visible extensions in themselves are little regarded and have no settled determinate greatness, and that men measure altogether by the application of tangible extension to tangible extension. All which makes it evident that visible extension and figures are not the object of geometry.

**152** It is therefore plain that visible figures are of the same use in geometry that words are, and the one may as well be accounted the object of that science as the other, neither of them being otherwise concerned therein than as they represent or suggest to the mind the particular tangible figures connected with them. There is indeed this difference between the signification of tangible figures by visible figures, and of ideas by words: that whereas the latter is variable and uncertain, depending altogether on the arbitrary appointment of men, the former is fixed and immutably the same in all times and places. A visible square, for instance, suggests to the mind the same tangible figure in Europe that it does in America. Hence it is that the voice of [the Author of][27] nature, which speaks to our eyes, is not liable to that misinterpretation and ambiguity that languages of human contrivance are unavoidably subject to.

**153** Though what has been said may suffice to show what ought to be determined with relation to the object of geometry, I shall nevertheless, for the fuller illustration thereof, consider the case of an intelligence, or unbodied spirit, which is supposed to see perfectly well, *i.e.* to have a clear perception of the proper and immediate objects of sight, but to have no sense of touch. Whether there be any such being in nature or no is beside my purpose to inquire. It suffices that the supposition contains no contradiction in it. Let us now examine what proficiency such a one may be able to make in geometry, which speculation will lead us more clearly to see whether the ideas of sight can possibly be the object of that science.

**154** *First*, then, it is certain the aforesaid intelligence could have no idea of a solid, or quantity of three dimensions, which follows from its not having any idea of distance. We indeed are prone to think that we have by sight the ideas of space and solids, which arise from our imagining that

[27] 'The Author of' was added in 1732.

we do, strictly speaking, see distance and some parts of an object at a greater distance than others; which has been demonstrated to be the effect of the experience we have had, what ideas of touch are connected with such and such ideas attending vision. But the intelligence here spoken of is supposed to have no experience of touch. He would not, therefore, judge as we do, nor have any idea of distance, outness, or profundity, nor consequently of space or body, either immediately or by suggestion. Whence it is plain he can have no notion of those parts of geometry which relate to the mensuration of solids and their convex or concave surfaces, and contemplate the properties of lines generated by the section of a solid. The conceiving of any part whereof is beyond the reach of his faculties.

**155** Farther, he cannot comprehend the manner wherein geometers describe a right line or circle, the rule and compass, with their use, being things of which it is impossible he should have any notion. Nor is it an easier matter for him to conceive the placing of one plane or angle on another, in order to prove their equality, since that supposes some idea of distance or external space. All which makes it evident our pure intelligence could never attain to know so much as the first elements of plane geometry. And perhaps upon a nice inquiry it will be found he cannot even have an idea of plane figures any more than he can of solids, since some idea of distance is necessary to form the idea of a geometrical plane, as will appear to whoever shall reflect a little on it.

**156** All that is properly perceived by the visive faculty amounts to no more than colours, with their variations and different proportions of light and shade. But the perpetual mutability and fleetingness of those immediate objects of sight render them incapable of being managed after the manner of geometrical figures; nor is it in any degree useful that they should. It is true there are divers of them perceived at once, and more of some and less of others; but accurately to compute their magnitude and assign precise determinate proportions between things so variable and inconstant, if we suppose it possible to be done, must yet be a very trifling and insignificant labour.

**157** I must confess men are tempted to think that flat or plane figures are immediate objects of sight, though they acknowledge solids are not. And this opinion is grounded on what is observed in painting, wherein (it seems) the ideas immediately imprinted on the mind are only of planes variously coloured, which by a sudden act of the judgment are changed into solids. But with a little attention we shall find the planes here mentioned as the immediate objects of sight are not visible but tangible planes. For when we say that pictures are planes, we mean thereby that they appear to the touch smooth and uniform. But then this smoothness and uniformity or, in other words, this planeness of the picture, is not perceived immediately by vision, for it appears to the eye various and multiform.

**158** From all which we may conclude that planes are no more the immediate object of sight than solids. What we strictly see are not solids, nor yet planes variously coloured; they are only diversity of colours. And some of these suggest to the mind solids, and others plane figures, just as they have been experienced to be connected with the one or the other. So that we see planes in the same way that we see solids, both being equally suggested by the immediate objects of sight, which accordingly are themselves denominated planes and solids. But though they are called by the same names with the things marked by them, they are nevertheless of a nature entirely different, as has been demonstrated.

**159** What has been said is, if I mistake not, sufficient to decide the question we proposed to examine, concerning the ability of a pure spirit, such as we have described, to know geometry. It is, indeed, no easy matter for us to enter precisely into the thoughts of such an intelligence, because we cannot without great pains cleverly separate and disentangle in our thoughts the proper objects of sight from those of touch, which are connected with them. This, indeed, in a complete degree seems scarce possible to be performed; which will not seem strange to us if we consider how hard it is for anyone to hear the words of his native language pronounced in his ears without understanding them. Though he endeavour to disunite the meaning from the sound, it will nevertheless intrude into his thoughts, and he shall find it extreme difficult, if not impossible, to put himself exactly in the posture of a foreigner that never learned the language, so as to be affected barely with the sounds themselves, and not perceive the signification annexed to them. By this time, I suppose, it is clear that neither abstract nor visible extension makes the object of geometry; the not discerning of which may perhaps have created some difficulty and useless labour in mathematics.[28]

---

[28] In the 1732 editions Berkeley omitted the final sentences of earlier editions, which complained of 'the abstruse and fine geometry' that was studied with such 'ardour' in his time.

# A Treatise Concerning the Principles of Human Knowledge

Wherein the Chief Causes of Error and Difficulty in the Sciences, with the grounds of Scepticism, Atheism, and Irreligion, are inquired into.

2nd edition 1734

## [The Preface

What I here make public has, after a long and scrupulous inquiry, seemed to me evidently true, and not unuseful to be known, particularly to those who are tainted with scepticism, or want a demonstration of the existence and immateriality of God, or the natural immortality of the soul. Whether it be so or no, I am content the reader should impartially examine, since I do not think my self any farther concerned for the success of what I have written, than as it is agreeable to truth. But to the end this may not suffer, I make it my request that the reader suspend his judgment, till he has once, at least, read the whole through with that degree of attention and thought which the subject matter shall seem to deserve. For as there are some passages that, taken by themselves, are very liable (nor could it be remedied) to gross misinterpretation, and to be charged with most absurd consequences, which, nevertheless, upon an entire perusal will appear not to follow from them: so likewise, though the whole should be read over, yet, if this be done transiently, it is very probable my sense may be mistaken; but to a thinking reader, I flatter my self, it will be throughout clear and obvious. As for the characters of novelty and singularity, which some of the following notions may seem to bear, it is, I hope, needless to make any apology on that account. He must surely be either very weak, or very little acquainted with the sciences, who shall reject a truth, that is capable of demonstration, for no other reason but because it is newly known and contrary to the prejudices of mankind. Thus much I thought fit to premise in order to prevent, if possible, the hasty censures of a sort of men, who are too apt to condemn an opinion before they rightly comprehend it.][1]

## Introduction

1   Philosophy being nothing else but the study of wisdom and truth, it may with reason be expected, that those who have spent most time and pains in it should enjoy a greater calm and serenity of mind, a greater clearness and evidence of knowledge, and be less disturbed with doubts and difficulties than other men. Yet so it is we see the illiterate bulk of mankind that walk the high-road of plain, common sense, and are governed by the dictates of nature, for the most part easy and undisturbed. To them nothing that's familiar appears unaccountable or difficult to comprehend. They complain not of any want of evidence in their senses, and are out of all danger of becoming sceptics. But no sooner do we depart from sense and instinct to follow the light of a superior principle, to reason, meditate, and reflect on the nature of things, but a thousand scruples spring up in our minds, concerning those things which before we seemed fully to comprehend. Prejudices and errors of sense do from all parts discover themselves to our view; and endeavouring to correct these by reason, we are insensibly drawn into uncouth paradoxes, difficulties, and inconsistences, which multiply and grow upon us as we advance in speculation; till at length, having wandered through many intricate mazes, we find our selves just where we were, or, which is worse, sit down in a forlorn scepticism.

2   The cause of this is thought to be the obscurity of things, or the natural weakness and imperfection of our understandings. It is said the faculties we have are few, and those designed by nature for the support and comfort of life, and not to penetrate into the inward essence and

---

[1] The Preface was omitted from the 1734 edition.

constitution of things.[2] Besides, the mind of man being finite, when it treats of things which partake of infinity, it is not to be wondered at, if it run into absurdities and contradictions; out of which it is impossible it should ever extricate it self, it being of the nature of infinite not to be comprehended by that which is finite.

3 But perhaps we may be too partial to our selves in placing the fault originally in our faculties, and not rather in the wrong use we make of them. It is a hard thing to suppose, that right deductions from true principles should ever end in consequences which cannot be maintained or made consistent. We should believe that God has dealt more bountifully with the sons of men, than to give them a strong desire for that knowledge, which He had placed quite out of their reach. This were not agreeable to the wonted, indulgent methods of Providence, which, whatever appetites it may have implanted in the creatures, usually furnishes them with such means as, if rightly made use of, will not fail to satisfy them. Upon the whole, I am inclined to think that the far greater part, if not all, of those difficulties which have hitherto amused philosophers, and blocked up the way to knowledge, are entirely owing to our selves. That we have first raised a dust, and then complain, we cannot see.

4 My purpose therefore is to try if I can discover what those principles are, which have introduced all that doubtfulness and uncertainty, those absurdities and contradictions into the several sects of philosophy; insomuch that the wisest men have thought our ignorance incurable, conceiving it to arise from the natural dullness and limitation of our faculties. And surely it is a work well deserving our pains, to make a strict inquiry concerning the first principles of human knowledge, to sift and examine them on all sides, especially since there may be some grounds to suspect that those lets and difficulties, which stay and embarrass the mind in its search after truth, do not spring from any darkness and intricacy in the objects, or natural defect in the understanding, so much as from false principles which have been insisted on, and might have been avoided.

5 How difficult and discouraging soever this attempt may seem, when I consider how many great and extraordinary men have gone before me in the same designs, yet I am not without some hopes, upon the consideration that the largest views are not always the clearest, and

---

[2] Locke argued in the *Essay* that it was impossible to know the 'internal Fabrick and real Essences of Bodies' (IV, xii, 11); the same theme is found in II, xxiii, 32; IV, iii, 6; IV, iii, 23.

that he who is short-sighted will be obliged to draw the object nearer, and may, perhaps, by a close and narrow survey discern that which had escaped far better eyes.

6  In order to prepare the mind of the reader for the easier conceiving what follows, it is proper to premise somewhat, by way of introduction, concerning the nature and abuse of language. But the unravelling this matter leads me in some measure to anticipate my design, by taking notice of what seems to have had a chief part in rendering speculation intricate and perplexed, and to have occasioned innumerable errors and difficulties in almost all parts of knowledge. And that is the opinion that the mind has a power of framing abstract ideas or notions of things. He who is not a perfect stranger to the writings and disputes of philosophers, must needs acknowledge that no small part of them are spent about abstract ideas. These are in a more especial manner, thought to be the object of those sciences which go by the name of 'logic' and 'metaphysics', and of all that which passes under the notion of the most abstracted and sublime learning, in all which one shall scarce find any question handled in such a manner, as does not suppose their existence in the mind, and that it is well acquainted with them.

7  It is agreed on all hands, that the qualities or modes of things do never really exist each of them apart by it self and separated from all others, but are mixed, as it were, and blended together, several in the same object. But we are told, the mind being able to consider each quality singly, or abstracted from those other qualities with which it is united, does by that means frame to it self abstract ideas. For example, there is perceived by sight an object extended, coloured, and moved; this mixed or compound idea the mind resolving into its simple, constituent parts, and viewing each by it self, exclusive of the rest, does frame the abstract ideas of extension, colour, and motion. Not that it is possible for colour or motion to exist without extension, but only that the mind can frame to it self by abstraction the idea of colour exclusive of extension, and of motion exclusive of both colour and extension.

8  Again, the mind having observed that in the particular extensions perceived by sense, there is something common and alike in all, and some other things peculiar, as this or that figure or magnitude, which distinguish them one from another, it considers apart or singles out by it self that which is common, making thereof a most abstract idea of extension, which is neither line, surface, nor solid, nor has any figure or magnitude

but is an idea entirely prescinded from all these. So likewise the mind, by leaving out of the particular colours perceived by sense that which distinguishes them one from another, and retaining that only which is common to all, makes an idea of colour in abstract which is neither red, nor blue, nor white, nor any other determinate colour. And in like manner by considering motion abstractedly not only from the body moved, but likewise from the figure it describes, and all particular directions and velocities, the abstract idea of motion is framed; which equally corresponds to all particular motions whatsoever that may be perceived by sense.

9 And as the mind frames to it self abstract ideas of qualities or modes, so does it, by the same precision or mental separation, attain abstract ideas of the more compounded beings, which include several coexistent qualities. For example, the mind having observed that Peter, James, and John, resemble each other, in certain common agreements of shape and other qualities, leaves out of the complex or compounded idea it has of Peter, James, and any other particular man, that which is peculiar to each, retaining only what is common to all; and so makes an abstract idea wherein all the particulars equally partake, abstracting entirely from and cutting off all those circumstances and differences, which might determine it to any particular existence. And after this manner it is said we come by the abstract idea of 'man' or, if you please, humanity or human nature; wherein it is true, there is included colour, because there is no man but has some colour, but then it can be neither white, nor black, nor any particular colour; because there is no one particular colour wherein all men partake. So likewise there is included stature, but then it is neither tall stature nor low stature, nor yet middle stature, but something abstracted from all these. And so of the rest.

Moreover, there being a great variety of other creatures that partake in some parts, but not all, of the complex idea of 'man', the mind leaving out those parts which are peculiar to men, and retaining those only which are common to all the living creatures, frames the idea of 'animal', which abstracts not only from all particular men, but also all birds, beasts, fishes, and insects. The constituent parts of the abstract idea of animal are body, life, sense, and spontaneous motion. By 'body' is meant body without any particular shape or figure, there being no one shape or figure common to all animals, without covering, either of hair or feathers, or scales, etc. nor yet naked: hair, feathers, scales, and nakedness being the distinguishing properties of particular animals, and for that reason left out of the abstract idea. Upon the same account the spontaneous motion must be neither walking, nor flying, nor creeping, it is nevertheless a motion, but what that motion is, it is not easy to conceive.

10    Whether others have this wonderful faculty of abstracting their ideas, they best can tell; for my self I find indeed I have a faculty of imagining, or representing to my self the ideas of those particular things I have perceived and of variously compounding and dividing them. I can imagine a man with two heads or the upper parts of a man joined to the body of a horse. I can consider the hand, the eye, the nose, each by it self abstracted or separated from the rest of the body. But then whatever hand or eye I imagine, it must have some particular shape and colour. Likewise the idea of man that I frame to my self must be either of a white, or a black, or a tawny, a straight, or a crooked, a tall, or a low, or a middle-sized man. I cannot by any effort of thought conceive the abstract idea above described. And it is equally impossible for me to form the abstract idea of motion distinct from the body moving, and which is neither swift nor slow, curvilinear nor rectilinear; and the like may be said of all other abstract general ideas whatsoever. To be plain, I own my self able to abstract in one sense, as when I consider some particular parts or qualities separated from others with which, though they are united in some object, yet it is possible they may really exist without them. But I deny that I can abstract one from another or conceive separately, those qualities which it is impossible should exist so separated, or that I can frame a general notion by abstracting from particulars in the manner aforesaid. Which two last are the proper acceptations of 'abstraction'. And there are grounds to think most men will acknowledge themselves to be in my case. The generality of men which are simple and illiterate never pretend to abstract notions. It is said they are difficult and not to be attained without pains and study. We may therefore reasonably conclude that, if such there be, they are confined only to the learned.

11    I proceed to examine what can be alleged in defence of the doctrine of abstraction, and try if I can discover what it is that inclines the men of speculation to embrace an opinion, so remote from common sense as that seems to be. There has been a late deservedly esteemed philosopher, who, no doubt, has given it very much countenance by

seeming to think the having abstract general ideas is what puts the widest difference in point of understanding betwixt man and beast.[3]

> The having of general ideas, (*saith he*) is that which puts a perfect distinction betwixt man and brutes, and is an excellency which the faculties of brutes do by no means attain unto. For it is evident we observe no footsteps in them of making use of general signs for universal ideas; from which we have reason to imagine that they have not the faculty of *abstracting* or making general ideas, since they have no use of words or any other general signs.

And a little after:

> Therefore, I think, we may suppose that it is in this that the species of brutes are discriminated from men, and 'tis that proper difference wherein they are wholly separated, and which at last widens to so wide a distance. For if they have any ideas at all, and are not bare machines (as some would have them) we cannot deny them to have some reason. It seems as evident to me that they do some of them in certain instances reason as that they have sense, but it is only in particular ideas, just as they receive them from their senses. They are the best of them tied up within those narrow bounds, and have not (as I think) the faculty to enlarge them by any kind of *abstraction.*[a]

I readily agree with this learned author, that the faculties of brutes can by no means attain to abstraction. But then if this be made the distinguishing property of that sort of animals, I fear a great many of those that pass for men must be reckoned into their number. The reason that is here assigned why we have no grounds to think brutes have abstract general ideas, is that we observe in them no use of words or any other general signs; which is built on this supposition, to wit, that the making use of words, implies the having general ideas. From which it follows, that men who use language are able to abstract or generalize their ideas. That this is the sense and arguing of the author will further appear by his answering the question he in another place puts. 'Since all things that exist are only particulars, how come we by general terms?' His answer is, 'Words

---

[a] *Essay on Human Understanding*, Book II, Chapter xi, Sections 10 and 11.

[3] John Locke.

become general by being made the signs of general ideas.'[b] But it seems that a word becomes general by being made the sign, not of an abstract general idea but of several particular ideas, any one of which it indifferently suggests to the mind. For example, when it is said 'the change of motion is proportional to the impressed force', or that 'whatever has extension is divisible', these propositions are to be understood of motion and extension in general; and nevertheless it will not follow that they suggest to my thoughts an idea of motion without a body moved, or any determinate direction and velocity, or that I must conceive an abstract general idea of extension, which is neither line, surface nor solid, neither great nor small, black, white, nor red, nor of any other determinate colour. It is only implied that whatever motion I consider, whether it be swift or slow, perpendicular, horizontal or oblique, or in whatever object, the axiom concerning it holds equally true. As does the other of every particular extension, it matters not whether line, surface or solid, whether of this or that magnitude or figure.

12   By observing how ideas become general, we may the better judge how words are made so. And here it is to be noted that I do not deny absolutely there are general ideas, but only that there are any abstract general ideas; for in the passage above quoted, wherein there is mention of general ideas, it is always supposed that they are formed by abstraction, after the manner set forth in Sections 8 and 9. Now if we will annex a meaning to our words, and speak only of what we can conceive, I believe we shall acknowledge that an idea, which considered in it self is particular, becomes general by being made to represent or stand for all other particular ideas of the same sort. To make this plain by an example, suppose a geometrician is demonstrating the method of cutting a line in two equal parts. He draws, for instance, a black line of an inch in length; this, which in it self is a particular line, is nevertheless with regard to its signification general, since as it is there used, it represents all particular lines whatsoever; so that what is demonstrated of it is demonstrated of all lines or, in other words, of a line in general. And as that particular line becomes general, by being made a sign, so the name 'line' which taken absolutely is particular, by being a sign is made general. And as the former owes its generality, not to its being the sign of an abstract or general line, but of all particular right lines that may possibly exist, so the

[b] *Essay on Human Understanding*, Book III, Chapter iii, Section 6.

latter must be thought to derive its generality from the same cause, namely, the various particular lines which it indifferently denotes.

**13** To give the reader a yet clearer view of the nature of abstract ideas, and the uses they are thought necessary to, I shall add one more passage out of the *Essay on Human Understanding*, which is as follows.

> Abstract ideas are not so obvious or easy to children or the yet unexercised mind as particular ones. If they seem so to grown men, it is only because by constant and familiar use they are made so. For when we nicely reflect upon them, we shall find that general ideas are fictions and contrivances of the mind, that carry difficulty with them, and do not so easily offer themselves, as we are apt to imagine. For example, does it not require some pains and skill to form the general idea of a triangle (which is yet none of the most abstract, comprehensive, and difficult) for it must be neither oblique nor rectangle, neither equilateral, equicrural, nor scalenon, but *all and none* of these at once. In effect, it is something imperfect that cannot exist, an idea wherein some parts of several different and *inconsistent* ideas are put together. It is true the mind in this imperfect state has need of such ideas, and makes all the haste to them it can, for the conveniency of communication and enlargement of knowledge, to both which it is naturally very much inclined. But yet one has reason to suspect such ideas are marks of our imperfection. At least this is enough to show that the most abstract and general ideas are not those that the mind is first and most easily acquainted with, nor such as its earliest knowledge is conversant about.[c]

If any man has the faculty of framing in his mind such an idea of a triangle as is here described, it is in vain to pretend to dispute him out of it, nor would I go about it. All I desire is that the reader would fully and certainly inform himself whether he has such an idea or no. And this, methinks, can be no hard task for any one to perform. What more easy than for any one to look a little into his own thoughts, and there try whether he has, or can attain to have, an idea that shall correspond with the description that is here given of the general idea of a triangle, which is 'neither oblique, nor rectangle, equilateral, equicrural, nor scalenon, but all and none of these at once'?

**14** Much is here said of the difficulty that abstract ideas carry with them, and the pains and skill requisite to the forming them. And it is on all hands agreed that there is need of great toil and labour of the mind, to emancipate our thoughts from particular objects, and raise them to those sublime speculations that are conversant about abstract ideas. From all which the natural consequence should seem to be, that so difficult a thing as the forming abstract ideas was not necessary for 'communication', which is so easy and familiar to all sorts of men. But we are told, if they seem obvious and easy to grown men, 'it is only because by constant and familiar use they are made so'. Now I would fain know at what time it is, men are employed in surmounting that difficulty, and furnishing themselves with those necessary helps for discourse. It cannot be when they are grown up, for then it seems they are not conscious of any such pains-taking; it remains therefore to be the business of their childhood. And surely, the great and multiplied labour of framing abstract notions, will be found a hard task for that tender age. Is it not a hard thing to imagine, that a couple of children cannot prate together, of their sugar-plums and rattles and the rest of their little trinkets, till they have first tacked together numberless inconsistencies, and so framed in their minds abstract general ideas, and annexed them to every common name they make use of?

**15**   Nor do I think them a whit more needful for the 'enlargement of knowledge' than for 'communication'. It is I know a point much insisted on, that all knowledge and demonstration are about universal notions, to which I fully agree. But then it does not appear to me that those notions are formed by abstraction in the manner premised; universality, so far as I can comprehend, not consisting in the absolute, positive nature or conception of any thing, but in the relation it bears to the particulars signified or represented by it, by virtue whereof it is that things, names, or notions, being in their own nature particular, are rendered universal. Thus when I demonstrate any proposition concerning triangles, it is to be supposed that I have in view the universal idea of a triangle; which ought not to be understood as if I could frame an idea of a triangle which was neither equilateral nor scalenon nor equicrural. But only that the particular triangle I consider, whether of this or that sort it matters not, equally stands for and represents all rectilinear triangles whatsoever, and is in that sense universal. All which seems very plain and not to include any difficulty in it.

**16**   But here it will be demanded, how we can know any proposition to be true of all particular triangles, except we have first seen it demonstrated of the abstract idea of a triangle which equally agrees to all? For because a property may be demonstrated to agree to some one particular triangle, it will not thence follow that it equally belongs to any other triangle, which in all respects is not the same with it. For example, having demonstrated that the three angles of an isosceles rectangular triangle are equal to two right ones, I cannot therefore conclude this affection agrees to all other triangles, which have neither a right angle, nor two equal sides. It seems therefore that, to be certain this proposition is universally true, we must either make a particular demonstration for every particular triangle, which is impossible, or once for all demonstrate it of the abstract idea of a triangle, in which all the particulars do indifferently partake and by which they are all equally represented.

To which I answer, that though the idea I have in view whilst I make the demonstration be, for instance, that of an isosceles rectangular triangle, whose sides are of a determinate length, I may nevertheless be certain it extends to all other rectilinear triangles, of what sort or bigness soever; and that, because neither the right angle, nor the equality, nor determinate length of the sides, are at all concerned in the demonstration. It is true, the diagram I have in view includes all these particulars, but then there is not the least mention made of them in the proof of the proposition. It is not said, the three angles are equal to two right ones, because one of them is a right angle, or because the sides comprehending it are of the same length. Which sufficiently shows that the right angle might have been oblique, and the sides unequal, and for all that the demonstration have held good. And for this reason it is, that I conclude that to be true of any obliquangular or scalenon, which I had demonstrated of a particular right-angled, equicrural triangle; and not because I demonstrated the proposition of the abstract idea of a triangle. [And here it must be acknowledged that a man may consider a figure merely as triangular, without attending to the particular qualities of the angles or relations of the sides. So far he may abstract; but this will never prove that he can frame an abstract general inconsistent idea of a triangle. In like manner we may consider Peter so far forth as man, or so far forth as animal, without framing the forementioned abstract idea, either of man or of animal, in as much as all that is perceived is not considered.][4]

[4] The text in parentheses was added in the 1734 edition.

17   It were an endless, as well as an useless thing, to trace the Schoolmen,[5] those great masters of abstraction, through all the manifold inextricable labyrinths of error and dispute, which their doctrine of abstract natures and notions seems to have led them into. What bickerings and controversies, and what a learned dust have been raised about those matters, and what mighty advantage has been from thence derived to mankind, are things at this day too clearly known to need being insisted on. And it had been well if the ill effects of that doctrine were confined to those only who make the most avowed profession of it. When men consider the great pains, industry and parts, that have for so many ages been laid out on the cultivation and advancement of the sciences and that, notwithstanding all this, the far greater part of them remain full of darkness and uncertainty and disputes that are like never to have an end, and even those that are thought to be supported by the most clear and cogent demonstrations contain in them paradoxes which are perfectly irreconcilable to the understandings of men, and that taking all together, a small portion of them supplies any real benefit to mankind, otherwise than by being an innocent diversion and amusement: I say, the consideration of all this is apt to throw them into a despondency, and perfect contempt of all study. But this may perhaps cease, upon a view of the false principles that have obtained in the world, amongst all which there is none, methinks, has a more wide influence over the thoughts of speculative men, than this of abstract general ideas.

18   I come now to consider the source of this prevailing notion, and that seems to me to be language. And surely nothing of less extent than reason it self could have been the source of an opinion so universally received. The truth of this appears as from other reasons, so also from the plain confession of the ablest patrons of abstract ideas, who acknowledge that they are made in order to naming; from which it is a clear consequence, that if there had been no such thing as speech or universal signs, there never had been any thought of abstraction.[d] Let us therefore examine the manner wherein words have contributed to the origin of that mistake. First then, it is thought that every name has, or ought to have, one only precise and settled signification, which inclines men to think there are certain abstract, determinate ideas, which constitute the true

---

[d] See Book III, Chapter vi, section 39 and elsewhere of the *Essay on Human Understanding*.

[5] i.e. Scholastic philosophers and theologians, such as Thomas Aquinas.

and only immediate signification of each general name, and that it is by the mediation of these abstract ideas that a general name comes to signify any particular thing. Whereas, in truth, there is no such thing as one precise and definite signification annexed to any general name, they all signifying indifferently a great number of particular ideas. All which evidently follows from what has been already said, and will clearly appear to any one by a little reflexion.

To this it will be objected, that every name that has a definition is thereby restrained to one certain signification. For example, a 'triangle' is defined to be a 'plane surface comprehended by three right lines', by which that name is limited to denote one certain idea and no other. To which I answer, that in the definition it is not said whether the surface be great or small, black or white, nor whether the sides are long or short, equal or unequal, nor with what angles they are inclined to each other; in all which there may be a great variety, and consequently there is no one settled idea which limits the signification of the word 'triangle'. It is one thing for to keep a name constantly to the same definition, and another to make it stand every where for the same idea; the one is necessary, the other useless and impracticable.

19   But to give a farther account how words came to produce the doctrine of abstract ideas, it must be observed that it is a received opinion that language has no other end but the communicating our ideas, and that every significant name stands for an idea. This being so, and it being withal certain that names, which yet are not thought altogether insignificant, do not always mark out particular conceivable ideas, it is straightway concluded that they stand for abstract notions. That there are many names in use amongst speculative men, which do not always suggest to others determinate particular ideas, is what no body will deny. And a little attention will discover, that it is not necessary (even in the strictest reasonings) significant names which stand for ideas should, every time they are used, excite in the understanding the ideas they are made to stand for: in reading and discoursing, names being for the most part used as letters are in algebra, in which though a particular quantity be marked by each letter, yet to proceed right it is not requisite that in every step each letter suggest to our thoughts that particular quantity it was appointed to stand for.

20   Besides, the communicating of ideas marked by words is not the chief and only end of language, as is commonly supposed. There are

other ends, as the raising of some passion, the exciting to, or deterring from an action, the putting the mind in some particular disposition; to which the former is in many cases barely subservient, and sometimes entirely omitted, when these can be obtained without it, as I think not infrequently happens in the familiar use of language. I entreat the reader to reflect with himself, and see if it does not often happen either in hearing or reading a discourse, that the passions of fear, love, hatred, admiration, disdain, and the like, arise immediately in his mind upon the perception of certain words, without any ideas coming between. At first, indeed, the words might have occasioned ideas that were fit to produce those emotions; but, if I mistake not, it will be found that when language is once grown familiar, the hearing of the sounds or sight of the characters is oft immediately attended with those passions, which at first were wont to be produced by the intervention of ideas that are now quite omitted. May we not, for example, be affected with the promise of a 'good thing', though we have not an idea of what it is? Or is not the being threatened with danger sufficient to excite a dread, though we think not of any particular evil likely to befall us, nor yet frame to our selves an idea of danger in abstract?

If any one shall join ever so little reflexion of his own to what has been said, I believe it will evidently appear to him, that general names are often used in the propriety of language without the speaker's designing them for marks of ideas in his own, which he would have them raise in the mind of the hearer. Even proper names themselves do not seem always spoken with a design to bring into our view the ideas of those individuals that are supposed to be marked by them. For example, when a Schoolman tells me 'Aristotle has said it', all I conceive he means by it is to dispose me to embrace his opinion with the deference and submission which custom has annexed to that name. And this effect may be so instantly produced in the minds of those who are accustomed to resign their judgment to the authority of that philosopher, as it is impossible any idea either of his person, writings, or reputation should go before. Innumerable examples of this kind may be given, but why should I insist on those things, which every one's experience will, I doubt not, plentifully suggest unto him?

21 We have, I think, shown the impossibility of abstract ideas. We have considered what has been said for them by their ablest patrons, and endeavoured to show they are of no use for those ends to which they are thought necessary. And lastly, we have traced them to the source from

whence they flow, which appears to be language. It cannot be denied that words are of excellent use, in that by their means all that stock of knowledge which has been purchased by the joint labours of inquisitive men in all ages and nations may be drawn into the view and made the possession of one single person. But at the same time it must be owned that most parts of knowledge have been strangely perplexed and darkened by the abuse of words, and general ways of speech wherein they are delivered. Since therefore words are so apt to impose on the understanding, whatever ideas I consider, I shall endeavour to take them bare and naked into my view, keeping out of my thoughts, so far as I am able, those names which long and constant use has so strictly united with them; from which I may expect to derive the following advantages.[6]

22 First, I shall be sure to get clear of all controversies purely verbal, the springing up of which weeds in almost all the sciences has been a main hindrance to the growth of true and sound knowledge. Secondly, this seems to be a sure way to extricate my self out of that fine and subtle net of abstract ideas, which has so miserably perplexed and entangled the minds of men, and that with this peculiar circumstance, that by how much the finer and more curious was the wit of any man, by so much the deeper was he like to be ensnared and faster held therein. Thirdly, so long as I confine my thoughts to my own ideas divested of words, I do not see how I can easily be mistaken. The objects I consider, I clearly and adequately know. I cannot be deceived in thinking I have an idea which I have not. It is not possible for me to imagine, that any of my own ideas are alike or unlike that are not truly so. To discern the agreements or disagreements there are between my ideas, to see what ideas are included in any compound idea, and what not, there is nothing more requisite than an attentive perception of what passes in my own understanding.

23 But the attainment of all these advantages presupposes an entire deliverance from the deception of words, which I dare hardly promise myself; so difficult a thing it is to dissolve an union so early begun, and confirmed by so long a habit as that betwixt words and ideas, which difficulty seems to have been very much increased by the doctrine of abstraction. For so long as men thought abstract ideas were annexed to their words, it does not seem strange that they should use words for ideas,

---

[6] This method of avoiding prejudicial judgements was recommended by Descartes in *The Principles of Philosophy*, Part I, section 74: *Oeuvres*, VIII-1, 37–38.

it being found an impracticable thing to lay aside the word and retain the abstract idea in the mind, which in it self was perfectly inconceivable. This seems to me the principal cause, why those men who have so emphatically recommended to others the laying aside all use of words in their meditations and contemplating their bare ideas, have yet failed to perform it themselves. Of late many have been very sensible of the absurd opinions and insignificant disputes, which grow out of the abuse of words. And in order to remedy these evils they advise well that we attend to the ideas signified, and draw off our attention from the words which signify them. But how good soever this advice may be, they have given others, it is plain they could not have a due regard to it themselves, so long as they thought the only immediate use of words was to signify ideas, and that the immediate signification of every general name was a determinate, abstract idea.

24    But these being known to be mistakes, a man may with greater ease prevent his being imposed on by words. He that knows he has no other than particular ideas, will not puzzle himself in vain to find out and conceive the abstract idea annexed to any name. And he that knows names do not always stand for ideas, will spare himself the labour of looking for ideas, where there are none to be had. It were therefore to be wished that every one would use his utmost endeavours to obtain a clear view of the ideas he would consider, separating from them all that dress and encumbrance of words which so much contribute to blind the judgment and divide the attention. In vain do we extend our view into the heavens, and pry into the entrails of the earth, in vain do we consult the writings of learned men, and trace the dark footsteps of antiquity. We need only draw the curtain of words to behold the fairest tree of knowledge, whose fruit is excellent, and within the reach of our hand.

25    Unless we take care to clear the first principles of knowledge from the embarrass and delusion of words, we may make infinite reasonings upon them to no purpose; we may draw consequences from consequences, and be never the wiser. The farther we go, we shall only lose our selves the more irrecoverably, and be the deeper entangled in difficulties and mistakes. Whoever therefore designs to read the following sheets, I entreat him to make my words the occasion of his own thinking, and endeavour to attain the same train of thoughts in reading that I had in writing them. By this means it will be easy for him to discover the truth or falsity of what I say. He will be out of all danger of being deceived by my

words, and I do not see how he can be led into an error by considering his own naked, undisguised ideas.

## Of the Principles of Human Knowledge

### Part I[7]

1   It is evident to any one who takes a survey of the objects of human knowledge, that they are either ideas actually imprinted on the senses, or else such as are perceived by attending to the passions and operations of the mind, or lastly ideas formed by help of memory and imagination, either compounding, dividing, or barely representing those originally perceived in the aforesaid ways. By sight I have the ideas of light and colours with their several degrees and variations. By touch I perceive, for example, hard and soft, heat and cold, motion and resistance, and of all these more and less either as to quantity or degree. Smelling furnishes me with odours; the palate with tastes, and hearing conveys sounds to the mind in all their variety of tone and composition. And as several of these are observed to accompany each other, they come to be marked by one name, and so to be reputed as one thing. Thus, for example, a certain colour, taste, smell, figure and consistence having been observed to go together, are accounted one distinct thing, signified by the name 'apple'. Other collections of ideas constitute a stone, a tree, a book, and the like sensible things; which, as they are pleasing or disagreeable, excite the passions of love, hatred, joy, grief, and so forth.

2   But besides all that endless variety of ideas or objects of knowledge, there is likewise something which knows or perceives them, and exercises divers operations, as willing, imagining, remembering about them. This perceiving, active being is what I call 'mind', 'spirit', 'soul' or 'my self'. By which words I do not denote any one of my ideas, but a thing entirely distinct from them, wherein they exist or, which is the same thing, whereby they are perceived; for the existence of an idea consists in being perceived.

3   That neither our thoughts, nor passions, nor ideas formed by the imagination, exist without the mind, is what every body will allow. And it seems no less evident that the various sensations or ideas imprinted on the sense, however blended or combined together (that is, whatever

---

[7]  Although this is entitled 'Part I', no subsequent part was published by Berkeley.

objects they compose) cannot exist otherwise than in a mind perceiving them. I think an intuitive knowledge may be obtained of this, by any one that shall attend to what is meant by the term 'exist' when applied to sensible things. The table I write on, I say, exists, that is, I see and feel it; and if I were out of my study I should say it existed, meaning thereby that if I was in my study I might perceive it, or that some other spirit actually does perceive it. There was an odour, that is, it was smelled; there was a sound, that is to say, it was heard; a colour or figure, and it was perceived by sight or touch. This is all that I can understand by these and the like expressions. For as to what is said of the absolute existence of unthinking things without any relation to their being perceived, that seems perfectly unintelligible. Their *esse* is *percipi*,[8] nor is it possible they should have any existence, out of the minds or thinking things which perceive them.

4    It is indeed an opinion strangely prevailing amongst men, that houses, mountains, rivers, and in a word all sensible objects have an existence natural or real, distinct from their being perceived by the understanding. But with how great an assurance and acquiescence soever this principle may be entertained in the world; yet whoever shall find in his heart to call it in question, may, if I mistake not, perceive it to involve a manifest contradiction. For what are the forementioned objects but the things we perceive by sense, and what do we perceive besides our own ideas or sensations; and is it not plainly repugnant that any one of these or any combination of them should exist unperceived?

5    If we throughly examine this tenet, it will, perhaps, be found at bottom to depend on the doctrine of abstract ideas. For can there be a nicer strain of abstraction than to distinguish the existence of sensible objects from their being perceived, so as to conceive them existing unperceived? Light and colours, heat and cold, extension and figures, in a word the things we see and feel, what are they but so many sensations, notions, ideas or impressions on the sense; and is it possible to separate, even in thought, any of these from perception? For my part I might as easily divide a thing from it self. I may indeed divide in my thoughts or conceive apart from each other those things which, perhaps, I never perceived by sense so divided. Thus I imagine the trunk of a human body without the limbs, or conceive the smell of a rose without thinking on the rose it self. So far I will not deny I can abstract, if that may properly be called 'abstraction', which

---

[8]  i.e. their being, existence, or reality is to be perceived.

extends only to the conceiving separately such objects as it is possible may really exist or be actually perceived asunder. But my conceiving or imagining power does not extend beyond the possibility of real existence or perception. Hence, as it is impossible for me to see or feel any thing without an actual sensation of that thing, so is it impossible for me to conceive in my thoughts any sensible thing or object distinct from the sensation or perception of it.

6    Some truths there are so near and obvious to the mind, that a man need only open his eyes to see them. Such I take this important one to be, to wit, that all the choir of heaven and furniture of the earth, in a word all those bodies which compose the mighty frame of the world, have not any subsistence without a mind, that their being is to be perceived or known; that consequently so long as they are not actually perceived by me, or do not exist in my mind or that of any other created spirit, they must either have no existence at all, or else subsist in the mind of some eternal spirit: it being perfectly unintelligible and involving all the absurdity of abstraction, to attribute to any single part of them an existence independent of a spirit. To be convinced of which, the reader need only reflect and try to separate in his own thoughts the being of a sensible thing from its being perceived.

7    From what has been said, it follows, there is not any other substance than spirit, or that which perceives. But for the fuller proof of this point, let it be considered, the sensible qualities are colour, figure, motion, smell, taste, and such like, that is, the ideas perceived by sense. Now for an idea to exist in an unperceiving thing is a manifest contradiction; for to have an idea is all one as to perceive; that therefore wherein colour, figure, and the like qualities exist, must perceive them. Hence it is clear there can be no unthinking substance or *substratum* of those ideas.

8    But say you, though the ideas themselves do not exist without the mind, yet there may be things like them whereof they are copies or resemblances, which things exist without the mind in an unthinking substance. I answer, an idea can be like nothing but an idea; a colour or figure can be like nothing but another colour or figure. If we look but ever so little into our thoughts, we shall find it impossible for us to conceive a likeness except only between our ideas. Again, I ask whether those supposed originals or external things, of which our ideas are the pictures or representations, be themselves perceivable or no? If they are, then they are ideas, and we have gained our point; but if you say they are not,

I appeal to any one whether it be sense to assert [that] a colour is like something which is invisible; hard or soft, like something which is intangible; and so of the rest.

9    Some there are who make a distinction betwixt *primary* and *secondary* qualities.[9] By the former they mean extension, figure, motion, rest, solidity or impenetrability and number; by the latter they denote all other sensible qualities, as colours, sounds, tastes, and so forth. The ideas we have of these they acknowledge not to be the resemblances of any thing existing without the mind or unperceived; but they will have our ideas of the primary qualities to be patterns or images of things which exist without the mind, in an unthinking substance which they call 'matter'. By 'matter' therefore we are to understand an inert, senseless substance, in which extension, figure, and motion do actually subsist. But it is evident from what we have already shown that extension, figure, and motion are only ideas existing in the mind, and that an idea can be like nothing but another idea, and that consequently neither they nor their archetypes can exist in an unperceiving substance. Hence it is plain that the very notion of what is called 'matter' or 'corporeal substance' involves a contradiction in it.

10    They who assert that figure, motion, and the rest of the primary or original qualities do exist without the mind, in unthinking substances, do at the same time acknowledge that colours, sounds, heat, cold, and such like secondary qualities do not, which they tell us are sensations existing in the mind alone, that depend on and are occasioned by the different size, texture, and motion of the minute particles of matter. This they take for an undoubted truth, which they can demonstrate beyond all exception. Now if it be certain that those original qualities are inseparably united with the other sensible qualities, and not, even in thought, capable of being abstracted from them, it plainly follows that they exist only in the mind. But I desire any one to reflect and try whether he can, by any abstraction of thought, conceive the extension and motion of a body without all other sensible qualities. For my own part, I see evidently that it is not in my power to frame an idea of a body extended and moved, but I must withal give it some colour or other sensible quality, which is acknowledged to exist only in the mind. In short, extension, figure,

---

[9]  This distinction was introduced by Galileo in *The Assayer* (1623), and was subsequently discussed by Descartes, Robert Boyle and especially by John Locke. The terms 'primary' and 'secondary' became familiar as a result of Locke's usage in the *Essay*. See editor's Introduction above.

and motion, abstracted from all other qualities, are inconceivable. Where therefore the other sensible qualities are, there must these be also, to wit, in the mind and no where else.

11 Again, great and small, swift and slow, are allowed to exist no where without the mind, being entirely relative, and changing as the frame or position of the organs of sense varies. The extension therefore which exists without the mind is neither great nor small, the motion neither swift nor slow, that is, they are nothing at all. But say you, they are extension in general, and motion in general; thus we see how much the tenet of extended, moveable substances existing without the mind, depends on that strange doctrine of abstract ideas. And here I cannot but remark how nearly the vague and indeterminate description of matter or corporeal substance, which the modern philosophers are run into by their own principles, resembles that antiquated and so much ridiculed notion of *materia prima*,[10] to be met with in Aristotle and his followers. Without extension, solidity cannot be conceived; since therefore it has been shown that extension exists not in an unthinking substance, the same must also be true of solidity.

12 That number is entirely the creature of the mind, even though the other qualities be allowed to exist without, will be evident to whoever considers that the same thing bears a different denomination of number, as the mind views it with different respects. Thus, the same extension is one or three or thirty six, according as the mind considers it with reference to a yard, a foot, or an inch. Number is so visibly relative and dependent on men's understanding, that it is strange to think how any one should give it an absolute existence without the mind. We say one book, one page, one line; all these are equally units, though some contain several of the others. And in each instance it is plain, the unit relates to some particular combination of ideas arbitrarily put together by the mind.

13 Unity I know some will have to be a simple or uncompounded idea, accompanying all other ideas into the mind. That I have any such idea, answering the word 'unity', I do not find; and if I had, methinks I could not miss finding it. On the contrary, it should be the most familiar to my understanding, since it is said to accompany all other ideas and to

---

[10] i.e. prime matter. Followers of Aristotle claimed that all things are composed of a form and an indeterminate stuff, called prime matter, which is incapable of existing without a form.

be perceived by all the ways of sensation and reflexion. To say no more, it is an abstract idea.

**14** I shall farther add that, after the same manner, as modern philosophers prove certain sensible qualities to have no existence in matter, or without the mind, the same thing may be likewise proved of all other sensible qualities whatsoever. Thus, for instance, it is said that heat and cold are affections only of the mind, and not at all patterns of real beings existing in the corporeal substances which excite them, for that the same body which appears cold to one hand seems warm to another. Now why may we not as well argue that figure and extension are not patterns or resemblances of qualities existing in matter, because to the same eye at different stations, or eyes of a different texture at the same station, they appear various, and cannot therefore be the images of any thing settled and determinate without the mind? Again, it is proved that sweetness is not really in the sapid thing because, the thing remaining unaltered, the sweetness is changed into bitter, as in the case of a fever or otherwise vitiated palate. Is it not as reasonable to say that motion is not without the mind, since if the succession of ideas in the mind become swifter, the motion, it is acknowledged, shall appear slower without any alteration in any external object.

**15** In short, let anyone consider those arguments, which are thought manifestly to prove that colours and tastes exist only in the mind, and he shall find they may with equal force be brought to prove the same thing of extension, figure, and motion. Though it must be confessed this method of arguing does not so much prove that there is no extension or colour in an outward object, as that we do not know by sense which is the true extension or colour of the object. But the arguments foregoing plainly show it to be impossible that any colour or extension at all, or other sensible quality whatsoever, should exist in an unthinking subject without the mind, or in truth, that there should be any such thing as an outward object.

**16** But let us examine a little the received opinion. It is said extension is a mode or accident of matter, and that matter is the *substratum* that supports it. Now I desire that you would explain what is meant by matter's 'supporting' extension: say you, I have no idea of matter, and therefore cannot explain it. I answer, though you have no positive, yet if you have any meaning at all, you must at least have a relative idea of matter; though you know not what it is, yet you must be supposed to know what relation it bears to accidents, and what is meant by its support-ing them. It is evident 'support' cannot here be taken in its usual or literal sense, as when we say that pillars support a building. In what sense therefore must it be taken?

17  If we inquire into what the most accurate philosophers declare themselves to mean by 'material substance', we shall find them acknowl-edge, they have no other meaning annexed to those sounds, but the idea of being in general, together with the relative notion of its supporting accidents. The general idea of being appears to me the most abstract and incomprehensible of all other; and as for its supporting accidents, this, as we have just now observed, cannot be understood in the common sense of those words. It must therefore be taken in some other sense, but what that is they do not explain. So that when I consider the two parts or branches which make the signification of the words 'material substance', I am convinced there is no distinct meaning annexed to them. But why should we trouble ourselves any farther, in discussing this material *substratum* or support of figure and motion, and other sensible qualities? Does it not suppose they have an existence without the mind? And is not this a direct repugnancy, and altogether inconceivable?

18  But though it were possible that solid, figured, moveable sub-stances may exist without the mind, corresponding to the ideas we have of bodies, yet how is it possible for us to know this? Either we must know it by sense, or by reason. As for our senses, by them we have the knowl-edge only of our sensations, ideas, or those things that are immediately perceived by sense, call them what you will. But they do not inform us that things exist without the mind, or unperceived, like to those which are perceived. This the materialists themselves acknowledge. It remains therefore that, if we have knowledge at all of external things, it must be by reason, inferring their existence from what is immediately perceived by sense. But what reason can induce us to believe the existence of bodies without the mind, from what we perceive, since the very patrons of matter themselves do not pretend there is any necessary connexion betwixt them and our ideas? I say it is granted on all hands (and what happens in dreams, phrensies, and the like, puts it beyond dispute) that it is possible we might be affected with all the ideas we have now, though no bodies existed without, resembling them. Hence it is evident the suppo-sition of external bodies is not necessary for the producing our ideas,

since it is granted they are produced sometimes, and might possibly be produced always in the same order we see them in at present, without their concurrence.

**19** But though we might possibly have all our sensations without them, yet perhaps it may be thought easier to conceive and explain the manner of their production by supposing external bodies in their likeness rather than otherwise; and so it might be at least probable there are such things as bodies that excite their ideas in our minds. But neither can this be said. For though we give the materialists their external bodies, they by their own confession are never the nearer knowing how our ideas are produced, since they own themselves unable to comprehend in what manner body can act upon spirit, or how it is possible it should imprint any idea in the mind. Hence it is evident the production of ideas or sensations in our minds, can be no reason why we should suppose matter or corporeal substances, since that is acknowledged to remain equally inexplicable with, or without, this supposition. If therefore it were possible for bodies to exist without the mind, yet to hold they do so must needs be a very precarious opinion, since it is to suppose, without any reason at all, that God has created innumerable beings that are entirely useless, and serve to no manner of purpose.

**20** In short, if there were external bodies, it is impossible we should ever come to know it; and if there were not, we might have the very same reasons to think there were that we have now. Suppose, what no one can deny possible, an intelligence, without the help of external bodies, to be affected with the same train of sensations or ideas that you are, imprinted in the same order and with like vividness in his mind. I ask whether that intelligence has not all the reason to believe the existence of corporeal substances, represented by his ideas and exciting them in his mind, that you can possibly have for believing the same thing? Of this there can be no question; which one consideration is enough to make any reasonable person suspect the strength of whatever arguments he may think himself to have for the existence of bodies without the mind.

**21** Were it necessary to add any farther proof against the existence of matter, after what has been said, I could instance several of those errors and difficulties (not to mention impieties) which have sprung from that tenet. It has occasioned numberless controversies and disputes in philosophy, and not a few of far greater moment in religion. But I shall not enter into the detail of them in this place, as well because I think arguments *a posteriori* are unnecessary for confirming what has been, if I mistake not, sufficiently demonstrated *a priori*, as because I shall here-after find occasion to say somewhat of them.

**22**  I am afraid I have given cause to think me needlessly prolix in handling this subject. For to what purpose is it to dilate on that which may be demonstrated with the utmost evidence in a line or two, to any one that is capable of the least reflexion? It is but looking into your own thoughts, and so trying whether you can conceive it possible for a sound, or figure, or motion, or colour, to exist without the mind, or unperceived? This easy trial may make you see, that what you contend for is a downright contradiction. Insomuch that I am content to put the whole upon this issue: if you can but conceive it possible for one extended moveable substance, or in general, for any one idea or any thing like an idea, to exist otherwise than in a mind perceiving it, I shall readily give up the cause. And as for all that compages of external bodies which you contend for, I shall grant you its existence, though you cannot either give me any reason why you believe it exists, or assign any use to it when it is supposed to exist. I say, the bare possibility of your opinion's being true shall pass for an argument that it is so.

**23**  But say you, surely there is nothing easier than to imagine trees, for instance, in a park, or books existing in a closet, and no body by to perceive them. I answer, you may so, there is no difficulty in it; but what is all this, I beseech you, more than framing in your mind certain ideas which you call 'books' and 'trees', and at the same time omitting to frame the idea of any one that may perceive them? But do not you your self perceive or think of them all the while? This therefore is nothing to the purpose; it only shows you have the power of imagining or forming ideas in your mind. But it does not show that you can conceive it possible, the objects of your thought may exist without the mind. To make out this, it is necessary that you conceive them existing unconceived or unthought of, which is a manifest repugnancy. When we do our utmost to conceive the existence of external bodies, we are all the while only contemplating our own ideas. But the mind taking no notice of itself, is deluded to think it can and does conceive bodies existing unthought of or without the mind; though at the same time they are apprehended by or exist in it self. A little attention will discover to any one the truth and evidence of what is here said, and make it unnecessary to insist on any other proofs against the existence of material substance.

**24** It is very obvious, upon the least inquiry into our own thoughts, to know whether it be possible for us to understand what is meant by the 'absolute existence of sensible objects in themselves, or without the mind.' To me it is evident those words make out either a direct contradiction, or else nothing at all. And to convince others of this, I know no readier or fairer way, than to entreat they would calmly attend to their own thoughts; and if by this attention the emptiness or repugnancy of those expressions does appear, surely nothing more is requisite for their conviction. It is on this therefore that I insist, to wit, that 'the absolute existence of unthinking things' are words without a meaning, or which include a contradiction. This is what I repeat and inculcate, and earnestly recommend to the attentive thoughts of the reader.

**25** All our ideas, sensations, or the things which we perceive, by whatsoever names they may be distinguished, are visibly inactive; there is nothing of power or agency included in them,[11] so that one idea or object of thought cannot produce, or make any alteration in another. To be satisfied of the truth of this, there is nothing else requisite but a bare observation of our ideas. For since they and every part of them exist only in the mind, it follows that there is nothing in them but what is perceived. But whoever shall attend to his ideas, whether of sense or reflexion, will not perceive in them any power or activity; there is therefore no such thing contained in them. A little attention will discover to us that the very being of an idea implies passiveness and inertness in it, insomuch that it is impossible for any idea to do any thing, or, strictly speaking, to be the cause of any thing; neither can it be the resemblance or pattern of any active being, as is evident from Section 8. Whence it plainly follows that extension, figure and motion cannot be the cause of our sensations. To say, therefore, that these are the effects of powers resulting from the configuration, number, motion, and size of corpuscles must certainly be false.[12]

**26** We perceive a continual succession of ideas, some are anew excited, others are changed or totally disappear. There is therefore some cause of these ideas whereon they depend, and which produces and changes them. That this cause cannot be any quality or idea or combination of ideas, is clear from the preceding section. It must therefore be a substance. But it

[11] Berkeley argues in the *Essay on Motion* that physical bodies lack power or force.
[12] Locke claimed, in the *Essay* (II, viii, 11) that external phenomena cause ideas in our mind 'by impulse'.

has been shown that there is no corporeal or material substance; it remains therefore that the cause of ideas is an incorporeal active substance or spirit.

**27** A spirit is one simple, undivided, active being. As it perceives ideas, it is called the 'understanding', and as it produces or otherwise operates about them, it is called the 'will'. Hence there can be no idea formed of a soul or spirit; for all ideas whatever, being passive and inert,[e] they cannot represent unto us, by way of image or likeness, that which acts. A little attention will make it plain to any one that to have an idea, which shall be like that active principle of motion and change of ideas, is absolutely impossible. Such is the nature of spirit, or that which acts, that it cannot be it self perceived, but only by the effects which it produces. If any man shall doubt of the truth of what is here delivered, let him but reflect and try if he can frame the idea of any power or active being; and whether he has ideas of two principal powers, marked by the names 'will' and 'understanding', distinct from each other as well as from a third idea of substance or being in general, with a relative notion of its supporting or being the subject of the aforesaid powers, which is signified by the name 'soul' or 'spirit'. This is what some hold; but so far as I can see, the words 'will', 'soul', 'spirit'[13] do not stand for different ideas or, in truth, for any idea at all, but for something which is very different from ideas, and which being an agent cannot be like unto, or represented by, any idea whatsoever. [Though it must be owned at the same time, that we have some notion of soul, spirit, and the operations of the mind, such as willing, loving, hating, in as much as we know or understand the meaning of those words.][14]

**28** I find I can excite ideas in my mind at pleasure, and vary and shift the scene as oft as I think fit. It is no more than willing, and straightway this or that idea arises in my fancy; and by the same power it is obliterated, and makes way for another. This making and unmaking of ideas very properly denominates the mind active. Thus much is certain, and grounded on experience; but when we talk of unthinking agents, or of exciting ideas exclusive of volition, we only amuse our selves with words.

---

[e] See Section 25.

[13] The 1710 edition has 'will', 'understanding', 'mind', 'soul', 'spirit'.
[14] The sentence in parentheses was added in the 1734 edition.

**29**   But whatever power I may have over my own thoughts, I find the ideas actually perceived by sense have not a like dependence on my will. When in broad daylight I open my eyes, it is not in my power to choose whether I shall see or no, or to determine what particular objects shall present themselves to my view; and so likewise as to the hearing and other senses, the ideas imprinted on them are not creatures of my will. There is therefore some other will or spirit that produces them.

**30**   The ideas of sense are more strong, lively, and distinct than those of the imagination. They have likewise a steadiness, order, and coherence, and are not excited at random, as those which are the effects of human wills often are, but in a regular train or series, the admirable connexion whereof sufficiently testifies the wisdom and benevolence of its Author. Now the set of rules or established methods, wherein the mind we depend on excites in us the ideas of sense, are called the 'laws of nature'; and these we learn by experience, which teaches us that such and such ideas are attended with such and such other ideas in the ordinary course of things.

**31**   This gives us a sort of foresight, which enables us to regulate our actions for the benefit of life; and without this we should be eternally at a loss. We could not know how to act any thing that might procure us the least pleasure, or remove the least pain of sense. That food nourishes, sleep refreshes, and fire warms us; that to sow in the seed-time is the way to reap in the harvest and, in general, that to obtain such or such ends, such or such means are conducive; all this we know, not by discovering any necessary connexion between our ideas, but only by the observation of the settled laws of nature, without which we should be all in uncertainty and confusion, and a grown man no more know how to manage himself in the affairs of life than an infant just born.

**32**   And yet this consistent uniform working, which so evidently displays the goodness and wisdom of that governing spirit whose will constitutes the laws of nature, is so far from leading our thoughts to him, that it rather sends them a wandering after second causes. For when we perceive certain ideas of sense constantly followed by other ideas, and we know this is not of our doing, we forthwith attribute power and agency to the ideas themselves, and make one the cause of another, than which nothing can be more absurd and unintelligible. Thus, for example, having observed that when we perceive by sight a certain round luminous figure, we at the same time perceive by touch the idea or sensation called 'heat', we do from thence conclude the sun to be the cause of heat. And in like manner perceiving the motion and collision of bodies to be attended with sound, we are inclined to think the latter an effect of the former.

**33** The ideas imprinted on the senses by the Author of nature are called 'real things'; and those excited in the imagination being less regular, vivid, and constant, are more properly termed 'ideas', or 'images of things', which they copy and represent. But then our sensations, be they never so vivid and distinct, are nevertheless ideas, that is, they exist in the mind, or are perceived by it, as truly as the ideas of its own framing. The ideas of sense are allowed to have more reality in them, that is, to be more strong, orderly, and coherent than the creatures of the mind; but this is no argument that they exist without the mind. They are also less dependent on the spirit or thinking substance which perceives them, in that they are excited by the will of another and more powerful spirit. Yet still they are ideas, and certainly no idea, whether faint or strong, can exist otherwise than in a mind perceiving it.

**34** Before we proceed any farther, it is necessary to spend some time in answering objections which may probably be made against the principles hitherto laid down. In doing of which, if I seem too prolix to those of quick apprehensions, I hope it may be pardoned, since all men do not equally apprehend things of this nature; and I am willing to be understood by every one. First then, it will be objected that, by the foregoing principles, all that is real and substantial in nature is banished out of the world, and instead thereof a chimerical scheme of ideas takes place. All things that exist, exist only in the mind, that is, they are purely notional. What therefore becomes of the sun, moon, and stars? What must we think of houses, rivers, mountains, trees, stones, nay, even of our own bodies? Are all these but so many chimeras and illusions of the fancy? To all which, and whatever else of the same sort may be objected, I answer, that by the principles premised, we are not deprived of any one thing in nature. Whatever we see, feel, hear, or any wise conceive or understand, remains as secure as ever and is as real as ever. There is a *rerum natura*,[15] and the distinction between realities and chimeras retains its full force. This is evident from Sections 29, 30, and 33, where we have shown what is meant by 'real things' in opposition to 'chimeras' or ideas of our own

[15] i.e. a nature of things.

framing; but then they both equally exist in the mind, and in that sense are alike ideas.

**35**  I do not argue against the existence of any one thing that we can apprehend, either by sense or reflexion. That the things I see with mine eyes and touch with my hands do exist, really exist, I make not the least question. The only thing whose existence we deny is that which philosophers call matter or corporeal substance. And in doing of this, there is no damage done to the rest of mankind, who, I dare say, will never miss it. The atheist indeed will want the colour of an empty name to support his impiety, and the philosophers may possibly find, they have lost a great handle for trifling and disputation.

**36**  If any man thinks this detracts from the existence or reality of things, he is very far from understanding what has been premised in the plainest terms I could think of. Take here an abstract of what has been said. There are spiritual substances, minds, or human souls, which will or excite ideas in themselves at pleasure; but these are faint, weak, and unsteady in respect of others they perceive by sense, which being impressed upon them according to certain rules or laws of nature, speak themselves the effects of a mind more powerful and wise than human spirits. These latter are said to have more reality in them than the former: by which is meant that they are more affecting, orderly, and distinct, and that they are not fictions of the mind perceiving them. And in this sense, the sun that I see by day is the real sun, and that which I imagine by night is the idea of the former. In the sense here given of 'reality', it is evident that every vegetable, star, mineral, and in general each part of the mundane system, is as much a real being by our principles as by any other. Whether others mean any thing by the term 'reality' different from what I do, I entreat them to look into their own thoughts and see.

**37**  It will be urged that thus much at least is true, to wit, that we take away all corporeal substances. To this my answer is, that if the word 'substance' be taken in the vulgar sense, for a combination of sensible qualities, such as extension, solidity, weight, and the like, this we cannot be accused of taking away. But if it be taken in a philosophic sense, for the support of accidents or qualities without the mind, then indeed I acknowledge that we take it away, if one may be said to take away that which never had any existence, not even in the imagination.

**38**  But, say you, it sounds very harsh to say we eat and drink ideas, and are clothed with ideas. I acknowledge it does so, the word 'idea' not being used in common discourse to signify the several combinations of sensible qualities, which are called 'things'; and it is certain that any expression which varies from the familiar use of language will seem harsh and ridiculous. But this does not concern the truth of the proposition, which in other words is no more than to say: we are fed and clothed with those things which we perceive immediately by our senses. The hardness or softness, the colour, taste, warmth, figure, and such like qualities, which combined together constitute the several sorts of victuals and apparel, have been shown to exist only in the mind that perceives them. And this is all that is meant by calling them 'ideas'; which word, if it was not ordinarily used as 'thing', would sound no harsher nor more ridiculous than it. I am not for disputing about the propriety, but the truth of the expression. If therefore you agree with me that we eat and drink, and are clad with the immediate objects of sense, which cannot exist unperceived or without the mind, I shall readily grant it is more proper or conformable to custom that they should be called things rather than ideas.

**39** If it be demanded why I make use of the word 'idea', and do not rather in compliance with custom call them things, I answer: I do it for two reasons. First, because the term 'thing', in contradistinction to 'idea', is generally supposed to denote somewhat existing without the mind; secondly, because 'thing' has a more comprehensive signification than 'idea', including spirits or thinking things as well as ideas. Since therefore the objects of sense exist only in the mind, and are withal thoughtless and inactive, I chose to mark them by the word 'idea', which implies those properties.

**40** But say what we can, some one perhaps may be apt to reply: he will still believe his senses, and never suffer any arguments, how plausible soever, to prevail over the certainty of them. Be it so, assert the evidence of sense as high as you please, we are willing to do the same. That what I see, hear, and feel does exist, that is to say, is perceived by me, I no more doubt than I do of my own being. But I do not see how the testimony of sense can be alleged, as a proof for the existence of any thing, which is not perceived by sense. We are not for having any man turn sceptic, and disbelieve his senses; on the contrary we give them all the stress and assurance imaginable. Nor are there any principles more opposite to scepticism, than those we have laid down, as shall be hereafter clearly shown.

**41** Secondly, it will be objected that there is a great difference betwixt real fire, for instance, and the idea of fire, betwixt dreaming or imagining one's self burnt, and actually being so; this and the like may be urged in opposition to our tenets. To all which the answer is evident from what has been already said; and I shall only add in this place, that if real fire be very different from the idea of fire, so also is the real pain that it occasions very different from the idea of the same pain. And yet no body will pretend that real pain either is, or can possibly be, in an unperceiving thing or without the mind, any more than its idea.

**42** Thirdly, it will be objected that we see things actually without or at a distance from us, and which consequently do not exist in the mind, it being absurd that those things which are seen at the distance of several miles, should be as near to us as our own thoughts. In answer to this, I desire it may be considered, that in a dream we do oft perceive things as existing at a great distance off, and yet for all that, those things are acknowledged to have their existence only in the mind.

**43** But for the fuller clearing of this point, it may be worth while to consider, how it is that we perceive distance and things placed at a distance by sight. For that we should in truth see external space, and bodies actually existing in it, some nearer, others farther off, seems to carry with it some opposition to what has been said of their existing no where without the mind. The consideration of this difficulty it was, that gave birth to my *Essay towards a New Theory of Vision*, which was published not long since.[16] Wherein it is shown that distance or outness is neither immediately of it self perceived by sight, nor yet apprehended or judged of by lines and angles, or any thing that has a necessary connexion with it; but that it is only suggested to our thoughts by certain visible ideas and sensations attending vision, which in their own nature have no manner of similitude or relation, either with distance, or things placed at a distance. But by a connexion taught us by experience, they come to signify and suggest them to us, after the same manner that words of any language suggest the ideas they are made to stand for. Insomuch that a man born blind, and afterwards made to see,[17] would not, at first

---

[16] The *Essay* was published in 1709, one year before the first edition of the *Principles*.

[17] William Molyneux (1656–98) asked Locke in 1688 the question about a man who is blind from birth, and Locke reported it in the second edition of the *Essay*, II, ix, 8. If there were a necessary connection between sensations, the newly sighted man would not require any experience to recognize things that he had previously failed to see.

sight, think the things he saw to be without his mind, or at any distance from him.[f]

**44**   The ideas of sight and touch make two species, entirely distinct and heterogeneous. The former are marks and prognostics of the latter. That the proper objects of sight neither exist without the mind, nor are the images of external things, was shown even in that treatise; though throughout the same, the contrary be supposed true of tangible objects. Not that to suppose that vulgar error was necessary for establishing the notion therein laid down; but because it was beside my purpose to examine and refute it in a discourse concerning vision. So that in strict truth the ideas of sight, when we apprehend by them distance and things placed at a distance, do not suggest or mark out to us things actually existing at a distance, but only admonish us what ideas of touch will be imprinted in our minds at such and such distances of time, and in consequence of such and such actions. It is, I say, evident from what has been said in the foregoing parts of this treatise, and in Section 147 and elsewhere of the essay concerning vision, that visible ideas are the language whereby the governing spirit on whom we depend, informs us what tangible ideas he is about to imprint upon us, in case we excite this or that motion in our bodies. But for a fuller information in this point I refer to the essay it self.

**45**   Fourthly, it will be objected that from the foregoing principles it follows, things are every moment annihilated and created anew. The objects of sense exist only when they are perceived. The trees therefore are in the garden, or the chairs in the parlour, no longer than while there is some body by to perceive them. Upon shutting my eyes all the furniture in the room is reduced to nothing, and barely upon opening them it is again created. In answer to all which, I refer the reader to what has been said in Sections 3, 4 *etc.* and desire he will consider whether he means any thing by the actual existence of an idea, distinct from its being perceived. For my part, after the nicest inquiry I could make, I am not able to discover that any thing else is meant by those words. And I once more entreat the reader to sound his own thoughts, and not suffer himself to be imposed on by words. If he can conceive it possible either for his ideas or their archetypes to exist without being perceived, then I give up the cause; but if he cannot, he will acknowledge it is unreasonable for him

[f]   See Section 41 of the forementioned treatise [i.e. *An Essay towards a New Theory of Vision*].

to stand up in defence of he knows not what, and pretend to charge on me, as an absurdity, the not assenting to those propositions which at bottom have no meaning in them.

**46** It will not be amiss to observe how far the received principles of philosophy are themselves chargeable with those pretended absurdities. It is thought strangely absurd that upon closing my eyelids, all the visible objects round me should be reduced to nothing; and yet is not this what philosophers commonly acknowledge, when they agree on all hands that light and colours, which alone are the proper and immediate objects of sight, are mere sensations that exist no longer than they are perceived? Again, it may to some perhaps seem very incredible, that things should be every moment creating, yet this very notion is commonly taught in the Schools. For the Schoolmen, though they acknowledge the existence of matter, and that the whole mundane fabric is framed out of it, are nevertheless of opinion that it cannot subsist without the divine conservation, which by them is expounded to be a continual creation.

**47** Farther, a little thought will discover to us that, though we allow the existence of matter or corporeal substance, yet it will unavoidably follow from the principles which are now generally admitted, that the particular bodies of what kind soever, do none of them exist whilst they are not perceived. For it is evident from Section 11 and the following sections, that the matter philosophers contend for is an incomprehensible somewhat which has none of those particular qualities, whereby the bodies falling under our senses are distinguished one from another.

But to make this more plain, it must be remarked that the infinite divisibility of matter is now universally allowed, at least by the most approved and considerable philosophers, who on the received principles demonstrate it beyond all exception. Hence it follows, that there is an infinite number of parts in each particle of matter, which are not perceived by sense. The reason, therefore, that any particular body seems to be of a finite magnitude, or exhibits only a finite number of parts to sense, is not because it contains no more, since in itself it contains an infinite number of parts, but because the sense is not acute enough to discern them. In proportion therefore as the sense is rendered more acute, it perceives a greater number of parts in the object, that is, the object appears greater, and its figure varies, those parts in its extremities which were before unperceivable, appearing now to bound it in very different lines and angles from those perceived by an obtuser sense. And at length, after various changes of size and shape, when the sense becomes infinitely acute, the body shall seem infinite. During all which there is no alteration in the body, but only in the sense. Each body, therefore, considered in it self, is infinitely extended and consequently void of all shape or figure. From which it follows, that though we should grant the existence of matter to be ever so certain, yet it is withal as certain, the materialists themselves are by their own principles forced to acknowledge, that neither the particular bodies perceived by sense, nor any thing like them, exists without the mind. Matter, I say, and each particle thereof, is according to them infinite and shapeless, and it is the mind that frames all that variety of bodies which compose the visible world, any one whereof does not exist longer than it is perceived.

**48** If we consider it, the objection proposed in Section 45 will not be found reasonably charged on the principles we have premised, so as in truth to make any objection at all against our notions. For though we hold indeed the objects of sense to be nothing else but ideas which cannot exist unperceived; yet we may not hence conclude they have no existence except only while they are perceived by us, since there may be some other spirit that perceives them, though we do not. Wherever bodies are said to have no existence without the mind, I would not be understood to mean this or that particular mind, but all minds whatsoever. It does not therefore follow from the foregoing principles that bodies are annihilated and created every moment, or exist not at all during the intervals between our perception of them.

**49** Fifthly, it may perhaps be objected, that if extension and figure exist only in the mind, it follows that the mind is extended and figured, since extension is a mode or attribute, which (to speak with the Schools) is predicated of the subject in which it exists. I answer, those qualities are in the mind only as they are perceived by it, that is, not by way of mode or attribute, but only by way of idea; and it no more follows that the soul or mind is extended because extension exists in it alone, than it does that it is red or blue, because those colours are on all hands acknowledged to exist in it, and no where else. As to what philosophers say of subject and mode, that seems very groundless and unintelligible. For instance, in this proposition, 'a die is hard, extended and square', they will have it that the word 'die' denotes a subject or substance, distinct from the hardness, extension, and figure, which are predicated of it and in which they exist. This I cannot comprehend. To me a die seems to be nothing distinct from those things which are termed its modes or accidents. And to say a die is hard, extended, and square, is not to attribute those qualities to a subject distinct from and supporting them, but only an explication of the meaning of the word 'die'.

**50** Sixthly, you will say there have been a great many things explained by matter and motion; take away these, and you destroy the whole corpuscular philosophy, and undermine those mechanical principles which have been applied with so much success to account for the phenomena. In short, whatever advances have been made, either by ancient or modern philosophers, in the study of nature, do all proceed on the supposition that corporeal substance or matter does really exist. To this I answer, that there is not any one phenomenon explained on that supposition, which may not as well be explained without it, as might easily be made appear by an induction of particulars. To explain the phenomena is all one as to show why, upon such and such occasions, we are affected with such and such ideas. But how matter should operate on a spirit, or produce any idea in it, is what no philosopher will pretend to explain. It is therefore evident, there can be no use of matter in natural philosophy. Besides, they who attempt to account for things do it, not by corporeal substance, but by figure, motion, and other qualities, which are in truth no more than mere ideas, and therefore cannot be the cause of any thing, as has been already shown.[g]

**51** Seventhly, it will upon this be demanded whether it does not seem absurd to take away natural causes, and ascribe every thing to the immediate operation of spirits? We must no longer say upon these principles that fire heats, or water cools, but that a spirit heats, and so forth. Would not a man be deservedly laughed at, who should talk after this manner? I answer, he would so; in such things we ought to 'think with the learned, and speak with the vulgar'.[18] They who to demonstration are convinced of the truth of the Copernican system, do nevertheless say the sun rises, the sun sets, or comes to the meridian; and if they affect a contrary style in common talk, it would without doubt appear very ridiculous. A little reflexion on what is here said will make it manifest,

---

[g] See Section 25.

[18] Quoted from Francis Bacon, *The two Bookes of the Advancement of Learning, divine and humane* (London, 1605), Book II, p. 57: '*Loquendum ut vulgus, sentiendum ut sapientes.*'

that the common use of language would receive no manner of alteration or disturbance from the admission of our tenets.

52 In the ordinary affairs of life, any phrases may be retained so long as they excite in us proper sentiments, or dispositions to act in such a manner as is necessary for our well-being, how false soever they may be if taken in a strict and speculative sense. Nay this is unavoidable, since propriety being regulated by custom, language is suited to the received opinions, which are not always the truest. Hence it is impossible, even in the most rigid philosophic reasonings, so far to alter the bent and genius of the tongue we speak, as never to give a handle for cavillers to pretend difficulties and inconsistencies. But a fair and ingenuous reader will collect the sense, from the scope and tenor and connexion of a discourse, making allowances for those inaccurate modes of speech, which use has made inevitable.

53 As to the opinion that there are no corporeal causes, this has been heretofore maintained by some of the Schoolmen, as it is of late by others among the modern philosophers, who though they allow matter to exist, yet will have God alone to be the immediate efficient cause of all things.[19] These men saw that, amongst all the objects of sense, there was none which had any power or activity included in it, and that by consequence this was likewise true of whatever bodies they supposed to exist without the mind, like unto the immediate objects of sense. But then, that they should suppose an innumerable multitude of created beings, which they acknowledge are not capable of producing any one effect in nature, and which therefore are made to no manner of purpose, since God might have done every thing as well without them: this I say, though we should allow it possible, must yet be a very unaccountable and extravagant supposition.

54 In the eighth place, the universal concurrent assent of mankind may be thought by some an invincible argument in behalf of matter or the existence of external things. Must we suppose the whole world to be mistaken? And if so, what cause can be assigned of so widespread and predominant an error? I answer, first, that upon a narrow inquiry, it will not perhaps be found so many as is imagined do really believe the

---

[19] Refers to supporters of occasionalism, a theory that what appear to be the causes of natural phenomena are not genuinely such, but are merely the occasions on which God directly causes everything. See especially Nicolas Malebranche (1638–1715).

existence of matter or things without the mind. Strictly speaking, to believe that which involves a contradiction, or has no meaning in it, is impossible; and whether the foregoing expressions are not of that sort, I refer it to the impartial examination of the reader. In one sense indeed, men may be said to believe that matter exists, that is, they act as if the immediate cause of their sensations, which affects them every moment and is so nearly present to them, were some senseless unthinking being. But that they should clearly apprehend any meaning marked by those words, and form thereof a settled speculative opinion, is what I am not able to conceive. This is not the only instance wherein men impose upon themselves, by imagining they believe those propositions they have often heard, though at bottom they have no meaning in them.

55 But secondly, though we should grant a notion to be ever so universally and steadfastly adhered to, yet this is but a weak argument of its truth, to whoever considers what a vast number of prejudices and false opinions are every where embraced with the utmost tenaciousness, by the unreflecting (which are the far greater) part of mankind. There was a time when the Antipodes and motion of the earth were looked upon as monstrous absurdities, even by men of learning; and if it be considered what a small proportion they bear to the rest of mankind, we shall find that at this day those notions have gained but a very inconsiderable footing in the world.

56 But it is demanded that we assign a cause of this prejudice, and account for its obtaining in the world. To this I answer, that men knowing they perceived several ideas, whereof they themselves were not the authors, as not being excited from within nor depending on the operation of their wills, this made them maintain, those ideas or objects of perception had an existence independent of, and without the mind, without ever dreaming that a contradiction was involved in those words. But philosophers having plainly seen that the immediate objects of perception do not exist without the mind, they in some degree corrected the mistake of the vulgar, but at the same time run into another which seems no less absurd, to wit: that there are certain objects really existing without the mind, or having a subsistence distinct from being perceived, of which our ideas are only images or resemblances, imprinted by those objects on the mind. And this notion of the philosophers owes its origin to the same cause with the former, namely, their being conscious that they were not the authors of their own sensations, which they evidently

knew were imprinted from without, and which therefore must have some cause distinct from the minds on which they are imprinted.

**57** But why they should suppose the ideas of sense to be excited in us by things in their likeness, and not rather have recourse to spirit, which alone can act, may be accounted for, first, because they were not aware of the repugnancy there is, as well in supposing things like unto our ideas existing without, as in attributing to them power or activity. Secondly, because the supreme spirit, which excites those ideas in our minds, is not marked out and limited to our view by any particular finite collection of sensible ideas, as human agents are by their size, complexion, limbs, and motions. And thirdly, because his operations are regular and uniform. Whenever the course of nature is interrupted by a miracle, men are ready to own the presence of a superior agent. But when we see things go on in the ordinary course, they do not excite in us any reflexion; their order and concatenation, though it be an argument of the greatest wisdom, power, and goodness in their Creator, is yet so constant and familiar to us, that we do not think them the immediate effects of a free spirit, especially since inconstancy and mutability in acting, though it be an imperfection, is looked on as a mark of freedom.

**58** Tenthly, it will be objected that the notions we advance are inconsistent with several sound truths in philosophy and mathematics. For example, the motion of the earth is now universally admitted by astronomers, as a truth grounded on the clearest and most convincing reasons; but on the foregoing principles, there can be no such thing. For motion being only an idea, it follows that if it be not perceived, it exists not; but the motion of the earth is not perceived by sense. I answer, that tenet, if rightly understood, will be found to agree with the principles we have premised. For the question, whether the earth moves or no, amounts in reality to no more than this, to wit: whether we have reason to conclude from what has been observed by astronomers, that if we were placed in such and such circumstances, and such and such a position and distance, both from the earth and sun, we should perceive the former to move among the choir of the planets, and appearing in all respects like one of them; and this, by the established rules of nature, which we have no reason to mistrust, is reasonably collected from the phenomena.

**59** We may, from the experience we have had of the train and succession of ideas in our minds, often make, I will not say uncertain conjectures, but sure and well-grounded predictions, concerning the ideas we shall be affected with, pursuant to a great train of actions, and be enabled to pass a right judgment of what would have appeared to us in case we were placed in circumstances very different from those we are in at present. Herein consists the knowledge of nature, which may preserve its use and certainty very consistently with what has been said. It will be easy to apply this to whatever objections of the like sort may be drawn from the magnitude of the stars, or any other discoveries in astronomy or nature.

**60** In the eleventh place, it will be demanded to what purpose serves that curious organization of plants, and the admirable mechanism in the parts of animals; might not vegetables grow, and shoot forth leaves and blossoms, and animals perform all their motions, as well without as with all that variety of internal parts so elegantly contrived and put together, which being ideas have nothing powerful or operative in them, nor have any necessary connexion with the effects ascribed to them? If it be a spirit that immediately produces every effect by a *fiat*, or act of his will, we must think all that is fine and artificial in the works, whether of man or nature, to be made in vain. By this doctrine, though an artist has made the spring and wheels, and every movement of a watch, and adjusted them in such a manner as he knew would produce the motions he designed; yet he must think all this done to no purpose, and that it is an intelligence which directs the index, and points to the hour of the day. If so, why may not the intelligence do it, without his being at the pains of making the movements and putting them together? Why does not an empty case serve as well as another? And how comes it to pass, that whenever there is any fault in the going of a watch, there is some corresponding disorder to be found in the movements, which being mended by a skilful hand, all is right again? The like may be said of all the clockwork of nature, [a] great part whereof is so wonderfully fine and subtle as scarce to be discerned by the best microscope. In short, it will be asked, how upon our principles any tolerable account can be given, or any final cause assigned, of an innumerable multitude of bodies and machines framed with the most exquisite art, which in the common philosophy have very apposite uses assigned them and serve to explain abundance of phenomena.

**61** To all which I answer, first, that though there were some difficulties relating to the administration of providence, and the uses by it assigned to the several parts of nature, which I could not solve by the foregoing principles, yet this objection could be of small weight against the truth and certainty of those things which may be proved *a priori*, with the utmost evidence. Secondly, but neither are the received principles free from the like difficulties; for it may still be demanded, to what end God should take those round-about methods of effecting things by instruments and machines, which no one can deny might have been effected by the mere command of his will, without all that apparatus. Nay, if we narrowly consider it, we shall find the objection may be retorted with greater force on those who hold the existence of those machines without the mind; for it has been made evident that solidity, bulk, figure, motion and the like, have no activity or efficacy in them, so as to be capable of producing any one effect in nature.[h] Whoever therefore supposes them to exist (allowing the supposition possible) when they are not perceived, does it manifestly to no purpose, since the only use that is assigned to them, as they exist unperceived, is that they produce those perceivable effects, which in truth cannot be ascribed to any thing but spirit.

62   But to come nearer the difficulty, it must be observed, that though the fabrication of all those parts and organs be not absolutely necessary to the producing any effect, yet it is necessary to the producing of things in a constant, regular way, according to the laws of nature. There are certain general laws that run through the whole chain of natural effects. These are learned by the observation and study of nature, and are by men applied as well to the framing artificial things for the use and ornament of life as to the explaining the various phenomena: which explication consists only in showing the conformity any particular phenomenon has to the general laws of nature or, which is the same thing, in discovering the uniformity there is in the production of natural effects, as will be evident to whoever shall attend to the several instances, wherein philosophers pretend to account for appearances. That there is a great and conspicuous use in these regular constant methods of working observed by the Supreme Agent, has been shown in Section 31. And it is no less visible that a particular size, figure, motion, and disposition of parts are necessary, though not absolutely, to the producing any effect, yet to the producing it according to the standing mechanical laws of nature. Thus, for instance, it cannot be denied that God, or the intelligence which sustains and rules the ordinary course of things might, if he

[h]  See Section 25.

were minded to produce a miracle, cause all the motions on the dial-plate of a watch, though no body had ever made the movements, and put them in it. But yet, if he will act agreeably to the rules of mechanism, by him for wise ends established and maintained in the Creation, it is necessary that those actions of the watchmaker, whereby he makes the movements and rightly adjusts them, precede the production of the aforesaid motions; as also that any disorder in them be attended with the perception of some corresponding disorder in the movements, which being once corrected, all is right again.

**63** It may indeed on some occasions be necessary that the Author of nature display his overruling power in producing some appearance out of the ordinary series of things. Such exceptions from the general rules of nature are proper to surprise and awe men into an acknowledgment of the Divine Being. But then they are to be used but seldom; otherwise there is a plain reason why they should fail of that effect. Besides, God seems to choose the convincing our reason of his attributes by the works of nature, which discover so much harmony and contrivance in their make, and are such plain indications of wisdom and beneficence in their Author, rather than to astonish us into a belief of his being by anomalous and surprising events.

**64** To set this matter in a yet clearer light, I shall observe that what has been objected in Section 60 amounts in reality to no more than this. Ideas are not any how and at random produced, there being a certain order and connexion between them, like to that of cause and effect. There are also several combinations of them, made in a very regular and artificial manner, which seem like so many instruments in the hand of nature, that being hid as it were behind the scenes, have a secret operation in producing those appearances which are seen on the theatre of the world, being themselves discernible only to the curious eye of the philosopher. But since one idea cannot be the cause of another, to what purpose is that connexion? And since those instruments, being barely inefficacious perceptions in the mind, are not subservient to the production of natural effects, it is demanded why they are made or, in other words, what reason can be assigned why God should make us, upon a close inspection into his works, behold so great variety of ideas, so artfully laid together and so much according to rule; it not being credible, that he would be at the expense (if one may so speak) of all that art and regularity to no purpose?

65  To all which my answer is, first, that the connexion of ideas does not imply the relation of cause and effect, but only of a mark or sign with the thing signified. The fire which I see is not the cause of the pain I suffer upon my approaching it, but the mark that forewarns me of it. In like manner, the noise that I hear is not the effect of this or that motion or collision of the ambient bodies, but the sign thereof. Secondly, the reason why ideas are formed into machines, that is, artificial and regular combinations, is the same with that for combining letters into words. That a few original ideas may be made to signify a great number of effects and actions, it is necessary they be variously combined together: and to the end their use be permanent and universal, these combinations must be made by rule, and with wise contrivance. By this means abundance of information is conveyed unto us, concerning what we are to expect from such and such actions, and what methods are proper to be taken for the exciting such and such ideas; which in effect is all that I conceive to be distinctly meant when it is said that, by discerning the figure, texture, and mechanism of the inward parts of bodies, whether natural or artificial, we may attain to know the several uses and properties depending thereon or the nature of the thing.

66  Hence it is evident that those things, which under the notion of a cause co-operating or concurring to the production of effects, are altogether inexplicable and run us into great absurdities, may be very naturally explained and have a proper and obvious use assigned them, when they are considered only as marks or signs for our information. And it is the searching after, and endeavouring to understand those signs instituted by the Author of nature,[20] that ought to be the employment of the natural philosopher, and not the pretending to explain things by corporeal causes; which doctrine seems to have too much estranged the minds of men from that active principle, that supreme and wise spirit, 'in whom we live, move, and have our being'.[21]

67  In the twelfth place, it may perhaps be objected, that though it be clear from what has been said, that there can be no such thing as an inert, senseless, extended, solid, figured, moveable substance, existing without the mind, such as philosophers describe matter; yet if any man shall leave

---

[20]  In the 1710 edition, this phrase reads: 'to understand this language (if I may so call it) of the Author of nature.'

[21]  Acts 17: 28. This was also quoted frequently by Malebranche, in support of the thesis that God alone is the true cause of everything that occurs in the natural world.

out of his idea of 'matter' the positive ideas of extension, figure, solidity, and motion, and say that he means only by that word an inert senseless substance, that exists without the mind or unperceived, which is the occasion of our ideas, or at the presence whereof God is pleased to excite ideas in us: it does not appear, but that matter taken in this sense may possibly exist. In answer to which I say, first, that it seems no less absurd to suppose a substance without accidents, than it is to suppose accidents without a substance. But secondly, though we should grant this unknown substance may possibly exist, yet where can it be supposed to be? That it exists not in the mind is agreed; and that it exists not in place is no less certain, since all extension exists only in the mind, as has been already proved. It remains therefore that it exists no where at all.

**68** Let us examine a little the description that is here given us of matter. It neither acts, nor perceives, nor is perceived; for this is all that is meant by saying it is an inert, senseless, unknown substance, which is a definition entirely made up of negatives, excepting only the relative notion of its standing under or supporting. But then it must be observed that it 'supports' nothing at all; and how nearly this comes to the description of a non-entity, I desire may be considered. But, say you, it is the unknown occasion, at the presence of which ideas are excited in us by the will of God. Now I would fain know how any thing can be present to us, which is neither perceivable by sense nor reflexion, nor capable of producing any idea in our minds, nor is at all extended, nor has any form, nor exists in any place. The words 'to be present', when thus applied, must needs be taken in some abstract and strange meaning, and which I am not able to comprehend.

**69** Again, let us examine what is meant by 'occasion'. So far as I can gather from the common use of language, that word signifies either the agent which produces any effect, or else something that is observed to accompany or go before it in the ordinary course of things. But when it is applied to matter as above described, it can be taken in neither of those senses. For matter is said to be passive and inert, and so cannot be an agent or efficient cause. It is also unperceivable, as being devoid of all sensible qualities, and so cannot be the occasion of our perceptions in the latter sense, as when the burning my finger is said to be the occasion of the pain that attends it. What therefore can be meant by calling matter an 'occasion'? This term is either used in no sense at all, or else in some sense very distant from its received signification.

**70**  You will perhaps say that matter, though it be not perceived by us, is nevertheless perceived by God, to whom it is the occasion of exciting ideas in our minds. For, say you, since we observe our sensations to be imprinted in an orderly and constant manner, it is but reasonable to suppose there are certain constant and regular occasions of their being produced. That is to say, that there are certain permanent and distinct parcels of matter corresponding to our ideas, which, though they do not excite them in our minds or any ways immediately affect us, as being altogether passive and unperceivable to us, they are nevertheless to God, by whom they are perceived, as it were so many occasions to remind him when and what ideas to imprint on our minds, that so things may go on in a constant uniform manner.

**71**  In answer to this I observe, that as the notion of matter is here stated, the question is no longer concerning the existence of a thing distinct from spirit and idea, from perceiving and being perceived, but whether there are not certain ideas, of I know not what sort, in the mind of God, which are so many marks or notes that direct him how to produce sensations in our minds in a constant and regular method: much after the same manner as a musician is directed by the notes of music to produce that harmonious train and composition of sound, which is called a 'tune'; though they who hear the music do not perceive the notes, and may be entirely ignorant of them. But this notion of matter (which after all is the only intelligible one that I can pick, from what is said of unknown occasions) seems too extravagant to deserve a confutation.[22] Besides, it is in effect no objection against what we have advanced, to wit, that there is no senseless, unperceived substance.

**72**  If we follow the light of reason we shall, from the constant uniform method of our sensations, collect the goodness and wisdom of the spirit who excites them in our minds. But this is all that I can see reasonably concluded from thence. To me, I say, it is evident that the being of a spirit infinitely wise, good, and powerful is abundantly sufficient to explain all the appearances of nature. But as for inert senseless matter, nothing that I perceive has any the least connexion with it or leads to the thoughts of it. And I would fain see any one explain any the meanest phenomenon in nature by it, or show any manner of reason,

[22]  The phrase in parentheses was included as a parenthetical remark in 1710 and omitted in the 1734 edition.

though in the lowest rank of probability, that he can have for its existence; or even make any tolerable sense or meaning of that supposition. For as to its being an occasion, we have, I think, evidently shown that with regard to us it is no occasion. It remains therefore that it must be, if at all, the occasion to God of exciting ideas in us; and what this amounts to, we have just now seen.

73    It is worth while to reflect a little on the motives which induced men to suppose the existence of material substance, that so having observed the gradual ceasing and expiration of those motives or reasons, we may proportionably withdraw the assent that was grounded on them. First therefore, it was thought that colour, figure, motion, and the rest of the sensible qualities or accidents did really exist without the mind; and for this reason, it seemed needful to suppose some unthinking substratum or substance wherein they did exist, since they could not be conceived to exist by themselves. Afterwards, in process of time, men being convinced that colours, sounds, and the rest of the sensible secondary qualities had no existence without the mind, they stripped this substratum or material substance of those qualities, leaving only the primary ones, figure, motion, and such like, which they still conceived to exist without the mind, and consequently to stand in need of a material support. But it having been shown that none, even of these, can possibly exist otherwise than in a spirit or mind which perceives them, it follows that we have no longer any reason to suppose the being of matter. Nay, that it is utterly impossible there should be any such thing, so long as that word is taken to denote an 'unthinking substratum' of qualities or accidents, wherein they exist without the mind.

74    But though it be allowed by the materialists themselves, that matter was thought of only for the sake of supporting accidents; and the reason entirely ceasing, one might expect the mind should naturally, and without any reluctance at all, quit the belief of what was solely grounded thereon. Yet the prejudice is riveted so deeply in our thoughts, that we can scarce tell how to part with it, and are therefore inclined, since the thing it self is indefensible, at least to retain the name; which we apply to I know not what abstracted and indefinite notions of being, or occasion, though without any show of reason, at least so far as I can see. For what is there on our part, or what do we perceive amongst all the ideas, sensations, notions, which are imprinted on our minds, either by sense or reflexion, from whence may be inferred the existence of an inert,

thoughtless, unperceived occasion? And on the other hand, on the part of an all-sufficient spirit, what can there be that should make us believe, or even suspect, he is directed by an inert occasion to excite ideas in our minds?

75 It is a very extraordinary instance of the force of prejudice, and much to be lamented, that the mind of man retains so great a fondness against all the evidence of reason for a stupid thoughtless somewhat, by the interposition whereof it would, as it were, screen it self from the providence of God and remove him farther off from the affairs of the world. But though we do the utmost we can to secure the belief of matter, though when reason forsakes us, we endeavour to support our opinion on the bare possibility of the thing, and though we indulge our selves in the full scope of an imagination not regulated by reason, to make out that poor possibility, yet the upshot of all is that there are certain unknown ideas in the mind of God. For this, if any thing, is all that I can conceive to be meant by 'occasion' with regard to God. And this, at bottom, is no longer contending for the thing, but for the name.

76 Whether therefore there are such ideas in the mind of God, and whether they may be called by the name 'matter', I shall not dispute. But if you stick to the notion of an unthinking substance or support of extension, motion, and other sensible qualities, then to me it is most evidently impossible there should be any such thing. Since it is a plain repugnancy that those qualities should exist in, or be supported by, an unperceiving substance.

77 But say you, though it be granted that there is no thoughtless support of extension, and the other qualities or accidents which we perceive; yet there may, perhaps, be some inert unperceiving substance or *substratum* of some other qualities, as incomprehensible to us as colours are to a man born blind, because we have not a sense adapted to them. But if we had a new sense, we should possibly no more doubt of their existence than a blind man made to see does of the existence of light and colours. I answer, first, if what you mean by the word 'matter' be only the unknown support of unknown qualities, it is no matter whether there is such a thing or no, since it no way concerns us; and I do not see the advantage there is in disputing about we know not what, and we know not why.

78 But secondly, if we had a new sense, it could only furnish us with new ideas or sensations; and then we should have the same reason against

their existing in an unperceiving substance, that has been already offered with relation to figure, motion, colour, and the like. Qualities, as has been shown, are nothing else but sensations or ideas, which exist only in a mind perceiving them; and this is true not only of the ideas we are acquainted with at present, but likewise of all possible ideas whatsoever.

79 But you will insist, what if I have no reason to believe the existence of matter, what if I cannot assign any use to it, or explain any thing by it, or even conceive what is meant by that word? Yet still it is no contradiction to say that matter exists, and that this matter is in general a substance, or occasion of ideas; though, indeed, to go about to unfold the meaning, or adhere to any particular explication of those words, may be attended with great difficulties. I answer, when words are used without a meaning, you may put them together as you please, without danger of running into a contradiction. You may say, for example, that 'twice two is equal to seven', so long as you declare you do not take the words of that proposition in their usual acceptation, but for marks of you know not what. And by the same reason you may say, there is an inert thoughtless substance without accidents, which is the occasion of our ideas. And we shall understand just as much by one proposition as the other.

80 In the last place, you will say, what if we give up the cause of material substance, and assert that matter is an unknown somewhat, neither substance nor accident, spirit nor idea, inert, thoughtless, indivisible, immoveable, unextended, existing in no place? For, say you, whatever may be urged against substance or occasion, or any other positive or relative notion of matter, has no place at all, so long as this negative definition of matter is adhered to. I answer, you may, if so it shall seem good, use the word 'matter' in the same sense that other men use 'nothing', and so make those terms convertible in your style. For after all, this is what appears to me to be the result of that definition, the parts whereof when I consider with attention, either collectively or separate from each other, I do not find that there is any kind of effect or impression made on my mind different from what is excited by the term 'nothing'.

81 You will reply perhaps, that in the foresaid definition is included, what sufficiently distinguishes it from nothing, the positive, abstract idea of quiddity, entity, or existence. I own, indeed, that those who pretend to the faculty of framing abstract general ideas do talk as if they had such an idea, which is, say they, the most abstract and general notion of all, that is

to me the most incomprehensible of all others. That there are a great variety of spirits of different orders and capacities, whose faculties, both in number and extent, are far exceeding those the Author of my being has bestowed on me, I see no reason to deny. As for me to pretend to determine by my own few, stinted, narrow inlets of perception, what ideas the inexhaustible power of the Supreme Spirit may imprint upon them, were certainly the utmost folly and presumption. Since there may be, for aught that I know, innumerable sorts of ideas or sensations, as different from one another and from all that I have perceived, as colours are from sounds. But how ready soever I may be, to acknowledge the scantiness of my comprehension with regard to the endless variety of spirits and ideas that might possibly exist, yet for any one to pretend to a notion of entity or existence, abstracted from spirit and idea, from perceiving and being perceived, is, I suspect, a downright repugnancy and trifling with words. It remains that we consider the objections, which may possibly be made on the part of religion.

82  Some there are who think that, though the arguments for the real existence of bodies, which are drawn from reason, be allowed not to amount to demonstration, yet the Holy Scriptures are so clear in the point as will sufficiently convince every good Christian that bodies do really exist, and are something more than mere ideas, there being in Holy Writ innumerable facts related, which evidently suppose the reality of timber, and stone, mountains, and rivers, and cities, and human bodies. To which I answer, that no sort of writings whatever, sacred or profane, which use those and the like words in the vulgar acceptation, or so as to have a meaning in them, are in danger of having their truth called in question by our doctrine. That all those things do really exist, that there are bodies, even corporeal substances, when taken in the vulgar sense, has been shown to be agreeable to our principles; and the difference betwixt things and ideas, realities and chimeras, has been distinctly explained.[i] And I do not think that either what philosophers call 'matter', or the existence of objects without the mind, is any where mentioned in Scripture.

83  Again, whether there be or be not external things, it is agreed on all hands that the proper use of words, is the marking our conceptions, or things only as they are known and perceived by us; whence it plainly

[i] Sections 29, 30, 33, 36, etc.

follows that, in the tenets we have laid down, there is nothing inconsistent with the right use and significancy of language, and that discourse of what kind soever, so far as it is intelligible, remains undisturbed. But all this seems so manifest, from what has been set forth in the premises, that it is needless to insist any farther on it.

84   But, it will be urged, that miracles do, at least, lose much of their stress and import by our principles. What must we think of Moses's rod, was it not really turned into a serpent, or was there only a change of ideas in the minds of the spectators? And can it be supposed that our Saviour did no more, at the marriage-feast in Cana, than impose on the sight, and smell, and taste of the guests, so as to create in them the appearance or idea only of wine?[23] The same may be said of all other miracles, which, in consequence of the foregoing principles, must be looked upon only as so many cheats or illusions of fancy. To this I reply, that the rod was changed into a real serpent, and the water into real wine. That this does not, in the least, contradict what I have elsewhere said, will be evident from Sections 34 and 35. But this business of real and imaginary has been already so plainly and fully explained, and so often referred to, and the difficulties about it are so easily answered from what has gone before, that it were an affront to the reader's understanding to resume the explication of it in this place. I shall only observe that if, at table, all who were present should see, and smell, and taste, and drink wine, and find the effects of it, with me there could be no doubt of its reality. So that, at bottom, the scruple concerning real miracles has no place at all on ours, but only on the received principles, and consequently makes rather for than against what has been said.

85   Having done with the objections, which I endeavoured to propose in the clearest light, and gave them all the force and weight I could, we proceed in the next place to take a view of our tenets in their consequences. Some of these appear at first sight, as that several difficult and obscure questions, on which abundance of speculation has been thrown away, are entirely banished from philosophy. Whether corporeal substance can think? Whether matter be infinitely divisible? And how it operates on spirit? – these and the like inquiries have given infinite amusement to philosophers in all ages. But depending on the existence

[23] References to the biblical accounts of Moses turning a rod into a serpent (Exodus 4: 3), and of Jesus performing a miracle at a wedding feast when he turned water into wine (John 2: 1–11).

of matter, they have no longer any place in our principles. Many other advantages there are, as well with regard to religion and the sciences, which it is easy for any one to deduce from what has been premised. But this will appear more plainly in the sequel.

**86** From the principles we have laid down it follows, human knowledge may naturally be reduced to two heads, that of ideas, and that of spirits. Of each of these I shall treat in order. And first as to ideas or unthinking things, our knowledge of these has been very much obscured and confounded, and we have been led into very dangerous errors, by supposing a twofold existence of the objects of sense, the one intelligible or in the mind, the other real and without the mind, whereby unthinking things are thought to have a natural subsistence of their own, distinct from being perceived by spirits. This which, if I mistake not, has been shown to be a most groundless and absurd notion, is the very root of scepticism. For so long as men thought that real things subsisted without the mind, and that their knowledge was only so far forth real as it was conformable to real things, it follows, they could not be certain that they had any real knowledge at all. For how can it be known that the things, which are perceived, are conformable to those which are not perceived or exist without the mind?

**87** Colour, figure, motion, extension and the like, considered only as so many sensations in the mind, are perfectly known, there being nothing in them which is not perceived. But if they are looked on as notes or images, referred to things or archeytpes existing without the mind, then are we involved all in scepticism. We see only the appearances, and not the real qualities of things. What may be the extension, figure, or motion of any thing really and absolutely, or in it self, it is impossible for us to know, but only the proportion or the relation they bear to our senses. Things remaining the same, our ideas vary, and which of them, or even whether any of them at all represent the true quality really existing in the thing, it is out of our reach to determine. So that, for aught we know, all we see, hear, and feel, may be only phantom and vain chimera, and not at all agree with the real things, existing in *rerum natura*. All this scepticism follows from our supposing a difference between things and ideas, and that the former have a subsistence without the mind or unperceived. It were easy to dilate on this subject, and show how the arguments urged by sceptics in all ages, depend on the supposition of external things.

**88** So long as we attribute a real existence to unthinking things, distinct from their being perceived, it is not only impossible for us to know with evidence the nature of any real unthinking being, but even that it exists. Hence it is that we see philosophers distrust their senses, and doubt of the existence of heaven and earth, of every thing they see or feel, even of their own bodies. And after all their labour and struggle of thought, they are forced to own, we cannot attain to any self-evident or demonstrative knowledge of the existence of sensible things. But all this doubtfulness, which so bewilders and confounds the mind, and makes philosophy ridiculous in the eyes of the world, vanishes if we annex a meaning to our words, and do not amuse our selves with the terms 'absolute', 'external', 'exist', and such like, signifying we know not what. I can as well doubt of my own being as of the being of those things which I actually perceive by sense, it being a manifest contradiction that any sensible object should be immediately perceived by sight or touch, and at the same time have no existence in nature, since the very existence of an unthinking being consists in being perceived.

**89** Nothing seems of more importance towards erecting a firm system of sound and real knowledge, which may be proof against the assaults of scepticism, than to lay the beginning in a distinct explication of what is meant by 'thing', 'reality', 'existence'. For in vain shall we dispute concerning the real existence of things, or pretend to any knowledge thereof, so long as we have not fixed the meaning of those words. 'Thing' or 'being' is the most general name of all; it comprehends under it two kinds entirely distinct and heterogeneous, and which have nothing in common but the name, to wit, spirits and ideas. The former are active, indivisible substances; the latter are inert, fleeting, dependent beings, which subsist not by themselves but are supported by, or exist in, minds or spiritual substances. [We comprehend our own existence by inward feeling or reflexion, and that of other spirits by reason. We may be said to have some knowledge or notion of our own minds, of spirits and active beings, whereof in a strict sense we have not ideas. In like manner we know and have a notion of relations between things or ideas, which relations are distinct from the ideas or things related, inasmuch as the latter may be perceived by us without our perceiving the former. To me it seems that ideas, spirits, and relations are all in their respective kinds the object of human knowledge and subject of discourse, and that the term 'idea' would be improperly extended to signify every thing we know or have any notion of.][24]

90   Ideas imprinted on the senses are real things, or do really exist. This we do not deny, but we deny they can subsist without the minds which perceive them, or that they are resemblances of any archetypes existing without the mind, since the very being of a sensation or idea consists in being perceived, and an idea can be like nothing but an idea. Again, the things perceived by sense may be termed 'external' with regard to their origin, in that they are not generated from within, by the mind it self, but imprinted by a spirit distinct from that which perceives them. Sensible objects may likewise be said to be without the mind, in another sense, namely when they exist in some other mind. Thus when I shut my eyes, the things I saw may still exist, but it must be in another mind.

91   It were a mistake to think that what is here said derogates in the least from the reality of things. It is acknowledged on the received principles that extension, motion, and in a word all sensible qualities, have need of a support, as not being able to subsist by themselves. But the objects perceived by sense are allowed to be nothing but combinations of those qualities, and consequently cannot subsist by themselves. Thus far it is agreed on all hands. So that in denying the things perceived by sense an existence independent of a substance, or support wherein they may exist, we detract nothing from the received opinion of their reality, and are guilty of no innovation in that respect. All the difference is, that according to us the unthinking beings perceived by sense, have no existence distinct from being perceived, and cannot therefore exist in any other substance, than those unextended, indivisible substances, or spirits, which act, and think, and perceive them. Whereas philosophers vulgarly hold, that the sensible qualities exist in an inert, extended, unperceiving substance, which they call 'matter', to which they attribute a natural subsistence, exterior to all thinking beings, or distinct from being perceived by any mind whatsoever, even the eternal mind of the Creator, wherein they suppose only ideas of the corporeal substances created by him, if indeed they allow them to be at all created.

92   For as we have shown the doctrine of matter or corporeal substance to have been the main pillar and support of scepticism, so likewise

---

[24] The material in parentheses was added in the 1734 edition, during a period when Berkeley was concerned that his theory of ideas precluded knowledge of minds or God. See below, in the *Alciphron*.

upon the same foundation have been raised all the impious schemes of atheism and irreligion. Nay so great a difficulty has it been thought, to conceive matter produced out of nothing, that the most celebrated among the ancient philosophers, even of these who maintained the being of a God, have thought matter to be uncreated and coeternal with him.[25] How great a friend material substance has been to atheists in all ages, were needless to relate. All their monstrous systems have so visible and necessary a dependence on it, that when this corner-stone is once removed, the whole fabric cannot choose but fall to the ground; insomuch that it is no longer worth while, to bestow a particular consideration on the absurdities of every wretched sect of atheists.

93  That impious and profane persons should readily fall in with those systems which favour their inclinations by deriding immaterial substance, and supposing the soul to be divisible and subject to corruption as the body; which exclude all freedom, intelligence, and design from the formation of things, and instead thereof make a self-existent, stupid, unthinking substance the root and origin of all beings; that they should hearken to those who deny a providence, or inspection of a superior mind over the affairs of the world, attributing the whole series of events either to blind chance or fatal necessity, arising from the impulse of one body on another: all this is very natural. And on the other hand, when men of better principles observe the enemies of religion lay so great a stress on unthinking matter, and all of them use so much industry and artifice to reduce every thing to it, methinks they should rejoice to see them deprived of their grand support, and driven from that only fortress, without which your Epicureans, Hobbists, and the like,[26] have not even the shadow of a pretence, but become the most cheap and easy triumph in the world.

94  The existence of matter, or bodies unperceived, has not only been the main support of atheists and fatalists, but on the same principles idolatry likewise in all its various forms depends. Did men but consider that the sun, moon, and stars, and every other object of the senses, are only so many sensations in their minds, which have no other existence but barely being perceived, doubtless they would never fall down and

---

[25] Many philosophers in the ancient period claimed that matter was eternal. See for example Aristotle, *Physics*, I, 8, *On the Heavens*, I, 9–10.
[26] Followers of Epicurus (341–271 BC) and Thomas Hobbes (1588–1679), both of whom were regarded as either implicit or explicit supporters of atheism.

worship their own ideas, but rather address their homage to that Eternal Invisible Mind which produces and sustains all things.

**95** The same absurd principle, by mingling it self with the articles of our faith, has occasioned no small difficulties to Christians. For example, about the resurrection, how many scruples and objections have been raised by Socinians and others?[27] But do not the most plausible of them depend on the supposition that a body is denominated the 'same', with regard not to the form or that which is perceived by sense, but the material substance which remains the same under several forms? Take away this material substance, about the identity whereof all the dispute is, and mean by 'body' what every plain ordinary person means by that word, to wit, that which is immediately seen and felt, which is only a combination of sensible qualities, or ideas, and then their most unanswerable objections come to nothing.

**96** Matter being once expelled out of nature, drags with it so many sceptical and impious notions, such an incredible number of disputes and puzzling questions, which have been thorns in the sides of divines, as well as philosophers, and made so much fruitless work for mankind, that if the arguments we have produced against it are not found equal to demonstration (as to me they evidently seem) yet I am sure all friends to knowledge, peace, and religion, have reason to wish they were.

**97** Besides the external existence of the objects of perception, another great source of errors and difficulties, with regard to ideal knowledge, is the doctrine of abstract ideas, such as it has been set forth in the Introduction. The plainest things in the world, those we are most intimately acquainted with and perfectly know, when they are considered in an abstract way, appear strangely difficult and incomprehensible. Time, place, and motion, taken in particular or concrete, are what every body knows; but having passed through the hands of a metaphysician, they become too abstract and fine to be apprehended by men of ordinary sense. Bid your servant meet you at such a time, in such a place, and he shall never stay to deliberate on the meaning of those words; in conceiving that particular time and place, or the motion by which he is to get

---

[27] Fausto Sozzini (1539–1604) was an anti-trinitarian theologian who denied that Christ was God. 'Socinians' was used as a more comprehensive term in seventeenth- and eighteenth-century controversies for those accused of denying important features of the Christian tradition. Here it is applied to those who denied that each human being recovers, in heaven, the same body (in some sense) that they had during their life on earth.

thither, he finds not the least difficulty. But if 'time' be taken, exclusive of all those particular actions and ideas that diversify the day, merely for the continuation of existence or duration in abstract, then it will perhaps gravel even a philosopher to comprehend it.

98   Whenever I attempt to frame a simple idea of time, abstracted from the succession of ideas in my mind, which flows uniformly and is participated by all beings, I am lost and embrangled in inextricable difficulties. I have no notion of it at all; only I hear others say, it is infinitely divisible, and speak of it in such a manner as leads me to entertain odd thoughts of my existence, since that doctrine lays one under an absolute necessity of thinking, either that he passes away innumerable ages without a thought, or else that he is annihilated every moment of his life: both which seem equally absurd. Time therefore being nothing abstracted from the succession of ideas in our minds, it follows that the duration of any finite spirit must be estimated by the number of ideas or actions succeeding each other in that same spirit or mind. Hence it is a plain consequence that the soul always thinks; and in truth whoever shall go about to divide in his thoughts, or abstract the existence of a spirit from its cogitation, will, I believe, find it no easy task.

99   So likewise, when we attempt to abstract extension and motion from all other qualities, and consider them by themselves, we presently lose sight of them and run into great extravagancies. All which depend on a two-fold abstraction: first, it is supposed that extension, for example, may be abstracted from all other sensible qualities; and secondly, that the entity of extension may be abstracted from its being perceived. But whoever shall reflect and take care to understand what he says, will, if I mistake not, acknowledge that all sensible qualities are alike sensations, and alike real; that where the extension is, there is the colour too, to wit, in his mind, and that their archetypes can exist only in some other mind; and that the objects of sense are nothing but those sensations combined, blended, or (if one may so speak) concreted together, none of all which can be supposed to exist unperceived.

100   What it is for a man to be happy, or an object good, every one may think he knows. But to frame an abstract idea of 'happiness' prescinded from all particular pleasure, or of 'goodness' from every thing that is good, this is what few can pretend to. So likewise, a man may be just and virtuous, without having precise ideas of 'justice' and 'virtue'. The opinion that those and the like words stand for general notions,

abstracted from all particular persons and actions, seems to have rendered morality difficult and the study thereof of less use to mankind.[28] And in effect, the doctrine of abstraction has not a little contributed towards spoiling the most useful parts of knowledge.

**101** The two great provinces of speculative science, conversant about the ideas received from sense and their relations, are natural philosophy and mathematics; with regard to each of these I shall make some observations. And first, I shall say somewhat of natural philosophy. On this subject it is that the sceptics triumph. All that stock of arguments they produce to depreciate our faculties, and make mankind appear ignorant and low, are drawn principally from this head, to wit, that we are under an invincible blindness as to the true and real nature of things. This they exaggerate, and love to enlarge on. We are miserably bantered, say they, by our senses, and amused only with the outside and show of things. The real essence, the internal qualities and constitution of every the meanest object, is hid from our view;[29] something there is in every drop of water, every grain of sand, which it is beyond the power of human understanding to fathom or comprehend. But it is evident from what has been shown, that all this complaint is groundless, and that we are influenced by false principles to that degree as to mistrust our senses, and think we know nothing of those things which we perfectly comprehend.

**102** One great inducement to our pronouncing our selves ignorant of the nature of things is the current opinion that every thing includes within it self the cause of its properties, or that there is in each object an inward essence, which is the source whence its discernible qualities flow and whereon they depend. Some have pretended to account for appearances by occult qualities, but of late they are mostly resolved into mechanical causes, to wit, the figure, motion, weight, and such like qualities of insensible particles, whereas in truth there is no other agent or efficient cause than spirit, it being evident that motion, as well as all

[28] The 1710 edition has the following extra sentence: 'And in effect, one may make a great progress in School-Ethics, without ever being the wiser or better man for it, or knowing how to behave himself in the affairs of life, more to the advantage of himself or his neighbours than he did before. This hint may suffice, to let any one see the doctrine of *abstraction* ...'

[29] While the distinction between appearance and reality was a commonplace in the seventeenth century, the claim that the real essence of things cannot be known was characteristic of Locke. See note 2 above.

other ideas, is perfectly inert.[j] Hence, to endeavour to explain the production of colours or sounds by figure, motion, magnitude and the like, must needs be labour in vain. And accordingly, we see the attempts of that kind are not at all satisfactory. Which may be said, in general, of those instances, wherein one idea or quality is assigned for the cause of another. I need not say how many hypotheses and speculations are left out, and how much the study of nature is abridged by this doctrine.

**103** The great mechanical principle now in vogue is attraction.[30] That a stone falls to the earth, or the sea swell towards the moon, may to some appear sufficiently explained thereby. But how are we enlightened by being told this is done by attraction? Is it that that word signifies the manner of the tendency, and that it is by the mutual drawing of bodies, instead of their being impelled or protruded towards each other? But nothing is determined of the manner or action, and it may as truly (for aught we know) be termed 'impulse' or 'protrusion' as 'attraction'. Again, the parts of steel we see cohere firmly together, and this also is accounted for by attraction; but in this, as in the other instances, I do not perceive that any thing is signified beside the effect itself. For as to the manner of the action whereby it is produced, or the cause which produces it, these are not so much as aimed at.

**104** Indeed, if we take a view of the several phenomena and compare them together, we may observe some likeness and conformity between them. For example, in the falling of a stone to the ground, in the rising of the sea towards the moon, in cohesion and crystallization, there is something alike, namely an union or mutual approach of bodies. So that any one of these or the like phenomena, may not seem strange or surprising to a man who has nicely observed and compared the effects of nature. For that only is thought so which is uncommon, or a thing by it self, and out of the ordinary course of our observation. That bodies should tend towards the centre of the earth is not thought strange, because it is what we perceive every moment of our lives. But that they should have a like gravitation towards the centre of the moon may seem odd and unaccountable to most men, because it is discerned only in the tides. But a philosopher, whose thoughts take in a larger compass of nature, having

[j] See Section 25.

[30] Refers to the popularity of Isaac Newton's physics, according to which gravitational attraction causes stones to fall to earth and the seas to move in a tidal attraction towards the moon.

observed a certain similitude of appearances, as well in the heavens as the earth, that argue innumerable bodies to have a mutual tendency towards each other, which he denotes by the general name 'attraction', whatever can be reduced to that, he thinks justly accounted for. Thus he explains the tides by the attraction of the terraqueous globe towards the moon, which to him does not appear odd or anomalous, but only a particular example of a general rule or law of nature.

**105** If therefore we consider the difference there is betwixt natural philosophers and other men with regard to their knowledge of the phenomena, we shall find it consists, not in an exacter knowledge of the efficient cause that produces them, for that can be no other than the will of a spirit, but only in a greater largeness of comprehension whereby analogies, harmonies, and agreements are discovered in the works of nature, and the particular effects explained, that is, reduced to general rules, [k] which rules grounded on the analogy and uniformness observed in the production of natural effects, are most agreeable and sought after by the mind; for that they extend our prospect beyond what is present, and near to us, and enable us to make very probable conjectures, touching things that may have happened at very great distances of time and place, as well as to predict things to come; which sort of endeavour towards omniscience is much affected by the mind.

**106** But we should proceed warily in such things, for we are apt to lay too great a stress on analogies and, to the prejudice of truth, humour that eagerness of the mind whereby it is carried to extend its knowledge into general theorems. For example, gravitation or mutual attraction, because it appears in many instances, some are straightway for pronouncing 'universal'; and that to 'attract, and be attracted by every body, is an essential quality inherent in all bodies whatsoever.' Whereas it appears the fixed stars have no such tendency towards each other; and so far is that gravitation from being 'essential' to bodies that, in some instances, a quite contrary principle seems to show it self, as in the perpendicular growth of plants and the elasticity of the air. There is nothing necessary or essential in the case, but it depends entirely on the will of the governing spirit, who causes certain bodies to cleave together or tend towards each other according to various laws, whilst he keeps others at a fixed distance; and to some he gives a quite contrary tendency to fly asunder, just as he sees convenient.

[k] See Section 62.

**107** After what has been premised, I think we may lay down the following conclusions. First, it is plain philosophers amuse themselves in vain, when they inquire for any natural efficient cause, distinct from a mind or spirit. Secondly, considering the whole creation is the workmanship of a wise and good agent, it should seem to become philosophers to employ their thoughts (contrary to what some hold) about the final causes of things. And I must confess, I see no reason why pointing out the various ends, to which natural things are adapted and for which they were originally with unspeakable wisdom contrived, should not be thought one good way of accounting for them, and altogether worthy a philosopher.[31] Thirdly, from what has been premised no reason can be drawn why the history of nature should not still be studied, and observations and experiments made, which, that they are of use to mankind, and enable us to draw any general conclusions, is not the result of any immutable habitudes or relations between things themselves, but only of God's goodness and kindness to men in the administration of the world.[1] Fourthly, by a diligent observation of the phenomena within our view, we may discover the general laws of nature, and from them deduce the other phenomena. I do not say demonstrate, for all deductions of that kind depend on a supposition that the Author of nature always operates uniformly, and in a constant observance of those rules we take for principles, which we cannot evidently know.

**108** [It appears from Section 66 etc. that the steady, consistent methods of nature, may not unfitly be styled the language of its Author, whereby He discovers His attributes to our view, and directs us how to act for the convenience and felicity of life. And to me,][32] Those men who frame general rules from the phenomena, and afterwards derive the phenomena from those rules, seem to consider signs rather than causes. A man may well understand natural signs without knowing their analogy,[33] or being able to say by what rule a thing is so or so.

---

[1] See Sections 30 and 31.

[31] Most likely refers to Descartes, who argued that philosophers cannot discern God's plans. See his *Principles of Philosophy*, Part I, art. 28: *Oeuvres*, VIII-1, 15.

[32] The material in parentheses was included in the 1710 edition and omitted from the 1734 edition.

[33] The phrase 'seem to consider ... analogy', in the 1734 edition, replaced the following from 1710: 'seem to be grammarians, and their art the grammar of nature. Two ways there are of learning a language, either by rule or by practice: a man may well read in the language of nature, without understanding the grammar of it, ...'

And as it is very possible to write improperly, through too strict an observance of general grammar-rules, so in arguing from general rules of nature it is not impossible we may extend the analogy too far, and by that means run into mistakes.

**109** As in reading other books, a wise man will choose to fix his thoughts on the sense and apply it to use, rather than lay them out in grammatical remarks on the language; so in perusing the volume of nature, it seems beneath the dignity of the mind to affect an exactness in reducing each particular phenomenon to general rules, or showing how it follows from them. We should propose to our selves nobler views, such as to recreate and exalt the mind, with a prospect of the beauty, order, extent, and variety of natural things; hence, by proper inferences, to enlarge our notions of the grandeur, wisdom, and beneficence of the Creator; and lastly, to make the several parts of the Creation, so far as in us lies, subservient to the ends they were designed for, God's glory, and the sustentation and comfort of our selves and fellow-creatures.

**110** The best key for the aforesaid analogy, or natural science, will be easily acknowledged to be a certain celebrated treatise on mechanics, in the entrance of which justly admired treatise time, space and motion, are distinguished into 'absolute' and 'relative', 'true' and 'apparent', 'mathematical' and 'vulgar'.[34] Which distinction, as it is at large explained by the author, supposes those quantities to have an existence without the mind, and that they are ordinarily conceived with relation to sensible things, to which nevertheless in their own nature, they bear no relation at all.

**111** As for time, as it is there taken in an absolute or abstracted sense, for the duration or perseverance of the existence of things, I have nothing more to add concerning it, after what has been already said on that subject.[m] For the rest, this celebrated author holds there is an 'absolute

---

[m] Sections 97 and 98.

[34] The opening sentence, 'the best … mechanics', replaces the following paragraph from the 1710 edition: 'The best grammar of the kind we are speaking of will be easily acknowledged to be a treatise of mechanics, demonstrated and applied to Nature, by a philosopher of a neighbouring nation whom all the world admire. I shall not take upon me to make remarks on the performance of that extraordinary person: only some things he has advanced, so directly opposite to the doctrine we have hitherto laid down, that we should be wanting, in the regard due to the authority of so great a man, did we not take some notice of them.' In a Scholium to the definitions with which Newton begins Book I of the *Principles*, he claims that it is not necessary to define 'time, space and motion, as being well known to all' (p. 9). However, he distinguishes absolute from relative time, space, place and motion, as Berkeley reports (pp. 9–18).

space' which, being unperceivable to sense, remains in it self similar and immoveable, and relative space to be the measure thereof, which being moveable, and defined by its situation in respect of sensible bodies, is vulgarly taken for immoveable space. 'Place' he defines to be that part of space which is occupied by any body. And according as the space is absolute or relative, so also is the place. 'Absolute motion' is said to be the translation of a body from absolute place to absolute place, as relative motion is from one relative place to another. And because the parts of absolute space do not fall under our senses, instead of them we are obliged to use their sensible measures, and so define both place and motion with respect to bodies, which we regard as immoveable. But it is said in philosophical matters we must abstract from our senses, since it may be that none of those bodies which seem to be quiescent are truly so, and the same thing which is moved relatively may be really at rest. As likewise one and the same body may be in relative rest and motion, or even moved with contrary relative motions at the same time, according as its place is variously defined. All which ambiguity is to be found in the apparent motions, but not at all in the true or absolute, which should therefore be alone regarded in philosophy. And the true, we are told, are distinguished from apparent or relative motions by the following properties. First, in true or absolute motion, all parts which preserve the same position with respect to the whole, partake of the motions of the whole. Secondly, the place being moved, that which is placed therein is also moved; so that a body moving in a place which is in motion, participates [in] the motion of its place. Thirdly, true motion is never generated or changed, otherwise than by force impressed on the body it self. Fourthly, true motion is always changed by force impressed on the body moved. Fifthly, in circular motion barely relative, there is no centrifugal force, which nevertheless in that which is true or absolute is proportional to the quantity of motion.

112   But not withstanding what has been said, it does not appear to me that there can be any motion other than relative; so that to conceive motion, there must be at least conceived two bodies, whereof the distance or position in regard to each other is varied. Hence if there was one only body in being, it could not possibly be moved. This seems evident, in that the idea I have of motion necessarily includes relation.

113   But though in every motion it be necessary to conceive more bodies than one, yet it may be that one only is moved, namely that on

which the force causing the change of distance is impressed, or in other words, that to which the action is applied. For however some may define relative motion, so as to term that body 'moved' which changes its distance from some other body, whether the force or action causing that change were applied to it or no; yet as relative motion is that which is perceived by sense, and regarded in the ordinary affairs of life, it should seem that every man of common sense knows what it is, as well as the best philosopher. Now I ask any one, whether in his sense of motion as he walks along the streets, the stones he passes over may be said to move, because they change distance with his feet? To me it seems that though motion includes a relation of one thing to another, yet it is not necessary that each term of the relation be denominated from it. As a man may think of somewhat which does not think, so a body may be moved to or from another body, which is not therefore itself in motion, [I mean relative motion, for other I am not able to conceive.][35]

114  As the place happens to be variously defined, the motion which is related to it varies. A man in a ship may be said to be quiescent with relation to the sides of the vessel, and yet move with relation to the land. Or he may move eastward in respect of the one, and westward in respect of the other. In the common affairs of life, men never go beyond the earth to define the place of any body; and what is quiescent in respect of that, is accounted absolutely to be so. But philosophers, who have a greater extent of thought and juster notions of the system of things, discover even the earth it self to be moved. In order therefore to fix their notions, they seem to conceive the corporeal world as finite, and the utmost unmoved walls or shell thereof to be the place, whereby they estimate true motions. If we sound our own conceptions, I believe we may find all the absolute motion we can frame an idea of, to be at bottom no other than relative motion thus defined. For as has been already observed, absolute motion exclusive of all external relation is incomprehensible; and to this kind of relative motion, all the above-mentioned properties, causes, and effects ascribed to absolute motion will, if I mistake not, be found to agree. As to what is said of the centrifugal force, that it does not at all belong to circular relative motion, I do not see how this follows from

[35] The phrase in parentheses was omitted from the 1734 edition.

the experiment which is brought to prove it.ⁿ For the water in the vessel, at that time wherein it is said to have the greatest relative circular motion, has, I think, no motion at all, as is plain from the foregoing section.[36]

**115** For to denominate a body 'moved' it is requisite, first, that it change its distance or situation with regard to some other body; and secondly, that the force or action occasioning that change be applied to it. If either of these be wanting, I do not think that agreeably to the sense of mankind, or the propriety of language, a body can be said to be in motion. I grant indeed, that it is possible for us to think a body, which we see change its distance from some other, to be moved, though it have no force applied to it (in which sense there may be apparent motion); but then it is, because the force causing the change of distance is imagined by us to be applied or impressed on that body thought to move. Which indeed shows we are capable of mistaking a thing to be in motion which is not, [and that is all.][37]

**116** From what has been said, it follows that the philosophic consideration of motion does not imply the being of an absolute space, distinct from that which is perceived by sense, and related to bodies: which that it cannot exist without the mind, is clear upon the same principles that demonstrate the like of all other objects of sense. And perhaps, if we inquire narrowly, we shall find we cannot even frame an idea of pure space, exclusive of all body. This I must confess seems impossible, as being a most abstract idea. When I excite a motion in some

---

ⁿ See *Philosophiae Naturalis Principia Mathematica*, in Scholium to Definition VIII [*Principles*, vol. I, 15–16].

[36] The experiment was to suspend a bucket from a long rope, twist the rope many times and, having filled the bucket with water and released it, allow the rope to unwind and the bucket to spin in the opposite direction. Berkeley disagreed with Newton who claimed that, as the bucket spins and the surface of the water assumes a concave shape, the water in the bucket must be moving in an absolute sense (as is indicated by the centrifugal forces that cause the surface of the water to change) but not relative to the bucket.

[37] The final phrase in parentheses replaces, in the 1734 edition, the following in 1710: 'but does not prove that, in the common acceptation of "motion", a body is moved merely because it changes distance from another; since as soon as we are undeceived, and find that the moving force was not communicated to it, we no longer hold it to be moved. So on the other hand, when one only body (the parts whereof preserve a given position between themselves) is imagined to exist; some there are who think that it can be moved all manner of ways, though without any change of distance or situation to any other bodies; which we should not deny, if they meant only that it might have an impressed force, which, upon the bare creation of other bodies, would produce a motion of any certain quantity and determination. But that an actual motion (distinct from the impressed force, or power productive of change of place in case there were bodies present whereby to define it) can exist in such a single body, I must confess I am not able to comprehend.'

part of my body, if it be free or without resistance, I say there is space: but if I find a resistance, then I say there is body; and in proportion as the resistance to motion is lesser or greater, I say the space is more or less pure. So that when I speak of pure or empty space, it is not to be supposed that the word 'space' stands for an idea distinct from, or conceivable without, body and motion. Though indeed we are apt to think [that] every noun substantive stands for a distinct idea that may be separated from all others, which has occasioned infinite mistakes. When therefore supposing all the world to be annihilated besides my own body, I say there still remains pure space: thereby nothing else is meant, but only that I conceive it possible, for the limbs of my body to be moved on all sides without the least resistance. But if that too were annihilated, then there could be no motion, and consequently no space. Some perhaps may think the sense of seeing furnishes them with the idea of pure space; but it is plain from what we have elsewhere shown, that the ideas of space and distance are not obtained by that sense.[o]

117    What is here laid down seems to put an end to all those disputes and difficulties, which have sprung up amongst the learned concerning the nature of pure space. But the chief advantage arising from it is that we are freed from that dangerous dilemma, to which several who have employed their thoughts on this subject imagine themselves reduced, to wit, of thinking either that real space is God, or else that there is something beside God which is eternal, uncreated, infinite, indivisible, immutable. Both which may justly be thought pernicious and absurd notions. It is certain that not a few divines, as well as philosophers of great note, have, from the difficulty they found in conceiving either limits or annihilation of space, concluded it must be divine. And some of late have set themselves particularly to show, that the incommunicable attributes of God agree to it. Which doctrine, how unworthy soever it may seem to the Divine Nature, yet I do not see how we can get clear of it, so long as we adhere to the received opinions.

118    Hitherto of natural philosophy: we come now to make some inquiry concerning that other great branch of speculative knowledge, to wit, mathematics. These, how celebrated soever they may be, for their clearness and certainty of demonstration, which is hardly any where else to be found, cannot nevertheless be supposed altogether free from

[o] See the *Essay concerning Vision* [section 126].

mistakes, if in their principles there lurks some secret error, which is common to the professors of those sciences with the rest of mankind. Mathematicians, though they deduce their theorems from a great height of evidence, yet their first principles are limited by the consideration of quantity; and they do not ascend into any inquiry concerning those transcendental maxims, which influence all the particular sciences, each part whereof, mathematics not excepted, consequently participates of the errors involved in them. That the principles laid down by mathematicians are true, and their way of deduction from those principles clear and incontestable, we do not deny. But we hold, there may be certain erroneous maxims of greater extent than the object of mathematics, and for that reason not expressly mentioned, though tacitly supposed throughout the whole progress of that science; and that the ill effects of those secret unexamined errors are diffused through all the branches thereof. To be plain, we suspect the mathematicians are, as well as other men, concerned in the errors arising from the doctrine of abstract general ideas, and the existence of objects without the mind.

**119**   Arithmetic has been thought to have for its object abstract ideas of number, of which to understand the properties and mutual habitudes is supposed no mean part of speculative philosophy. The opinion of the pure and intellectual nature of numbers in abstract has made them in esteem with those philosophers, who seem to have affected an uncommon fineness and elevation of thought. It has set a price on the most trifling numerical speculations which in practice are of no use, but serve only for amusement; and has therefore so far infected the minds of some, that they have dreamt of mighty mysteries involved in numbers, and attempted the explication of natural things by them. But if we inquire into our own thoughts, and consider what has been premised, we may perhaps entertain a low opinion of those high flights and abstractions, and look on all inquiries about numbers, only as so many *difficiles nugae*,[38] so far as they are not subservient to practice and promote the benefit of life.

**120**   Unity in abstract we have before considered in Section 13, from which, and what has been said in the Introduction, it plainly follows there is not any such idea. But number being defined a 'collection of units', we may conclude that, if there be no such thing as unity or unit in abstract,

[38] i.e. difficult trifles.

there are not ideas of number in abstract denoted by the numeral names and figures. The theories therefore in arithmetic, if they are abstracted from the names and figures, as likewise from all use and practice, as well as from the particular things numbered, can be supposed to have nothing at all for their object. Hence we may see how entirely the science of numbers is subordinate to practice, and how jejune and trifling it becomes when considered as a matter of mere speculation.

121 However since there may be some who, deluded by the specious show of discovering abstracted verities, waste their time in arithmetical theorems and problems, which have not any use, it will not be amiss, if we more fully consider and expose the vanity of that pretence; and this will plainly appear, by taking a view of arithmetic in its infancy, and observing what it was that originally put men on the study of that science, and to what scope they directed it. It is natural to think that at first, men, for ease of memory and help of computation, made use of counters, or in writing of single strokes, points or the like, each whereof was made to signify an unit, that is, some one thing of whatever kind they had occasion to reckon. Afterwards they found out the more compendious ways of making one character stand in place of several strokes, or points. And lastly, the notation of the Arabians or Indians came into use, wherein by the repetition of a few characters or figures, and varying the signification of each figure according to the place it obtains, all numbers may be most aptly expressed: which seems to have been done in imitation of language, so that an exact analogy is observed betwixt the notation by figures and names, the nine simple figures answering the nine first numeral names and places in the former, corresponding to denominations in the latter.

And agreeably to those conditions of the simple and local value of figures, were contrived methods of finding from the given figures or marks of the parts, what figures and how placed, are proper to denote the whole or vice versa. And having found the sought figures, the same rule or analogy being observed throughout, it is easy to read them into words; and so the number becomes perfectly known. For then the number of any particular things is said to be known, when we know the name or figures (with their due arrangement) that according to the standing analogy belong to them. For these signs being known, we can by the operations of arithmetic, know the signs of any part of the particular sums signified by them; and thus computing in signs (because of the connexion established betwixt them and the distinct multitudes of things, whereof one is taken for an unit), we may be able rightly to sum up, divide, and proportion the things themselves that we intend to number.

**122**  In arithmetic therefore we regard not the things but the signs, which nevertheless are not regarded for their own sake, but because they direct us how to act with relation to things and dispose rightly of them. Now agreeably to what we have before observed, of words in general,[P] it happens here likewise that abstract ideas are thought to be signified by numeral names or characters, while they do not suggest ideas of particular things to our minds. I shall not at present enter into a more particular dissertation on this subject, but only observe that it is evident from what has been said, those things which pass for abstract truths and theorems concerning numbers are, in reality, conversant about no object distinct from particular numerable things, except only names and characters; which originally came to be considered, on no other account but their being signs, or capable to represent aptly, whatever particular things men had need to compute. Whence it follows that to study them for their own sake would be just as wise, and to as good purpose, as if a man, neglecting the true use or original intention and subserviency of language, should spend his time in impertinent criticisms upon words, or reasonings and controversies purely verbal.

**123**  From numbers we proceed to speak of extension, which considered as relative, is the object of geometry. The infinite divisibility of finite extension, though it is not expressly laid down, either as an axiom or theorem in the elements of that science, yet is throughout the same every where supposed, and thought to have so inseparable and essential a connexion with the principles and demonstrations in geometry, that mathematicians never admit it into doubt, or make the least question of it. And as this notion is the source from whence do spring all those amusing geometrical paradoxes, which have such a direct repugnancy to the plain common sense of mankind, and are admitted with so much reluctance into a mind not yet debauched by learning, so is it the principal occasion of all that nice and extreme subtlety, which renders the study of mathematics so difficult and tedious. Hence if we can make it appear that no finite extension contains innumerable parts, or is infinitely divisible, it follows that we shall at once clear the science of geometry from a great number of difficulties and contradictions, which have ever

[P] Section 19, Introduction.

been esteemed a reproach to human reason, and withal make the attainment thereof a business of much less time and pains than it hitherto has been.

**124** Every particular finite extension, which may possibly be the object of our thought, is an idea existing only in the mind, and consequently each part thereof must be perceived. If therefore I cannot perceive innumerable parts in any finite extension that I consider, it is certain they are not contained in it. But it is evident that I cannot distinguish innumerable parts in any particular line, surface, or solid, which I either perceive by sense, or figure to my self in my mind; wherefore I conclude they are not contained in it. Nothing can be plainer to me than that the extensions I have in view are no other than my own ideas, and it is no less plain that I cannot resolve any one of my ideas into an infinite number of other ideas, that is, that they are not infinitely divisible. If by 'finite extension' be meant something distinct from a finite idea, I declare I do not know what that is, and so cannot affirm or deny any thing of it. But if the terms 'extension', 'parts', and the like, are taken in any sense conceivable, that is, for ideas; then to say a finite quantity or extension consists of parts infinite in number is so manifest a contradiction, that every one at first sight acknowledges it to be so. And it is impossible it should ever gain the assent of any reasonable creature who is not brought to it by gentle and slow degrees, as a converted Gentile to the belief of transubstantiation. Ancient and rooted prejudices do often pass into principles; and those propositions, which once obtain the force and credit of a principle, are not only themselves, but likewise whatever is deducible from them, thought privileged from all examination. And there is no absurdity so gross, which by this means the mind of man may not be prepared to swallow.

**125** He whose understanding is prepossessed with the doctrine of abstract general ideas, may be persuaded, that (whatever be thought of the ideas of sense), extension in abstract is infinitely divisible. And one who thinks the objects of sense exist without the mind, will perhaps in virtue thereof be brought to admit that a line but an inch long may contain innumerable parts really existing, though too small to be discerned. These errors are grafted as well in the minds of geometricians as of other men, and have a like influence on their reasonings; and it were no difficult thing to show how the arguments from geometry, [which are] made use of to support the infinite divisibility of extension, are bottomed on them. At present we shall only observe in general, whence it is that the mathematicians are all so fond and tenacious of this doctrine.

**126** It has been observed in another place, that the theorems and demonstrations in geometry are conversant about universal ideas.[q] Where it is explained in what sense this ought to be understood, to wit, that the particular lines and figures included in the diagram, are supposed to stand for innumerable others of different sizes: or in other words, the geometer considers them abstracting from their magnitude. Which does not imply that he forms an abstract idea, but only that he cares not what the particular magnitude is, whether great or small, but looks on that as a thing indifferent to the demonstration. Hence it follows that a line in the scheme, but an inch long, must be spoken of as though it contained ten thousand parts, since it is regarded not in it self but as it is universal; and it is universal only in its signification, whereby it represents innumerable lines greater than it self, in which may be distinguished ten thousand parts or more, though there may not be above an inch in it. After this manner the properties of the lines signified are (by a very usual figure) transferred to the sign, and thence through mistake thought to appertain to it considered in its own nature.

**127** Because there is no number of parts so great, but it is possible there may be a line containing more, the inch-line is said to contain parts more than any assignable number; which is true, not of the inch taken absolutely, but only for the things signified by it. But men not retaining that distinction in their thoughts, slide into a belief that the small particular line described on paper contains in it self parts innumerable. There is no such thing as the ten-thousandth part of an inch; but there is of a mile or diameter of the earth, which may be signified by that inch. When therefore I delineate a triangle on paper, and take one side not above an inch, for example, in length to be the radius: this I consider as divided into ten thousand or an hundred thousand parts or more. For though the ten-thousandth part of that line, considered in it self, is nothing at all and consequently may be neglected without any error or inconveniency; yet these described lines being only marks standing for greater quantities, whereof it may be the ten-thousandth part is very considerable, it follows, that to prevent notable errors in practice, the radius must be taken of ten thousand parts, or more.

[q] Section 15, Introduction.

128    From what has been said the reason is plain why, to the end any theorem may become universal in its use, it is necessary we speak of the lines described on paper, as though they contained parts which really they do not. In doing of which, if we examine the matter throughly, we shall perhaps discover that we cannot conceive an inch it self as consisting of, or being divisible into a thousand parts, but only some other line which is far greater than an inch and represented by it. And that when we say a line is 'infinitely divisible', we must mean a line is 'infinitely great'. What we have here observed seems to be the chief cause, why to suppose the infinite divisibility of finite extension has been thought necessary in geometry.

129    The several absurdities and contradictions which flowed from this false principle might, one would think, have been esteemed so many demonstrations against it. But, by I know not what logic, it is held proofs *a posteriori* are not to be admitted against propositions relating to infinity – as though it were not impossible even for an infinite mind to reconcile contradictions, or as if any thing absurd and repugnant could have a necessary connexion with truth, or flow from it. But whoever considers the weakness of this pretence, will think it was contrived on purpose to humour the laziness of the mind, which had rather acquiesce in an indolent scepticism than be at the pains to go through with a severe examination of those principles it has ever embraced for true.

130    Of late the speculations about infinities have run so high, and grown to such strange notions, as have occasioned no small scruples and disputes among the geometers of the present age.[39] Some there are of great note, who not content with holding that finite lines may be divided into an infinite number of parts, do yet farther maintain that each of those infinitesimals is it self subdivisible into an infinity of other parts, or infinitesimals of a second order, and so on *ad infinitum*. These, I say, assert there are infinitesimals of infinitesimals of infinitesimals, without ever coming to an end. So that according to them an inch does not barely contain an infinite number of parts, but an infinity of an infinity of an infinity *ad infinitum* of parts. Others there be who hold all orders of infinitesimals below the first to be nothing at all, thinking it with good reason absurd to imagine there is any positive quantity or part of extension,

---

[39] Here and in the following section Berkeley questions the validity of mathematical theories of infinitesimals, such as had recently been developed by Leibniz and Newton. See *The Analyst* (1734).

which though multiplied infinitely, can never equal the smallest given extension. And yet on the other hand it seems no less absurd to think the square, cube, or other power of a positive real root, should it self be nothing at all; which they who hold infinitesimals of the first order, denying all of the subsequent orders, are obliged to maintain.

131 Have we not therefore reason to conclude that they are both in the wrong, and that there is in effect no such thing as parts infinitely small, or an infinite number of parts contained in a finite quantity? But you will say, that if this doctrine obtains, it will follow the very foundations of geometry are destroyed, and those great men who have raised that science to so astonishing an height, have been all the while building a castle in the air. To this it may be replied, that whatever is useful in geometry and promotes the benefit of human life, does still remain firm and unshaken on our principles. That science, considered as practical, will rather receive advantage than any prejudice from what has been said. But to set this in a due light may be the subject of a distinct inquiry. For the rest, though it should follow that some of the more intricate and subtle parts of speculative mathematics may be pared off without any prejudice to truth, yet I do not see what damage will be thence derived to mankind. On the contrary, it were highly to be wished that men of great abilities and obstinate application would draw off their thoughts from those amusements, and employ them in the study of such things as lie nearer the concerns of life, or have a more direct influence on the manners.

132 If it be said that several theorems undoubtedly true are discovered by methods in which infinitesimals are made use of, which could never have been, if their existence included a contradiction in it. I answer, that upon a thorough examination it will not be found, that in any instance it is necessary to make use of or conceive infinitesimal parts of finite lines, or even quantities less than the *minimum sensibile*;[40] nay, it will be evident this is never done, it being impossible.

133 By what we have premised, it is plain that very numerous and important errors have taken their rise from those false principles, which were impugned in the foregoing parts of this treatise. And the opposites of those erroneous tenets at the same time appear to be most fruitful principles, from whence do flow innumerable consequences highly

[40] i.e. the smallest quantity that can be observed by using the senses.

advantageous to true philosophy as well as to religion. Particularly matter, or the absolute existence of corporeal objects, has been shown to be that wherein the most avowed and pernicious enemies of all knowledge, whether human or divine, have ever placed their chief strength and confidence. And surely, if by distinguishing the real existence of unthinking things from their being perceived, and allowing them a subsistence of their own out of the minds of spirits, no one thing is explained in nature, but on the contrary a great many inexplicable difficulties arise; if the supposition of matter is barely precarious, as not being grounded on so much as one single reason; if its consequences cannot endure the light of examination and free inquiry, but screen themselves under the dark and general pretence of infinites being incomprehensible; if withal the removal of this matter be not attended with the least evil consequence, if it be not even missed in the world but every thing as well, nay much easier, conceived without it; if lastly, both sceptics and atheists are for ever silenced upon supposing only spirits and ideas, and this scheme of things is perfectly agreeable both to reason and religion; methinks we may expect it should be admitted and firmly embraced, though it were supposed only as an hypothesis, and the existence of matter had been allowed possible, which yet I think we have evidently demonstrated that it is not.

**134** True it is that, in consequence of the foregoing principles, several disputes and speculations, which are esteemed no mean parts of learning, are rejected as useless. But how great a prejudice soever against our notions this may give to those who have already been deeply engaged, and made large advances in studies of that nature, yet by others we hope it will not be thought any just ground of dislike to the principles and tenets herein laid down, that they abridge the labour of study, and make human sciences more clear, compendious, and attainable, than they were before.

**135** Having dispatched what we intended to say concerning the knowledge of ideas, the method we proposed leads us, in the next place, to treat of spirits; with regard to which, perhaps human knowledge is not so deficient as is vulgarly imagined. The great reason that is assigned for our being thought ignorant of the nature of spirits, is our not having an idea of it. But surely it ought not to be looked on as a defect in a human understanding that it does not perceive the idea of spirit, if it is manifestly impossible there should be any such idea. And this, if I mistake not, has been demonstrated in Section 27; to which I shall here add that a spirit has been shown to be the only substance or support, wherein the unthinking beings or ideas can exist. But that this substance which supports or perceives ideas should it self be an idea, or like an idea, is evidently absurd.

**136** It will perhaps be said that we want a sense (as some have imagined) proper to know substances withal, which if we had, we might know our own soul as we do a triangle. To this I answer, that in case we had a new sense bestowed upon us, we could only receive thereby some new sensations or ideas of sense. But I believe no body will say, that what he means by the terms 'soul' and 'substance', is only some particular sort of idea or sensation. We may therefore infer, that all things duly considered, it is not more reasonable to think of faculties defective, in that they do not furnish us with an idea of spirit or active thinking substance, than it would be if we should blame them for not being able to comprehend a 'round square'.

**137** From the opinion that spirits are to be known after the manner of an idea or sensation have risen many absurd and heterodox tenets, and much scepticism about the nature of the soul. It is even probable, that this opinion may have produced a doubt in some, whether they had any soul at all distinct from their body, since upon inquiry they could not find they had an idea of it. That an idea which is inactive, and the existence whereof consists in being perceived, should be the image or likeness of an agency subsisting by it self, seems to need no other refutation than barely attending to what is meant by those words. But perhaps you will say that, though an *idea* cannot resemble a *spirit*, in its thinking, acting, or subsisting by it self, yet it may in some other respects, and it is not necessary that an idea or image be in all respects like the original.

**138** I answer, if it does not in those mentioned, it is impossible it should represent it in any other thing. Do but leave out the power of willing, thinking, and perceiving ideas, and there remains nothing else wherein the idea can be like a spirit. For by the word 'spirit' we mean only that which thinks, wills, and perceives; this, and this alone, constitutes the signification of that term. If therefore it is impossible that any degree of those powers should be represented in an idea, it is evident there can be no idea [or notion]⁴¹ of a spirit.

---

⁴¹ The phrase 'or notion' was deleted in the 1734 edition, by which time Berkeley wished to defend the possibility of having a notion of a spirit.

139 But it will be objected, that if there is no idea signified by the terms 'soul', 'spirit', and 'substance', they are wholly insignificant or have no meaning in them. I answer, those words do mean or signify a real thing, which is neither an idea nor like an idea, but that which perceives ideas and wills and reasons about them. What I am my self, that which I denote by the term 'I', is the same with what is meant by 'soul' or 'spiritual substance'. If it be said that this is only quarrelling at a word, and that since the immediate significations of other names are by common consent called 'ideas', no reason can be assigned, why that which is signified by the name 'spirit' or 'soul' may not partake in the same appellation. I answer, all the unthinking objects of the mind agree, in that they are entirely passive and their existence consists only in being perceived; whereas a soul or spirit is an active being, whose existence consists not in being perceived, but in perceiving ideas and thinking. It is therefore necessary, in order to prevent equivocation and confounding natures perfectly disagreeing and unlike, that we distinguish between 'spirit' and 'idea'.<sup>r</sup>

140 In a large sense indeed, we may be said to have an idea, [or rather a notion]<sup>42</sup> of spirit, that is, we understand the meaning of the word; otherwise we could not affirm or deny any thing of it. Moreover, as we conceive the ideas that are in the minds of other spirits by means of our own, which we suppose to be resemblances of them, so we know other spirits by means of our own soul, which in that sense is the image or idea of them, it having a like respect to other spirits that blueness or heat by me perceived has to those ideas perceived by another.

141 It must not be supposed that they who assert the natural immortality of the soul are of opinion, that it is absolutely incapable of annihilation even by the infinite power of the Creator who first gave it being, but only that it is not liable to be broken or dissolved by the ordinary laws of nature or motion. They indeed, who hold the soul of man to be only a thin vital flame or system of animal spirits, make it perishing and corruptible as the body, since there is nothing more easily dissipated than such a being, which it is naturally impossible should survive the ruin of the tabernacle wherein it is enclosed. And this notion has been greedily embraced and cherished by the worst part of mankind, as the most

---

<sup>r</sup> See Section 27.

<sup>42</sup> The phrase 'or rather a notion' was added in 1734.

effectual antidote against all impressions of virtue and religion. But it has been made evident that bodies of what frame or texture soever are barely passive ideas in the mind, which is more distant and heterogeneous from them than light is from darkness. We have shown that the soul is indivisible, incorporeal, unextended, and it is consequently incorruptible. Nothing can be plainer than that the motions, changes, decays, and dissolutions which we hourly see befall natural bodies (and which is what we mean by the 'course of nature') cannot possibly affect an active, simple, uncompounded substance. Such a being therefore is indissoluble by the force of nature, that is to say, the soul of man is naturally immortal.

**142** After what has been said, it is I suppose plain that souls are not to be known in the same manner as senseless inactive objects, or by way of idea. Spirits and ideas are things so wholly different that, when we say 'they exist', 'they are known', or the like, these words must not be thought to signify any thing common to both natures. There is nothing alike or common in them; and to expect that by any multiplication or enlargement of our faculties, we may be enabled to know a spirit as we do a triangle, seems as absurd as if we should hope to see a sound. This is inculcated because I imagine it may be of moment towards clearing several important questions, and preventing some very dangerous errors concerning the nature of the soul. [We may not I think strictly be said to have an idea of an active being, or of an action, although we may be said to have a notion of them. I have some knowledge or notion of my mind, and its acts about ideas, inasmuch as I know or understand what is meant by those words. What I know, that I have some notion of. I will not say, that the terms 'idea' and 'notion' may not be used convertibly, if the world will have it so. But yet it conduces to clearness and propriety that we distinguish things very different by different names. It is also to be remarked that, all relations including an act of the mind, we cannot so properly be said to have an idea, but rather a notion, of the relations or habitudes between things. But if in the modern way the word 'idea' is extended to spirits, and relations and acts, this is after all an affair of verbal concern.][43]

**143** It will not be amiss to add that the doctrine of abstract ideas has had no small share in rendering those sciences intricate and obscure, which are particularly conversant about spiritual things. Men have

---

[43] The material in parentheses was added in the 1734 edition.

imagined they could frame abstract notions of the powers and acts of the mind, and consider them prescinded, as well from the mind or spirit it self as from their respective objects and effects. Hence a great number of dark and ambiguous terms, presumed to stand for abstract notions, have been introduced into metaphysics and morality, and from these have grown infinite distractions and disputes amongst the learned.

**144** But nothing seems more to have contributed towards engaging men in controversies and mistakes with regard to the nature and operations of the mind, than the being used to speak of those things in terms borrowed from sensible ideas. For example, the will is termed the 'motion' of the soul; this infuses a belief that the mind of man is as a ball in motion, impelled and determined by the objects of sense, as necessarily as that is by the stroke of a racket.[44] Hence arise endless scruples and errors of dangerous consequences in morality. All which I doubt not may be cleared, and truth appear plain, uniform, and consistent, could but philosophers be prevailed on [to retire into themselves, and attentively consider their own meaning.][45]

**145** From what has been said, it is plain that we cannot know the existence of other spirits, otherwise than by their operations, or the ideas by them excited in us. I perceive several motions, changes, and combinations of ideas that inform me there are certain particular agents like my self, which accompany them and concur in their production. Hence the knowledge I have of other spirits is not immediate, as is the knowledge of my ideas, but depending on the intervention of ideas, by me referred to agents or spirits distinct from myself, as effects or concomitant signs.

**146** But though there be some things which convince us, human agents are concerned in producing them; yet it is evident to every one that those things which are called the works of nature, that is, the far greater part of the ideas or sensations perceived by us, are not produced by or dependent on the wills of men. There is therefore some other spirit that causes them, since it is repugnant that they should subsist by themselves.[s] But if we attentively consider the constant regularity,

---

[s] See Section 29.

[44] Probably a reference to Hobbes, for whom acts of the will are reducible to properties of a body.

[45] The phrase in parentheses was substituted, in 1734, for the following in the 1710 edition: 'to depart from some received prejudices and modes of speech, and retiring into themselves attentively consider their own meaning. But the difficulties arising on this head demand a more particular disquisition than suits with the design of this treatise.'

order, and concatenation of natural things, the surprising magnificence, beauty, and perfection of the larger, and the exquisite contrivance of the smaller parts of the creation, together with the exact harmony and correspondence of the whole, but above all, the never enough admired laws of pain and pleasure, and the instincts or natural inclinations, appetites, and passions of animals; I say if we consider all these things, and at the same time attend to the meaning and import of the attributes, one, eternal, infinitely wise, good, and perfect, we shall clearly perceive that they belong to the aforesaid spirit, 'who works all in all', and 'by whom all things consist.'[46]

**147** Hence it is evident, that God is known as certainly and immediately as any other mind or spirit whatsoever, distinct from our selves. We may even assert that the existence of God is far more evidently perceived than the existence of men, because the effects of nature are infinitely more numerous and considerable, than those ascribed to human agents. There is not any one mark that denotes a man, or effect produced by him, which does not more strongly evince the being of that spirit who is the Author of nature. For it is evident that, in affecting other persons, the will of man has no other object than barely the motion of the limbs of his body; but that such a motion should be attended by, or excite any idea in the mind of another, depends wholly on the will of the Creator. He alone it is who 'upholding all things by the Word of his Power',[47] maintains that intercourse between spirits, whereby they are able to perceive the existence of each other. And yet this pure and clear light which enlightens every one, is it self invisible [to the greatest part of mankind].[48]

**148** It seems to be a general pretence of the unthinking herd that they cannot see God. Could we but see him, say they, as we see a man, we should believe that he is and, believing, obey his commands. But alas we need only open our eyes to see the sovereign Lord of all things with a more full and clear view, than we do any one of our fellow-creatures. Not that I imagine we see God (as some will have it) by a direct and immediate view, or see corporeal things, not by themselves, but by seeing that which represents them in the essence of God, which doctrine is I must confess to me incomprehensible.[49] But I shall explain my meaning. A human

---

[46] I Corinthians 12: 6 and Colossians 1: 17.    [47] Hebrews 1: 3.
[48] The phrase in parentheses was deleted in 1734.
[49] Refers to Malebranche's theory, that we see all things by perceiving their ideas in God.

spirit or person is not perceived by sense, as not being an idea. When therefore we see the colour, size, figure, and motions of a man, we perceive only certain sensations or ideas excited in our own minds; and these being exhibited to our view in sundry distinct collections, serve to mark out unto us the existence of finite and created spirits like our selves. Hence it is plain, we do not see a man, if by 'man' is meant that which lives, moves, perceives, and thinks as we do, but only such a certain collection of ideas, as directs us to think there is a distinct principle of thought and motion like to our selves accompanying and represented by it. And after the same manner we see God. All the difference is that, whereas some one finite and narrow assemblage of ideas denotes a particular human mind, whithersoever we direct our view, we do at all times and in all places perceive manifest tokens of the divinity, every thing we see, hear, feel, or any wise perceive by sense, being a sign or effect of the power of God, as is our perception of those very motions, which are produced by men.

149 It is therefore plain that nothing can be more evident to any one that is capable of the least reflexion than the existence of God, or a spirit who is intimately present to our minds, producing in them all that variety of ideas or sensations, which continually affect us, on whom we have an absolute and entire dependence, in short, 'in whom we live, and move, and have our being'.[50] That the discovery of this great truth, which lies so near and obvious to the mind, should be attained to by the reason of so very few is a sad instance of the stupidity and inattention of men, who, though they are surrounded with such clear manifestations of the Deity, are yet so little affected by them that they seem as it were blinded with excess of light.

150 But you will say, has nature no share in the production of natural things, and must they be all ascribed to the immediate and sole operation of God? I answer, if by 'nature' is meant only the visible series of effects or sensations imprinted on our minds, according to certain fixed and general laws, then it is plain that nature taken in this sense cannot produce any thing at all. But if by 'nature' is meant some being distinct from God, as well as from the laws of nature and things perceived by sense, I must confess that word is to me an empty sound, without any intelligible meaning annexed to it. Nature in this acceptation is a vain

[50] Acts 17: 28.

chimera introduced by those heathens, who had not just notions of the omnipresence and infinite perfection of God. But it is more unaccountable that it should be received among Christians professing belief in the Holy Scriptures, which constantly ascribe those effects to the immediate hand of God, that heathen philosophers are wont to impute to nature. 'The Lord, he causeth the vapours to ascend; he maketh lightnings with rain; he bringeth forth the wind out of his treasures.'ᵗ 'He turneth the shadow of death into the morning, and maketh the day dark with night.'ᵘ 'He visiteth the earth, and maketh it soft with showers: he blesseth the springing thereof, and crowneth the year with his goodness; so that the pastures are clothed with flocks, and the valleys are covered over with corn.'ᵛ But notwithstanding that this is the constant language of Scripture, yet we have I know not what aversion from believing that God concerns himself so nearly in our affairs. Fain would we suppose him at a great distance off, and substitute some blind unthinking deputy in his stead, though (if we may believe Saint Paul) 'he be not far from every one of us.'⁵¹

**151** It will I doubt not be objected that the slow and gradual methods observed in the production of natural things, do not seem to have for their cause the immediate hand of an almighty Agent. Besides, monsters, untimely births, fruits blasted in the blossom, rains falling in desert places, miseries incident to human life, are so many arguments that the whole frame of nature is not immediately actuated and superintended by a spirit of infinite wisdom and goodness. But the answer to this objection is in a good measure plain from Section 62, it being visible, that the aforesaid methods of nature are absolutely necessary, in order to working by the most simple and general rules, and after a steady and consistent manner; which argue both the wisdom and goodness of God. Such is the artificial contrivance of this mighty machine of nature that, whilst its motions and various phenomena strike on our senses, the hand which actuates the whole is itself unperceivable to men of flesh and blood. 'Verily (saith the prophet) thou art a God that hidest thy self.'ʷ But though God conceal himself from the eyes of the sensual and lazy, who will not be at the least expense of thought; yet to an unbiased and

---

ᵗ Jeremiah 10: 13.   ᵘ Amos 5: 8.
ᵛ See Psalm 65 [Berkeley borrows phrases from verses 9–13].   ʷ Isaiah 45: 15.

⁵¹ Acts 17: 27.

attentive mind, nothing can be more plainly legible than the intimate presence of an all-wise Spirit, who fashions, regulates, and sustains the whole system of being. It is clear from what we have elsewhere observed that the operating according to general and stated laws, is so necessary for our guidance in the affairs of life, and letting us into the secret of nature, that without it all reach and compass of thought, all human sagacity and design, could serve to no manner of purpose; it were even impossible there should be any such faculties or powers in the mind.[x] Which one consideration abundantly out-balances whatever particular inconveniences may thence arise.

152 We should further consider that the very blemishes and defects of nature are not without their use, in that they make an agreeable sort of variety, and augment the beauty of the rest of the creation, as shades in a picture serve to set off the brighter and more enlightened parts. We would likewise do well to examine whether our taxing the waste of seeds and embryos, and accidental destruction of plants and animals before they come to full maturity, as an imprudence in the Author of nature, be not the effect of prejudice contracted by our familiarity with impotent and saving mortals. In man indeed a thrifty management of those things, which he cannot procure without much pains and industry, may be esteemed wisdom. But we must not imagine that the inexplicably fine machine of an animal or vegetable costs the great Creator any more pains or trouble in its production than a pebble does, nothing being more evident, than that an omnipotent spirit can indifferently produce every thing by a mere *fiat* or act of the will. Hence it is plain, that the splendid profusion of natural things should not be interpreted weakness or prodigality in the agent who produces them, but rather be looked on as an argument of the riches of his power.

153 As for the mixture of pain or uneasiness which is in the world, pursuant to the general laws of nature and the actions of finite imperfect spirits: this, in the state we are in at present, is indispensably necessary to our well-being. But our prospects are too narrow. We take, for instance, the idea of some one particular pain into our thoughts, and account it evil; whereas if we enlarge our view, so as to comprehend the various ends, connexions, and dependencies of things, on what occasions and in what proportions we are affected with pain and pleasure, the nature of human

---

[x] See Section 31.

freedom, and the design with which we are put into the world, we shall be forced to acknowledge that those particular things, which considered in themselves appear to be evil, have the nature of good when considered as linked with the whole system of beings.

**154** From what has been said it will be manifest to any considering person, that it is merely for want of attention and comprehensiveness of mind, that there are any favourers of atheism and the Manichean heresy to be found.[52] Little and unreflecting souls may indeed burlesque the works of Providence, the beauty and order whereof they have not capacity, or will not be at the pains, to comprehend. But those who are masters of any justness and extent of thought, and are withal used to reflect, can never sufficiently admire the divine traces of wisdom and goodness that shine throughout the economy of nature. But what truth is there which shines so strongly on the mind, that by an aversion of thought, a wilful shutting of the eyes, we may not escape seeing it? Is it therefore to be wondered at if the generality of men, who are ever intent on business or pleasure, and little used to fix or open the eye of their mind, should not have all that conviction and evidence of the being of God, which might be expected in reasonable creatures?

**155** We should rather wonder that men can be found so stupid as to neglect, than that neglecting they should be unconvinced of such an evident and momentous truth. And yet it is to be feared that too many of parts and leisure, who live in Christian countries, are merely through a supine and dreadful negligence sunk into a sort of atheism. Since it is downright impossible that a soul pierced and enlightened with a thorough sense of the omnipresence, holiness, and justice of that Almighty Spirit should persist in a remorseless violation of his laws. We ought therefore earnestly to meditate and dwell on those important points, that so we may attain conviction without all scruple 'that the eyes of the Lord are in every place beholding the evil and the good'; 'that he is with us and keepeth us in all places whither we go, and giveth us bread to eat, and raiment to put on';[53] that he is present and conscious in our innermost thoughts; and that we have a most absolute and immediate dependence on him. A clear view of which great truths cannot choose but fill our

---

[52] Manicheanism was a theory that originated in the third century, and emphasized the dualism of opposing forces of good and evil in nature.

[53] Proverbs 15: 3; Genesis 28: 20.

hearts with an awful circumspection and holy fear, which is the strongest incentive to virtue, and the best guard against vice.

**156** For after all, what deserves the first place in our studies is the consideration of God, and our duty; which to promote, as it was the main drift and design of my labours, so shall I esteem them altogether useless and ineffectual, if by what I have said I cannot inspire my readers with a pious sense of the presence of God; and having shown the falseness or vanity of those barren speculations, which make the chief employment of learned men, the better dispose them to reverence and embrace the salutary truths of the Gospel, which to know and to practise is the highest perfection of human nature.

# Three Dialogues between Hylas and Philonous

[The Design of which is plainly to demonstrate the reality and perfection
of human knowledge, the incorporeal nature of the soul, and the immediate providence of a Deity:] In opposition to sceptics and atheists. [Also,
to open a method for rendering the sciences more easy, useful, and
compendious.][1]

3rd edition 1734

## [The Preface                                          [167]

Though it seems the general opinion of the world, no less than the design
of nature and providence, that the end of speculation be practice, or the
improvement and regulation of our lives and actions; yet those who are
most addicted to speculative studies seem as generally of another mind.
And, indeed, if we consider the pains that have been taken to perplex the
plainest things, that distrust of the senses, those doubts and scruples,
those abstractions and refinements that occur in the very entrance of the
sciences; it will not seem strange that men of leisure and curiosity should
lay themselves out in fruitless disquisitions, without descending to the
practical parts of life, or informing themselves in the more necessary and
important parts of knowledge.

Upon the common principles of philosophers, we are not assured of
the existence of things from their being perceived. And we are taught to
distinguish their real nature from that which falls under our senses.

---

[1] The phrases in parentheses were omitted from the 1734 edition.

Hence arise scepticism and paradoxes. It is not enough that we see and feel, that we taste and smell a thing. Its true nature, its absolute external entity, is still concealed. For, though it be the fiction of our own brain, we have made it inaccessible to all our faculties. Sense is fallacious, reason defective. We spend our lives in doubting of those things which other men evidently know, and believing those things which they laugh at and despise.

In order, therefore, to divert the busy mind of man from vain researches, it seemed necessary to inquire into the source of its perplexities; and, if possible, to lay down such principles as, by an easy solution of them, together with their own native evidence, may at once recommend themselves for genuine to the mind, and rescue it from those endless pursuits it is engaged in. Which, with a plain demonstration of the immediate providence of an all-seeing God, and the natural immortality of the soul, should seem the readiest preparation, as well as the strongest motive, to the study and practice of virtue.

[168] This design I proposed, in the First Part of a Treatise concerning the *Principles of Human Knowledge*, published in the year 1710. But, before I proceed to publish the Second Part, I thought it requisite to treat more clearly and fully of certain principles laid down in the First, and to place them in a new light.[2] Which is the business of the following *Dialogues*.

In this treatise, which does not presuppose in the reader any knowledge of what was contained in the former, it has been my aim to introduce the notions I advance, into the mind, in the most easy and familiar manner; especially because they carry with them a great opposition to the prejudices of philosophers, which have so far prevailed against the common sense and natural notions of mankind.

If the principles, which I here endeavour to propagate, are admitted for true; the consequences which, I think, evidently flow from thence are that atheism and scepticism will be utterly destroyed, many intricate points made plain, great difficulties solved, several useless parts of science retrenched, speculation referred to practice, and men reduced from paradoxes to common sense.

And although it may, perhaps, seem an uneasy reflection to some, that when they have taken a circuit through so many refined and unvulgar notions, they should at last come to think like other men: yet, methinks,

---

[2] Berkeley never published a second part of the *Principles*.

this return to the simple dictates of nature, after having wandered through the wild mazes of philosophy, is not unpleasant. It is like coming home from a long voyage; a man reflects with pleasure on the many difficulties and perplexities he has passed through, sets his heart at ease, and enjoys himself with more satisfaction for the future.

As it was my intention to convince sceptics and infidels by reason, so it has been my endeavour strictly to observe the most rigid laws of reasoning. And, to an impartial reader, I hope, it will be manifest that the sublime notion of a God, and the comfortable expectation of immortality, do naturally arise from a close and methodical application of thought: whatever may be the result of that loose, rambling way, not altogether improperly termed 'free-thinking' by certain libertines in thought, who can no more endure the restraints of logic than those of religion or government.

It will, perhaps, be objected to my design, that so far as it tends to ease the mind of difficult and useless inquiries, it can affect only a few speculative persons. But, if by their speculations rightly placed, the study of morality and the law of nature were brought more into fashion among men of parts and genius, the discouragements that draw to scepticism removed, the measures of right and wrong accurately defined, and the principles of natural religion reduced into regular systems, as artfully disposed and clearly connected as those of some other sciences, there are grounds to think, these effects would not only have a gradual influence in repairing the too much defaced sense of virtue in the world; but also, by showing that such parts of revelation as lie within the reach of human inquiry are most agreeable to right reason, would dispose all prudent, unprejudiced persons to a modest and wary treatment of [169] those sacred mysteries, which are above the comprehension of our faculties.

It remains that I desire the reader to withhold his censure of these Dialogues till he has read them through. Otherwise, he may lay them aside in the mistake of their design, or on account of difficulties or objections which he would find answered in the sequel. A treatise of this nature would require to be once read over coherently, in order to comprehend its design, the proofs, solution of difficulties, and the connection and disposition of its parts. If it be thought to deserve a second reading, this, I imagine, will make the entire scheme very plain, especially if recourse be had to an Essay I wrote some years since upon *Vision*, and the Treatise concerning the *Principles of Human Knowledge*, wherein divers notions advanced in these *Dialogues* are farther pursued or placed in different lights, and other points handled, which naturally tend to confirm and illustrate them.][3]

[171]          **Three Dialogues between Hylas and Philonous**

                        **The First Dialogue**

*Philonous.*   Good morrow, Hylas. I did not expect to find you abroad so early.

*Hylas.*   It is indeed something unusual; but my thoughts were so taken up with a subject I was discoursing of last night, that finding I could not sleep, I resolved to rise and take a turn in the garden.

*Phil.*   It happened well, to let you see what innocent and agreeable pleasures you lose every morning. Can there be a pleasanter time of the day, or a more delightful season of the year? That purple sky, these wild but sweet notes of birds, the fragrant bloom upon the trees and flowers, the gentle influence of the rising sun, these and a thousand nameless beauties of nature inspire the soul with secret transports; its faculties too being at this time fresh and lively, are fit for those meditations, which the solitude of a garden and tranquillity of the morning naturally dispose us to. But I am afraid I interrupt your thoughts, for you seemed very intent on something.

*Hyl.*   It is true, I was, and shall be obliged to you if you will permit me to go on in the same vein; not that I would by any means deprive myself of your company, for my thoughts always flow more easily in conversation with a friend than when I am alone. But my request is that you would suffer me to impart my reflections to you.

*Phil.*   With all my heart, it is what I should have requested myself, if you had not prevented me.

*Hyl.*   I was considering the odd fate of those men who have in all ages, through an affectation of being distinguished from the vulgar, or some unaccountable turn of thought, pretended either to believe nothing at all or to believe the most extravagant things in the world. This however might be borne, if their paradoxes and scepticism did

---

[3] The Preface was omitted from the 1734 edition.

not draw after them some consequences of general disadvantage to mankind. But the mischief lies here; that when men of less leisure see [172] them who are supposed to have spent their whole time in the pursuits of knowledge, professing an entire ignorance of all things, or advancing such notions as are repugnant to plain and commonly received principles, they will be tempted to entertain suspicions concerning the most important truths, which they had hitherto held sacred and unquestionable.

*Phil.* I entirely agree with you, as to the ill tendency of the affected doubts of some philosophers and fantastical conceits of others. I am even so far gone of late in this way of thinking that I have quitted several of the sublime notions I had got in their schools for vulgar opinions. And I give it you on my word, since this revolt from metaphysical notions to the plain dictates of nature and common sense, I find my understanding strangely enlightened, so that I can now easily comprehend a great many things which before were all mystery and riddle.

*Hyl.* I am glad to find there was nothing in the accounts I heard of you.

*Phil.* Pray, what were those?

*Hyl.* You were represented in last night's conversation as one who maintained the most extravagant opinion that ever entered into the mind of man, to wit, that there is no such thing as material substance in the world.

*Phil.* That there is no such thing as what philosophers call 'material substance', I am seriously persuaded; but if I were made to see anything absurd or sceptical in this, I should then have the same reason to renounce this that I imagine I have now to reject the contrary opinion.

*Hyl.* What! Can anything be more fantastical, more repugnant to common sense, or a more manifest piece of scepticism, than to believe there is no such thing as matter?

*Phil.* Softly, good Hylas. What if it should prove that you, who hold there is, are by virtue of that opinion a greater sceptic, and maintain more paradoxes and repugnancies to common sense, than I who believe no such thing?

*Hyl.* You may as soon persuade me the part is greater than the whole as that, in order to avoid absurdity and scepticism, I should ever be obliged to give up my opinion in this point.

*Phil.* Well, then, are you content to admit that opinion for true, which upon examination shall appear most agreeable to common sense and remote from scepticism?

[173] *Hyl.* With all my heart. Since you are for raising disputes about the plainest things in nature, I am content for once to hear what you have to say.

*Phil.* Pray, Hylas, what do you mean by a sceptic?

*Hyl.* I mean what all men mean, one that doubts of everything.

*Phil.* He then who entertains no doubt concerning some particular point, with regard to that point cannot be thought a sceptic.

*Hyl.* I agree with you.

*Phil.* Whether does doubting consist in embracing the affirmative or negative side of a question?

*Hyl.* In neither; for whoever understands English, cannot but know that 'doubting' signifies a suspense between both.

*Phil.* He then that denies any point, can no more be said to doubt of it, than he who affirms it with the same degree of assurance.

*Hyl.* True.

*Phil.* And consequently, for such his denial is no more to be esteemed a sceptic than the other.

*Hyl.* I acknowledge it.

*Phil.* How comes it to pass then, Hylas, that you pronounce me a sceptic, because I deny what you affirm, to wit, the existence of matter? Since, for aught you can tell, I am as peremptory in my denial as you in your affirmation.

*Hyl.* Hold, Philonous, I have been a little out in my definition; but every false step a man makes in discourse is not to be insisted on. I said indeed, that a sceptic was one who doubted of everything; but I should have added: or who denies the reality and truth of things.

*Phil.* What things? Do you mean the principles and theorems of sciences? But these you know are universal intellectual notions, and consequently independent of matter; the denial therefore of this does not imply the denying them.

*Hyl.* I grant it. But are there no other things? What think you of distrusting the senses, of denying the real existence of sensible things, or pretending to know nothing of them? Is not this sufficient to denominate a man a sceptic?

*Phil.* Shall we therefore examine which of us it is that denies the reality of sensible things or professes the greatest ignorance of them; since, if I take you rightly, he is to be esteemed the greatest sceptic? [174]

*Hyl.* That is what I desire.

*Phil.* What mean you by 'sensible things'?

*Hyl.* Those things which are perceived by the senses. Can you imagine that I mean anything else?

*Phil.* Pardon me, Hylas, if I am desirous clearly to apprehend your notions, since this may much shorten our inquiry. Suffer me then to ask you this farther question. Are those things only perceived by the senses which are perceived immediately? Or, may those things properly be said to be 'sensible' which are perceived mediately, or not without the intervention of others?

*Hyl.* I do not sufficiently understand you.

*Phil.* In reading a book, what I immediately perceive are the letters; but mediately, or by means of these, are suggested to my mind the notions of God, virtue, truth, &c. Now, that the letters are truly sensible things or perceived by sense, there is no doubt; but I would know whether you take the things suggested by them to be so too.

*Hyl.* No certainly, it were absurd to think God or virtue sensible things, though they may be signified and suggested to the mind by sensible marks, with which they have an arbitrary connection.

*Phil.* It seems then, that by 'sensible things' you mean those only which can be perceived immediately by sense.

*Hyl.* Right.

*Phil.* Does it not follow from this, that though I see one part of the sky red, and another blue, and that my reason does thence evidently conclude there must be some cause of that diversity of colours, yet that cause cannot be said to be a sensible thing, or perceived by the sense of seeing?

*Hyl.* It does.

*Phil.* In like manner, though I hear [a] variety of sounds, yet I cannot be said to hear the causes of those sounds.

*Hyl.* You cannot.

*Phil.* And when by my touch I perceive a thing to be hot and heavy, I cannot say with any truth or propriety that I feel the cause of its heat or weight.

*Hyl.* To prevent any more questions of this kind, I tell you once for all, that by 'sensible things' I mean those only which are perceived by

[175] sense, and that in truth the senses perceive nothing which they do not perceive immediately, for they make no inferences. The deducing therefore of causes or occasions from effects and appearances, which alone are perceived by sense, entirely relates to reason.[4]

*Phil.* This point then is agreed between us, that 'sensible things are those only which are immediately perceived by sense.' You will farther inform me, whether we immediately perceive by sight anything beside light, and colours, and figures; or by hearing, anything but sounds; by the palate, anything beside tastes; by the smell, beside odours; or by the touch, more than tangible qualities.

*Hyl.* We do not.

*Phil.* It seems therefore, that if you take away all sensible qualities, there remains nothing sensible.

*Hyl.* I grant it.

*Phil.* Sensible things therefore are nothing else but so many sensible qualities, or combinations of sensible qualities.

*Hyl.* Nothing else.

*Phil.* Heat then is a sensible thing.

*Hyl.* Certainly.

*Phil.* Does the reality of sensible things consist in being perceived? or, is it something distinct from their being perceived, and that bears no relation to the mind?

*Hyl.* To *exist* is one thing, to be *perceived* is another.

*Phil.* I speak with regard to sensible things only; and of these I ask, whether by their real existence you mean a subsistence exterior to the mind, and distinct from their being perceived?

*Hyl.* I mean a real absolute being, distinct from, and without any relation to their being perceived.

*Phil.* Heat therefore, if it be allowed a real being, must exist without the mind.

*Hyl.* It must.

*Phil.* Tell me, Hylas, is this real existence equally compatible to all degrees of heat, which we perceive; or is there any reason why we should

---

[4] Berkeley uses the term 'occasion' here (and later in the text) to avoid endorsing any account of causal relations between natural phenomena. Malebranche and other occasionalists had argued that God alone is the only true cause, and that natural phenomena are merely the occasions on which He exercises causal agency.

attribute it to some, and deny it [to] others? And if there be, pray let me know that reason.

*Hyl.* Whatever degree of heat we perceive by sense, we may be sure the same exists in the object that occasions it.

*Phil.* What, the greatest as well as the least?

*Hyl.* I tell you, the reason is plainly the same in respect of both. They are both perceived by sense; nay, the greater degree of heat is more sensibly perceived; and consequently, if there is any difference, we are more certain of its real existence than we can be of the reality of a lesser degree.                                                                [176]

*Phil.* But is not the most vehement and intense degree of heat a very great pain?

*Hyl.* No one can deny it.

*Phil.* And is any unperceiving thing capable of pain or pleasure?

*Hyl.* No, certainly.

*Phil.* Is your material substance a senseless being, or a being endowed with sense and perception?

*Hyl.* It is senseless, without doubt.

*Phil.* It cannot therefore be the subject of pain.

*Hyl.* By no means.

*Phil.* Nor consequently of the greatest heat perceived by sense, since you acknowledge this to be no small pain.

*Hyl.* I grant it.

*Phil.* What shall we say then of your external object; is it a material substance, or no?

*Hyl.* It is a material substance with the sensible qualities inhering in it.

*Phil.* How then can a great heat exist in it, since you own it cannot in a material substance? I desire you would clear this point.

*Hyl.* Hold, Philonous, I fear I was out in yielding intense heat to be a pain. It should seem rather, that pain is something distinct from heat, and the consequence or effect of it.

*Phil.* Upon putting your hand near the fire, do you perceive one simple uniform sensation, or two distinct sensations?

*Hyl.* But one simple sensation.

*Phil.* Is not the heat immediately perceived?

*Hyl.* It is.

*Phil.* And the pain?

*Hyl.* True.

*Phil.* Seeing therefore they are both immediately perceived at the same time, and the fire affects you only with one simple or uncompounded idea, it follows that this same simple idea is both the intense heat immediately perceived and the pain; and consequently, that the intense heat immediately perceived is nothing distinct from a particular sort of pain.

*Hyl.* It seems so.

*Phil.* Again, try in your thoughts, Hylas, if you can conceive a
[177] vehement sensation to be without pain, or pleasure?

*Hyl.* I cannot.

*Phil.* Or can you frame to yourself an idea of sensible pain or pleasure in general, abstracted from every particular idea of heat, cold, tastes, smells? *&c.*

*Hyl.* I do not find that I can.

*Phil.* Does it not therefore follow, that sensible pain is nothing distinct from those sensations or ideas, in an intense degree?

*Hyl.* It is undeniable; and to speak the truth, I begin to suspect a very great heat cannot exist but in a mind perceiving it.

*Phil.* What! are you then in that sceptical state of suspense, between affirming and denying?

*Hyl.* I think I may be positive in the point. A very violent and painful heat cannot exist without the mind.

*Phil.* It has not therefore, according to you, any real being.

*Hyl.* I own it.

*Phil.* Is it therefore certain, that there is no body in nature really hot?

*Hyl.* I have not denied there is any real heat in bodies. I only say, there is no such thing as an intense real heat.

*Phil.* But did you not say before that all degrees of heat were equally real; or if there was any difference, that the greater were more undoubtedly real than the lesser?

*Hyl.* True; but it was because I did not then consider the ground there is for distinguishing between them, which I now plainly see. And it is this: because intense heat is nothing else but a particular kind of painful sensation, and pain cannot exist but in a perceiving being, it follows that no intense heat can really exist in an unperceiving corporeal substance. But this is no reason why we should deny heat in an inferior degree to exist in such a substance.

*Phil.* But how shall we be able to discern those degrees of heat which exist only in the mind, from those which exist without it?

*Hyl.* That is no difficult matter. You know the least pain cannot exist unperceived; whatever, therefore, degree of heat is a pain, exists only in the mind. But as for all other degrees of heat, nothing obliges us to think the same of them.

*Phil.* I think you granted before that no unperceiving being was capable of pleasure, any more than of pain.

*Hyl.* I did.                                                                  [178]

*Phil.* And is not warmth, or a more gentle degree of heat than what causes uneasiness, a pleasure?

*Hyl.* What then?

*Phil.* Consequently it cannot exist without the mind in any unperceiving substance or body.

*Hyl.* So it seems.

*Phil.* Since therefore, as well those degrees of heat that are not painful, as those that are, can exist only in a thinking substance; may we not conclude that external bodies are absolutely incapable of any degree of heat whatsoever?

*Hyl.* On second thoughts, I do not think it so evident that warmth is a pleasure, as that a great degree of heat is a pain.

*Phil.* I do not pretend that warmth is as great a pleasure as heat is a pain. But if you grant it to be even a small pleasure, it serves to make good my conclusion.

*Hyl.* I could rather call it an 'indolence'. It seems to be nothing more than a privation of both pain and pleasure. And that such a quality or state as this may agree to an unthinking substance, I hope you will not deny.

*Phil.* If you are resolved to maintain that warmth, or a gentle degree of heat, is no pleasure, I know not how to convince you otherwise than by appealing to your own sense. But what think you of cold?

*Hyl.* The same that I do of heat. An intense degree of cold is a pain; for to feel a very great cold is to perceive a great uneasiness: it cannot therefore exist without the mind; but a lesser degree of cold may, as well as a lesser degree of heat.

*Phil.* Those bodies, therefore, upon whose application to our own, we perceive a moderate degree of heat, must be concluded to have a moderate degree of heat or warmth in them; and those, upon whose application we feel a like degree of cold, must be thought to have cold in them.

*Hyl.* They must.

*Phil.* Can any doctrine be true that necessarily leads a man into an absurdity?

*Hyl.* Without doubt it cannot.

*Phil.* Is it not an absurdity to think that the same thing should be at the same time both cold and warm?

*Hyl.* It is.

*Phil.* Suppose now one of your hands hot, and the other cold, and [179] that they are both at once put into the same vessel of water, in an intermediate state; will not the water seem cold to one hand and warm to the other?

*Hyl.* It will.

*Phil.* Ought we not therefore by your principles to conclude, it is really both cold and warm at the same time, that is, according to your own concession, to believe an absurdity?

*Hyl.* I confess it seems so.

*Phil.* Consequently, the principles themselves are false, since you have granted that no true principle leads to an absurdity?

*Hyl.* But after all, can anything be more absurd than to say, 'there is no heat in the fire'?

*Phil.* To make the point still clearer: tell me, whether in two cases exactly alike, we ought not to make the same judgment?

*Hyl.* We ought.

*Phil.* When a pin pricks your finger, does it not rend and divide the fibres of your flesh?

*Hyl.* It does.

*Phil.* And when a coal burns your finger, does it any more?

*Hyl.* It does not.

*Phil.* Since therefore you neither judge the sensation itself occasioned by the pin, nor anything like it, to be in the pin; you should not, conformably to what you have now granted, judge the sensation occasioned by the fire, or anything like it, to be in the fire.

*Hyl.* Well, since it must be so, I am content to yield this point, and acknowledge that heat and cold are only sensations existing in our minds; but there still remain qualities enough to secure the reality of external things.

*Phil.* But what will you say, Hylas, if it shall appear that the case is the same with regard to all other sensible qualities, and that they can no more be supposed to exist without the mind than heat and cold?

*Hyl.* Then indeed you will have done something to the purpose; but that is what I despair of seeing proved.

*Phil.* Let us examine them in order. What think you of tastes, do they exist without the mind, or no?

*Hyl.* Can any man in his senses doubt whether sugar is sweet, or wormwood bitter?

*Phil.* Inform me, Hylas. Is a sweet taste a particular kind of pleasure or pleasant sensation, or is it not? [180]

*Hyl.* It is.

*Phil.* And is not bitterness some kind of uneasiness or pain?

*Hyl.* I grant it.

*Phil.* If therefore sugar and wormwood are unthinking corporeal substances existing without the mind, how can sweetness and bitterness, that is, pleasure and pain, agree to them?

*Hyl.* Hold, Philonous, I now see what it was deluded me all this time. You asked whether heat and cold, sweetness and bitterness, were not particular sorts of pleasure and pain; to which I answered simply, that they were. Whereas I should have thus distinguished: those qualities, as perceived by us, are pleasures and pains, but not as existing in the external objects. We must not therefore conclude absolutely that there is no heat in the fire, or sweetness in the sugar, but only that heat or sweetness, as perceived by us, are not in the fire or sugar. What say you to this?

*Phil.* I say it is nothing to the purpose. Our discourse proceeded altogether concerning sensible things, which you defined to be the things we 'immediately perceive by our senses'. Whatever other qualities therefore you speak of, as distinct from these, I know nothing of them, neither do they at all belong to the point in dispute. You may indeed pretend to have discovered certain qualities which you do not perceive, and assert those insensible qualities exist in fire and sugar. But what use can be made of this to your present purpose, I am at a loss to conceive. Tell me then once more, do you acknowledge that heat and cold, sweetness and bitterness (meaning those qualities which are perceived by the senses), do not exist without the mind?

*Hyl.* I see it is to no purpose to hold out, so I give up the cause as to those mentioned qualities. Though, I profess, it sounds oddly to say that sugar is not sweet.

*Phil.* But for your farther satisfaction, take this along with you: that which at other times seems sweet, shall to a distempered palate appear bitter. And nothing can be plainer than that divers persons perceive different tastes in the same food, since that which one man delights in, another abhors. And how could this be, if the taste was something really inherent in the food?

*Hyl.* I acknowledge I know not how.

*Phil.* In the next place, odours are to be considered. And, with regard to these, I would fain know whether what has been said of tastes does not exactly agree to them? Are they not so many pleasing or displeasing sensations?

[181]

*Hyl.* They are.

*Phil.* Can you then conceive it possible that they should exist in an unperceiving thing?

*Hyl.* I cannot.

*Phil.* Or can you imagine that filth and ordure affect those brute animals, that feed on them out of choice, with the same smells which we perceive in them?

*Hyl.* By no means.

*Phil.* May we not therefore conclude of smells, as of the other forementioned qualities, that they cannot exist in any but a perceiving substance or mind?

*Hyl.* I think so.

*Phil.* Then as to sounds, what must we think of them: are they accidents really inherent in external bodies or not?

*Hyl.* That they inhere not in the sonorous bodies is plain from hence: because a bell struck in the exhausted receiver of an air-pump sends forth no sound. The air therefore must be thought the subject of sound.

*Phil.* What reason is there for that, Hylas?

*Hyl.* Because when any motion is raised in the air, we perceive a sound greater or lesser, in proportion to the air's motion; but without some motion in the air, we never hear any sound at all.

*Phil.* And granting that we never hear a sound but when some motion is produced in the air, yet I do not see how you can infer from thence that the sound itself is in the air.

*Hyl.* It is this very motion in the external air that produces in the mind the sensation of sound. For, striking on the drum of the ear, it causes a vibration, which by the auditory nerves being communicated to the brain, the soul is thereupon affected with the sensation called 'sound'.

*Phil.* What! Is sound then a sensation?

*Hyl.* I tell you, as perceived by us, it is a particular sensation in the mind.

*Phil.* And can any sensation exist without the mind?

*Hyl.* No certainly.

*Phil.* How then can sound, being a sensation, exist in the air, if by the 'air' you mean a senseless substance existing without the mind?

*Hyl.* You must distinguish, Philonous, between sound as it is per- [182] ceived by us, and as it is in itself; or (which is the same thing) between the sound we immediately perceive and that which exists without us. The former indeed is a particular kind of sensation, but the latter is merely a vibrative or undulatory motion in the air.

*Phil.* I thought I had already obviated that distinction by the answer I gave when you were applying it in a like case before. But to say no more of that; are you sure then that sound is really nothing but motion?

*Hyl.* I am.

*Phil.* Whatever therefore agrees to real sound, may with truth be attributed to motion.

*Hyl.* It may.

*Phil.* It is then good sense to speak of motion, as of a thing that is loud, sweet, acute, or grave.

*Hyl.* I see you are resolved not to understand me. Is it not evident, those accidents or modes belong only to sensible sound, or sound in the common acceptation of the word, but not to sound in the real and philosophic sense, which, as I just now told you, is nothing but a certain motion of the air?

*Phil.* It seems then there are two sorts of sound, the one vulgar, or that which is heard, the other philosophical and real.

*Hyl.* Even so.

*Phil.* And the latter consists in motion.

*Hyl.* I told you so before.

*Phil.* Tell me, Hylas, to which of the senses, think you, the idea of motion belongs: to the hearing?

*Hyl.* No certainly, but to the sight and touch.

*Phil.* It should follow then that, according to you, real sounds may possibly be seen or felt, but never heard.

*Hyl.* Look you, Philonous, you may if you please make a jest of my opinion, but that will not alter the truth of things. I own indeed, the inferences you draw me into sound something oddly; but common language, you know, is framed by, and for the use of, the vulgar. We must not therefore wonder, if expressions adapted to exact philosophic notions seem uncouth and out of the way.

[183] *Phil.* Is it come to that? I assure you, I imagine myself to have gained no small point, since you make so light of departing from common phrases and opinions; it being a main part of our inquiry, to examine whose notions are widest of the common road, and most repugnant to the general sense of the world. But can you think it no more than a philosophical paradox, to say that 'real sounds are never heard' and that the idea of them is obtained by some other sense. And is there nothing in this contrary to nature and the truth of things?

*Hyl.* To deal ingenuously, I do not like it. And after the concessions already made, I had as well grant that sounds too have no real being without the mind.

*Phil.* And I hope you will make no difficulty to acknowledge the same of colours.

*Hyl.* Pardon me: the case of colours is very different. Can anything be plainer than that we see them on the objects?

*Phil.* The objects you speak of are, I suppose, corporeal substances existing without the mind.

*Hyl.* They are.

*Phil.* And have true and real colours inhering in them?

*Hyl.* Each visible object has that colour which we see in it.

*Phil.* How! Is there anything visible but what we perceive by sight.

*Hyl.* There is not.

*Phil.* And do we perceive anything by sense, which we do not perceive immediately?

*Hyl.* How often must I be obliged to repeat the same thing? I tell you, we do not.

*Phil.* Have patience, good Hylas; and tell me once more, whether there is anything immediately perceived by the senses, except sensible qualities. I know you asserted there was not; but I would now be informed, whether you still persist in the same opinion.

*Hyl.* I do.

*Phil.* Pray, is your corporeal substance either a sensible quality, or made up of sensible qualities?

*Hyl.* What a question that is! who ever thought it was?

*Phil.* My reason for asking was because, in saying 'each visible object has that colour which we see in it,' you make visible objects to be corporeal substances; which implies either that corporeal substances are sensible qualities, or else that there is something beside sensible qualities perceived by sight. But as this point was formerly agreed between us and is still maintained by you, it is a clear consequence that your corporeal substance is nothing distinct from sensible qualities.                                                                      [184]

*Hyl.* You may draw as many absurd consequences as you please, and endeavour to perplex the plainest things; but you shall never persuade me out of my senses. I clearly understand my own meaning.

*Phil.* I wish you would make me understand it too. But since you are unwilling to have your notion of corporeal substance examined, I shall urge that point no farther. Only be pleased to let me know whether the same colours which we see, exist in external bodies, or some other.

*Hyl.* The very same.

*Phil.* What! are then the beautiful red and purple we see on yonder clouds, really in them? Or do you imagine they have in themselves any other form, than that of a dark mist or vapour?

*Hyl.* I must own, Philonous, those colours are not really in the clouds as they seem to be at this distance. They are only apparent colours.

*Phil.* 'Apparent' call you them? how shall we distinguish these apparent colours from real?

*Hyl.* Very easily. Those are to be thought apparent, which appearing only at a distance, vanish upon a nearer approach.

*Phil.* And those I suppose are to be thought real, which are discovered by the most near and exact survey.

*Hyl.* Right.

*Phil.* Is the nearest and exactest survey made by the help of a microscope, or by the naked eye?

*Hyl.* By a microscope, doubtless.

*Phil.* But a microscope often discovers colours in an object different from those perceived by the unassisted sight. And in case we had microscopes magnifying to an assigned degree, it is certain that no object whatsoever, viewed through them, would appear in the same colour which it exhibits to the naked eye.

*Hyl.* And what will you conclude from all this? You cannot argue that there are really and naturally no colours on objects because, by artificial managements, they may be altered or made to vanish.

*Phil.* I think it may evidently be concluded, from your own concessions, that all the colours we see with our naked eyes are only apparent as those on the clouds, since they vanish upon a more close and accurate inspection, which is afforded us by a microscope. Then as to what you say [185] by way of prevention: I ask you, whether the real and natural state of an object is better discovered by a very sharp and piercing sight, or by one which is less sharp?

*Hyl.* By the former without doubt.

*Phil.* Is it not plain from dioptrics that microscopes make the sight more penetrating, and represent objects as they would appear to the eye in case it were naturally endowed with the most exquisite sharpness?

*Hyl.* It is.

*Phil.* Consequently the microscopical representation is to be thought that which best sets forth the real nature of the thing, or what it is in itself. The colours, therefore, by it perceived are more genuine and real than those perceived otherwise.

*Hyl.* I confess there is something in what you say.

*Phil.* Besides, it is not only possible but manifest, that there actually are animals, whose eyes are by nature framed to perceive those things, which by reason of their minuteness escape our sight. What think you of those inconceivably small animals perceived by glasses? Must we suppose they are all stark blind? Or, in case they see, can it be imagined their sight has not the same use in preserving their bodies from injuries, which appears in that of all other animals? And if it has, is it not evident, they must see particles less than their own bodies, which will present them with a far different view in each object, from that which strikes our senses? Even our own eyes do not always represent objects to us after the same manner. In the jaundice, everyone knows that all things seem yellow. Is it not therefore highly probable, those animals in whose eyes we discern a very different texture from that of ours and whose bodies abound with different humours, do not see the same colours in every object that we do? From all which should it not seem to follow, that all colours are equally apparent, and that none of those which we perceive are really inherent in any outward object?

*Hyl.* It should.

*Phil.* The point will be past all doubt if you consider that, in case colours were real properties or affections inherent in external bodies, they could admit of no alteration without some change wrought in the very bodies themselves. But is it not evident from what has been said that, upon the use of microscopes, upon a change happening in the humours of the eye or a variation of distance, without any manner of real alteration in the thing itself, the colours of any object are either [186] changed or totally disappear? Nay, all other circumstances remaining the same, change but the situation of some objects and they shall present different colours to the eye. The same thing happens upon viewing an object in various degrees of light. And what is more known, than that the same bodies appear differently coloured by candle-light from what they do in the open day? Add to these the experiment of a prism, which separating the heterogeneous rays of light, alters the colour of any object; and will cause the whitest to appear of a deep blue or red to the naked eye. And now tell me, whether you are still of opinion that every body has its true real colour inhering in it; and if you think it has, I would fain know farther from you, what certain distance and position of the object, what peculiar texture and formation of the eye, what degree or kind of light is necessary for ascertaining that true colour and distinguishing it from apparent ones.

*Hyl.* I own myself entirely satisfied that they are all equally apparent, and that there is no such thing as colour really inhering in external bodies, but that it is altogether in the light. And what confirms me in this opinion is that, in proportion to the light, colours are still more or less vivid; and if there be no light, then are there no colours perceived. Besides, allowing there are colours on external objects, yet how is it possible for us to perceive them? For no external body affects the mind, unless it act first on our organs of sense. But the only action of bodies is motion; and motion cannot be communicated otherwise than by impulse. A distant object therefore cannot act on the eye, nor consequently make itself or its properties perceivable to the soul. Whence it plainly follows that it is immediately some contiguous substance, which operating on the eye occasions a perception of colours: and such is light.

*Phil.* How! is light then a substance?

*Hyl.* I tell you, Philonous, external light is nothing but a thin fluid substance whose minute particles, being agitated with a brisk motion and in various manners reflected from the different surfaces of outward objects to the eyes, communicate different motions to the optic nerves; which, being propagated to the brain, cause therein various impressions, and these are attended with the sensations of red, blue, yellow, &c.

*Phil.* It seems, then, the light does no more than shake the optic
[187] nerves.

*Hyl.* Nothing else.

*Phil.* And consequent to each particular motion of the nerves the mind is affected with a sensation, which is some particular colour.

*Hyl.* Right.

*Phil.* And these sensations have no existence without the mind.

*Hyl.* They have not.

*Phil.* How then do you affirm that colours are in the light, since by 'light' you understand a corporeal substance external to the mind?

*Hyl.* Light and colours, as immediately perceived by us, I grant cannot exist without the mind. But in themselves they are only the motions and configurations of certain insensible particles of matter.

*Phil.* Colours then, in the vulgar sense, or taken for the immediate objects of sight, cannot agree to any but a perceiving substance.

*Hyl.* That is what I say.

*Phil.* Well then, since you give up the point as to those sensible qualities, which are alone thought colours by all mankind beside, you may hold what you please with regard to those invisible ones of the philosophers. It is not my business to dispute about them; only I would advise you to bethink yourself, whether considering the inquiry we are upon, it be prudent for you to affirm 'the red and blue which we see are not real colours, but certain unknown motions and figures which no man ever did or can see are truly so.' Are not these shocking notions, and are not they subject to as many ridiculous inferences, as those you were obliged to renounce before in the case of sounds?

*Hyl.* I frankly own, Philonous, that it is in vain to stand out any longer. Colours, sounds, tastes, in a word, all those termed 'secondary qualities' have certainly no existence without the mind. But by this acknowledgment I must not be supposed to derogate anything from the reality of matter or external objects, seeing it is no more than several philosophers maintain, who nevertheless are the farthest imaginable from denying matter. For the clearer understanding of this, you must know sensible qualities are by philosophers divided into 'primary' and 'secondary'. The former are extension, figure, solidity, gravity, motion, and rest. And these they hold exist really in bodies. The latter are those [188] above enumerated; or briefly, all sensible qualities beside the primary, which they assert are only so many sensations or ideas existing nowhere but in the mind. But all this, I doubt not, you are already apprised of. For my part, I have been a long time sensible there was such an opinion current among philosophers, but was never thoroughly convinced of its truth till now.

*Phil.* You are still then of opinion that extension and figures are inherent in external unthinking substances.

*Hyl.* I am.

*Phil.* But what if the same arguments which are brought against secondary qualities, will hold good against these too?

*Hyl.* Why then I shall be obliged to think, they too exist only in the mind.

*Phil.* Is it your opinion, the very figure and extension which you perceive by sense, exist in the outward object or material substance?

*Hyl.* It is.

*Phil.* Have all other animals as good grounds to think the same of the figure and extension which they see and feel?

*Hyl.* Without doubt, if they have any thought at all.

*Phil.* Answer me, Hylas. Think you the senses were bestowed upon all animals for their preservation and well-being in life? or were they given to men alone for this end?

*Hyl.* I make no question but they have the same use in all other animals.

*Phil.* If so, is it not necessary they should be enabled by them to perceive their own limbs, and those bodies which are capable of harming them?

*Hyl.* Certainly.

*Phil.* A mite therefore must be supposed to see his own foot, and things equal or even less than it, as bodies of some considerable dimension; though at the same time they appear to you scarce discernible or at best as so many visible points.

*Hyl.* I cannot deny it.

*Phil.* And to creatures less than the mite they will seem yet larger.

*Hyl.* They will.

*Phil.* Insomuch that what you can hardly discern, will to another extremely minute animal appear as some huge mountain. [189]

*Hyl.*   All this I grant.

*Phil.*   Can one and the same thing be at the same time in itself of different dimensions?

*Hyl.*   That were absurd to imagine.

*Phil.*   But from what you have laid down it follows, that both the extension by you perceived, and that perceived by the mite itself, as likewise all those perceived by lesser animals, are each of them the true extension of the mite's foot; that is to say, by your own principles you are led into an absurdity.

*Hyl.*   There seems to be some difficulty in the point.

*Phil.*   Again, have you not acknowledged that no real inherent property of any object can be changed, without some change in the thing itself?

*Hyl.*   I have.

*Phil.*   But as we approach to or recede from an object, the visible extension varies, being at one distance ten or a hundred times greater than at another. Does it not therefore follow from hence likewise, that it is not really inherent in the object?

*Hyl.*   I own I am at a loss what to think.

*Phil.*   Your judgment will soon be determined, if you will venture to think as freely concerning this quality as you have done concerning the rest. Was it not admitted as a good argument that neither heat nor cold was in the water, because it seemed warm to one hand and cold to the other?

*Hyl.*   It was.

*Phil.*   Is it not the very same reasoning to conclude, there is no extension or figure in an object because to one eye it shall seem little, smooth, and round, when at the same time it appears to the other, great, uneven, and angular?

*Hyl.*   The very same. But does this latter fact ever happen?

*Phil.*   You may at any time make the experiment, by looking with one eye bare, and with the other through a microscope.

*Hyl.*   I know not how to maintain it, and yet I am loath to give up extension; I see so many odd consequences following upon such a concession.

*Phil.*   Odd, say you? After the concessions already made, I hope you will stick at nothing for its oddness. [But on the other hand should it not [190] seem very odd, if the general reasoning which includes all other sensible qualities did not also include extension? If it be allowed that no idea nor anything like an idea can exist in an unperceiving substance, then surely it follows that no figure or mode of extension, which we can either perceive or imagine, or have any idea of, can be really inherent in matter; not to mention the peculiar difficulty there must be in conceiving a material substance, prior to and distinct from extension, to be the *substratum* of extension. Be the sensible quality what it will, figure, or sound, or colour; it seems alike impossible it should subsist in that which does not perceive it.][5]

*Hyl.* I give up the point for the present, reserving still a right to retract my opinion, in case I shall hereafter discover any false step in my progress to it.

*Phil.* That is a right you cannot be denied. Figures and extension being dispatched, we proceed next to motion. Can a real motion in any external body be at the same time both very swift and very slow?

*Hyl.* It cannot.

*Phil.* Is not the motion of a body swift in a reciprocal proportion to the time it takes up in describing any given space? Thus a body that describes a mile in an hour, moves three times faster than it would in case it described only a mile in three hours.

*Hyl.* I agree with you.

*Phil.* And is not time measured by the succession of ideas in our minds?

*Hyl.* It is.

*Phil.* And is it not possible [that] ideas should succeed one another twice as fast in your mind, as they do in mine, or in that of some spirit of another kind.

*Hyl.* I own it.

*Phil.* Consequently the same body may to another seem to perform its motion over any space in half the time that it does to you. And the same reasoning will hold as to any other proportion: that is to say, according to your principles (since the motions perceived are both really in the object), it is possible one and the same body shall be really moved the same way at once, both very swift and very slow. How is this consistent with common sense, or with what you just now granted?

*Hyl.* I have nothing to say to it.                                        [191]

---

[5] The material in parentheses was added in the 1734 edition.

*Phil.* Then as for 'solidity': either you do not mean any sensible quality by that word, and so it is beside our inquiry; or if you do, it must be either hardness or resistance. But both the one and the other are plainly relative to our senses: it being evident, that what seems hard to one animal may appear soft to another, who has greater force and firmness of limbs. Nor is it less plain, that the resistance I feel is not in the body.

*Hyl.* I own the very sensation of resistance, which is all you immediately perceive, is not in the body; but the cause of that sensation is.

*Phil.* But the causes of our sensations are not things immediately perceived, and therefore not sensible. This point I thought had been already determined.

*Hyl.* I own it was; but you will pardon me if I seem a little embarrassed. I know not how to quit my old notions.

*Phil.* To help you out, do but consider that if extension be once acknowledged to have no existence without the mind, the same must necessarily be granted of motion, solidity, and gravity, since they all evidently suppose extension. It is therefore superfluous to inquire particularly concerning each of them. In denying extension, you have denied them all to have any real existence.

*Hyl.* I wonder, Philonous, if what you say be true, why those philosophers who deny the secondary qualities any real existence should yet attribute it to the primary. If there is no difference between them, how can this be accounted for?

*Phil.* It is not my business to account for every opinion of the philosophers. But among other reasons which may be assigned for this, it seems probable, that pleasure and pain being rather annexed to the former than the later, may be one. Heat and cold, tastes and smells, have something more vividly pleasing or disagreeable than the ideas of extension, figure, and motion, affect us with. And it being too visibly absurd to hold that pain or pleasure can be in an unperceiving substance, men are more easily weaned from believing the external existence of the secondary than the primary qualities. You will be satisfied there is something in this, if you recollect the difference you made between an intense and more moderate degree of heat, allowing the one a real existence, while you denied it to the other. But after all, there is no rational ground for
[192] that distinction. For surely an indifferent sensation is as truly a sensation as one more pleasing or painful, and consequently should not any more than they be supposed to exist in an unthinking subject.

*Hyl.* It is just come into my head, Philonous, that I have somewhere heard of a distinction between absolute and sensible extension.[6] Now though it be acknowledged that great and small, consisting merely in the relation which other extended beings have to the parts of our own bodies, do not really inhere in the substances themselves; yet nothing obliges us to hold the same with regard to absolute extension, which is something abstracted from great and small, from this or that particular magnitude or figure. So likewise as to motion, swift and slow are altogether relative to the succession of ideas in our own minds. But it does not follow, because those modifications of motion exist not without the mind, that therefore absolute motion abstracted from them does not.

*Phil.* Pray what is it that distinguishes one motion, or one part of extension, from another? Is it not something sensible, as some degree of swiftness or slowness, some certain magnitude or figure peculiar to each?

*Hyl.* I think so.

*Phil.* These qualities, therefore, stripped of all sensible properties, are without all specific and numerical differences, as the Schools call them.

*Hyl.* They are.

*Phil.* That is to say, they are extension in general, and motion in general.

*Hyl.* Let it be so.

*Phil.* But it is a universally received maxim, that 'everything which exists, is particular'.[7] How then can motion in general, or extension in general, exist in any corporeal substance? [193]

*Hyl.* I will take time to solve your difficulty.

*Phil.* But I think the point may be speedily decided. Without doubt you can tell whether you are able to frame this or that idea. Now I am content to put our dispute on this issue. If you can frame in your thoughts a distinct abstract idea of motion or extension, divested of all those sensible modes, as swift and slow, great and small, round and square, and the like, which are acknowledged to exist only in the mind, I will then yield the point you contend for. But if you cannot, it will be unreasonable on your side to insist any longer upon what you have no notion of.

*Hyl.* To confess ingenuously, I cannot.

[6] See *PHK*, 110, 116.  [7] Cf. Locke, *Essay*, III, iii, i: 'All things, that exist, being Particulars ... '

*Phil.* Can you even separate the ideas of extension and motion from the ideas of all those qualities, which they who make the distinction term 'secondary'.

*Hyl.* What! is it not an easy matter, to consider extension and motion by themselves, abstracted from all other sensible qualities? Pray how do the mathematicians treat of them?

*Phil.* I acknowledge, Hylas, it is not difficult to form general propositions and reasonings about those qualities, without mentioning any other; and in this sense to consider or treat of them abstractedly. But how does it follow that, because I can pronounce the word 'motion' by itself, I can form the idea of it in my mind exclusive of body? Or because theorems may be made of extension and figures, without any mention of 'great' or 'small', or any other sensible mode or quality; that therefore it is possible such an abstract idea of extension, without any particular size or figure, or sensible quality, should be distinctly formed and apprehended by the mind? Mathematicians treat of quantity, without regarding what other sensible qualities it is attended with, as being altogether indifferent to their demonstrations. But when laying aside the words, they contemplate the bare ideas; I believe you will find they are not the pure abstracted ideas of extension.

*Hyl.* But what say you to 'pure intellect'? May not abstracted ideas be framed by that faculty?

[194] *Phil.* Since I cannot frame abstract ideas at all, it is plain, I cannot frame them by the help of 'pure intellect', whatsoever faculty you understand by these words. Besides, not to inquire into the nature of pure intellect and its spiritual objects, as virtue, reason, God, or the like; thus much seems manifest, that sensible things are only to be perceived by sense or represented by the imagination. Figures, therefore, and extension, being originally perceived by sense, do not belong to pure intellect. But for your farther satisfaction, try if you can frame the idea of any figure, abstracted from all particularities of size, or even from other sensible qualities.

*Hyl.* Let me think a little – I do not find that I can.

*Phil.* And can you think it possible, that should really exist in nature, which implies a repugnancy in its conception?

*Hyl.* By no means.

*Phil.* Since therefore it is impossible even for the mind to disunite the ideas of extension and motion from all other sensible qualities, does it not follow, that where the one exist, there necessarily the other exist likewise?

*Hyl.* It should seem so.

*Phil.* Consequently the very same arguments which you admitted as conclusive against the secondary qualities are, without any farther application of force, against the primary too. Besides, if you will trust your senses, is it not plain, all sensible qualities coexist, or, to them, appear as being in the same place? Do they ever represent a motion, or figure, as being divested of all other visible and tangible qualities?

*Hyl.* You need say no more on this head. I am free to own, if there be no secret error or oversight in our proceedings hitherto, that all sensible qualities are alike to be denied existence without the mind. But my fear is, that I have been too liberal in my former concessions, or overlooked some fallacy or other. In short, I did not take time to think.

*Phil.* For that matter, Hylas, you may take what time you please in reviewing the progress of our inquiry. You are at liberty to recover any slips you might have made, or offer whatever you have omitted, which makes for your first opinion.

*Hyl.* One great oversight I take to be this: that I did not sufficiently distinguish the object from the sensation. Now though this latter may not exist without the mind, yet it will not thence follow that the former cannot.

*Phil.* What object do you mean? the object of the senses?

*Hyl.* The same.

*Phil.* It is then immediately perceived. [195]

*Hyl.* Right.

*Phil.* Make me understand the difference between what is immediately perceived and a sensation.

*Hyl.* The sensation I take to be an act of the mind perceiving; beside which there is something perceived, and this I call the object. For example, there is red and yellow on that tulip. But then the act of perceiving those colours is in me only, and not in the tulip.

*Phil.* What tulip do you speak of? is it that which you see?

*Hyl.* The same.

*Phil.* And what do you see beside colour, figure, and extension?

*Hyl.* Nothing.

*Phil.* What you would say then is that the red and yellow are coexistent with the extension; is it not?

*Hyl.* That is not all; I would say, they have a real existence without the mind, in some unthinking substance.

*Phil.* That the colours are really in the tulip, which I see, is manifest. Neither can it be denied that this tulip may exist independent of your mind or mine; but that any immediate object of the senses, that is, any idea or combination of ideas, should exist in an unthinking substance or exterior to all minds, is in itself an evident contradiction. Nor can I imagine how this follows from what you said just now, to wit, that the red and yellow were on the tulip you saw, since you do not pretend to see that unthinking substance.

*Hyl.* You have an artful way, Philonous, of diverting our inquiry from the subject.

*Phil.* I see you have no mind to be pressed that way. To return then to your distinction between 'sensation' and 'object'; if I take you right, you distinguish in every perception two things, the one an action of the mind, the other not.

*Hyl.* True.

*Phil.* And this action cannot exist in, or belong to, any unthinking [196] thing; but whatever beside is implied in a perception, may.

*Hyl.* That is my meaning.

*Phil.* So that if there was a perception without any act of the mind, it were possible such a perception should exist in an unthinking substance.

*Hyl.* I grant it. But it is impossible there should be such a perception.

*Phil.* When is the mind said to be active?

*Hyl.* When it produces, puts an end to, or changes anything.

*Phil.* Can the mind produce, discontinue, or change anything but by an act of the will?

*Hyl.* It cannot.

*Phil.* The mind therefore is to be accounted active in its perceptions, so far forth as volition is included in them.

*Hyl.* It is.

*Phil.* In plucking a flower, I am active, because I do it by the motion of my hand, which was consequent upon my volition; so likewise in applying it to my nose. But is either of these smelling?

*Hyl.* No.

*Phil.* I act too in drawing the air through my nose; because my breathing so, rather than otherwise, is the effect of my volition. But neither can this be called 'smelling'; for if it were, I should smell every time I breathed in that manner.

*Hyl.* True.

*Phil.* Smelling then is somewhat consequent to all this.

*Hyl.* It is.

*Phil.* But I do not find my will concerned any farther. Whatever more there is, as that I perceive such a particular smell or any smell at all, this is independent of my will, and therein I am altogether passive. Do you find it otherwise with you, Hylas?

*Hyl.* No, the very same.

*Phil.* Then as to seeing, is it not in your power to open your eyes, or keep them shut; to turn them this or that way?

*Hyl.* Without doubt.

*Phil.* But does it in like manner depend on your will that, in looking on this flower, you perceive white rather than any other colour? Or directing your open eyes toward yonder part of the heaven, can you avoid seeing the sun? Or is light or darkness the effect of your volition?

*Hyl.* No, certainly.

*Phil.* You are then in these respects altogether passive. [197]

*Hyl.* I am.

*Phil.* Tell me now, whether seeing consists in perceiving light and colours, or in opening and turning the eyes?

*Hyl.* Without doubt, in the former.

*Phil.* Since therefore you are in the very perception of light and colours altogether passive, what is become of that action you were speaking of as an ingredient in every sensation? And does it not follow from your own concessions that the perception of light and colours, including no action in it, may exist in an unperceiving substance? And is not this a plain contradiction?

*Hyl.* I know not what to think of it.

*Phil.* Besides, since you distinguish the active and passive in every perception, you must do it in that of pain. But how is it possible that pain, be it as little active as you please, should exist in an unperceiving substance? In short, do but consider the point, and then confess ingenuously whether light and colours, tastes, sounds, &c. are not all equally passions or sensations in the soul. You may indeed call them 'external objects', and give them in words what subsistence you please. But examine your own thoughts, and then tell me whether it be not as I say?

179

*Hyl.* I acknowledge, Philonous, that upon a fair observation of what passes in my mind, I can discover nothing else, but that I am a thinking being, affected with [a] variety of sensations; neither is it possible to conceive how a sensation should exist in an unperceiving substance. But then on the other hand, when I look on sensible things in a different view, considering them as so many modes and qualities, I find it necessary to suppose a material *substratum*, without which they cannot be conceived to exist.

*Phil.* 'Material *substratum*' call you it? Pray, by which of your senses came you acquainted with that being?

*Hyl.* It is not itself sensible, its modes and qualities only being perceived by the senses.

*Phil.* I presume then it was by reflection and reason you obtained the idea of it.

*Hyl.* I do not pretend to any proper positive idea of it. However I conclude it exists, because qualities cannot be conceived to exist without a support.

*Phil.* It seems then you have only a relative notion of it, or that you conceive it not otherwise than by conceiving the relation it bears to sensible qualities.

[198]

*Hyl.* Right.

*Phil.* Be pleased therefore to let me know wherein that relation consists.

*Hyl.* Is it not sufficiently expressed in the term '*substratum*' or 'substance'?

*Phil.* If so, the word '*substratum*' should import that it is spread under the sensible qualities or accidents.

*Hyl.* True.

*Phil.* And consequently under extension.

*Hyl.* I own it.

*Phil.* It is therefore somewhat in its own nature entirely distinct from extension.

*Hyl.* I tell you, extension is only a mode, and matter is something that supports modes. And is it not evident the thing supported is different from the thing supporting?

*Phil.* So that something distinct from, and exclusive of, extension is supposed to be the *substratum* of extension.

*Hyl.* Just so.

*Phil.*    Answer me, Hylas. Can a thing be spread without extension? or is not the idea of extension necessarily included in 'spreading'?

*Hyl.*    It is.

*Phil.*    Whatsoever therefore you suppose spread under anything, must have in itself an extension distinct from the extension of that thing under which it is spread.

*Hyl.*    It must.

*Phil.*    Consequently every corporeal substance, being the *substratum* of extension, must have in itself another extension by which it is qualified to be a *substratum*: and so on to infinity. And I ask whether this be not absurd in itself, and repugnant to what you granted just now, to wit, that the *substratum* was something distinct from, and exclusive of, extension.

*Hyl.*    Aye but, Philonous, you take me wrong. I do not mean that matter is 'spread' in a gross literal sense under extension. The word '*substratum*' is used only to express in general the same thing with 'substance'.

*Phil.*    Well then, let us examine the relation implied in the term 'substance'. Is it not that it stands under accidents?

*Hyl.*    The very same.

*Phil.*    But that one thing may stand under or support another, must it not be extended?

*Hyl.*    It must.                                                                          [199]

*Phil.*    Is not therefore this supposition liable to the same absurdity with the former?

*Hyl.*    You still take things in a strict literal sense: that is not fair, Philonous.

*Phil.*    I am not for imposing any sense on your words: you are at liberty to explain them as you please. Only I beseech you, make me understand something by them. You tell me, matter supports or stands under accidents. How! is it as your legs support your body?

*Hyl.*    No; that is the literal sense.

*Phil.*    Pray let me know any sense, literal or not literal, that you understand it in. – How long must I wait for an answer, Hylas?

*Hyl.*    I declare I know not what to say. I once thought I understood well enough what was meant by matter's supporting accidents. But now, the more I think on it the less can I comprehend it; in short, I find that I know nothing of it.

*Phil.* It seems then you have no idea at all, neither relative nor positive, of matter; you know neither what it is in itself, nor what relation it bears to accidents.

*Hyl.* I acknowledge it.

*Phil.* And yet you asserted that you could not conceive how qualities or accidents should really exist, without conceiving at the same time a material support of them.

*Hyl.* I did.

*Phil.* That is to say, when you conceive the real existence of qualities, you do withal conceive something which you cannot conceive.

*Hyl.* It was wrong I own. But still I fear there is some fallacy or other. Pray what think you of this? It is just come into my head that the ground of all our mistakes lies in your treating of each quality by itself. Now, I grant that each quality cannot singly subsist without the mind. Colour cannot without extension, neither can figure without some other sensible quality. But as the several qualities united or blended together form entire sensible things, nothing hinders why such things may not be supposed to exist without the mind.

*Phil.* Either, Hylas, you are jesting or have a very bad memory. Though indeed we went through all the qualities by name one after another; yet my arguments, or rather your concessions, nowhere tended to prove that the secondary qualities did not subsist each alone by itself; [200] but that they were not at all without the mind. Indeed in treating of figure and motion, we concluded they could not exist without the mind, because it was impossible even in thought to separate them from all secondary qualities so as to conceive them existing by themselves. But then this was not the only argument made use of upon that occasion. But (to pass by all that has been hitherto said, and reckon it for nothing, if you will have it so) I am content to put the whole upon this issue. If you can conceive it possible for any mixture or combination of qualities, or any sensible object whatever, to exist without the mind, then I will grant it actually to be so.

*Hyl.* If it comes to that, the point will soon be decided. What more easy than to conceive a tree or house existing by itself, independent of, and unperceived by, any mind whatsoever? I do at this present time conceive them existing after that manner.

*Phil.* How say you, Hylas, can you see a thing which is at the same time unseen?

*Hyl.*    No, that were a contradiction.

*Phil.*    Is it not as great a contradiction to talk of 'conceiving' a thing which is 'unconceived'?

*Hyl.*    It is.

*Phil.*    The tree or house therefore, which you think of, is conceived by you.

*Hyl.*    How should it be otherwise?

*Phil.*    And what is conceived is surely in the mind?

*Hyl.*    Without question, that which is conceived is in the mind.

*Phil.*    How then came you to say, you conceived a house or tree existing independent and out of all minds whatsoever?

*Hyl.*    That was I own an oversight; but stay, let me consider what led me into it. – It is a pleasant mistake enough. As I was thinking of a tree in a solitary place, where no one was present to see it, methought that was to conceive a tree as existing unperceived or unthought of, not considering that I myself conceived it all the while. But now I plainly see that all I can do is to frame ideas in my own mind. I may indeed conceive in my own thoughts the idea of a tree, or a house, or a mountain, but that is all. And this is far from proving that I can conceive them 'existing out of the minds of all spirits'.

*Phil.*    You acknowledge then that you cannot possibly conceive how any one corporeal sensible thing should exist otherwise than in a mind.    [201]

*Hyl.*    I do.

*Phil.*    And yet you will earnestly contend for the truth of that which you cannot so much as conceive.

*Hyl.*    I profess I know not what to think, but still there are some scruples remain with me. Is it not certain I see things at a distance? Do we not perceive the stars and moon, for example, to be a great way off? Is not this, I say, manifest to the senses?

*Phil.*    Do you not in a dream too perceive those or the like objects?

*Hyl.*    I do.

*Phil.*    And have they not then the same appearance of being distant?

*Hyl.*    They have.

*Phil.*    But you do not thence conclude the apparitions in a dream to be without the mind?

*Hyl.*    By no means.

*Phil.*    You ought not therefore to conclude that sensible objects are without the mind, from their appearance or manner wherein they are perceived.

*Hyl.* I acknowledge it. But does not my sense deceive me in those cases?

*Phil.* By no means. The idea or thing which you immediately perceive, neither sense nor reason informs you that it actually exists without the mind. By sense you only know that you are affected with such certain sensations of light and colours, *&c.* And these you will not say are without the mind.

*Hyl.* True: but beside all that, do you not think the sight suggests something of outness or distance?

*Phil.* Upon approaching a distant object, do the visible size and figure change perpetually, or do they appear the same at all distances?

*Hyl.* They are in a continual change.

*Phil.* Sight therefore does not suggest, or any way inform you, that the visible object you immediately perceive exists at a distance,[a] or will be perceived when you advance farther onward, there being a continued series of visible objects succeeding each other, during the whole time of your approach.

[202] *Hyl.* It does not. But still I know, upon seeing an object, what object I shall perceive after having passed over a certain distance; no matter whether it be exactly the same or no, there is still something of distance suggested in the case.

*Phil.* Good Hylas, do but reflect a little on the point, and then tell me whether there be any more in it than this. From the ideas you actually perceive by sight, you have by experience learned to collect what other ideas you will (according to the standing order of nature) be affected with, after such a certain succession of time and motion.

*Hyl.* Upon the whole, I take it to be nothing else.

*Phil.* Now is it not plain, that if we suppose a man born blind was on a sudden made to see, he could at first have no experience of what may be suggested by sight.[8]

*Hyl.* It is.

*Phil.* He would not then, according to you, have any notion of distance annexed to the things he saw, but would take them for a new set of sensations existing only in his mind.

---

[a] See the Essay towards a New Theory of Vision; and its Vindication. [This reference to the *New Theory of Vision* (1709) and *The Theory of Vision Vindicated and Explained* (1733) was added to the third edition in 1734.]

[8] See *NTV*, 40, and *PHK*, note 17 above.

*Hyl.* It is undeniable.

*Phil.* But to make it still more plain: is not distance a line turned endwise to the eye?[9]

*Hyl.* It is.

*Phil.* And can a line so situated be perceived by sight?

*Hyl.* It cannot.

*Phil.* Does it now therefore follow that distance is not properly and immediately perceived by sight?

*Hyl.* It should seem so.

*Phil.* Again, is it your opinion that colours are at a distance?

*Hyl.* It must be acknowledged, they are only in the mind.

*Phil.* But do not colours appear to the eye as coexisting in the same place with extension and figures?

*Hyl.* They do.

*Phil.* How can you then conclude from sight that figures exist without, when you acknowledge colours do not, the sensible appearance being the very same with regard to both?

*Hyl.* I know not what to answer.

*Phil.* But allowing that distance was truly and immediately perceived by the mind, yet it would not thence follow it existed out of the mind. For whatever is immediately perceived is an idea; and can any idea exist out of the mind?

*Hyl.* To suppose that were absurd; but inform me, Philonous, can we perceive or know nothing beside our ideas?

*Phil.* As for the rational deducing of causes from effects, that is [203] beside our inquiry. And by the senses you can best tell, whether you perceive anything which is not immediately perceived. And I ask you, whether the things immediately perceived are other than your own sensations or ideas? You have indeed more than once, in the course of this conversation, declared yourself on those points; but you seem by this last question to have departed from what you then thought.

*Hyl.* To speak the truth, Philonous, I think there are two kinds of objects, the one perceived immediately, which are likewise called 'ideas'; the other are real things or external objects perceived by the mediation of ideas, which are their images and representations. Now I own, ideas do not exist without the mind; but the latter sort of objects do. I am sorry

---

[9] This repeats an argument borrowed from Molyneux and used in *NTV*, 2.

I did not think of this distinction sooner; it would probably have cut short your discourse.

*Phil.* Are those external objects perceived by sense, or by some other faculty?

*Hyl.* They are perceived by sense.

*Phil.* How! is there anything perceived by sense, which is not immediately perceived?

*Hyl.* Yes, Philonous, in some sort there is. For example, when I look on a picture or statue of Julius Caesar, I may be said after a manner to perceive him (though not immediately) by my senses.

*Phil.* It seems then, you will have our ideas, which alone are immediately perceived, to be pictures of external things; and that these also are perceived by sense, inasmuch as they have a conformity or resemblance to our ideas.

*Hyl.* That is my meaning.

*Phil.* And in the same way that Julius Caesar, in himself invisible, is nevertheless perceived by sight, real things, in themselves imperceptible, are perceived by sense.

*Hyl.* In the very same.

*Phil.* Tell me, Hylas, when you behold the picture of Julius Caesar, do you see with your eyes any more than some colours and figures, with a certain symmetry and composition of the whole?

*Hyl.* Nothing else.

*Phil.* And would not a man, who had never known anything of Julius [204] Caesar, see as much?

*Hyl.* He would.

*Phil.* Consequently he has his sight, and the use of it, in as perfect a degree as you.

*Hyl.* I agree with you.

*Phil.* Whence comes it then that your thoughts are directed to the Roman Emperor, and his are not? This cannot proceed from the sensations or ideas of sense by you then perceived, since you acknowledge you have no advantage over him in that respect. It should seem therefore to proceed from reason and memory, should it not?

*Hyl.* It should.

*Phil.* Consequently it will not follow from that instance that anything is perceived by sense, which is not immediately perceived. Though I grant we may in one acceptation be said to perceive sensible things mediately by sense: that is, when from a frequently perceived connection, the immediate perception of ideas by one sense suggests to the mind others, perhaps belonging to another sense, which are wont to be connected with them. For instance, when I hear a coach drive along the streets, immediately I perceive only the sound; but from the experience I have had that such a sound is connected with a coach, I am said to hear the coach. It is nevertheless evident, that in truth and strictness, nothing can be heard but sound; and the coach is not then properly perceived by sense, but suggested from experience. So likewise when we are said to see a red-hot bar of iron, the solidity and heat of the iron are not the objects of sight, but suggested to the imagination by the colour and figure, which are properly perceived by that sense. In short, those things alone are actually and strictly perceived by any sense, which would have been perceived, in case that same sense had then been first conferred on us. As for other things, it is plain they are only suggested to the mind by experience grounded on former perceptions. But to return to your comparison of Caesar's picture, it is plain, if you keep to that, you must hold the real things, or archetypes of our ideas, are not perceived by sense, but by some internal faculty of the soul, as reason or memory. I would therefore fain know, what arguments you can draw from reason for the existence of what you call 'real things' or 'material objects'. Or whether you remember to have seen them formerly as they are in themselves? or if you have heard or read of any one that did.          [205]

*Hyl.*     I see, Philonous, you are disposed to raillery; but that will never convince me.

*Phil.*     My aim is only to learn from you, the way to come at the knowledge of material beings. Whatever we perceive, is perceived immediately or mediately: by sense, or by reason and reflection. But as you have excluded sense, pray show me what reason you have to believe their existence, or what medium you can possibly make use of, to prove it either to mine or your own understanding.

*Hyl.*     To deal ingenuously, Philonous, now I consider the point, I do not find I can give you any good reason for it. But thus much seems pretty plain, that it is at least possible such things may really exist. And as long as there is no absurdity in supposing them, I am resolved to believe as I did, till you bring good reasons to the contrary.

*Phil.*     What! is it come to this, that you only believe the existence of material objects, and that your belief is founded barely on the possibility of its being true? Then you will have me bring reasons against it, though another would think it reasonable, the proof should lie on him who holds the affirmative. And after all, this very point which you are now resolved to maintain without any reason, is in effect what you have more than once during this discourse seen good reason to give up. But to pass over all this; if I understand you rightly, you say our ideas do not exist without the mind, but that they are copies, images, or representations of certain originals that do.

*Hyl.* You take me right.

*Phil.* They are then like external things.

*Hyl.* They are.

*Phil.* Have those things a stable and permanent nature independent of our senses; or are they in a perpetual change, upon our producing any motions in our bodies, suspending, exerting, or altering our faculties or organs of sense?

*Hyl.* Real things, it is plain, have a fixed and real nature, which remains the same, notwithstanding any change in our senses, or in the posture and motion of our bodies; which indeed may affect the ideas in our minds, but it were absurd to think they had the same effect on things existing without the mind.

*Phil.* How then is it possible, that things perpetually fleeting and variable as our ideas should be copies or images of anything fixed [206] and constant? Or in other words, since all sensible qualities, as size, figure, colour, &c., that is, our ideas, are continually changing upon every alteration in the distance, medium, or instruments of sensation; how can any determinate material objects be properly represented or painted forth by several distinct things, each of which is so different from and unlike the rest? Or if you say it resembles some one only of our ideas, how shall we be able to distinguish the true copy from all the false ones?

*Hyl.* I profess, Philonous, I am at a loss. I know not what to say to this.

*Phil.* But neither is this all. Which are material objects in themselves, perceptible or imperceptible?

*Hyl.* Properly and immediately nothing can be perceived but ideas. All material things therefore are in themselves insensible, and to be perceived only by their ideas.

*Phil.* Ideas then are sensible, and their archetypes or originals insensible.

*Hyl.* Right.

*Phil.* But how can that which is sensible be like that which is insensible? Can a real thing in itself invisible be like a colour, or a real thing which is not audible be like a sound? In a word, can anything be like a sensation or idea, but another sensation or idea?

*Hyl.* I must own, I think not.

*Phil.* Is it possible there should be any doubt in the point? Do you not perfectly know your own ideas?

*Hyl.* I know them perfectly; since what I do not perceive or know can be no part of my idea.

*Phil.* Consider therefore, and examine them, and then tell me if there be anything in them which can exist without the mind, or if you can conceive anything like them existing without the mind.

*Hyl.* Upon inquiry, I find it is impossible for me to conceive or understand how anything but an idea can be like an idea. And it is most evident, that 'no idea can exist without the mind'.

*Phil.* You are therefore by your principles forced to deny the reality of sensible things, since you made it to consist in an absolute existence exterior to the mind. That is to say, you are a downright sceptic. So I have gained my point, which was to show your principles led to scepticism. [207]

*Hyl.* For the present I am, if not entirely convinced, at least silenced.

*Phil.* I would fain know what more you would require in order to a perfect conviction. Have you not had the liberty of explaining yourself all manner of ways? Were any little slips in discourse laid hold and insisted on? Or were you not allowed to retract or reinforce anything you had offered, as best served your purpose? Has not everything you could say been heard and examined with all the fairness imaginable? In a word, have you not in every point been convinced out of your own mouth? And if you can at present discover any flaw in any of your former concessions, or think of any remaining subterfuge, any new distinction, colour, or comment whatsoever, why do you not produce it?

*Hyl.* A little patience, Philonous. I am at present so amazed to see myself ensnared and as it were imprisoned in the labyrinths you have drawn me into, that on the sudden it cannot be expected I should find my way out. You must give me time to look about me, and recollect myself.

*Phil.* Hark; is not this the college bell?

*Hyl.* It rings for prayers.

*Phil.* We will go in then if you please, and meet here again tomorrow morning. In the mean time you may employ your thoughts on this morning's discourse, and try if you can find any fallacy in it, or invent any new means to extricate yourself.

*Hyl.* Agreed.

## The Second Dialogue

*Hylas.* I beg your pardon, Philonous, for not meeting you sooner. All this morning my head was so filled with our late conversation, that I had not leisure to think of the time of the day, or indeed of anything else.

*Philonous.* I am glad you were so intent upon it, in hopes if there were any mistakes in your concessions, or fallacies in my reasonings from them, you will now discover them to me.

*Hyl.* I assure you, I have done nothing ever since I saw you but search after mistakes and fallacies, and with that view have minutely examined the whole series of yesterday's discourse; but all in vain, for the notions it led me into, upon review, appear still more clear and evident. And the more I consider them, the more irresistibly do they force my assent.

*Phil.* And is not this, think you, a sign that they are genuine, that they proceed from nature and are conformable to right reason? Truth and beauty are in this alike, that the strictest survey sets them both off to advantage, while the false lustre of error and disguise cannot endure being reviewed or too nearly inspected.

*Hyl.* I own there is a great deal in what you say. Nor can any one be more entirely satisfied of the truth of those odd consequences, so long as I have in view the reasonings that lead to them. But when these are out of my thoughts, there seems on the other hand something so satisfactory, so natural and intelligible in the modern way of explaining things, that I profess I know not how to reject it.

*Phil.* I know not what way you mean.

*Hyl.* I mean the way of accounting for our sensations or ideas.

*Phil.* How is that?

*Hyl.* It is supposed the soul makes her residence in some part of the brain, from which the nerves take their rise, and are thence extended to all parts of the body, and that outward objects, by the different impressions they make on the organs of sense, communicate certain vibrative

motions to the nerves; and these being filled with spirits, propagate them
to the brain  or seat of the soul, which according to the various impres-    [209]
sions or traces thereby made in the brain, is variously affected with
ideas.[10]

*Phil.*   And call you this an explication of the manner whereby we are
affected with ideas?

*Hyl.*   Why not, Philonous, have you anything to object against it?

*Phil.*   I would first know whether I rightly understand your hypothesis. You make certain traces in the brain to be the causes or occasions of
our ideas. Pray tell me, whether by the 'brain' you mean any sensible
thing?

*Hyl.*   What else think you I could mean?

*Phil.*   Sensible things are all immediately perceivable; and those
things which are immediately perceivable are ideas; and these exist
only in the mind. Thus much you have, if I mistake not, long since
agreed to.

*Hyl.*   I do not deny it.

*Phil.*   The brain therefore you speak of, being a sensible thing, exists
only in the mind. Now, I would fain know whether you think it reasonable to suppose, that one idea or thing existing in the mind, occasions all
other ideas. And if you think so, pray how do you account for the origin
of that primary idea or brain itself?

*Hyl.*   I do not explain the origin of our ideas by that brain which is
perceivable by sense, this being itself only a combination of sensible
ideas, but by another which I imagine.

*Phil.*   But are not things imagined as truly 'in the mind' as things
perceived?

*Hyl.*   I must confess they are.

*Phil.*   It comes therefore to the same thing; and you have been all this
while accounting for ideas, by certain motions or impressions in the
brain, that is, by some alterations in an idea, whether sensible or imaginable it matters not.

*Hyl.*   I begin to suspect my hypothesis.

[10] In the theory of nerves commonly accepted in the seventeenth and eighteenth centuries, the term
'spirits' refers to a very subtle fluid, often called animal spirits, which was believed to flow in thin
tubes throughout the body. Such spirits are completely different to what Berkeley usually means
by 'spirit'. However, Berkeley seems to accept the theory of animal spirits and of mind–brain
interaction in *Siris*, 87.

*Phil.* Beside spirits, all that we know or conceive are our own ideas. When therefore you say, all ideas are occasioned by impressions in the brain, do you conceive this brain or no? If you do, then you talk of ideas imprinted in an idea, causing that same idea, which is absurd. If you do not conceive it, you talk unintelligibly, instead of forming a reasonable [210] hypothesis.

*Hyl.* I now clearly see it was a mere dream. There is nothing in it.

*Phil.* You need not be much concerned at it; for after all, this way of explaining things, as you call it, could never have satisfied any reasonable man. What connection is there between a motion in the nerves, and the sensations of sound or colour in the mind? or how is it possible these should be the effect of that?

*Hyl.* But I could never think it had so little in it, as now it seems to have.

*Phil.* Well then, are you at length satisfied that no sensible things have real existence, and that you are in truth an arrant sceptic?

*Hyl.* It is too plain to be denied.

*Phil.* Look! are not the fields covered with a delightful verdure? Is there not something in the woods and groves, in the rivers and clear springs, that soothes, that delights, that transports the soul? At the prospect of the wide and deep ocean, or some huge mountain whose top is lost in the clouds, or of an old gloomy forest, are not our minds filled with a pleasing horror? Even in rocks and deserts, is there not an agreeable wildness? How sincere a pleasure is it to behold the natural beauties of the earth! To preserve and renew our relish for them, is not the veil of night alternately drawn over her face, and does she not change her dress with the seasons? How aptly are the elements disposed? What variety and use [in the meanest productions of nature]?[11] What delicacy, what beauty, what contrivance in animal and vegetable bodies? How exquisitely are all things suited, as well to their particular ends as to constitute apposite parts of the whole! And while they mutually aid and support, do they not also set off and illustrate each other? Raise now your thoughts from this ball of earth, to all those glorious luminaries that adorn the high arch of heaven. The motion and situation of the planets, are they not admirable for use and order? Were those (miscalled 'erratic') globes ever known to stray, in their repeated journeys through the

[11] The first two editions (1713 and 1725) have: 'in stones and minerals'.

pathless void? Do they not measure areas round the sun ever proportioned to the times? So fixed, so immutable are the laws by which the unseen Author of nature actuates the universe. How vivid and radiant is [211] the lustre of the fixed stars! How magnificent and rich that negligent profusion, with which they appear to be scattered throughout the whole azure vault! Yet if you take the telescope, it brings into your sight a new host of stars that escape the naked eye. Here they seem contiguous and minute, but to a nearer view immense orbs of light at various distances, far sunk in the abyss of space.

Now you must call imagination to your aid. The feeble narrow sense cannot descry innumerable worlds revolving round the central fires, and in those worlds the energy of an all-perfect mind displayed in endless forms. But neither sense nor imagination are big enough to comprehend the boundless extent with all its glittering furniture. Though the labouring mind exert and strain each power to its utmost reach, there still stands out ungrasped a surplusage immeasurable. Yet all the vast bodies that compose this mighty frame, how distant and remote soever, are by some secret mechanism, some divine art and force, linked in a mutual dependence and intercourse with each other, even with this earth, which was almost slipped from my thoughts and lost in the crowd of worlds. Is not the whole system immense, beautiful, glorious beyond expression and beyond thought! What treatment then do those philosophers deserve, who would deprive these noble and delightful scenes of all reality? How should those principles be entertained, that lead us to think all the visible beauty of the creation a false imaginary glare? To be plain, can you expect this scepticism of yours will not be thought extravagantly absurd by all men of sense?

*Hyl.* Other men may think as they please; but for your part, you have nothing to reproach me with. My comfort is, you are as much a sceptic as I am.

*Phil.* There, Hylas, I must beg leave to differ from you.

*Hyl.* What! have you all along agreed to the premises, and do you now deny the conclusion, and leave me to maintain those paradoxes by myself which you led me into? This surely is not fair.

*Phil.* I deny that I agreed with you in those notions that led to scepticism. You indeed said, the reality of sensible things consisted in an 'absolute existence' out of the minds of spirits, or distinct from their being perceived. And pursuant to this notion of reality, you are obliged to deny sensible things any real existence; that is, according to your own [212]

193

definition, you profess yourself a sceptic. But I neither said nor thought the reality of sensible things was to be defined after that manner. To me it is evident, for the reasons you allow of, that sensible things cannot exist otherwise than in a mind or spirit. Whence I conclude, not that they have no real existence, but that seeing they depend not on my thought, and have an existence distinct from being perceived by me, there must be some other mind wherein they exist. As sure therefore as the sensible world really exists, so sure is there an infinite omnipresent spirit who contains and supports it.

*Hyl.* What! this is no more than I and all Christians hold; nay, and all others too who believe there is a God, and that he knows and comprehends all things.

*Phil.* Aye, but here lies the difference. Men commonly believe that all things are known or perceived by God, because they believe the being of a God, whereas I, on the other side, immediately and necessarily conclude the being of a God because all sensible things must be perceived by him.

*Hyl.* But so long as we all believe the same thing, what matter is it how we come by that belief?

*Phil.* But neither do we agree in the same opinion. For philosophers, though they acknowledge all corporeal beings to be perceived by God, yet they attribute to them an absolute subsistence distinct from their being perceived by any mind whatever, which I do not. Besides, is there no difference between saying: 'there is a God, therefore he perceives all things', and saying: 'sensible things do really exist; and if they really exist, they are necessarily perceived by an infinite mind. Therefore there is an infinite mind, or God.' This furnishes you with a direct and immediate demonstration, from a most evident principle, of the being of a God. Divines and philosophers have proved beyond all controversy, from the beauty and usefulness of the several parts of the creation, that it was the workmanship of God. But that, setting aside all help of astronomy and natural philosophy, all contemplation of the contrivance, order, and adjustment of things, an infinite mind should be necessarily inferred from the bare existence of the sensible world, is an advantage peculiar to them only who have made this easy reflection: that the sensible world is that which we perceive by our several senses; and that nothing is perceived by the senses beside ideas; and that no idea or archetype of an idea can exist otherwise than in a mind.

[213]

You may now, without any laborious search into the sciences, without any subtlety of reason or tedious length of discourse, oppose and baffle the most strenuous advocate for atheism. Those miserable refuges, whether in an eternal succession of unthinking causes and effects, or in a fortuitous concourse of atoms; those wild imaginations of Vanini, Hobbes, and Spinoza;[12] in a word the whole system of atheism, is it not entirely overthrown by this single reflection on the repugnancy included in supposing the whole, or any part, even the most rude and shapeless of the visible world, to exist without a mind? Let any one of those abettors of impiety but look into his own thoughts, and there try if he can conceive how so much as a rock, a desert, a chaos, or confused jumble of atoms, how anything at all, either sensible or imaginable, can exist independent of a mind, and he need go no farther to be convinced of his folly. Can anything be fairer than to put a dispute on such an issue, and leave it to a man himself to see if he can conceive, even in thought, what he holds to be true in fact, and from a notional to allow it a real existence?

*Hyl.* It cannot be denied, there is something highly serviceable to religion in what you advance. But do you not think it looks very like a notion entertained by some eminent moderns, of 'seeing all things in God'?[13]

*Phil.* I would gladly know that opinion; pray explain it to me.

*Hyl.* They conceive that the soul, being immaterial, is incapable of being united with material things, so as to perceive them in themselves, but that she perceives them by her union with the substance of God, which being spiritual is therefore purely intelligible, or capable of being the immediate object of a spirit's thought. Besides, the divine essence contains in it perfections correspondent to each created being, and which are for that reason proper to exhibit or represent them to the mind.

*Phil.* I do not understand how our ideas, which are things altogether passive and inert, can be the essence or any part (or like any part) of the essence or substance of God, who is an impassive, indivisible, purely [214] active being. Many more difficulties and objections there are, which

---

[12] Giulio Cesare Vanini (1585–1619) was burned at the stake in Toulouse for atheism and blasphemy. Berkeley concluded that Hobbes (1588–1679) was an atheist because of his materialism, and that Baruch Spinoza (1632–77) was an atheist because he defended the identity of the universe with God.

[13] Refers to Nicolas Malebranche (1638–1715), whose *Search after Truth* was published in 1674–5, or to John Norris, who defended Malebranche's theory in various publications in English, including *An Essay towards the Theory of the Ideal or Intelligible World*, 2 vols. (London, 1701–4).

occur at first view against this hypothesis; but I shall only add that it is liable to all the absurdities of the common hypothesis, in making a created world exist otherwise than in the mind of a spirit. Beside all which, it has this peculiar to itself; that it makes that material world serve no purpose. And if it pass for a good argument against other hypotheses in the sciences, that they suppose nature or the divine wisdom to make something in vain, or do that by tedious roundabout methods, which might have been performed in a much more easy and compendious way, what shall we think of that hypothesis which supposes the whole world made in vain?

*Hyl.* But what say you, are not you too of opinion that we see all things in God? If I mistake not, what you advance comes near it.

*Phil.* [Few men think, yet all will have opinions. Hence men's opinions are superficial and confused. It is nothing strange that tenets, which in themselves are ever so different, should nevertheless be confounded with each other by those who do not consider them attentively. I shall not therefore be surprised if some men imagine that I run into the enthusiasm of Malebranche, though in truth I am very remote from it. He builds on the most abstract general ideas, which I entirely disclaim. He asserts an absolute external world, which I deny. He maintains that we are deceived by our senses, and know not the real natures or the true forms and figures of extended beings; of all which I hold the direct contrary. So that, upon the whole, there are no principles more fundamentally opposite than his and mine. It must be owned][14] I entirely agree with what the holy Scripture says, 'that in God we live, and move, and have our being'.[15] But that we see things in his essence after the manner above set forth, I am far from believing. Take here in brief my meaning. It is evident that the things I perceive are my own ideas, and that no idea can exist unless it be in a mind. Nor is it less plain that these ideas or things by me perceived, either themselves or their archetypes, exist independently of my mind, since I know myself not to be their author, it being out of my power to determine at pleasure what particular ideas I shall be affected with upon opening my eyes or ears. They must [215] therefore exist in some other mind, whose will it is they should be exhibited to me. The things, I say, immediately perceived are ideas or sensations, call them which you will. But how can any idea or sensation

---

[14] The sentences in parentheses were added to the third edition.    [15] Acts 17: 28.

exist in, or be produced by, anything but a mind or spirit? This indeed is inconceivable; and to assert that which is inconceivable is to talk nonsense: is it not?

*Hyl.* Without doubt.

*Phil.* But on the other hand, it is very conceivable that they should exist in, and be produced by, a spirit; since this is no more than I daily experience in myself, inasmuch as I perceive numberless ideas; and by an act of my will can form a great variety of them, and raise them up in my imagination; though it must be confessed, these creatures of the fancy are not altogether so distinct, so strong, vivid, and permanent, as those perceived by my senses, which latter are called 'real things'. From all which I conclude, there is a mind which affects me every moment with all the sensible impressions I perceive. And from the variety, order, and manner of these, I conclude the Author of them to be wise, powerful, and good, beyond comprehension. Mark it well; I do not say, I see things by perceiving that which represents them in the intelligible substance of God. This I do not understand; but I say, the things by me perceived are known by the understanding, and produced by the will, of an infinite spirit. And is not all this most plain and evident? Is there any more in it than what a little observation of our own minds, and that which passes in them, not only enables us to conceive but also obliges us to acknowledge?

*Hyl.* I think I understand you very clearly; and own the proof you give of a Deity seems no less evident than it is surprising. But allowing that God is the supreme and universal cause of all things, yet may not there be still a third nature besides spirits and ideas? May we not admit a subordinate and limited cause of our ideas? In a word, may there not for all that be matter?

*Phil.* How often must I inculcate the same thing? You allow the things immediately perceived by sense to exist nowhere without the mind; but there is nothing perceived by sense, which is not perceived immediately. Therefore there is nothing sensible that exists without the mind. The matter, therefore, which you still insist on is something intelligible, I suppose, something that may be discovered by reason and not by sense.

*Hyl.* You are in the right.                                                   [216]

*Phil.* Pray let me know what reasoning your belief of matter is grounded on, and what this matter is in your present sense of it.

*Hyl.* I find myself affected with various ideas, whereof I know I am not the cause; neither are they the cause of themselves, or of one another, or capable of subsisting by themselves, as being altogether inactive, fleeting, dependent beings. They have therefore some cause distinct from me and them, of which I pretend to know no more than that it is 'the cause of my ideas'. And this thing, whatever it be, I call matter.

*Phil.* Tell me, Hylas, has everyone a liberty to change the current proper signification annexed to a common name in any language? For example, suppose a traveller should tell you that in a certain country men might pass unhurt through the fire; and, upon explaining himself, you found he meant by the word 'fire' that which others call 'water'; or if he should assert there are trees which walk upon two legs, meaning men by the term 'trees'. Would you think this reasonable?

*Hyl.* No; I should think it very absurd. Common custom is the standard of propriety in language. And for any man to affect speaking improperly is to pervert the use of speech, and can never serve to a better purpose than to protract and multiply disputes where there is no difference in opinion.

*Phil.* And does not 'matter', in the common current acceptation of the word, signify an extended, solid, moveable, unthinking, inactive substance?

*Hyl.* It does.

*Phil.* And has it not been made evident that no such substance can possibly exist? And though it should be allowed to exist, yet how can that which is inactive be a cause, or that which is unthinking be a cause of thought? You may indeed, if you please, annex to the word 'matter' a contrary meaning to what is vulgarly received, and tell me you understand by it an unextended, thinking, active being, which is the cause of our ideas. But what else is this than to play with words, and run into that very fault you just now condemned with so much reason? I do by no means find fault with your reasoning, in that you collect a cause from the phenomena; but I deny that the cause deducible by reason can properly be termed 'matter'.

[217] *Hyl.* There is indeed something in what you say. But I am afraid you do not thoroughly comprehend my meaning. I should by no means be thought to deny that God or an Infinite Spirit is the supreme cause of all things. All I contend for is that, subordinate to the supreme agent, there is a cause of a limited and inferior nature, which concurs in the

production of our ideas, not by any act of will or spiritual efficiency but by that kind of action which belongs to matter, *viz.* motion.

*Phil.* I find you are at every turn relapsing into your old exploded conceit, of a moveable and consequently an extended substance existing without the mind. What! Have you already forgot you were convinced, or are you willing I should repeat what has been said on that head? In truth this is not fair dealing in you, still to suppose the being of that which you have so often acknowledged to have no being. But not to insist farther on what has been so largely handled, I ask whether all your ideas are not perfectly passive and inert, including nothing of action in them?

*Hyl.* They are.

*Phil.* And are sensible qualities anything else but ideas?

*Hyl.* How often have I acknowledged that they are not?

*Phil.* But is not motion a sensible quality?

*Hyl.* It is.

*Phil.* Consequently it is no action.

*Hyl.* I agree with you. And indeed it is very plain, that when I stir my finger, it remains passive; but my will, which produced the motion, is active.

*Phil.* Now I desire to know in the first place whether motion, being allowed to be no action, you can conceive any action besides volition; and in the second place, whether to say something and conceive nothing be not to talk nonsense. And lastly, whether having considered the premises, you do not perceive that to suppose any efficient or active cause of our ideas, other than spirit, is highly absurd and unreasonable?

*Hyl.* I give up the point entirely. But though matter may not be a cause, yet what hinders its being an instrument subservient to the supreme agent in the production of our ideas?

*Phil.* An instrument, say you; pray what may be the figure, springs, wheels, and motions of that instrument?

*Hyl.* Those I pretend to determine nothing of, both the substance and its qualities being entirely unknown to me.

*Phil.* What? You are then of opinion, it is made up of unknown parts, [218] that it has unknown motions, and an unknown shape.

*Hyl.* I do not believe that it has any figure or motion at all, being already convinced that no sensible qualities can exist in an unperceiving substance.

*Phil.* But what notion is it possible to frame of an instrument void of all sensible qualities, even extension itself?

*Hyl.* I do not pretend to have any notion of it.

*Phil.* And what reason have you to think this unknown, this inconceivable somewhat, does exist? Is it that you imagine God cannot act as well without it, or that you find by experience the use of some such thing, when you form ideas in your own mind?

*Hyl.* You are always teasing me for reasons of my belief. Pray, what reasons have you not to believe it?

*Phil.* It is for me a sufficient reason not to believe the existence of anything, if I see no reason for believing it. But not to insist on reasons for believing, you will not so much as let me know what it is you would have me believe, since you say you have no manner of notion of it. After all, let me entreat you to consider whether it be like a philosopher, or even like a man of common sense, to pretend to believe you know not what, and you know not why.

*Hyl.* Hold, Philonous. When I tell you matter is an 'instrument', I do not mean altogether nothing. It is true, I know not the particular kind of instrument; but however I have some notion of 'instrument in general', which I apply to it.

*Phil.* But what if it should prove that there is something, even in the most general notion of 'instrument', as taken in a distinct sense from 'cause', which makes the use of it inconsistent with the divine attributes?

*Hyl.* Make that appear, and I shall give up the point.

*Phil.* What mean you by the general nature or notion of 'instrument'?

*Hyl.* That which is common to all particular instruments composes the general notion.

*Phil.* Is it not common to all instruments that they are applied to the doing those things only, which cannot be performed by the mere act of our wills? Thus, for instance, I never use an instrument to move my finger because it is done by a volition. But I should use one, if I were to remove part of a rock or tear up a tree by the roots. Are you of the same

[219] mind? Or can you show any example where an instrument is made use of in producing an effect immediately depending on the will of the agent?

*Hyl.* I own, I cannot.

*Phil.* How therefore can you suppose, that an all-perfect spirit, on whose will all things have an absolute and immediate dependence, should need an instrument in his operations or, not needing it, make use of it? Thus it seems to me that you are obliged to own the use of a lifeless inactive instrument to be incompatible with the infinite perfection of God; that is, by your own confession, to give up the point.

*Hyl.* It does not readily occur what I can answer you.

*Phil.* But methinks you should be ready to own the truth, when it has been fairly proved to you. We indeed, who are beings of finite powers, are forced to make use of instruments. And the use of an instrument shows the agent to be limited by rules of another's prescription, and that he cannot obtain his end but in such a way and by such conditions. Whence it seems a clear consequence, that the supreme unlimited agent uses no tool or instrument at all. The will of an omnipotent spirit is no sooner exerted than executed, without the application of means which, if they are employed by inferior agents, it is not upon account of any real efficacy that is in them, or necessary aptitude to produce any effect, but merely in compliance with the laws of nature, or those conditions prescribed to them by the first cause, who is himself above all limitation or prescription whatsoever.

*Hyl.* I will no longer maintain that matter is an instrument. However, I would not be understood to give up its existence neither; since notwithstanding what has been said, it may still be an occasion.

*Phil.* How many shapes is your matter to take? Or how often must it be proved not to exist, before you are content to part with it? But to say no more of this (though by all the laws of disputation I may justly blame you for so frequently changing the signification of the principal term), I would fain know what you mean by affirming that matter is an occasion, having already denied it to be a cause. And when you have shown in what sense you understand 'occasion', pray in the next place be pleased to show me what reason induces you to believe there is such an occasion of our ideas.

*Hyl.* As to the first point: by 'occasion' I mean an inactive unthink- [220] ing being, at the presence whereof God excites ideas in our minds.

*Phil.* And what may be the nature of that inactive unthinking being?

*Hyl.* I know nothing of its nature.

*Phil.* Proceed then to the second point, and assign some reason why we should allow an existence to this inactive, unthinking, unknown thing.

*Hyl.* When we see ideas produced in our minds after an orderly and constant manner, it is natural to think they have some fixed and regular occasions, at the presence of which they are excited.

*Phil.* You acknowledge then God alone to be the cause of our ideas, and that he causes them at the presence of those occasions.

*Hyl.* That is my opinion.

*Phil.* Those things which you say are present to God, without doubt he perceives.

*Hyl.* Certainly; otherwise they could not be in him an occasion of acting.

*Phil.* Not to insist on your making sense of this hypothesis, or answering all the puzzling questions and difficulties it is liable to: I only ask whether the order and regularity observable in the series of our ideas, or the course of nature, be not sufficiently accounted for by the wisdom and power of God; and whether it does not derogate from those attributes to suppose He is influenced, directed, or put in mind, when and what He is to act, by an unthinking substance. And lastly whether, in case I granted all you contend for, it would make anything to your purpose, it not being easy to conceive how the external and absolute existence of an unthinking substance, distinct from its being perceived, can be inferred from my allowing that there are certain things perceived by the mind of God, which are to Him the occasion of producing ideas in us.

*Hyl.* I am perfectly at a loss what to think, this notion of 'occasion' seeming now altogether as groundless as the rest.

*Phil.* Do you not at length perceive that, in all these different accept-ations of 'matter', you have been only supposing you know not what, for no manner of reason and to no kind of use?

*Hyl.* I freely own myself less fond of my notions, since they have been so accurately examined. But still, methinks I have some confused
[221] perception that there is such a thing as matter.

*Phil.* Either you perceive the being of matter immediately, or medi-ately. If immediately, pray inform me by which of the senses you perceive it. If mediately, let me know by what reasoning it is inferred from those things which you perceive immediately. So much for the perception. Then for the matter itself, I ask whether it is object, *substratum*, cause, instrument, or occasion? You have already pleaded for each of these, shifting your notions, and making matter to appear sometimes in one shape, then in another. And what you have offered has been disapproved and rejected by yourself. If you have anything new to advance, I would gladly hear it.

*Hyl.* I think I have already offered all I had to say on those heads. I am at a loss what more to urge.

*Phil.* And yet you are loath to part with your old prejudice. But to make you quit it more easily, I desire that, beside what has been hitherto suggested, you will farther consider whether, upon supposition that matter exists, you can possibly conceive how you should be affected by it? Or supposing it did not exist, whether it be not evident you might for all that be affected with the same ideas you now are, and consequently have the very same reasons to believe its existence that you now can have.

*Hyl.* I acknowledge it is possible we might perceive all things just as we do now, though there was no matter in the world; neither can I conceive, if there be matter, how it should produce any idea in our minds. And I do farther grant, you have entirely satisfied me, that it is impossible there should be such a thing as matter in any of the foregoing acceptations. But still I cannot help supposing that there is matter in some sense or other. What that is I do not indeed pretend to determine.

*Phil.* I do not expect you should define exactly the nature of that unknown being. Only be pleased to tell me, whether it is a substance; and if so, whether you can suppose a substance without accidents. Or in case you suppose it to have accidents or qualities, I desire you will let me know what those qualities are, at least what is meant by matter's supporting them.

*Hyl.* We have already argued on those points. I have no more to say to them. But to prevent any farther questions, let me tell you: I at present understand by 'matter' neither substance nor accident, thinking nor extended being, neither cause, instrument, nor occasion, but something entirely unknown, distinct from all these. [222]

*Phil.* It seems then you include, in your present notion of matter, nothing but the general abstract idea of 'entity'.

*Hyl.* Nothing else, save only that I superadd to this general idea the negation of all those particular things, qualities, or ideas that I perceive, imagine, or in any wise apprehend.

*Phil.* Pray where do you suppose this unknown matter to exist?

*Hyl.* Oh Philonous! now you think you have entangled me. For if I say it exists in place, then you will infer that it exists in the mind, since it is agreed that place or extension exists only in the mind; but I am not ashamed to own my ignorance. I know not where it exists; only I am sure

*Philosophical Writings*

it exists not in place. There is a negative answer for you; and you must expect no other to all the questions you put for the future about matter.

*Phil.*   Since you will not tell me where it exists, be pleased to inform me after what manner you suppose it to exist, or what you mean by its 'existence'.

*Hyl.*   It neither thinks nor acts, neither perceives, nor is perceived.

*Phil.*   But what is there positive in your abstracted notion of its existence?

*Hyl.*   Upon a nice observation, I do not find I have any positive notion or meaning at all. I tell you again I am not ashamed to own my ignorance. I know not what is meant by its existence, or how it exists.

*Phil.*   Continue, good Hylas, to act the same ingenuous part, and tell me sincerely whether you can frame a distinct idea of entity in general, prescinded from and exclusive of all thinking and corporeal beings, all particular things whatsoever.

*Hyl.*   Hold, let me think a little – I profess, Philonous, I do not find that I can. At first glance methought I had some dilute and airy notion of pure entity in abstract; but upon closer attention it has quite vanished out of sight. The more I think on it, the more am I confirmed in my prudent resolution of giving none but negative answers, and not pretending to the least degree of any positive knowledge or conception of matter, its where, its how, its entity, or anything belonging to it.

*Phil.*   When therefore you speak of the existence of matter, you have not any notion in your mind.

*Hyl.*   None at all.

*Phil.*   Pray tell me if the case stands not thus. At first, from a belief of [223]   material substance you would have it that the immediate objects existed without the mind; then that their archetypes; then causes; next instruments; then occasions; lastly, 'something in general', which being interpreted proves 'nothing'. So matter comes to nothing. What think you, Hylas, is not this a fair summary of your whole proceeding?

*Hyl.*   Be that as it will, yet I still insist upon it, that our not being able to conceive a thing is no argument against its existence.

*Phil.*   That from a cause, effect, operation, sign, or other circumstance, there may reasonably be inferred the existence of a thing not immediately perceived, and that it were absurd for any man to argue against the existence of that thing from his having no direct and positive notion of it, I freely own. But where there is nothing of all this: where neither reason nor revelation induce us to believe the existence of a thing; where we have not even a relative notion of it; where an abstraction is made from perceiving and being perceived, from spirit and idea; lastly, where there is not so much as the most inadequate or faint idea pretended to; I will not indeed thence conclude against the reality of any notion or existence of anything. But my inference shall be that you mean nothing at all, that you employ words to no manner of purpose, without any design or signification whatsoever. And I leave it to you to consider how mere jargon should be treated.

*Hyl.* To deal frankly with you, Philonous, your arguments seem in themselves unanswerable, but they have not so great an effect on me as to produce that entire conviction, that hearty acquiescence which attends demonstration. I find myself still relapsing into an obscure surmise of I know not what, matter.

*Phil.* But are you not sensible, Hylas, that two things must concur to take away all scruple, and work a plenary assent in the mind? Let a visible object be set in never so clear a light, yet if there is any imperfection in the sight, or if the eye is not directed towards it, it will not be distinctly seen. And though a demonstration be never so well grounded and fairly proposed, yet if there is withal a stain of prejudice, or a wrong bias on the understanding, can it be expected on a sudden to perceive clearly and adhere firmly to the truth? No, there is need of time and pains; the attention must be awakened and detained by a frequent repetition of the same thing placed oft in the same, oft in different lights. I have said it already, and find I must still repeat and inculcate, that it is an unaccountable licence you take in pretending to maintain you know not what, [224] for you know not what reason, to you know not what purpose? Can this be paralleled in any art or science, any sect or profession of men? Or is there anything so barefacedly groundless and unreasonable to be met with even in the lowest of common conversation? But perhaps you will still say: matter may exist, though at the same time you neither know what is meant by 'matter' or by its 'existence'. This indeed is surprising, and the more so because it is altogether voluntary, you not being led to it by any one reason; for I challenge you to show me that thing in nature which needs matter to explain or account for it.

*Hyl.* The reality of things cannot be maintained without supposing the existence of matter. And is not this, think you, a good reason why I should be earnest in its defence?

*Phil.* The reality of things! What things, sensible or intelligible?

*Hyl.* Sensible things.

*Phil.* My glove, for example?

*Hyl.* That or any other thing perceived by the senses.

*Phil.* But to fix on some particular thing; is it not a sufficient evidence to me of the existence of this glove, that I see it, and feel it, and wear it? Or if this will not do, how is it possible I should be assured of the reality of this thing, which I actually see in this place, by supposing that some unknown thing, which I never did or can see, exists after an unknown manner, in an unknown place, or in no place at all? How can the supposed reality of that which is intangible be a proof that anything tangible really exists? or of that which is invisible, that any visible thing, or in general of anything which is imperceptible, that a perceptible exists? Do but explain this, and I shall think nothing too hard for you.

*Hyl.* Upon the whole, I am content to own the existence of matter is highly improbable; but the direct and absolute impossibility of it does not appear to me.

*Phil.* But granting matter to be possible, yet, upon that account merely, it can have no more claim to existence than a golden mountain or a centaur.

*Hyl.* I acknowledge it. But still you do not deny it is possible; and that which is possible, for aught you know, may actually exist.

[225]  *Phil.* I deny it to be possible, and have, if I mistake not, evidently proved from your own concessions that it is not. In the common sense of the word 'matter', is there any more implied than an extended, solid, figured, moveable substance existing without the mind? And have not you acknowledged over and over, that you have seen evident reason for denying the possibility of such a substance?

*Hyl.* True, but that is only one sense of the term 'matter'.

*Phil.* But is it not the only proper genuine received sense? And if matter in such a sense be proved impossible, may it not be thought with good grounds absolutely impossible? Else how could anything be proved impossible? Or indeed how could there be any proof at all one way or other, to a man who takes the liberty to unsettle and change the common signification of words?

*Hyl.* I thought philosophers might be allowed to speak more accurately than the vulgar, and were not always confined to the common acceptation of a term.

*Phil.* But this now mentioned is the common received sense among philosophers themselves. But not to insist on that, have you not been allowed to take matter in what sense you pleased? And have you not used this privilege in the utmost extent, sometimes entirely changing, at others leaving out or putting into the definition of it whatever for the present best served your design, contrary to all the known rules of reason and logic? And has not this shifting unfair method of yours spun out our dispute to an unnecessary length, matter having been particularly examined, and by your own confession refuted in each of those senses? And can any more be required to prove the absolute impossibility of a thing than the proving it impossible, in every particular sense, that either you or any one else understands it in?

*Hyl.* But I am not so thoroughly satisfied that you have proved the impossibility of matter in the last most obscure, abstracted, and indefinite sense.

*Phil.* When is a thing shown to be impossible?

*Hyl.* When a repugnancy is demonstrated between the ideas comprehended in its definition.

*Phil.* But where there are no ideas, there no repugnancy can be demonstrated between ideas.

*Hyl.* I agree with you.

*Phil.* Now in that which you call the obscure indefinite sense of the word 'matter' it is plain, by your own confession, there was included no [226] idea at all, no sense except an unknown sense, which is the same thing as none. You are not therefore to expect I should prove a repugnancy between ideas where there are no ideas, or the impossibility of matter taken in an unknown sense, that is no sense at all. My business was only to show, you meant nothing; and this you were brought to own. So that, in all your various senses, you have been shown either to mean nothing at all or, if anything, an absurdity. And if this be not sufficient to prove the impossibility of a thing, I desire you will let me know what is.

*Hyl.* I acknowledge you have proved that matter is impossible; nor do I see what more can be said in defence of it. But at the same time that I give up this, I suspect all my other notions. For surely none could be more seemingly evident than this once was; and yet it now seems as false and absurd as ever it did true before. But I think we have discussed the point sufficiently for the present. The remaining part of the day I would willingly spend, in running over in my thoughts the several heads of this morning's conversation, and tomorrow shall be glad to meet you here again about the same time.

*Phil.* I will not fail to attend you.

## The Third Dialogue

*Philonous.* Tell me, Hylas, what are the fruits of yesterday's meditation? Has it confirmed you in the same mind you were in at parting? or have you since seen cause to change your opinion?

*Hylas.* Truly, my opinion is that all our opinions are alike vain and uncertain. What we approve today, we condemn tomorrow. We keep a stir about knowledge and spend our lives in the pursuit of it when, alas! we know nothing all the while; nor do I think it possible for us ever to know anything in this life. Our faculties are too narrow and too few. Nature certainly never intended us for speculation.

*Phil.* What! say you we can know nothing, Hylas?

*Hyl.* There is not that single thing in the world, whereof we can know the real nature or what it is in itself.

*Phil.* Will you tell me I do not really know what fire or water is?

*Hyl.* You may indeed know that fire appears hot, and water fluid; but this is no more than knowing what sensations are produced in your own mind, upon the application of fire and water to your organs of sense. Their internal constitution, their true and real nature, you are utterly in the dark as to that.

*Phil.* Do I not know this to be a real stone that I stand on, and that which I see before my eyes to be a real tree?

*Hyl.* Know! No, it is impossible you or any man alive should know it. All you know is that you have such a certain idea or appearance in your own mind. But what is this to the real tree or stone? I tell you that colour, figure, and hardness, which you perceive, are not the real natures of those things, or in the least like them. The same may be said of all other real things or corporeal substances which compose the world. They have none of them anything in themselves, like those sensible qualities by us perceived. We should not therefore pretend to affirm or know anything of them, as they are in their own nature.

*Phil.* But surely, Hylas, I can distinguish gold, for example, from iron; and how could this be, if I knew not what either truly was?

*Hyl.* Believe me, Philonous, you can only distinguish between your own ideas. That yellowness, that weight, and other sensible qualities, think you they are really in the gold? They are only relative to the senses, and have no absolute existence in nature. And in pretending to distinguish the species of real things by the appearances in your mind, you may perhaps act as wisely as he that should conclude two men were of a different species because their clothes were not of the same colour.

*Phil.* It seems then we are altogether put off with the appearances of things, and those false ones too. The very meat I eat, and the cloth I wear, have nothing in them like what I see and feel.

*Hyl.* Even so.

*Phil.* But is it not strange the whole world should be thus imposed on, and so foolish as to believe their senses? And yet I know not how it is, but men eat, and drink, and sleep, and perform all the offices of life, as comfortably and conveniently, as if they really knew the things they are conversant about.

*Hyl.* They do so; but you know ordinary practice does not require a nicety of speculative knowledge. Hence the vulgar retain their mistakes, and for all that, make a shift to bustle through the affairs of life. But philosophers know better things.

*Phil.* You mean, they know that they 'know nothing'.

*Hyl.* That is the very top and perfection of human knowledge.

*Phil.* But are you all this while in earnest, Hylas, and are you seriously persuaded that you know nothing real in the world? Suppose you are going to write, would you not call for pen, ink, and paper, like another man; and do you not know what it is you call for?

*Hyl.* How often must I tell you, that I know not the real nature of any one thing in the universe? I may indeed upon occasion make use of pen, ink, and paper. But what any one of them is, in its own true nature, I declare positively I know not. And the same is true with regard to every other corporeal thing. And, what is more, we are not only ignorant of the true and real nature of things but even of their existence. It cannot be denied that we perceive such certain appearances or ideas; but it cannot be concluded from thence that bodies really exist. Nay, now I think on it, [229] I must agreeably to my former concessions farther declare, that it is impossible any real corporeal thing should exist in nature.

*Phil.* You amaze me. Was ever anything more wild and extravagant than the notions you now maintain; and is it not evident you are led into all these extravagancies by the belief of material substance? This makes you dream of those unknown natures in everything. It is this occasions your distinguishing between the reality and sensible appearances of things. It is to this you are indebted for being ignorant of what everybody else knows perfectly well. Nor is this all: you are not only ignorant of the true nature of everything, but you know not whether anything really exists or whether there are any true natures at all, forasmuch as you attribute to your material beings an absolute or external existence, wherein you suppose their reality consists. And as you are forced in the end to acknowledge such an existence means either a direct repugnancy, or nothing at all, it follows that you are obliged to pull down your own hypothesis of material substance, and positively to deny the real existence of any part of the universe. And so you are plunged into the deepest and most deplorable scepticism that ever man was. Tell me, Hylas, is it not as I say?

*Hyl.* I agree with you. Material substance was no more than an hypothesis, and a false and groundless one too. I will no longer spend my breath in defence of it. But whatever hypothesis you advance, or whatsoever scheme of things you introduce in its stead, I doubt not it will appear every whit as false; let me but be allowed to question you upon it. That is, suffer me to serve you in your own kind, and I warrant it shall conduct you, through as many perplexities and contradictions, to the very same state of scepticism that I myself am in at present.

*Phil.* I assure you, Hylas, I do not pretend to frame any hypothesis at all.[16] I am of a vulgar cast, simple enough to believe my senses, and leave things as I find them. To be plain, it is my opinion that the real things are those very things I see and feel, and perceive by my senses. These I know, and finding they answer all the necessities and purposes of life, have no reason to be solicitous about any other unknown beings. A piece of sensible bread, for instance, would stay my stomach better than ten thousand times as much of that insensible, unintelligible, real bread you speak of. It is likewise my opinion that colours and other sensible

[230] qualities are on the objects. I cannot for my life help thinking that snow is white and fire hot. You indeed, who by 'snow' and 'fire' mean certain external, unperceived, unperceiving substances, are in the right to deny

---

[16] This reflects the claim made by Isaac Newton, in the General Scholium to the second edition of the *Principles*: 'I do not feign hypotheses.'

whiteness or heat to be affections inherent in them. But I, who understand by those words the things I see and feel, am obliged to think like
other folks. And as I am no sceptic with regard to the nature of things, so
neither am I as to their existence. That a thing should be really perceived
by my senses, and at the same time not really exist, is to me a plain
contradiction, since I cannot prescind or abstract, even in thought, the
existence of a sensible thing from its being perceived. Wood, stones, fire,
water, flesh, iron, and the like things, which I name and discourse of, are
things that I know; [otherwise I should never have thought of them or
named them].[17] And I should not have known them, but that I perceived
them by my senses; and things perceived by the senses are immediately
perceived; and things immediately perceived are ideas; and ideas cannot
exist without the mind. Their existence therefore consists in being perceived; when therefore they are actually perceived, there can be no doubt
of their existence. Away then with all that scepticism, all those ridiculous
philosophical doubts. What a jest is it for a philosopher to question the
existence of sensible things, till he has it proved to him from the veracity of
God;[18] or to pretend our knowledge in this point falls short of intuition and
demonstration?[19] I might as well doubt of my own being, as of the being of
those things I actually see and feel.

*Hyl.* No so fast, Philonous. You say you cannot conceive how
sensible things should exist without the mind. Do you not?

*Phil.* I do.

*Hyl.* Supposing you were annihilated, cannot you conceive it possible that things perceivable by sense may still exist?

*Phil.* I can, but then it must be in another mind. When I deny
sensible things an existence out of the mind, I do not mean my mind in
particular, but all minds. Now it is plain they have an existence exterior
to my mind, since I find them by experience to be independent of it.
There is therefore some other mind wherein they exist, during the

[17] The phrase in parentheses was omitted from the third edition (1734).
[18] Descartes argued in the Sixth Meditation that he was certain about the existence of external physical
things – not about the existence of 'sensible things' in Berkeley's sense of that phrase – because
God's veracity underpins the reliability of our cognitive faculties. See *Oeuvres*, VII, 78–80.
[19] The target here is Locke's *Essay*, IV, xi, 3, which argues that our knowledge of external physical
objects falls short of the certainty with which we know of relations between ideas, by intuition and
demonstration (*Essay*, IV, ii, 1, 3). Locke's concern was the certainty or otherwise of our knowledge of external things, not of 'sensible things' in Berkeley's sense.

[231] intervals between the times of my perceiving them, as likewise they did before my birth and would do after my supposed annihilation. And as the same is true with regard to all other finite created spirits, it necessarily follows, there is an omnipresent eternal Mind, which knows and comprehends all things and exhibits them to our view in such a manner, and according to such rules as he himself has ordained, and are by us termed the 'laws of nature'.

*Hyl.* Answer me, Philonous. Are all our ideas perfectly inert beings? Or have they any agency included in them?

*Phil.* They are altogether passive and inert.

*Hyl.* And is not God an agent, a being purely active?

*Phil.* I acknowledge it.

*Hyl.* No idea therefore can be like unto, or represent, the nature of God.

*Phil.* It cannot.

*Hyl.* Since therefore you have no idea of the mind of God, how can you conceive it possible that things should exist in his mind? Or, if you can conceive the mind of God without having an idea of it, why may not I be allowed to conceive the existence of matter, notwithstanding that I have no idea of it?

*Phil.* As to your first question, I own I have properly no idea, either of God or any other spirit; for these being active, cannot be represented by things perfectly inert, as our ideas are. I do nevertheless know that I, who am a spirit or thinking substance, exist as certainly as I know my ideas exist. Farther, I know what I mean by the terms 'I' and 'myself'; and I know this immediately, or intuitively, though I do not perceive it as I perceive a triangle, a colour, or a sound. The mind, spirit, or soul, is that indivisible unextended thing, which thinks, acts, and perceives. I say 'indivisible' because unextended; and 'unextended' because extended, figured, moveable things are ideas. And that which perceives ideas, which thinks and wills, is plainly itself no idea, nor like an idea. Ideas are things inactive, and perceived, and spirits a sort of beings altogether different from them. I do not therefore say my soul is an idea or like an idea.

However, taking the word 'idea' in a large sense, my soul may be said to furnish me with an idea, that is, an image or likeness of God, though indeed extremely inadequate. For all the notion I have of God is obtained by reflecting on my own soul, heightening its powers, and removing its imperfections.[20] I have therefore, though not an inactive idea, yet in [232] myself some sort of an active thinking image of the Deity. And though I perceive him not by sense, yet I have a notion of Him or know Him by reflection and reasoning. My own mind and my own ideas I have an immediate knowledge of; and by the help of these, do mediately apprehend the possibility of the existence of other spirits and ideas. Farther, from my own being, and from the dependency I find in myself and my ideas, I do, by an act of reason, necessarily infer the existence of a God, and of all created things in the mind of God. So much for your first question. For the second: I suppose by this time you can answer it yourself. For you neither perceive matter objectively, as you do an inactive being or idea, nor know it, as you do yourself, by a reflex act. Neither do you mediately apprehend it by similitude of the one or the other, nor yet collect it by reasoning from that which you know immediately. All which makes the case of matter widely different from that of the Deity.

[*Hyl.* You say your own soul supplies you with some sort of an idea or image of God. But at the same time you acknowledge you have, properly speaking, no idea of your own soul. You even affirm that spirits are a sort of beings altogether different from ideas; consequently that no idea can be like a spirit. We have therefore no idea of any spirit. You admit nevertheless that there is spiritual substance, although you have no idea of it; while you deny there can be such a thing as material substance, because you have no notion or idea of it. Is this fair dealing? To act consistently, you must either admit matter or reject spirit. What say you to this?

*Phil.* I say in the first place, that I do not deny the existence of material substance, merely because I have no notion of it, but because the notion of it is inconsistent, or in other words, because it is repugnant that there should be a notion of it. Many things, for aught I know, may exist, whereof neither I nor any other man has or can have any idea or notion whatsoever. But then those things must be possible, that is, nothing [233] inconsistent must be included in their definition. I say secondly, that although we believe things to exist which we do not perceive, yet we may not believe that any particular thing exists, without some reason for such

[20] Both Descartes and Locke argued that we construct an idea of God by combining ideas derived from the awareness of ourselves as finite spirits. See Descartes, *Meditations* (*Oeuvres*, VII, 188), and Locke, *Essay*, II, xxiii, 33–5.

belief. But I have no reason for believing the existence of matter. I have no immediate intuition thereof; neither can I mediately from my sensations, ideas, notions, actions or passions, infer an unthinking, unperceiving, inactive substance, either by probable deduction or necessary consequence. Whereas the being of my self, that is, my own soul, mind or thinking principle, I evidently know by reflection. You will forgive me if I repeat the same things in answer to the same objections. In the very notion or definition of material substance, there is included a manifest repugnance and inconsistency. But this cannot be said of the notion of spirit. That ideas should exist in what does not perceive, or be produced by what does not act, is repugnant. But it is no repugnancy to say that a perceiving thing should be the subject of ideas, or an active thing the cause of them. It is granted we have neither an immediate evidence nor a demonstrative knowledge of the existence of other finite spirits; but it will not thence follow that such spirits are on a foot with material substances, if to suppose the one be inconsistent, and it be not inconsistent to suppose the other; if the one can be inferred by no argument, and there is a probability for the other; if we see signs and effects indicating distinct finite agents like ourselves, and see no sign or symptom whatever that leads to a rational belief of matter. I say lastly, that I have a notion of spirit, though I have not, strictly speaking, an idea of it. I do not perceive it as an idea or by means of an idea, but know it by reflection.

*Hyl.* Notwithstanding all you have said, to me it seems that, according to your own way of thinking and in consequence of your own principles, it should follow that you are only a system of floating ideas, without any substance to support them. Words are not to be used without a meaning. And as there is no more meaning in spiritual substance than in material substance, the one is to be exploded as well as the other.[21]

*Phil.* How often must I repeat that I know or am conscious of my own being; and that I myself am not my ideas, but somewhat else, a thinking active principle that perceives, knows, wills, and operates about
[234]    ideas. I know that I, one and the same self, perceive both colours and sounds; that a colour cannot perceive a sound, nor a sound a colour; that I am therefore one individual principle, distinct from colour and sound

---

[21] The equally contestable status of both concepts, of a spiritual substance or a material substance, was argued by Locke in the *Essay*, II, xxiii, 5.

and, for the same reason, from all other sensible things and inert ideas. But I am not in like manner conscious either of the existence or essence of matter. On the contrary, I know that nothing inconsistent can exist, and that the existence of matter implies an inconsistency. Farther, I know what I mean when I affirm that there is a spiritual substance or support of ideas, that is, that a spirit knows and perceives ideas. But I do not know what is meant when it is said that an unperceiving substance has inherent in it and supports either ideas or the archetypes of ideas. There is therefore upon the whole no parity of case between spirit and matter.][22]

*Hyl.* I own myself satisfied in this point. But do you in earnest think the real existence of sensible things consists in their being actually perceived? If so, how comes it that all mankind distinguish between them? Ask the first man you meet, and he shall tell you: 'to be perceived' is one thing, and 'to exist' is another.

*Phil.* I am content, Hylas, to appeal to the common sense of the world for the truth of my notion. Ask the gardener why he thinks yonder cherry tree exists in the garden, and he shall tell you, because he sees and feels it; in a word, because he perceives it by his senses. Ask him why he thinks an orange tree not to be there, and he shall tell you, because he does not perceive it. What he perceives by sense, that he terms a real being, and says it 'is' or 'exists'; but that which is not perceivable, the same, he says, has no being.

*Hyl.* Yes, Philonous, I grant the existence of a sensible thing consists in being perceivable, but not in being actually perceived.

*Phil.* And what is perceivable but an idea? And can an idea exist without being actually perceived? These are points long since agreed between us.

*Hyl.* But be your opinion never so true, yet surely you will not deny it is shocking, and contrary to the commonsense of men. Ask the fellow, [235] whether yonder tree has an existence out of his mind. What answer think you he would make?

*Phil.* The same that I should myself, to wit, that it does exist out of his mind. But then to a Christian it cannot surely be shocking to say, the real tree existing without his mind is truly known and comprehended by (that is, exists in) the infinite mind of God. Probably he may not at first glance be aware of the direct and immediate proof there is of this,

---

[22] The paragraphs in parentheses were added in the third edition (1734).

inasmuch as the very being of a tree, or any other sensible thing, implies a mind wherein it is. But the point itself he cannot deny. The question between the materialists and me is not whether things have a real existence out of the mind of this or that person, but whether they have an absolute existence, distinct from being perceived by God, and exterior to all minds. This indeed some heathens and philosophers have affirmed, but whoever entertains notions of the Deity suitable to the Holy Scriptures will be of another opinion.

*Hyl.* But according to your notions, what difference is there between real things and chimeras formed by the imagination or the visions of a dream, since they are all equally in the mind?

*Phil.* The ideas formed by the imagination are faint and indistinct; they have, besides, an entire dependence on the will. But the ideas perceived by sense, that is, real things, are more vivid and clear, and being imprinted on the mind by a spirit distinct from us, have not a like dependence on our will. There is therefore no danger of confounding these with the foregoing; and there is as little of confounding them with the visions of a dream, which are dim, irregular, and confused. And though they should happen to be never so lively and natural, yet by their not being connected, and of a piece with the preceding and subsequent transactions of our lives, they might easily be distinguished from realities. In short, by whatever method you distinguish things from chimeras on your own scheme, the same, it is evident, will hold also upon mine. For it must be, I presume, by some perceived difference, and I am not for depriving you of any one thing that you perceive.

*Hyl.* But still, Philonous, you hold, there is nothing in the world but spirits and ideas. And this, you must needs acknowledge, sounds very oddly.

*Phil.* I own the word 'idea', not being commonly used for 'thing', sounds something out of the way. My reason for using it was because a

[236]  necessary relation to the mind is understood to be implied by that term; and it is now commonly used by philosophers to denote the immediate objects of the understanding. But however oddly the proposition may sound in words, yet it includes nothing so very strange or shocking in its sense, which in effect amounts to no more than this, to wit: that there are only things perceiving, and things perceived; or that every unthinking being is necessarily, and from the very nature of its existence, perceived by some mind; if not by any finite created mind, yet certainly by the

infinite mind of God, in whom 'we live, and move, and have our being'.[23] Is this as strange as to say, the sensible qualities are not on the objects: or, that we cannot be sure of the existence of things, or know anything of their real natures, though we both see and feel them, and perceive them by all our senses?

*Hyl.* And in consequences of this, must we not think there are no such things as physical or corporeal causes, but that a spirit is the immediate cause of all the phenomena in nature? Can there be anything more extravagant than this?

*Phil.* Yes, it is infinitely more extravagant to say: a thing which is inert operates on the mind, and which is unperceiving, is the cause of our perceptions [without any regard either to consistency, or the old known axiom: 'Nothing can give to another that which it has not itself'].[24] Besides, that which to you, I know not for what reason, seems so extravagant, is no more than the Holy Scriptures assert in a hundred places. In them God is represented as the sole and immediate Author of all those effects, which some heathens and philosophers are wont to ascribe to nature, matter, fate, or the like unthinking principle. This is so much the constant language of Scripture that it were needless to confirm it by citations.

*Hyl.* You are not aware, Philonous, that in making God the immediate author of all the motions in nature, you make him the author of murder, sacrilege, adultery, and the like heinous sins.

*Phil.* In answer to that, I observe first that the imputation of guilt is the same, whether a person commits an action with or without an instrument. In case therefore you suppose God to act by the mediation of an instrument or occasion called 'matter', you as truly make Him the author of sin as I, who think Him the immediate agent in all those operations vulgarly ascribed to nature. I farther observe that sin or moral turpitude [237] does not consist in the outward physical action or motion, but in the internal deviation of the will from the laws of reason and religion. This is plain, in that the killing an enemy in a battle or putting a criminal legally to death is not thought sinful, though the outward act be the very same with that in the case of murder. Since therefore sin does not consist in the physical action, the making God an immediate cause of all such actions is

---

[23] Acts 17: 28.
[24] The phrase in parentheses was omitted from the third edition (1734). The axiom quoted by Berkeley was a Scholastic commonplace, usually in Latin: *nemo dat quod non habet.*

not making him the author of sin. Lastly, I have nowhere said that God is the only agent who produces all the motions in bodies. It is true, I have denied there are any other agents beside spirits; but this is very consistent with allowing to thinking rational beings, in the production of motions, the use of limited powers, ultimately indeed derived from God, but immediately under the direction of their own wills, which is sufficient to entitle them to all the guilt of their actions.

*Hyl.* But the denying matter, Philonous, or corporeal substance: there is the point. You can never persuade me that this is not repugnant to the universal sense of mankind. Were our dispute to be determined by most voices, I am confident you would give up the point without gathering the votes.

*Phil.* I wish both our opinions were fairly stated and submitted to the judgment of men who had plain common sense, without the prejudices of a learned education. Let me be represented as one who trusts his senses, who thinks he knows the things he sees and feels, and entertains no doubts of their existence; and you fairly set forth with all your doubts, your paradoxes, and your scepticism about you, and I shall willingly acquiesce in the determination of any indifferent person. That there is no substance wherein ideas can exist beside spirit, is to me evident. And that the objects immediately perceived are ideas, is on all hands agreed. And that sensible qualities are objects immediately perceived, no one can deny. It is therefore evident there can be no *substratum* of those qualities but spirit, in which they exist, not by way of mode or property, but as a thing perceived in that which perceives it. I deny therefore that there is any unthinking *substratum* of the objects of sense, and in that acceptation that there is any material substance. But if by 'material substance' is meant only sensible body, that which is seen and felt (and the unphilosophical part of the world, I dare say, mean no more), then I am more certain of matter's existence than you or any other philosopher pretend to [238] be. If there be anything which makes the generality of mankind averse from the notions I espouse, it is a misapprehension that I deny the reality of sensible things. But as it is you who are guilty of that and not I, it follows that in truth their aversion is against your notions and not mine. I do therefore assert that I am as certain of my own being, that there are bodies or corporeal substances (meaning the things I perceive by my senses), and that granting this, the bulk of mankind will take no thought about, nor think themselves at all concerned in, the fate of those unknown natures and philosophical quiddities, which some men are so fond of.

*Hyl.* What say you to this? Since, according to you, men judge of the reality of things by their senses, how can a man be mistaken in thinking the moon a plain lucid surface about a foot in diameter; or a square tower, seen at a distance, round; or an oar, with one end in the water, crooked?

*Phil.* He is not mistaken with regard to the ideas he actually perceives, but in the inferences he makes from his present perceptions. Thus in the case of the oar, what he immediately perceives by sight is certainly crooked; and so far he is in the right. But if he thence conclude, that upon taking the oar out of the water he shall perceive the same crookedness, or that it would affect his touch as crooked things are wont to do, in that he is mistaken. In like manner, if he shall conclude from what he perceives in one station, that in case he advances toward the moon or tower, he should still be affected with the like ideas, he is mistaken. But his mistake lies not in what he perceives immediately and at present (it being a manifest contradiction to suppose he should err in respect of that), but in the wrong judgment he makes concerning the ideas he apprehends to be connected with those immediately perceived, or concerning the ideas that, from what he perceives at present, he imagines would be perceived in other circumstances. The case is the same with regard to the Copernican system.[25] We do not here perceive any motion of the earth; but it were erroneous thence to conclude that, in case we were placed at as great a distance from that, as we are now from the other planets, we should not then perceive its motion.

*Hyl.* I understand you, and must needs own you say things plausible enough; but give me leave to put you in mind of one thing. Pray, [239] Philonous, were you not formerly as positive that matter existed, as you are now that it does not?

*Phil.* I was. But here lies the difference. Before, my positiveness was founded without examination, upon prejudice; but now, after inquiry, upon evidence.

*Hyl.* After all, it seems our dispute is rather about words than things. We agree in the thing, but differ in the name. That we are affected with ideas from without is evident; and it is no less evident, that there must be (I will not say archetypes, but) powers without the mind, corresponding to those ideas. And as these powers cannot subsist by themselves, there is

---

[25] The theory that the planets, including the Earth, move in orbits around a central Sun.

some subject of them necessarily to be admitted, which I call 'matter', and you call 'spirit'. This is all the difference.

*Phil.*    Pray, Hylas, is that powerful Being, or subject of powers, extended?

*Hyl.*    It has not extension; but it has the power to raise in you the idea of extension.

*Phil.*    It is therefore itself unextended.

*Hyl.*    I grant it.

*Phil.*    Is it not also active?

*Hyl.*    Without doubt: otherwise, how could we attribute powers to it?

*Phil.*    Now let me ask you two questions: *first*, whether it be agreeable to the usage, either of philosophers or others, to give the name 'matter' to an unextended active being? And *secondly*, whether it be not ridiculously absurd to misapply names contrary to the common use of language?

*Hyl.*    Well then, let it not be called matter, since you will have it so, but some third nature distinct from matter and spirit. For, what reason is there why you should call it spirit? does not the notion of spirit imply that it is thinking as well as active and unextended?

*Phil.*    My reason is this: because I have a mind to have some notion or meaning in what I say. But I have no notion of any action distinct from volition; neither can I conceive volition to be anywhere but in a spirit. Therefore when I speak of an active being, I am obliged to mean a spirit. Besides, what can be plainer than that a thing which has no ideas in itself, cannot impart them to me; and if it has ideas, surely it must be a spirit.

[240]    To make you comprehend the point still more clearly, if it be possible: I assert as well as you that since we are affected from without, we must allow powers to be without in a being distinct from ourselves. So far we are agreed. But then we differ as to the kind of this powerful being. I will have it to be spirit, you matter or I know not what (I may add too, you know not what) third nature. Thus I prove it to be spirit. From the effects I see produced, I conclude there are actions; and because actions, volitions; and because there are volitions, there must be a will. Again, the things I perceive must have an existence, they or their archetypes, out of my mind; but being ideas, neither they nor their archetypes can exist otherwise than in an understanding. There is therefore an understanding. But will and understanding constitute in the strictest sense a mind or spirit. The powerful cause, therefore, of my ideas is in strict propriety of speech a spirit.

*Hyl.* And now I warrant you think you have made the point very clear, little suspecting that what you advance leads directly to a contradiction. Is it not an absurdity to imagine any imperfection in God?

*Phil.* Without a doubt.

*Hyl.* To suffer pain is an imperfection.

*Phil.* It is.

*Hyl.* Are we not sometimes affected with pain and uneasiness by some other being?

*Phil.* We are.

*Hyl.* And have you not said that being is a spirit, and is not that spirit God?

*Phil.* I grant it.

*Hyl.* But you have asserted that whatever ideas we perceive from without, are in the mind which affects us. The ideas therefore of pain and uneasiness are in God or, in other words, God suffers pain; that is to say, there is an imperfection in the Divine Nature, which you acknowledged was absurd. So you are caught in a plain contradiction.

*Phil.* That God knows or understands all things, and that he knows among other things what pain is, even every sort of painful sensation, and what it is for his creatures to suffer pain, I make no question. But that God, though he knows and sometimes causes painful sensations in us, can himself suffer pain, I positively deny. We who are limited and dependent spirits are liable to impressions of sense, the effects of an external agent, which being produced against out wills, are sometimes painful and uneasy. But God, whom no external being can affect, who perceives nothing by sense as we do, whose will is absolute and independent, causing all things, and liable to be thwarted or resisted by nothing: it is evident, such a being as this can suffer nothing, nor be affected with any painful sensation or indeed any sensation at all. We are chained to a body, that is to say, our perceptions are connected with corporeal motions. By the law of our nature we are affected upon every alteration in the nervous parts of our sensible body: which sensible body, rightly considered, is nothing but a complexion of such qualities or ideas, as have no existence distinct from being perceived by a mind. So that this connection of sensations with corporeal motions means no more than a correspondence, in the order of nature, between two sets of ideas or things immediately perceivable. But God is a pure spirit, disengaged from all such sympathy or natural ties. No corporeal motions are attended [241] with the sensations of pain or pleasure in his mind. To know everything knowable is certainly a perfection; but to endure, or suffer, or feel anything by sense, is an imperfection. The former, I say, agrees to God, but not the latter. God knows, or has ideas; but his ideas are not conveyed to him by sense, as ours are. Your not distinguishing, where there is so manifest a difference, makes you fancy you see an absurdity where there is none.

*Hyl.* But all this while you have not considered that the quantity of matter has been demonstrated to be proportional to the gravity of bodies. And what can withstand demonstration?

*Phil.* Let me see how you demonstrate that point?

*Hyl.* I lay it down for a principle, that the moments or quantities of motion in bodies are in a direct compounded reason of the velocities and quantities of matter contained in them. Hence, where the velocities are equal, it follows, the moments are directly as the quantity of matter in each. But it is found by experience that all bodies (bating the small inequalities, arising from the resistance of the air) descend with an equal velocity; the motion therefore of descending bodies, and consequently their gravity, which is the cause or principle of that motion, is proportional to the quantity of matter; which was to be demonstrated.

*Phil.* You lay it down as a self-evident principle that the quantity of [242] motion in any body is proportional to the velocity and matter taken together: and this is made use of to prove a proposition, from whence the existence of matter is inferred. Pray is not this arguing in a circle?

*Hyl.* In the premise I only mean that the motion is proportional to the velocity, jointly with the extension and solidity.

*Phil.* But allowing this to be true, yet it will not thence follow that gravity is proportional to matter, in your philosophic sense of the word; except you take it for granted, that unknown *substratum*, or whatever else you call it, is proportional to those sensible qualities; which to suppose, is plainly begging the question. That there is magnitude and solidity, or resistance, perceived by sense, I readily grant; as likewise that gravity may be proportional to those qualities, I will not dispute. But that either [of] these qualities, as perceived by us, or the powers producing them, do exist in a material *substratum*; this is what I deny, and you indeed affirm, but notwithstanding your demonstration, have not yet proved.

*Hyl.* I shall insist no longer on that point. Do you think, however, you shall persuade me that natural philosophers have been dreaming all this while; pray what becomes of all their hypotheses and explications of the phenomena, which suppose the existence of matter?

*Phil.* What mean you, Hylas, by the 'phenomena'?

*Hyl.* I mean the appearances which I perceive by my senses.

*Phil.* And the appearances perceived by sense, are they not ideas?

*Hyl.* I have told you so a hundred times.

*Phil.* Therefore, to explain the phenomena is to show how we come to be affected with ideas, in that manner and order wherein they are imprinted on our senses. Is it not?

*Hyl.* It is.

*Phil.* Now if you can prove that any philosopher has explained the production of any one idea in our minds by the help of matter, I shall for ever acquiesce and look on all that has been said against it as nothing; but if you cannot, it is in vain to urge the explication of phenomena. That a being endowed with knowledge and will should produce or exhibit ideas is easily understood. But that a being which is utterly destitute of these faculties should be able to produce ideas, or in any sort to affect an intelligence, this I can never understand. This I say, though we had some positive conception of matter, though we knew its qualities and could [243] comprehend its existence, would yet be so far from explaining things that it is itself the most inexplicable thing in the world. And yet for all this, it will not follow that philosophers have been doing nothing; for by observing and reasoning upon the connection of ideas, they discover the laws and methods of nature, which is a part of knowledge both useful and entertaining.

*Hyl.* After all, can it be supposed God would deceive all mankind? Do you imagine he would have induced the whole world to believe the being of matter, if there was no such thing?

*Phil.* That every epidemical opinion arising from prejudice, or passion, or thoughtlessness, may be imputed to God as the Author of it, I believe you will not affirm. Whatsoever opinion we father on him, it must be either because he has discovered it to us by supernatural revelation, or because it is so evident to our natural faculties, which were framed and given us by God, that it is impossible we should withhold our assent from it. But where is the revelation, or where is the evidence that extorts the belief of matter? Nay, how does it appear that matter, taken for something distinct from what we perceive by our senses, is thought to exist by all mankind, or indeed by any except a few philosophers who do not know what they would be at? Your question supposes these points are clear; and when you have cleared them, I shall think myself obliged to give you another answer. In the mean time let it suffice that I tell you, I do not suppose God has deceived mankind at all.

*Hyl.* But the novelty, Philonous, the novelty! There lies the danger. New notions should always be discountenanced; they unsettle men's minds, and nobody knows where they will end.

*Phil.* Why the rejecting a notion that has no foundation either in sense or in reason, or in divine authority, should be thought to unsettle the belief of such opinions as are grounded on all or any of these, I cannot imagine. That innovations in government and religion are dangerous, and ought to be discountenanced, I freely own. But is there the like reason why they should be discouraged in philosophy? The making anything known which was unknown before, is an innovation in knowl-

[244] edge; and if all such innovations had been forbidden, men would [not][26] have made a notable progress in the arts and sciences. But it is none of my business to plead for novelties and paradoxes. That the qualities we perceive are not on the objects; that we must not believe our senses; that we know nothing of the real nature of things, and can never be assured even of their existence; that real colours and sounds are nothing but certain unknown figures and motions; that motions are in themselves neither swift nor slow; that there are in bodies absolute extensions, without any particular magnitude or figure; that a thing stupid, thought-less and inactive, operates on a spirit; that the least particle of a body contains innumerable extended parts. These are the novelties, these are the strange notions which shock the genuine uncorrupted judgment of all mankind and, being once admitted, embarrass the mind with endless doubts and difficulties. And it is against these and the like innovations [that] I endeavour to vindicate common sense. It is true, in doing this, I may perhaps be obliged to use some ambages and ways of speech not common. But if my notions are once thoroughly understood, that which is most singular in them will in effect be found to amount to no more than this: that it is absolutely impossible, and a plain contradiction to suppose, any unthinking being should exist without being perceived by a mind. And if this notion be singular, it is a shame it should be so at this time of day, and in a Christian country.

---

[26] The word 'not' seems to have been omitted in the first three editions.

*Hyl.*   As for the difficulties other opinions may be liable to, those are out of the question. It is your business to defend your own opinion. Can anything be plainer than that you are for changing all things into ideas? – you, I say, who are not ashamed to charge me with scepticism. This is so plain, there is no denying it.

*Phil.*   You mistake me. I am not for changing things into ideas, but rather ideas into things; since those immediate objects of perception, which according to you are only appearances of things, I take to be the real things themselves.

*Hyl.*   Things! you may pretend what you please; but it is certain, you leave us nothing but the empty forms of things, the outside only which strikes the senses.

*Phil.*   What you call the empty forms and outside of things seems to me the very things themselves. Nor are they empty or incomplete otherwise than, upon your supposition, that matter is an essential part of   [245] all corporeal things. We both therefore agree in this, that we perceive only sensible forms; but herein we differ, you will have them to be empty appearances, I real beings. In short you do not trust your senses, I do.

*Hyl.*   You say you believe your senses; and seem to applaud yourself that in this you agree with the vulgar. According to you, therefore, the true nature of a thing is discovered by the senses. If so, whence comes that disagreement? Why is not the same figure, and other sensible qualities, perceived all manner of ways? And why should we use a microscope, the better to discover the true nature of a body, if it were discoverable to the naked eye?

*Phil.*   Strictly speaking, Hylas, we do not see the same object that we feel; neither is the same object perceived by the microscope, which was by the naked eye. But in case every variation was thought sufficient to constitute a new kind or individual, the endless number or confusion of names would render language impracticable. Therefore to avoid this as well as other inconveniences which are obvious upon a little thought, men combine together several ideas, apprehended by divers senses, or by the same sense at different times or in different circumstances, but observed however to have some connection in nature, either with respect to co-existence or succession; all which they refer to one name and consider as one thing. Hence it follows that when I examine by my other senses a thing I have seen, it is not in order to understand better the same object which I had perceived by sight, the object of one sense not being perceived by the other senses. And when I look through a microscope, it is not that I may perceive more clearly what I perceived already with my bare eyes, the object perceived by the glass being quite different from the former. But in both cases my aim is only to know what ideas are connected together; and the more a man knows of the connection of ideas, the more he is said to know of the nature of things.

What therefore if our ideas are variable; what if our senses are not in all circumstances affected with the same appearances? It will not thence follow, they are not to be trusted, or that they are inconsistent either with themselves or anything else, except it be with your preconceived notion of (I know not what) one single, unchanged, unperceivable, real nature, marked by each name; which prejudice seems to have taken its rise from [246] not rightly understanding the common language of men speaking of several distinct ideas, as united into one thing by the mind. And indeed there is cause to suspect several erroneous conceits of the philosophers are owing to the same original, while they began to build their schemes, not so much on notions as words, which were framed by the vulgar, merely for conveniency and dispatch in the common actions of life, without any regard to speculation.

*Hyl.* Methinks I apprehend your meaning.

*Phil.* It is your opinion, the ideas we perceive by our senses are not real things but images or copies of them. Our knowledge therefore is no farther real, than as our ideas are the true representations of those originals. But as these supposed originals are in themselves unknown, it is impossible to know how far our ideas resemble them, or whether they resemble them at all. We cannot therefore be sure we have any real knowledge. Farther, as our ideas are perpetually varied, without any change in the supposed real things, it necessarily follows they cannot all be true copies of them. Or if some are, and others are not, it is impossible to distinguish the former from the latter. And this plunges us yet deeper in uncertainty. Again, when we consider the point, we cannot conceive how any idea, or anything like an idea, should have an absolute existence out of a mind; nor consequently, according to you, how there should be any real thing in nature. The result of all which is that we are thrown into the most hopeless and abandoned scepticism. Now give me leave to ask you, *first*, whether your referring ideas to certain absolutely existing unperceived substances, as their originals, be not the source of all this scepticism? *Secondly*, whether you are informed, either by sense or reason, of the existence of those unknown originals? And in case you are not, whether it be not absurd to suppose them? *Thirdly*, whether, upon inquiry, you find there is anything distinctly conceived or meant by the 'absolute or external existence of unperceiving substances'? *Lastly*, whether the premises considered, it be not the wisest way to follow nature, trust our senses, and laying aside all anxious thought about unknown natures or substances, admit with the vulgar those for real things which are perceived by the senses?

*Hyl.* For the present, I have no inclination to the answering part. I would much rather see how you can get over what follows. Pray are not the objects perceived by the senses of one, likewise perceivable to others [247] present? If there were an hundred more here, they would all see the garden, the trees, the flowers, as I see them. But they are not in the same manner affected with the ideas I frame in my imagination. Does not this make a difference between the former sort of objects and the latter?

*Phil.* I grant it does. Nor have I ever denied a difference between the objects of sense and those of imagination. But what would you infer from thence? You cannot say that sensible objects exist unperceived, because they are perceived by many?

*Hyl.* I own I can make nothing of that objection; but it has led me into another. Is it not your opinion that, by our senses, we perceive only the ideas existing in our minds?

*Phil.* It is.

*Hyl.* But the same idea, which is in my mind, cannot be in yours or in any other mind. Does it not therefore follow from your principles that no two can see the same thing? And is not this highly absurd?

*Phil.* If the term 'same' be taken in the vulgar acceptation, it is certain (and not at all repugnant to the principles I maintain) that different persons may perceive the same thing, or the same thing or idea exist in different minds. Words are of arbitrary imposition; and since men are used to apply the word 'same' where no distinction or variety is perceived, and I do not pretend to alter their perceptions, it follows that, as men have said before, 'several saw the same thing', so they may upon like occasions still continue to use the same phrase, without any deviation either from propriety of language or the truth of things. But if the term 'same' be used in the acceptation of philosophers, who pretend to an abstracted notion of identity, then, according to their sundry definitions of this notion (for it is not yet agreed wherein that philosophic identity consists), it may or may not be possible for divers persons to perceive the same thing. But whether philosophers shall think fit to call a thing the 'same' or no is, I conceive, of small importance.

Let us suppose several men together, all endued with the same faculties, and consequently affected in like sort by their senses, and who had yet never known the use of language; they would without question agree in their perceptions. Though perhaps, when they came to the use of speech, some regarding the uniformness of what was perceived, might [248] call it the 'same' thing; others especially regarding the diversity of persons who perceived, might choose the denomination of different things. But who sees not that all the dispute is about a word: to wit, whether what is perceived by different persons may yet have the term 'same' applied to it? Or suppose a house, whose walls or outward shell remaining unaltered, the chambers are all pulled down and new ones built in their place, and that you should call this the 'same', and I should say it was not the 'same' house. Would we not for all this perfectly agree in our thoughts of the house, considered in itself? And would not all the difference consist in a sound? If you should say, we differed in our notions; for that you superadded to your idea of the house the simple abstracted ideas of identity, whereas I did not; I would tell you I know not what you mean by that 'abstracted idea of identity', and should desire you to look into your own thoughts and be sure you understood yourself. –

Why so silent, Hylas? Are you not yet satisfied, men may dispute about identity and diversity, without any real difference in their thoughts and opinions, abstracted from names? Take this farther reflection with you: that whether matter be allowed to exist or no, the case is exactly the same as to the point in hand. For the materialists themselves acknowledge what we immediately perceive by our senses to be our own ideas. Your difficulty, therefore, that no two see the same thing makes equally against the materialists and me.

*Hyl.* But they suppose an external archetype to which, referring their several ideas, they may truly be said to perceive the same thing.

*Phil.* And (not to mention your having discarded those archetypes) so may you suppose an external archetype on my principles; external, I mean, to your own mind, though indeed it must be supposed to exist in that mind which comprehends all things; but then this serves all the ends of identity, as well as if it existed out of a mind. And I am sure you yourself will not say, it is less intelligible.

*Hyl.* You have indeed clearly satisfied me, either that there is no difficulty at bottom in this point; or if there be, that it makes equally against both opinions.

*Phil.* But that which makes equally against two contradictory opinions can be a proof against neither.

*Hyl.* I acknowledge it. But after all, Philonous, when I consider the [249] substance of what you advance against scepticism, it amounts to no more than this. We are sure that we really see, hear, feel; in a word, that we are affected with sensible impressions.

*Phil.* And how are we concerned any farther? I see this cherry, I feel it, I taste it; and I am sure nothing cannot be seen, or felt, or tasted. It is therefore real. Take away the sensations of softness, moisture, redness, tartness, and you take away the cherry. Since it is not a being distinct from sensations, a cherry, I say, is nothing but a congeries of sensible impressions or ideas perceived by various senses; which ideas are united into one thing (or have one name given them) by the mind, because they are observed to attend each other. Thus when the palate is affected with such a particular taste, the sight is affected with a red colour, the touch with roundness, softness, &c. Hence when I see, and feel, and taste, in such sundry certain manners, I am sure the cherry exists or is real, its reality being in my opinion nothing abstracted from those sensations. But if by the word 'cherry' you mean an unknown nature distinct from all those sensible qualities, and by its existence something distinct from its being perceived, then indeed I own, neither you nor I, nor anyone else, can be sure it exists.

*Hyl.* But what would you say, Philonous, if I should bring the very same reasons against the existence of sensible things in a mind, which you have offered against their existing in a material *substratum*?

*Phil.* When I see your reasons, you shall hear what I have to say to them.

*Hyl.* Is the mind extended or unextended?

*Phil.* Unextended, without doubt.

*Hyl.* Do you say the things you perceive are in your mind?

*Phil.* They are.

*Hyl.* Again, have I not heard you speak of sensible impressions?

*Phil.* I believe you may.

*Hyl.* Explain to me now, O Philonous! how it is possible there should be room for all those trees and houses to exist in your mind? Can extended things be contained in that which is unextended? Or are we to imagine impressions made on a thing void of all solidity? You cannot say objects are in your mind, as books in your study, or that things are imprinted on it as the figure of a seal upon wax. In what sense therefore are we to understand those expressions? Explain me this, if you can, and I shall then be able to answer all those queries you formerly put to me about my *substratum*.

[250]

*Phil.*   Look you, Hylas, when I speak of objects as existing in the mind or imprinted on the senses, I would not be understood in the gross literal sense, as when bodies are said to exist in a place or a seal to make an impression upon wax. My meaning is only that the mind comprehends or perceives them; and that it is affected from without or by some being distinct from itself. This is my explication of your difficulty; and how it can serve to make your tenet of an unperceiving material *substratum* intelligible, I would fain know.

*Hyl.*   Nay, if that be all, I confess I do not see what use can be made of it. But are you not guilty of some abuse of language in this?

*Phil.*   None at all. It is no more than common custom, which you know is the rule of language, has authorised, nothing being more usual than for philosophers to speak of the immediate objects of the understanding as things existing in the mind. Nor is there anything in this, but what is conformable to the general analogy of language; most part of the mental operations being signified by words borrowed from sensible things, as is plain in the terms 'comprehend', 'reflect', 'discourse', &c. which, being applied to the mind, must not be taken in their gross original sense.

*Hyl.*   You have, I own, satisfied me in this point. But there still remains one great difficulty, which I know not how you will get over. And indeed it is of such importance that, if you could solve all others without being able to find a solution for this, you must never expect to make me a proselyte to your principles.

*Phil.*   Let me know this mighty difficulty.

*Hyl.*   The Scripture account of the creation is what appears to me utterly irreconcilable with your notions.[27] Moses tells us of a creation: a creation of what? Of ideas? No, certainly, but of things, of real things,

---

[27] Refers to the account in Genesis, Chapter I.

solid corporeal substances. Bring your principles to agree with this, and I shall perhaps agree with you.

*Phil.*　Moses mentions the sun, moon, and stars, earth and sea, plants and animals: that all these do really exist, and were in the beginning created by God, I make no question. If by 'ideas' you mean fictions and fancies of the mind, then these are no ideas. If by 'ideas' you mean immediate objects of the understanding, or sensible things which cannot exist unperceived or out of a mind, then these things are ideas. But whether you do or do not call them 'ideas', it matters little. The difference is only about a name. And whether that name be retained or rejected, the sense, the truth, and reality of things continues the same. In common talk, the objects of our senses are not termed 'ideas' but 'things'. Call them so still, provided you do not attribute to them any absolute external existence, and I shall never quarrel with you for a word. The creation therefore I allow to have been a creation of things, of 'real' things. Neither is this the least inconsistent with my principles, as is evident from what I have now said; and would have been evident to you without this, if you had not forgotten what had been so often said before. But as for solid corporeal substances, I desire you to show where Moses makes any mention of them; and if they should be mentioned by him or any other inspired writer, it would still be incumbent on you to show those words were not taken in the vulgar acceptation, for things falling under our senses, but in the philosophic acceptation, for matter or an unknown quiddity with an absolute existence. When you have proved these points, then (and not till then) may you bring the authority of Moses into our dispute.

*Hyl.*　It is in vain to dispute about a point so clear. I am content to refer it to your own conscience. Are you not satisfied there is some peculiar repugnancy between the Mosaic account of the creation and your notions?

*Phil.*　If all possible sense, which can be put on the first chapter of Genesis, may be conceived as consistently with my principles as any other, then it has no peculiar repugnancy with them. But there is no sense you may not as well conceive, believing as I do. Since, beside spirits, all you conceive are ideas; and the existence of these I do not deny. Neither do you pretend they exist without the mind.

*Hyl.*　Pray let me see any sense you can understand it in.

*Phil.*　Why, I imagine that if I had been present at the creation, I should have seen things produced into being; that is, become perceptible,

[251]

in the order described by the sacred historian. I ever before believed the Mosaic account of the creation, and now find no alteration in my manner [252] of believing it. When things are said to begin or end their existence, we do not mean this with regard to God, but His creatures. All objects are eternally known by God or, which is the same thing, have an eternal existence in His mind. But when things, before imperceptible to creatures, are, by a decree of God made perceptible to them, then are they said to begin a relative existence with respect to created minds. Upon reading therefore the Mosaic account of the creation, I understand that the several parts of the world became gradually perceivable to finite spirits, endowed with proper faculties; so that whoever such were present, they were in truth perceived by them. This is the literal obvious sense suggested to me by the words of the Holy Scripture, in which is included no mention or no thought either of *substratum*, instrument, occasion, or absolute existence. And upon inquiry, I doubt not it will be found that most plain honest men, who believe the creation, never think of those things any more than I. What metaphysical sense you may understand it in, you only can tell.

*Hyl.* But, Philonous, you do not seem to be aware that you allow created things, in the beginning, only a relative and, consequently, hypothetical being: that is to say, upon supposition there were men to perceive them, without which they have no actuality of absolute existence wherein creation might terminate. Is it not therefore according to you plainly impossible, the creation of any inanimate creatures should precede that of man? And is not this directly contrary to the Mosaic account?[28]

*Phil.* In answer to that I say, *first*, created beings might begin to exist in the mind of other created intelligences beside men. You will not therefore be able to prove any contradiction between Moses and my notions, unless you first show there was no other order of finite created spirits in being before man.[29] I say farther, in case we conceive the creation, as we should at this time a parcel of plants or vegetables of all sorts, produced by an invisible power, in a desert where nobody was present: that this way of explaining or conceiving it is consistent with my principles, since they deprive you of nothing, either sensible or imaginable: that it exactly suits with the common,

[28] According to the Genesis account, God created inanimate objects and animals during the first five days of creation, before human beings were created on the sixth day. Hylas questions how, according to Philonous's theory, such inanimate things could have existed prior to the existence of human perceivers.

[29] For example, if God had created angels before he created men, the 'ideas' that resulted from creation could have existed in their minds.

natural, undebauched notions of mankind: that it manifests the dependence of all things on God; and consequently has all the good effect or influence, which it is possible that important article of our faith should have in making men humble, thankful, and resigned to their Creator. I say moreover, that in this naked conception of things, divested of words, there will not be found [253] any notion of what you call the 'actuality of absolute existence'. You may indeed raise a dust with those terms, and so lengthen our dispute to no purpose. But I entreat you calmly to look into your own thoughts, and then tell me if they are not an useless and unintelligible jargon.

*Hyl.*    I own, I have no very clear notion annexed to them. But what say you to this? Do you not make the existence of sensible things consist in their being in the mind? And were not all things eternally in the mind of God? Did they not therefore exist from all eternity, according to you? And how could that which was eternal be created in time? Can anything be clearer or better connected than this?

*Phil.*    And are not you too of opinion that God knew all things from eternity?

*Hyl.*    I am.

*Phil.*    Consequently they always had a being in the Divine Intellect.

*Hyl.*    This I acknowledge.

*Phil.*    By your own confession, therefore, nothing is new or begins to be, in respect of the mind of God. So we are agreed in that point.

*Hyl.*    What shall we make then of the creation?

*Phil.*    May we not understand it to have been entirely in respect of finite spirits, so that things, with regard to us, may properly be said to begin their existence or be created when God decreed they should become perceptible to intelligent creatures, in that order and manner which he then established and we now call the laws of nature? You may call this a 'relative' or 'hypo- thetical existence' if you please. But so long as it supplies us with the most natural, obvious, and literal sense of the Mosaic history of the creation; so long as it answers all the religious ends of that great article; in a word, so long as you can assign no other sense or meaning in its stead; why should we reject this? Is it to comply with a ridiculous sceptical humour of making everything nonsense and unintelligible? I am sure you cannot say, it is for the glory of God. For allowing it to be a thing possible and conceivable that the corporeal world should have an absolute subsistence extrinsical to the mind of God, as well as to the minds of all created spirits: yet how could this set forth either the immensity or omniscience of the Deity, or the necessary and immediate

[254]   dependence of all things on him? Nay, would it not rather seem to derogate from those attributes?

*Hyl.*   Well, but as to this decree of God's for making things perceptible, what say you, Philonous: is it not plain, God did either execute that decree from all eternity, or at some certain time began to will what he had not actually willed before, but only designed to will. If the former, then there could be no creation or beginning of existence in finite things. If the latter, then we must acknowledge something new to befall the Deity, which implies a sort of change; and all change argues imperfection.

*Phil.*   Pray consider what you are doing. Is it not evident, this objection concludes equally against a creation in any sense; nay, against every other act of the Deity, discoverable by the light of nature? None of which can we conceive otherwise than as performed in time and having a beginning. God is a being of transcendent and unlimited perfections; his nature therefore is incomprehensible to finite spirits. It is not therefore to be expected that any man, whether materialist or immaterialist, should have exactly just notions of the Deity, his attributes, and ways of operation. If then you would infer anything against me, your difficulty must not be drawn from the inadequateness of our conceptions of the Divine Nature, which is unavoidable on any scheme; but from the denial of matter, of which there is not one word, directly or indirectly, in what you have now objected.

*Hyl.*   I must acknowledge, the difficulties you are concerned to clear are such only as arise from the non-existence of matter and are peculiar to that notion. So far you are in the right. But I cannot by any means bring myself to think there is no such peculiar repugnancy between the creation and your opinion; though indeed where to fix it, I do not distinctly know.

*Phil.*   What would you have! do I not acknowledge a twofold state of things, the one ectypal or natural, the other archetypal and eternal? The former was created in time; the latter existed from everlasting in the mind of God. Is not this agreeable to the common notions of divines? or is any more than this necessary in order to conceive the creation? But you suspect some peculiar repugnancy, though you know not where it lies. To take away all possibility of scruple in the case, do but consider this one

[255]   point. Either you are not able to conceive the creation on any hypothesis whatsoever; and if so, there is no ground for dislike or complaint against my particular opinion on that score: or you are able to conceive it; and, if so, why not on my principles, since thereby nothing conceivable is taken away? You have all along been allowed the full scope of sense,

imagination, and reason. Whatever therefore you could before apprehend, either immediately or mediately by your senses, or by ratiocination
from your senses; whatever you could perceive, imagine, or understand,
remains still with you. If therefore the notion you have of the creation by
other principles be intelligible, you have it still upon mine; if it be not
intelligible, I conceive it to be no notion at all; and so there is no loss of it.
And indeed it seems to me very plain that the supposition of matter, that is,
a thing perfectly unknown and inconceivable, cannot serve to make us
conceive anything. And I hope it need not be proved to you that, if the
existence of matter does not make the creation conceivable, the creation's
being without it inconceivable can be no objection against its non-existence.

*Hyl.* I confess, Philonous, you have almost satisfied me in this point
of the creation.

*Phil.* I would fain know why you are not quite satisfied. You tell me
indeed of a repugnancy between the Mosaic history and immaterialism;
but you know not where it lies. Is this reasonable, Hylas? Can you expect
I should solve a difficulty without knowing what it is? But to pass by all
that, would not a man think you were assured there is no repugnancy
between the received notions of materialists and the inspired writings?

*Hyl.* And so I am.

*Phil.* Ought the historical part of Scripture to be understood in a plain
obvious sense, or in a sense which is metaphysical and out of the way?

*Hyl.* In the plain sense, doubtless.

*Phil.* When Moses speaks of herbs, earth, water, &c. as having been
created by God, think you not the sensible things, commonly signified by
those words, are suggested to every unphilosophical reader?

*Hyl.* I cannot help thinking so.

*Phil.* And are not all ideas, or things perceived by sense, to be denied
a real existence by the doctrine of the materialists?

*Hyl.* This I have already acknowledged.

*Phil.* The creation therefore, according to them, was not the creation [256]
of things sensible, which have only a relative being, but of certain unknown
natures, which have an absolute being, wherein creation might terminate?

*Hyl.* True.

*Phil.* Is it not therefore evident, the asserters of matter destroy the
plain obvious sense of Moses, with which their notions are utterly
inconsistent, and instead of it obtrude on us I know not what, something
equally unintelligible to themselves and me?

*Hyl.* I cannot contradict you.

*Phil.* Moses tells us of a creation. A creation of what? of unknown quiddities, or occasions, or *substratums?* No, certainly; but of things obvious to the senses. You must first reconcile this with your notions, if you expect I should be reconciled to them.

*Hyl.* I see you can assault me with my own weapons.

*Phil.* Then as to 'absolute existence': was there ever known a more jejune notion than that? Something it is, so abstracted and unintelligible, that you have frankly owned you could not conceive it, much less explain anything by it. But allowing matter to exist, and the notion of absolute existence to be as clear as light; yet was this ever known to make the creation more credible? Nay, has it not furnished the atheists and infidels of all ages with the most plausible argument against a creation? That a corporeal substance, which has an absolute existence without the minds of spirits, should be produced out of nothing by the mere will of a spirit, has been looked upon as a thing so contrary to all reason, so impossible and absurd, that not only the most celebrated among the ancients but even divers modern and Christian philosophers have thought matter co-eternal with the Deity.[30] Lay these things together, and then judge you whether materialism disposes men to believe the creation of things.

*Hyl.* I own, Philonous, I think it does not. This of the creation is the last objection I can think of, and I must needs own it has been sufficiently answered as well as the rest. Nothing now remains to be overcome, but a sort of unaccountable backwardness that I find in myself toward your notions.

*Phil.* When a man is swayed, he knows not why, to one side of the question, can this, think you, be anything else but the effect of prejudice, [257] which never fails to attend old and rooted notions? And indeed in this respect I cannot deny the belief of matter to have very much the advantage over the contrary opinion, with men of a learned education.

*Hyl.* I confess it seems to be as you say.

*Phil.* As a balance therefore to this weight of prejudice, let us throw into the scale the great advantages that arise from the belief of immaterialism, both in regard to religion and human learning. The being of a God, and incorruptibility of the soul, those great articles of religion, are they not proved with the clearest and most immediate evidence? When

---

[30] Berkeley had discussed belief in the eternity of matter in *PHK*, 92.

I say the being of a God, I do not mean an obscure general cause of things, whereof we have no conception, but God in the strict and proper sense of the word. A being whose spirituality, omnipresence, providence, omniscience, infinite power and goodness, are as conspicuous as the existence of sensible things, of which (notwithstanding the fallacious pretences and affected scruples of sceptics) there is no more reason to doubt than of our own being.

Then with relation to human sciences: in natural philosophy, what intricacies, what obscurities, what contradictions, has the belief of matter led men into! To say nothing of the numberless disputes about its extent, continuity, homogeneity, gravity, divisibility, &c. do they not pretend to explain all things by bodies operating on bodies, according to the laws of motion? And yet, are they able to comprehend how any one should move another? Nay, admitting there was no difficulty in reconciling the notion of an inert being with a cause, or in conceiving how an accident might pass from one body to another, yet by all their strained thoughts and extravagant suppositions, have they been able to reach the mechanical production of any one animal or vegetable body? Can they account, by the laws of motion, for sounds, tastes, smells, or colours, or for the regular course of things? Have they accounted by physical principles for the aptitude and contrivance, even of the most inconsiderable parts of the universe? But laying aside matter and corporeal causes, and admitting only the efficiency of an all-perfect mind, are not all the effects of nature easy and intelligible? If the phenomena are nothing else but ideas; God is a spirit, but matter an unintelligent, unperceiving being. If they demonstrate an unlimited power in their cause; God is active and omnipotent, but matter an inert mass. If the order, regularity, and usefulness of them, can never be sufficiently admired; God is infinitely wise and provident, [258] but matter destitute of all contrivance and design. These surely are great advantages in physics. Not to mention that the apprehension of a distant Deity naturally disposes men to a negligence in their moral actions, which they would be more cautious of in case they thought Him immediately present, and acting on their minds without the interposition of matter or unthinking second causes.[31]

---

[31] If God is described as the 'first cause' of everything that happens, then 'second causes' are all other causes which contribute to produce various effects, including human minds.

Then in metaphysics; what difficulties concerning entity in abstract, substantial forms, hylarchic principles, plastic natures, [substance and accident],[32] principle of individuation, possibility of matter's thinking, origin of ideas, the manner how two independent substances, so widely different as spirit and matter, should mutually operate on each other? What difficulties, I say, and endless disquisitions concerning these and innumerable other the like points, do we escape by supposing only spirits and ideas?

Even the mathematics themselves, if we take away the absolute existence of extended things, become much more clear and easy; the most shocking paradoxes and intricate speculations in those sciences, depending on the infinite divisibility of finite extension, which depends on that supposition.

But what need is there to insist on the particular sciences? Is not that opposition to all science whatsoever, that frenzy of the ancient and modern sceptics, built on the same foundation? Or can you produce so much as one argument against the reality of corporeal things, or in behalf of that avowed utter ignorance of their natures, which does not suppose their reality to consist in an external absolute existence? Upon this supposition, indeed, the objections from the change of colours in a pigeon's neck, or the appearances of a broken oar in the water, must be allowed to have weight. But those and the like objections vanish if we do not maintain the being of absolute external originals, but place the reality of things in ideas, fleeting indeed, and changeable: however not changed at random, but according to the fixed order of nature. For herein consists that constancy and truth of things, which secures all the concerns of life, and distinguishes that which
[259] is real from the irregular visions of the fancy.

*Hyl.* I agree to all you have now said, and must own that nothing can incline me to embrace your opinion more than the advantages I see it is attended with. I am by nature lazy, and this would be a mighty abridgment in knowledge. What doubts, what hypotheses, what labyrinths of amusement, what fields of disputation, what an ocean of false learning, may be avoided by that single notion of immaterialism?

*Phil.* After all, is there anything farther remaining to be done? You may remember you promised to embrace that opinion which upon

---

[32] The phrase in parentheses replaced, in the third edition, 'subjects and adjuncts' in the first two editions.

examination should appear most agreeable to common sense, and remote from scepticism. This by your own confession is that which denies matter, or the absolute existence of corporeal things. Nor is this all; the same notion has been proved several ways, viewed in different lights, pursued in its consequences, and all objections against it cleared. Can there be a greater evidence of its truth? Or is it possible it should have all the marks of a true opinion and yet be false?

*Hyl.* I own myself entirely satisfied for the present in all respects. But what security can I have that I shall still continue the same full assent to your opinion, and that no unthought-of objection or difficulty will occur hereafter?

*Phil.* Pray, Hylas, do you in other cases, when a point is once evidently proved, withhold your assent on account of objections or difficulties it may be liable to? Are the difficulties that attend the doctrine of incommensurable quantities, of the angle of contact, of the asymptotes to curves, or the like, sufficient to make you hold out against mathematical demonstration? Or will you disbelieve the providence of God, because there may be some particular things which you know not how to reconcile with it? If there are difficulties attending immaterialism, there are at the same time direct and evident proofs for it. But for the existence of matter, there is not one proof, and far more numerous and insurmountable objections lie against it. But where are those mighty difficulties you insist on? Alas! you know not where or what they are; something which may possibly occur hereafter. If this be a sufficient pretence for withholding your full assent, you should never yield it to any proposition, how free soever from exceptions, how clearly and solidly soever demonstrated.

*Hyl.* You have satisfied me, Philonous.

*Phil.* But to arm you against all future objections, do but consider that which bears equally hard on two contradictory opinions can be a [260] proof against neither. Whenever therefore any difficulty occurs, try if you can find a solution for it on the hypothesis of the materialists. Be not deceived by words, but sound your own thoughts. And in case you cannot conceive it easier by the help of materialism, it is plain it can be no objection against immaterialism. Had you proceeded all along by this rule, you would probably have spared yourself abundance of trouble in objecting; since of all your difficulties I challenge you to show one that is explained by matter; nay, which is not more unintelligible with than without that supposition, and consequently makes rather against than for it. You should consider, in each particular, whether the difficulty arises from the non-existence of matter. If it does not, you might as well argue from the infinite divisibility of extension against the divine prescience, as from such a difficulty against immaterialism. And yet upon recollection I believe you will find this to have been often, if not always, the case.

You should likewise take heed not to argue on a *petitio principii*.[33] One is apt to say, the unknown substances ought to be esteemed real things, rather than the ideas in our minds: and who can tell but the unthinking external substance may concur as a cause or instrument in the production of our ideas? But is this not proceeding on a supposition that there are such external substances? And to suppose this, is it not begging the question?

But above all things you should beware of imposing on yourself by that vulgar sophism, which is called *ignoratio elenchi*.[34] You talked often as if you thought I maintained the non-existence of sensible things, whereas in truth no one can be more thoroughly assured of their existence than I am; and it is you who doubt – I should have said, positively deny it. Everything that is seen, felt, heard, or any way perceived by the senses, is, on the principles I embrace, a real being, but not on yours. Remember, the matter you contend for is an unknown somewhat (if indeed it may be termed 'somewhat'), which is quite stripped of all sensible qualities, and can neither be perceived by sense nor apprehended by the mind. Remember, I say, that it is not any object which is hard or soft, hot or cold, blue or white, round or square, &c. For all these things I affirm do exist. Though indeed I deny they have an existence distinct from being perceived, or that they exist out of all minds whatsoever. Think on these points; let them be attentively considered and still kept in view. Otherwise you will not comprehend the state of the question; [261] without which your objections will always be wide of the mark, and instead of mine, may possibly be directed (as more than once they have been) against your own notions.

*Hyl.* I must needs own, Philonous, nothing seems to have kept me from agreeing with you more than this same 'mistaking the question'. In denying matter, at first glimpse I am tempted to imagine you deny the things we see and feel, but upon reflection find there is no ground

[33] The fallacy of begging the question, or assuming what needs to be proved.
[34] The fallacy of appearing to refute a position by arguing against a different thesis, thereby missing the target. Berkeley translates the phrase below as 'mistaking the question'.

for it. What think you therefore of retaining the name 'matter' and applying it to sensible things? This may be done without any change in your sentiments; and believe me it would be a means of reconciling them to some persons, who may be more shocked at an innovation in words than in opinion.

*Phil.* With all my heart: retain the word 'matter' and apply it to the objects of sense, if you please, provided you do not attribute to them any subsistence distinct from their being perceived. I shall never quarrel with you for an expression. 'Matter' or 'material substance' are terms introduced by philosophers; and, as used by them, imply a sort of independency, or a subsistence distinct from being perceived by a mind, but are never used by common people; or if ever, it is to signify the immediate objects of sense. One would think therefore, so long as the names of all particular things, with the terms 'sensible' 'substance', 'body', 'stuff', and the like, are retained, the word 'matter' should be never missed in common talk. And in philosophical discourses it seems the best way to leave it quite out; since there is not perhaps any one thing that has more favoured and strengthened the depraved bent of the mind toward atheism than the use of that general confused term.

*Hyl.* Well put, Philonous, since I am content to give up the notion of an unthinking substance exterior to the mind, I think you ought not to deny me the privilege of using the word 'matter' as I please, and annexing it to a collection of sensible qualities subsisting only in the mind. I freely own there is no other substance, in a strict sense, than spirit. But I have been so long accustomed to the term 'matter' that I know not how to part with it. To say 'there is no matter in the world' is still shocking to me. Whereas to say there is no matter, if by that term be meant an unthinking substance existing without the mind; but if by 'matter' is meant some sensible thing, whose existence consists in being perceived, then there is 'matter': this distinction gives it quite another turn, and men will come into your notions with small difficulty when they are proposed in that [262] manner. For after all, the controversy about 'matter' in the strict acceptation of it lies altogether between you and the philosophers, whose principles, I acknowledge, are not near so natural or so agreeable to the common sense of mankind and Holy Scripture as yours. There is nothing we either desire or shun but as it makes, or is apprehended to make, some part of our happiness or misery. But what has happiness or misery, joy or grief, pleasure or pain, to do with absolute existence, or with unknown entities, abstracted from all relation to us? It is evident, things regard us only as they are pleasing or displeasing; and they can please or displease, only so far forth as they are perceived. Farther therefore we are not concerned; and thus far you leave things as you found them. Yet still there is something new in this doctrine. It is plain, I do not now think with the philosophers, nor yet altogether with the vulgar. I would know how the case stands in that respect: precisely, what you have added to, or altered in my former notions.

*Phil.* I do not pretend to be a setter-up of 'new notions'. My endeavours tend only to unite, and place in a clearer light, that truth which was before shared between the vulgar and the philosophers: the former being of opinion, that 'those things they immediately perceive are the real things'; and the latter, that 'the things immediately perceived, are ideas which exist only in the mind'. Which two notions, put together, do in effect constitute the substance of what I advance.

*Hyl.* I have been a long time distrusting my senses; methought I saw things by a dim light, and through false glasses. Now the glasses are removed, and a new light breaks in upon my understanding. I am clearly convinced that I see things in their native forms, and am no longer in pain about their unknown natures or absolute existence. This is the state I find myself in at present, though indeed the course that brought me to it, I do not yet thoroughly comprehend. You set out upon the same principles that Academics, Cartesians, and the like sects usually do; and for a long time it looked as if you were advancing their philosophical scepticism; but in the end your conclusions are directly opposite to theirs.

[263]     *Phil.* You see, Hylas, the water of yonder fountain, how it is forced upwards, in a round column, to a certain height; at which it breaks and falls back into the basin from whence it rose, its ascent as well as descent, proceeding from the same uniform law or principle of gravitation. Just so, the same principles which at first view lead to scepticism, pursued to a certain point, bring men back to common sense.

# An Essay on Motion

## Motion; or the Principle and Nature of Motion, and the Cause of the Communication of Motions
### 1721

1 In order to discover the truth, it is most important that one avoid being obstructed by words that are poorly understood. While almost all philosophers give this advice, few observe it. Indeed, it hardly seems so difficult to do so, especially in matters that are discussed by physicists, in which sensation, experience, and geometrical reasoning are appropriate. Accordingly, having set aside as much as possible all prejudices that result either from common ways of speaking or from the authority of philosophers, one should examine diligently the very nature of things. Nor should the authority of anyone be valued to such an extent that their words and terms are prized even when nothing clear and certain can be found in them.

2 The consideration of motion troubled the minds of ancient philosophers very much; their thinking gave rise to a range of views which were extraordinarily difficult (not to say absurd) and which, since they have now lapsed almost into desuetude, hardly deserve that we devote much effort to discussing them. However, among the more recent and more sensible philosophers of the current period, when they discuss motion, one finds many words whose meaning is too abstract and obscure, such as the 'solicitation of gravity', 'striving', 'dead forces', etc.[1] These terms

---

[1] Berkeley gives as examples the following Latin terms: *solicitatio gravitatis, conatus, vires mortuae*, which are taken from Leibniz, *Specimen Dynamicum*. See G. W. Leibniz, *Philosophical Papers and Letters*, trans. Leroy E. Loemker, 2nd edn. (Dordrecht: Reidel, 1976), 435–52.

shroud in darkness what is otherwise very learned, and provide an opening for opinions that are as abhorrent to the truth as to the common sense of people. It is necessary to examine these carefully, in the interests of truth rather than with a view to refuting them.

3    'Solicitude' and 'effort' or 'striving' are terms that can be applied truthfully only to animate things. When they are attributed to other things, they must be understood in a metaphorical sense. A philosopher, however, should abstain from metaphor. Besides, anyone who considers this issue seriously acknowledges that these words have no clear and distinct meaning, apart from some affection of the mind or motion of a body.

4    Whenever we support heavy bodies, we experience in ourselves an effort, fatigue and discomfort. We also perceive, in falling bodies, an accelerating motion towards the earth's centre. We do not perceive anything else by using our senses. By reason, however, we conclude that there is some cause or principle of these phenomena, which is commonly called gravity. But since the cause of the descent of heavy bodies is unseen and unknown, gravity in that sense cannot be said to be a sensible quality. It is therefore an occult quality. But one can scarcely – and, indeed, not even scarcely – conceive what an occult quality is, or how any quality could act or could do anything. Therefore, it would be better if, having dismissed occult qualities, people were to consider only sensible effects and if their minds were focused on particular and concrete things, that is, on things themselves, by omitting abstract terms from their thinking (although they are useful for speaking).

5    'Force' is attributed to bodies in a similar way. This word is used, however, as if it signified a quality that is known and is distinct from motion, shape, and every other sensible thing and from every affection of living things. However, anyone who examines the matter more closely will find that it is nothing other than an occult quality. Animal effort and bodies in motion are commonly seen as symptoms of this occult quality, and as that by which force is measured.

6    It is obvious, therefore, that it is a mistake to propose gravity or force as the principle of motion; for how is it possible to know that principle more clearly by calling it an occult quality? The fact that it is itself occult explains nothing. Let us also overlook the fact that an unknown active cause could more correctly be called a substance rather than a quality. Besides, 'force', 'gravity' and similar words are more

frequently and not improperly used in a concrete way to signify a body that is moved, the difficulty of resisting, etc. However, when they are used by philosophers to signify certain natures, which are cut off and abstracted from all those things, which are not the objects of the senses and cannot be understood by any power of the mind or framed by the imagination, then they eventually give rise to errors and confusion.

7   The fact that general and abstract terms seem to be useful in speaking leads many people into error, even though they do not adequately understand the power of such terms. These terms were in fact invented partly to abbreviate speech, and partly by philosophers for teaching purposes – not because they are appropriate to the natures of things, which exist indeed in the concrete and singular, but because they are suitable for teaching disciplines to the extent that they make notions or, at least, propositions universal.

8   We assume, for the most part, that corporeal force is something that is easy to conceive. However, those who have looked into the issue carefully hold a different view, which becomes clear from the remarkable obscurity of the words with which they labour when they try to explain it. Torricelli says that force and impetus are certain abstract and subtle realities, and that they are quintessences that are included in corporeal substances, as if in a magical vase of Circe.[2] Likewise, Leibniz writes as follows when he explains the nature of force: 'primitive, active force, which is nothing other than the first entelechy, corresponds to the soul or substantial form.'[a] When even the greatest men are forced to indulge in abstractions, they search for words that have no definite meaning and are mere shadows of scholastic entities. It would be possible to provide other examples, and indeed quite a few, from the writings of more recent authors, which make it abundantly clear that metaphysical abstractions have not surrendered everywhere to mechanics and experiments but continue to provide a useless occupation for philosophers.

---

[a] See the *Acta Eruditorum* of Leipzig [published in April 1695; see *Specimen Dynamicum*, in Loemker, 426].

[2] Evangelista Torricelli (1608–47). His *Lezioni Academiche* were edited by Tommaso Bonaventuri and published posthumously. See *Lezioni Academiche* (Florence: Guiducci, 1740), Lecture IV, p. 27.

9  From this source various absurdities arise, one of which is that 'the force of percussion, no matter how small, is infinitely great.'³ This clearly assumes that gravity is some real quality that is different from all others, and that gravitation is an action of this quality that, in some sense, is really distinct from motion. However, the least percussion produces an effect that is greater than the greatest gravitation without motion. In other words, the former gives rise to some motion, the latter to none.ᵇ

10  Nevertheless it must be accepted that no force is itself felt immediately, nor can it be known and measured otherwise than by its effect. But a dead force or simple gravitation has no effect in a body at rest that is not subject to an actual change. A percussion, however, does have some effect. Therefore, since forces are proportional to their effects, one may conclude that a dead force is no force. However, we may not conclude for that reason that the force of a percussion is infinite, for one should not consider any positive quantity as infinite because it exceeds, by an infinite ratio, a null quantity or nothing.

11  The force of gravitation cannot be distinguished from momentum, but there is no momentum without speed, since it is mass multiplied by speed. Besides, it is impossible to understand speed without motion, nor therefore the force of gravitation. Thus, no force is known except by its action, by which it is measured; and we cannot separate the action of a body from motion. Therefore, as long as a heavy body changes the shape of lead that is placed underneath it or the shape of a string, it is moved. When it is at rest, however, it does not act or, what is the same thing, it is prevented from acting. In brief, the terms 'dead force' and 'gravitation' mean nothing, although they are assumed to signify something that, by a metaphysical abstraction, is distinct from a moving body, from what is moved, and from motion and rest.

ᵇ  See Galileo's experiments, and what Torricelli, Borelli and others have written about the infinite force of percussion. [Refers to Galileo's *Two New Sciences* (1638), trans. Stillman Drake (Madison, WI: University of Wisconsin Press, 1974), 281–306; Lectures 2–4 of Torricelli's *Lezioni* (see note 2); and Borelli's *De vi percussionis* (note 7).]

³  This is attributed indiscriminately to a number of authors, none of whom is identified more precisely. Galileo writes in *Two New Sciences*: 'one may deduce the force of impact to be infinite – or rather, let us say indeterminate, or undeterminable, being now greater and now less, according as it is applied to a greater or lesser resistance' (*Opere*, ed. Favaro, vol. VIII, 328; Eng. trans. 288). Leibniz endorses this in *Specimen Dynamicum*: 'This is what Galileo meant when, in an enigmatic way, he called the force of impact infinite as compared with the simple impulsion of gravity' (Loemker, 438). Torricelli discusses, in Lecture II, p. 4, the view attributed to Galileo that '*l'energia della percossa debba essere infinita.*'

**12**   If someone said that a weight suspended from or placed on a string acts on the string because it prevents it from recovering its original shape by an elastic force, I reply, by the same reasoning, that any lower body acts on a higher body that rests on it because it prevents the latter from descending. However, if one body prevents another body from existing in the same place that it occupies, that cannot be said to be an action of that body.

**13**   We sometimes feel the pressure of a gravitating body. That unpleasant sensation results from the communication of the motion of that heavy body to the nerves and fibres of our body and, since they remain in the same place, the sensation should be attributed to the percussion that is received. In these matters we labour under many serious prejudices, but they are controlled or, preferably, completely banished by keen and repeated reflection.

**14**   To prove that some quantity is infinite, one must show that some finite homogeneous part is contained in it infinitely many times. But, according to those authors who support the infinite force of percussion, a dead force is not related to the force of percussion as a part to a whole, but as a point to a line. One could add many things to this discussion, but I am concerned not to become prolix.

**15**   Well-known disputes that have greatly exercised learned men can be resolved by the principles that have been proposed above. One such example would be the controversy about the proportion between forces.[4] One side, while conceding that momenta, motions, and impetus are simply proportional to velocities for a given mass, claims that the forces are proportional to the squares of the velocities. Everyone sees that this opinion assumes that the force of a body is distinct from its momentum, its motion and its impetus, and that it collapses once that assumption is rejected.

**16**   To make it more clearly apparent that a strange confusion has been introduced by metaphysical abstractions into what is taught about motion, let us see how great is the difference between the notions of force and impetus proposed by famous men. Leibniz confuses impetus with motion.[5] According to Newton, impetus is in fact identical with the force

---

[4] The controversy between Leibniz and the Cartesians about the so-called *vis viva*.

[5] Berkeley seems to misrepresent Leibniz's view, according to which '*Impetus*, however, consists in the product of the mass of the body by its velocity, and so its quantity is that which Cartesians usually call the quantity of motion' (Loemker, 427).

of inertia.[6] Borelli claims that impetus is nothing other than a degree of velocity.[7] Some hold that impetus and effort are distinct from each other, while others hold that they do not differ. Many understand motive force as proportional to motion, while some believe that there is another force apart from motive force, and that it is measured in a different way insofar as they think it is proportional to the square of the velocity multiplied by the mass. But it would be an endless task to continue with this review.

17 'Force', 'gravity', 'attraction' and similar terms are useful for reasoning, and for calculations about motion and moving bodies, but not for understanding the simple nature of motion itself or for designating so many distinct qualities. It is certainly true that, in the case of attraction, it was used by Newton not as a genuine physical quality but merely as a mathematical hypothesis.[8] And even Leibniz, when he distinguished elementary effort or striving from impetus, confesses that those entities are not really found in the natures of things but are constructed by abstraction.[9]

18 This is similar to the understanding of the composition and resolution of direct forces into oblique forces by using the diagonal and sides of a parallelogram. These serve the needs of mechanics and computation; but it is one thing to be used in computation and mathematical demonstrations, and something else to reveal the nature of things.

19 Among recent authors, many hold the view that motion is neither destroyed nor generated anew but that the quantity of motion always remains the same. Aristotle raised this query a long time ago, whether

[6] Newton, *Principles*, Definition III, vol. I, 2.
[7] Giovanni Alfonso Borelli (1608–79), *De vi percussionis, et motionibus naturalibus* (Leiden: P. Vander, 1686), 2–3.
[8] Newton's use of gravity is more complicated than Berkeley reports. Newton claimed, in the General Scholium which was added to the second edition of the *Principles*, that 'we have explained the phenomena of the heavens and of our sea by the power of gravity, but have not yet assigned the cause of this power' (Vol. II, 546). For that purpose, 'to us it is enough that gravity does really exist, and act according to the laws which we have explained, and abundantly serves to account for all the motions of the celestial bodies, and of our sea' (ibid., 547). However, following publication of the *Principles*, Newton continued to look for an adequate explanation of gravity. See Introduction above.
[9] *Specimen Dynamicum*: 'Hence the nisus is obviously twofold, an elementary or infinitely small one which I also call a *solicitation*, and one formed by the continuation or repetition of these elementary impulsions, that is, the impetus itself. But I do not mean that these mathematical entities are really found in nature as such, but merely that they are means of making accurate calculations of an abstract mental kind' (Loemker, 438).

motion is created and perishes, or whether it is eternal.[c] It is evidently clear to the senses that perceptible motion perishes, but it seems as if these authors hold that the same impetus, effort, or sum of forces remains the same. Consequently Borelli claims that the force in a percussion is neither diminished nor increased, and even that contrary quantities of impetus are received and retained in the same body. Likewise, Leibniz claims that effort is present everywhere and always in matter and, where it is not apparent to the senses, it can be understood by reason.[10] It must be accepted, however, that these things are very abstract and obscure, and are almost like substantial forms and entelechies.

**20** Those who use a hylarchic principle, the needs of nature, an appetite or, finally, a natural instinct to explain the cause or origin of motion should be understood merely as having said something rather than as having understood anything.[11] Nor are others very different who, in order to assign a cause to the acceleration of falling bodies, have supposed that 'the parts of the earth move themselves, or even that there are spirits like forms implanted in them.'[12] Likewise, he is not very different who said that 'it is necessary to posit in bodies, in addition to solid extension, something else from which the consideration of forces may arise.'[13] All these people either say nothing that is specific and determinate or, if they do say something, it would be as difficult to explain it as the very things for which it is introduced as a source of explanation.

**21** Those things which are neither apparent to the senses nor intelligible to reason are used in vain to explain nature. Let us therefore see what is suggested by the senses, by experience, and finally by reason when supported by them. There are two supreme classes of things,

---

[c] Physics, Book 8 [250$^b$11–14].

[10] *Specimen Dynamicum*: 'This nisus sometimes appears to the senses, and is in my opinion to be understood on rational grounds, as present everywhere in matter, even where it does not appear to sense' (Loemker, 435).

[11] *Specimen Dynamicum*: 'Meanwhile, even though I hold that an active principle which is superior to material concepts and, so to speak, vital exists everywhere in bodies, I do not agree with Henry More and other men distinguished for piety and spirit, who make use of some Archeus – I know not what – or hylarchic principle, even to explain phenomena; as if there are some things in nature which cannot be explained mechanically and as if those who undertake a mechanical explanation aim to deny incorporeal beings, with a suspicion of impiety' (Loemker, 441). Cf. R. Cudworth, *The True Intellectual System of the Universe* (New York: Garland, 1978), 668 (1st edn. 1673).

[12] Borelli, *De vi percussionis*, Proposition 87.

[13] Leibniz wrote something rather different in the *Specimen Dynamicum*: 'I found a proof that something more than magnitude and impenetrability must be assumed in body, from which an interpretation of forces may arise' (Loemker, 440).

body and soul. We know with the help of the senses something that is extended, solid, mobile, shaped, and endowed with other qualities that strike the senses; however, we know by a certain internal consciousness something that is sentient, perceiving, and intelligent. Besides, we see that these things are obviously different from each other, and that they are very heterogeneous. I speak, however, of things that are known; there is no point in speaking about things that are unknown.

**22** The whole of that which we know, and to which we have given the name 'body', contains nothing in itself that could be the principle or efficient cause of motion, because impenetrability, extension, or shape include or connote no power to produce motion. On the contrary, when we review one by one not only those qualities but whatever other qualities that bodies possess, we see that they are all genuinely passive, and that there is nothing active in them which could be understood in any way as the source and principle of motion. As for gravity, we have already shown above that this term signifies nothing that is known and distinct from the sensible effect for which we seek a cause. Surely, when we say that a body is heavy we understand nothing except that it is carried downward, without thinking at all about the cause of this sensible effect.

**23** It is possible therefore boldly to proclaim about body, as something that is established, that it is not the principle of motion. Thus if anyone claims that, in addition to solid extension and its modifications, the term 'body' includes in its meaning some occult quality, some force, form or essence, he should be left to the useless occupation of disputing without ideas and abusing words that do not express anything distinctly. It seems to be a more reliable way of philosophizing to abstain, as much as possible, from abstract and general notions (on the assumption that things that cannot be understood could be called notions).

**24** We know what is contained in the idea of body. It has been established, however, that what is known to be present in body is not a principle of motion. Those who, in addition, invent something unknown in body of which they have no idea and which they call the principle of motion, are really saying nothing other than that the principle of motion is unknown. However, it is tiresome to delay further with such subtleties.

**25** In addition to bodily things, there is a separate class of thinking things. We have learned from our own experience that there is a power of moving bodies in these, since our mind may at will initiate or stop the movement of our limbs, however that is eventually explained. It is certainly established that bodies are moved at the command of the mind, and that the latter can therefore be called appropriately a principle of motion – a specific and subordinate principle, indeed, which itself depends on the first and universal principle.

**26** Heavy bodies are carried downward, although they are not moved by any apparent impulse; however, we ought not to think, as a result, that the principle of their motion is contained within them. Aristotle provides the following as an explanation of this phenomenon: 'heavy and light things,' he says, 'are not moved by themselves, for that would imply that they are vital and that they could stop themselves.'[14] All heavy bodies seek the centre of the earth by one and the same law that is certain and unchanging; no one observes any principle or faculty of stopping that motion, of reducing it, or of increasing it except at a proportionate rate, or finally of altering it in any way. Thus they behave passively. The same thing should also be said of colliding bodies, if one were to speak strictly and precisely. Such bodies, as long as they are moved, and also in the moment of collision, behave passively, just as when they are at rest. An inert body acts as much as a body in motion, if the truth were told; Newton recognises this when he says that the inertial force is identical to the impetus.[15] But an inert body at rest does nothing, and neither therefore does a body in motion.

**27** In truth, a body perseveres equally in either condition, in motion or at rest. However, that perseverance should not be called an action of the body any more than its existence. Perseverance is nothing other than the continuation of its existence in the same condition, and this cannot properly be called an action. But, deluded by mere appearances, we imagine that the resistance that we experience, when we stop a moving body, is its action. In fact, the resistance that we experience is a passion in us, and it does not imply that the body acts, but rather that we are affected; and it is known that we would have been affected in the same way whether that body was moved by itself or impelled by another principle.

**28** It is said that action and reaction are in bodies, and that this way of speaking is appropriate for mechanical demonstrations. But one should beware of believing that, because we assume that there is some real force which is the cause of motion or its principle, it is present in

---

[14] *Physics*, Bk. 8, ch. 4, 255$^a$ 5–7.    [15] *Principles*, Definition III, vol. 1, 2.

bodies. For those terms should be understood in the same way as the term 'attraction'. And just as attraction is merely a mathematical hypothesis rather than a physical quality, the other words should be understood in the same way and for the same reasons. The truth and usefulness of theorems about the mutual attraction of bodies remain unchanged in mechanical philosophy, insofar as they are based exclusively on the motion of bodies, whether that motion is assumed to be caused by the action of bodies which mutually attract each other or by the action of some agent, distinct from the body, which impels and controls them. By a similar reasoning, whatever is taught about the rules and laws of motion, and likewise about the theorems that are deduced from them, remains unchanged as long as the observable effects and reasoning based on them are granted – whether we assume that this action, or the force that causes these effects, is in the body or in some non-bodily agent.

29   If extension, solidity, and shape were subtracted from the idea of body, nothing would be left. These qualities, however, are indifferent to motion, and they contain nothing that could be said to be the principle of motion. This is clear from our ideas themselves. If therefore the term 'body' means what we conceive, it is evident that we cannot look for the principle of motion in body; for no part or attribute of body is a genuine efficient cause that produces motion. However, if we were to use a term and not conceive anything by it, that would be completely unworthy of a philosopher.

30   There is an active thinking thing that we experience in ourselves as a principle of motion. We call this 'soul', 'mind', and 'spirit.' There is also an extended, inert, impenetrable, mobile thing which is completely different from the former, and which constitutes a new kind of entity. Anaxagoras, a man of great wisdom, was the very first to comment on the difference between a thinking thing and an extended thing. He declared that the mind has nothing in common with bodies, which one can gather from the first book of Aristotle's *On the Soul*.[16] Among recent authors, Descartes has best drawn attention to the same thing. What he made adequately clear has been made difficult and complicated by others, using obscure terms.[17]

---

[16] *On the Soul*, Bk. I, Ch. 2, 405$^b$20.
[17] Descartes discusses this in the *Principles of Philosophy*, Part I, especially articles 8, 9; *Oeuvres*, VIII-1, 7.

31    From what has been said it is evident that those who claim that
there is genuinely an active force, an action, or a principle of motion in
bodies have adopted an opinion that is not based on any experience, and
that they have built on it with obscure and general terms and do not wish
to understand it adequately themselves. On the contrary, those who
choose the soul as the principle of motion propose an opinion that is
supported by their own experience and confirmed by the opinions of the
most learned men of every age.

32    Anaxagoras was the first to introduce the mind as that which
impresses motion on inert matter. Aristotle also approved the same
opinion and confirmed it in many ways, and claimed openly that the
first mover is immobile, indivisible, and has no magnitude. However, he
rightly observes that to say that every body that moves another is mobile,
is the same as saying that everything that builds must be capable of being
built.[d] Plato also teaches, in the *Timaeus*, that this bodily machine or the
visible world is moved and animated by a mind, which escapes every
sensation. Even today, Cartesian philosophers recognise that the principle of natural motions is God. And Newton intimates throughout his
work, clearly, not only that motion originated initially from the divine,
but that the true system of the world is still moved by the same action.
This is consistent with the sacred scriptures, and is confirmed by the
opinions of the scholastics. For although the peripatetics teach that
nature is the principle of motion and rest, they understand however
that 'naturing nature' is God.[18] They certainly understand that all the
bodies in this system of the world are moved by an omnipotent mind in
accordance with a design that is certain and constant.

33    But those who attribute a vital principle to bodies imagine something that is obscure and inappropriate to things. For what else is meant
by 'being endowed with a vital principle' apart from 'living'? And what is
meant by 'living' other than to move, to stop, and to change one's
condition? But the most learned philosophers of the current age propose,
as an indubitable principle, that every body remains in whatever condition it is in, either of rest or uniform motion in a straight line, unless

---

[d]  See *Physics*, Bk. 8 [ch. 5, 257ª15–20].

[18]  The phrase *natura naturans* (naturing nature) was used by scholastics to denote nature insofar as it
is active, in contrast with the effects that result from nature's activity, which were described
passively as 'natured nature'.

and to the extent that it is forced by something external to change its condition.[19] In contrast, we sense that there is a faculty in the mind for changing both its own condition and that of other things; that is properly called vital, and it distinguishes the soul completely from bodies.

**34**  Recent authors consider motion and rest in bodies as two ways of existing, in both of which every body remains inert by nature, as long as it is not affected by an external force. One may conclude from this that the cause of motion and rest is identical with that of the existence of bodies. It also seems that one should not look for a cause of the existence of a body successively in different parts of space elsewhere than in the cause of the existence of the same body successively in different parts of time. To discuss God, however, and the greatest and best creator and conserver of all things, and to demonstrate how all things depend on the highest and true being, although it is the most excellent part of human knowledge, appears to belong to first philosophy or metaphysics and theology rather than to natural philosophy, which today is almost completely restricted to experiments and mechanics. Therefore natural philosophy either presupposes knowledge of God, or it borrows it from some superior science. Nevertheless it is very true that the investigation of nature provides the higher sciences in every way with excellent arguments to show and prove the wisdom, goodness, and power of God.

**35**  Because these things are not well understood, some people reject the mathematical principles of physics undeservedly, on the pretext that they do not identify the efficient causes of things. However, it is the responsibility of the physicist or mechanist to provide only the rules, and not the efficient causes, of impulses or attractions and, in a word, the laws of motion; and once these are established properly, to assign the solution of a particular phenomenon, but not however the efficient cause.

**36**  It will be very important to have considered what is properly a principle, and in what sense this word should be understood by philosophers. The true efficient and conserving cause of all things is most appropriately called their source or principle. But the principles of experimental philosophy are properly said to be the foundations, on which it is built, or the sources from which is derived (I do not say the existence, but) the knowledge of bodily things. These are sense and experience. Likewise, in mechanical philosophy, the principles are said

---

[19] Newton's first law of motion, *Principles*, vol. I, 13.

to be those things in which are grounded and contained the whole discipline, those primary laws of motion which are confirmed by experience and are refined by reason and rendered universal. Those laws of motion are appropriately called principles, because both general mechanical theorems and particular explanations are derived from them.

**37** Accordingly, something can be said to be explained mechanically when it is reduced to such very simple and universal principles and is shown by careful reasoning to be consistent with and related to them. For, once the laws of nature have been discovered, it is the philosopher's task to show how any phenomenon necessarily follows by the consistent observance of those laws, that is, from those principles. That is what is meant by explaining and solving a phenomenon and assigning its cause, that is, the reason why it occurs.

**38** The human mind delights in extending and expanding its knowledge. To do so, however, it needs to form general notions and propositions, in which particular propositions and items of knowledge are somehow contained and are thought to be understood finally (since they are deduced from the former by an uninterrupted connection). Geometers are very well aware of this. Likewise, in mechanics, notions are initially established – that is, definitions, and first general statements about motion – from which more remote and less general conclusions are subsequently deduced by a mathematical method. And just as the magnitudes of particular bodies are measured by applying geometrical theorems, so likewise the motions of any parts of the system of the world, and the phenomena that depend on them, become known and determined by applying the universal theorems of mechanics. That is all that a physicist should aim to realize.

**39** Just as geometers, for the sake of their discipline, invent many things which they themselves cannot describe nor find in the nature of things, for exactly similar reasons a student of mechanics employs certain abstract and general terms and feigns in bodies a force, an action, an attraction or solicitation, *etc.* which are extremely useful in theories and propositions, as also in calculations of motion, even though it would be as vain to seek them in the very truth of things, or in bodies that actually exist, as it would be to seek the things that geometers invent by mathematical abstraction.

**40** In fact, by using our senses we perceive nothing other than sensible qualities or effects, and bodily things that are entirely passive, whether they are in motion or at rest. Reason and experience convince us that there is nothing active, apart from the mind or soul. Anything that is imagined beyond these must be assumed to be of the same kind as other mathematical hypotheses and abstractions, and this should be impressed deeply on the mind. If this is not done, we may easily lapse into the obscure subtlety of the scholastics, which corrupted philosophy for so many centuries like some kind of dire plague.

41   The mechanical principles and universal laws of motion, or of nature, which were happily discovered in the last century and have been discussed and applied with the assistance of geometry, have introduced a remarkable light into philosophy. However, the metaphysical principles and the real efficient causes of the motion and the existence of bodies, or of bodily attributes, do not in any way belong to mechanics or experiments, nor can they throw any light on them except insofar as, by being known first, they may be used to define in advance the limits of physics and, in that way, to remove irrelevant difficulties and questions.

42   Those who seek the principle of motion in spirits understand the term 'spirit' to mean either a corporeal or an incorporeal thing. If they mean a corporeal thing, no matter how subtle it is, the difficulty still remains. If they mean something that is not corporeal, however that is achieved, such a reality still does not belong properly to physics. For if someone were to extend natural philosophy beyond the limits of experiments and mechanics, so as to include knowledge even of incorporeal or unextended things, that wider understanding of the term would include discussion of the soul, the mind or the vital principle. However, it will be more convenient, and in accordance with already accepted usage, to distinguish among the sciences in such a way that each one is circumscribed within its own boundaries and the natural philosopher is wholly committed to experiments, the laws of motion, and the principles of mechanics, and to whatever may be deduced from them by reasoning. On the other hand, he should refer anything that he advances about other matters to what is assigned to some higher science. For many wonderful theories, together with mechanical devices that are useful for living, follow from the known laws of nature. However, considerations that are of outstanding importance arise from knowledge of the very Author of nature, but they are metaphysical, theological, and moral.

43   Up to this point we have discussed principles. Now we should speak about the nature of motion and, indeed, since this is perceived

clearly by the senses, it is made obscure, not by its own nature, but by the learned comments of philosophers. Motion never affects our senses without corporeal mass, space, and time. There are some people, however, who try to think about motion as if it were some kind of abstract, simple idea, separated from everything else. But that very tenuous and subtle idea eludes the keen perception of the intellect. Anyone can experience this themselves by meditating. Hence major difficulties arise concerning the nature of motion and definitions that are much more obscure than the reality that they are supposed to clarify. Such are the definitions of Aristotle and the scholastics, who state that motion is the act 'of a mobile thing, insofar as it is mobile, or the act of an entity in potency insofar as it is in potency.'[20] Such also is the definition of one of the most celebrated of recent authors, who claims that 'there is nothing real in motion apart from the momentary something which must consist in a force that is striving towards change.'[21] It is accepted, however, that the authors of these and similar definitions intended to explain the abstract nature of motion, while prescinding from every consideration of time and space; but I do not see how this abstract quintessence (as I call it) of motion can be understood.

**44** Since they are not content with this, they go further and divide and separate from one another the parts of motion itself, of which they try to form distinct ideas as if the parts were entities that were truly distinct from each other. For there are those who distinguish movement from motion, and consider the former as if it were an instantaneous element of motion.[22] Besides, they want velocity, force, impetus, to be so many things that are essentially distinct, each of which is presented to the intellect by its own abstract idea that is separated from all other ideas. But there is no reason to delay further in discussing these matters, if what we set out above is accepted.

**45** Many also define motion as 'transition', evidently forgetting that transition itself cannot be understood without motion and that the former should be defined by the latter.[23] It is so true that definitions,

---

[20] *Physics*, Bk. III, ch. 1, 200ᵃ10.    [21] Leibniz, *Specimen Dynamicum*, Loemker, 436.

[22] Cf. Leibniz, *Specimen Dynamicum*: 'so we can also distinguish the present or instantaneous element of motion from the motion extended through time and call it "motion." Then what is popularly called motion would be called quantity of motion' (Loemker, 437).

[23] Descartes defines motion as the translation of a body from the vicinity of one group of bodies to that of others, in *Principles of Philosophy*, Part II, article 25 (*Oeuvres*, VIII-1, 53). Borelli, *De vi percussionis*, pp. 1–2, was the likely source for Berkeley.

while they shed light on some things, in turn cast shadows on others. Indeed, someone could hardly make clearer or better known by definition whatever we perceive by the senses. The vain hope of doing so has caused philosophers to make easy things difficult and they have tied up their own minds in difficulties which, for the most part, they invented themselves. This zeal for defining and, at the same time, abstracting has given rise to many very subtle questions about motion and other things. Since these are of no use, they have tortured the intelligence of men in vain, to such an extent that Aristotle eventually, and frequently, conceded that motion is 'a certain act that is difficult to know.'[24] And some of the ancients became so accustomed to discussing such trifles that they denied motion altogether.[25]

**46**  However, it is tedious to delay on such trivialities. It is enough to have indicated the sources of solutions, to which the following may also be added; that what is taught in mathematics about the infinite division of time and space has, by the very nature of things, introduced paradoxes and thorny theories (such as all those that involve a discussion of the infinite) into speculations concerning motion. However, any problem of this kind is exclusively something that motion has in common with space and time or, rather, it is something that it has inherited from them.

**47**  Too much abstraction or the division of things that are truly inseparable, on the one hand, and likewise, on the other hand, the composition or rather the confusion of things that are very distinct, have made the nature of motion perplexing. For it is customary to confuse motion with the efficient cause of motion. One result is that motion is almost twofold, revealing one aspect to the senses while the other is hidden in the darkest night. Obscurity and confusion, and various paradoxes about motion, originate from this source, when something that can truly belong only to the cause is attributed to its effect.

**48**  This is the source of the opinion that the same quantity of motion is always conserved. This is false, as anyone can easily show, unless it is understood as applying to the force and power of the cause, or to the cause that is called nature or *nous* or whatever is ultimately the agent. Aristotle indeed, in Book 8 of the *Physics*, seems to have understood a vital principle rather than an external effect or a change of place when he

[24] Aristotle, *Physics*, Bk. III, ch. 1, 201[b]33.   [25] Refers to Zeno's paradoxes.

asked: 'is motion created and corrupted, or is it truly present in all things from eternity like an immortal life?'[26]

**49** That is also the reason why many suspect that motion is not simply a passion in bodies. If we understand it as that which is presented to the senses in the motion of a body, no one can doubt that it is completely passive. For what is involved in the successive existence of a body in different places that could imply action, or is there anything present there other than a bare, inert effect?

**50** Peripatetics, who say that motion is a single act of both the mover and the moved, do not adequately distinguish the cause from the effect. Likewise, those who imagine an effort or striving in motion, or who think that one and the same body is simultaneously carried in opposite directions, can be seen to be deluded by the same confusion of ideas and the same ambiguity of terms.

**51** It is very helpful to exercise great care in the science of motion, as in all other things, both in understanding the concepts used by others and in articulating one's own concepts. In this context I find it hard to believe, unless some mistake was committed, that the dispute could have lasted so long about whether or not a body is indifferent to motion or rest. For it is established by experience that it is a first law of nature that a body persists as it is 'in a state of motion or rest, as long as nothing extrinsic happens to change that state.'[27] For that reason, it is concluded that the force of inertia may be either a force for resistance or for impetus under different appearances. In that sense, a body can indeed be said to be naturally indifferent to motion or rest. Certainly, it is as difficult to induce rest into a moving body as it is to induce motion into a body at rest; since bodies preserve both states equally, why should they not be said to be disposed indifferently to both?

**52** The peripatetics distinguished different kinds of motion according to the various alterations that a thing could undergo. Those who discuss motion today understand it only as local motion. But they deny that local motion can be understood unless one also understands what is meant by 'location'. The latter is defined by modern authors as 'the part of space that a body occupies.'[28] This is accordingly distinguished into

---

[26] *Physics*, 250[b]11–14.
[27] Berkeley appears to be quoting here, but in fact is merely reporting a widely held view about the law of inertia, which was found in Descartes, Newton and others.
[28] Newton, *Principles*, Scholium to the Definitions (vol. I, 6).

absolute and relative location, depending on the space involved. For they distinguish between absolute or true space, and relative or apparent space. They claim, indeed, that there is space everywhere, that it is immense, immobile, insensible, and contains and permeates all bodies, and they call this absolute space. The space, however, that is comprehended or defined by bodies and, to that extent, is accessible to the senses, is called relative, apparent, or common space.

**53** Let us imagine therefore that all bodies have been destroyed and reduced to nothing. What remains is what they call absolute space, since every relation that results from the position and distances of bodies has been removed at the same time as the bodies themselves. This space, then, is infinite, immobile, indivisible, insensible, without relation or distinction. That is, all its attributes are privative or negative; it seems therefore to be a mere nothing. The only difficulty it raises is that it is extended. Extension, however, is a positive quality. But what kind of extension is that which cannot be divided, nor measured, which has no parts and which we cannot perceive by sensation nor depict in our imagination? For nothing enters the imagination that, of its nature, is impossible to perceive by sensation, because the imagination is nothing other than a faculty which represents sensible things, whether they exist actually or, at least, are possible. It also evades the pure intellect, since that faculty is concerned only with things that are spiritual and unextended, such as our minds, their habits, passions, powers, and such like. If we take away from absolute space only the words, nothing will remain in sensation, imagination, or intellect; the words therefore designate nothing other than a pure privation or negation, that is, a mere nothing.

**54** It must be fully acknowledged that, with respect to this question, we are in the grip of the most serious prejudices, from which we can be liberated only by applying all our mental efforts. Indeed, many people are so reluctant to consider absolute space as nothing, that they think it is the only thing (apart from God) which cannot be annihilated. They think it is eternal and uncreated and, to that extent, that it shares in the attributes of God. However, it is most certainly the case that all things that we designate by some term are known, at least in part, by qualities and relations (for it would be foolish to use terms which are not related to anything known, to any notion, idea, or concept). Let us therefore inquire diligently whether it is possible to form an idea of that pure, real, and absolute space, which continues to exist after the annihilation of all bodies.

However, when I examine that idea a little more keenly, I find it is an idea of the purest nothing, if indeed it can be called an idea at all. This is what I have found, having examined it very carefully; I anticipate that others will have the same experience if they apply a comparable diligence to the task.

**55** We are often deceived into believing that, when we have removed all other bodies in our imagination, our own body remains. Given that assumption, we imagine that our limbs can move very freely in every direction. However, it is impossible to conceive of motion without space. But if we reflect on the question with an attentive mind, it will be clear, first of all, that we conceive of a relative space that is defined by the parts of our body; secondly, we will conceive of the most free power of moving our limbs without being impeded by any obstacle. Over and above these two items, we conceive of nothing else. In spite of that, however, we believe falsely in some third thing, namely, an immense space which really exists, which provides us with the unimpeded power to move our own body. But this presupposes nothing other than the absence of other bodies. We must acknowledge that this absence or privation of bodies is nothing positive.[e]

**56** Terms and words are of little value unless one examines these matters with a free and keen scrutiny. However, unless I am mistaken, it will be obvious to someone who meditates and reflects on their reasons that all the same things that are said about pure and absolute space may be predicated of nothing. By this reasoning the human mind is liberated very easily from great difficulties, and at the same time from the absurdity of attributing necessary existence to any reality apart from the great and good God alone.

**57** It would be easy to confirm our opinion by *a posteriori* arguments (as they are called), by asking questions about absolute space – for example: is it a substance or an accident? is it created or uncreated? – and by showing the absurdities that result from either reply. But it is advisable to be brief. However, we should not fail to mention that Democritus formerly endorsed this opinion, for his own reasons. Aristotle reports this, in Book One of the *Physics*, when he says: 'Democritus establishes as principles the solid and the void, about which he says that one is that which

---

[e] See what is proposed against absolute space in the book, *The Principles of Human Knowledge*, which was published in English ten years ago. [See above, especially sections 112–16.]

is, while the other that which is not.'[29] If someone were to object that the distinction between absolute and relative space has been used by reputable philosophers and that many well-known theorems have been built on it as their foundation, it will be apparent from what is about to follow that there is no basis for that objection.

58   It is clear from what has been proposed thus far that it is inappropriate to define the true location of a body as the part of absolute space that the body occupies, and that real or absolute motion is a change in real or absolute location. Since all location is relative, so likewise is all motion. However, in order to make that conclusion more apparent, it should be noticed that it is impossible to understand any motion without some direction or determination, and that the latter cannot be understood unless, in addition to the body that is moved, either our own body or some other body is assumed to exist. For up, down, and all place or regions to the left or right are based on some relation, and they necessarily presuppose some body that is distinct from the body that is moved. Thus if one assumes that all bodies are reduced to nothing and, for example, that a single globe exists, it would be impossible to conceive of any motion in the latter; it is necessary that some other body be given by the location of which one could understand that the motion of the globe is determined. The truth of this opinion would appear most clearly if our assumption about the annihilation of all bodies were properly implemented, i.e. if it included both our own and all other bodies, except for the one solitary globe.

59   Let us assume then that two globes exist and that otherwise there is nothing corporeal.[30] Assume, secondly, that forces are applied to them in some way; whatever understanding of the application of forces is eventually adopted, the circular motion of two globes around a common centre cannot even be conceived by the imagination. Thirdly, let us assume that the heaven of fixed stars is created; suddenly, it is possible to conceive motion by the concept of the approach of the globes to different parts of that heaven. Thus, since motion is by its nature relative, it cannot be conceived unless other correlative bodies are given. Likewise, no other relation can be conceived without correlatives.

---

[29] *Physics*, Bk. I, ch. 5, 188ª22–23.
[30] This addresses an argument found in Newton's *Principles*, vol. I, 10, which is also mentioned in *PHK*, 114.

**60**   As regards circular motion, many think that, as true circular motion increases, a body necessarily tries to recede more and more from its axis of rotation. This however results from the fact that, as circular motion can be seen to derive its source at each moment of time from two directions, one along the radius and the other at a tangent, then if the impetus is increased only in the latter direction, the body in motion recedes from the centre and its orbit ceases to be circular. But if the forces are increased in both directions equally, the motion will remain circular but accelerated by an effort [*conatus*], which does not show that the forces of receding from the axis are increased any more than the forces of approaching it. It must therefore be said that water that is spinning in a bucket moves up the sides of the vessel because, as new forces are applied in the direction of the tangent to each particle of water, at the same instant no equal centripetal forces are applied to them. It does not follow by any means from this experiment that one can necessarily discern an absolute circular motion in the forces receding from the axis of motion. Besides, how the terms 'forces of bodies' and '*conatus*' are to be understood is more than adequately explained in what has already been proposed above.

**61**   Just as a curve can be considered as if it were an infinity of straight lines (even though in fact it is not composed of them) because that hypothesis is useful in geometry, in the same way a circular motion can be considered as if it results from an infinity of rectilinear directions, because that assumption is useful in mechanical philosophy. But one should not claim, for that reason, that it is impossible for the centre of gravity of any body to exist successively in single points on the circumference of a circle, by taking no account of any direction in a straight line, either at a tangent or along the radius.

**62**   We must add that the motion of a stone in a sling or of water in a spinning bucket cannot be described as truly circular motions, according to the view of those who define the true locations of bodies by reference to the parts of absolute space. These motions are composed wonderfully of the motions not only of the bucket or the sling, but also of the daily motion of the earth on its own axis, its monthly motion around the common centre of gravity of the earth and the moon, and its annual motion around the Sun. As a result of this, each particle of water or stone follows a path that is not remotely circular. Nor is it a real axifugal *conatus*, as some contend, because it does not have any single axis in relation to absolute space, even if we assume there is such a thing as absolute space. Accordingly, I cannot see how it can be described as a single *conatus*, which gives rise to a genuinely circular motion as its proper, proportionate effect.

**63** No motion can be distinguished or measured except through perceptible things. Since therefore absolute space does not affect the senses in any way, it follows necessarily that it is useless for distinguishing motions. Besides, it is essential for a motion to have some determination or direction, and the latter consists in a relation. Therefore, it is impossible to conceive of absolute motion.

**64** Furthermore, since the motion of any given body varies with changes in its relative location – and thus anything can be said to be moved in one respect, and to be at rest in another respect – in order to determine true motion and true rest, by which ambiguity is removed and the mechanics of philosophers who have a more comprehensive view of the system of things is developed, it would suffice to accept, instead of absolute space, the relative space of the fixed stars in a heaven that is regarded as at rest. The motion and rest that are defined by such a relative space can then be conveniently adopted instead of the corresponding absolutes, which cannot be distinguished from the former by any criterion. For no matter what way forces are applied and whatever kinds of *conatus* there may be, we acknowledge that we distinguish motions by the actions that they exert on bodies. However, it will never follow that we have an absolute space and location, and that some alteration in them is what is meant by true motion.[31]

**65** The laws of motion and effects, and the theorems that contain their calculations and the relations between them for paths of different shape, as well as for the accelerations and various directions for media that are more or less resistant – all of these are established without any reference to absolute motion. It is equally clear that since, according to the principles of those who introduce absolute motion, it is impossible to know by any test whether the whole framework of things is at rest or moving uniformly in a straight line, it is evident that it is impossible to know the absolute motion of any body.

**66** From what has been said it is clear that, in order to understand the true nature of motion, it will assist greatly: (i) to distinguish between

---

[31] Reading '*motus*' instead of '*locus*' in the final phrase.

mathematical hypotheses and the natures of things; (ii) to avoid abstractions; (iii) to consider motion as something that is perceptible or at least imaginable, and to be satisfied with relative measurements. If we were to do all that, two results would follow: first, it would leave untouched the clearest theorems of mechanical philosophy, by which the secrets of nature are revealed, and the system of the world would be subjected to human calculations. Secondly, the examination of motion would be liberated from a thousand trivial issues, subtleties, and abstract ideas. Let that be enough about motion.

**67**  It remains for us to discuss the cause of the communication of motions. Many think that the cause of motion is found in a force that is impressed by a body in motion. Nevertheless, it is clear from what was said above that they do not assign a cause of motion that is known and is distinct from the body and its motion. It is clear that force is not something that is certain and determinate, from the fact that the greatest men propose many different and even contradictory views of it, although they retain the truth in the conclusions they draw from them. Newton says that an impressed force consists in action alone, that it is the action applied to a body to change its state, and that it does not survive after the action.[32] Torricelli claims that a certain aggregation or accumulation of impressed forces is transmitted by percussion to a body that is moved, and that it remains in that body and constitutes its impetus.[33] Borelli and others say more or less the same thing.[34] However, although Newton and Torricelli seem to disagree with each other and each one proposes their own account, nonetheless the reality is adequately explained by both of them. For all forces that are attributed to bodies are mathematical hypotheses as much as the attractive forces between the planets and the Sun. Mathematical entities, however, have no stable essence in the nature of things. They depend on the notion of the person who defines them; therefore, one and the same thing can be explained in different ways.

**68**  Let us stipulate that the new motion in a body that is struck is conserved, either by means of the innate force by which every body perseveres in whatever state it is in, either of rest or of uniform motion in a straight line;[35] or by means of an impressed force that is received during

---

[32] *Principles*, Definition IV (vol. I, 2).    [33] *Lezioni Academiche*, Lecture III (1715, 15–17).
[34] *De vi percussionis*, Chapter VI, pp. 30ff.
[35] The final phrase in both editions reads: 'either of motion or of uniform rest in a straight line' and is assumed to be an error.

a percussion into the body that is struck and then remains there. There will be no difference between these two accounts as far as the realities are concerned; the difference occurs only in the words used. Likewise, when a striking mobile body loses motion, and the struck body acquires motion, it is trivial to dispute whether the motion that is acquired is numerically identical with the motion lost by the other body. That leads into metaphysical trivialities and even into nominal trivialities about identity.[36] Thus whether we say that the motion in transferred from the striking body to the struck body, or that motion is generated anew in a body that is struck and is destroyed in the striking body, it amounts to the same thing. In either case, it is understood that one body loses motion, another acquires motion, and there is nothing further involved.

**69** I would hardly deny that the mind which moves and contains this universe of corporeal mass is also the true, efficient cause of motion and is also, in a strict and proper sense, the cause of the communication of the same motion. However, in natural philosophy, one should look for the causes and explanations of phenomena in mechanical principles. Therefore, something is explained physically, not by assigning its true active, incorporeal cause, but by showing how it is connected to mechanical principles, one of which is this: 'action and reaction are always opposite and equal.'[37] The rules for the communication of motions are drawn from this, as from a source and primary principle, and have already been discovered and demonstrated by the moderns to the great benefit of the sciences.

**70** It would be enough for us to suggest that that principle could be expressed in a different way. For if one regards the true nature of things, rather than abstract mathematical calculations, it will be seen that one could more correctly say that, in attraction or collision, the passivity of bodies rather than their activity is equal on both sides. For example, a stone that is tied with a rope to a horse is drawn towards the horse just as much as the horse is drawn towards the stone;[38] likewise, a body in motion that collides with another body suffers the same change as the body at rest. And, as regards the real effect, the striking body is similar to the struck body, and the latter resembles the former. That change, however, in both – which is just as much in the horse's body as in the

---

[36] Cf. *D*, 247–8.    [37] Newton's Third Law of Motion, *Principles*, Vol. I, 13.
[38] Borrowed almost verbatim from Newton, *Principles*, Third Law of Motion, Vol. I, 14.

stone, or in a body in motion as in a body at rest – is a mere passion. But it is not the case that there is a force, power, or corporeal action which in a true and strict sense is causative of such effects. A moving body collides with a body at rest, and we speak in the active voice by saying that the former sets the latter in motion; and that is not absurd in mechanics, in which we are concerned with mathematical ideas rather than the true nature of things.

71   In physics, we rely on sensation and experience, which extend only to effects that are perceivable; in mechanics, the abstract notions of mathematics are accepted. In first philosophy or metaphysics, one discusses incorporeal things and the causes, truth, and existence of things. A physicist thinks about a series or succession of perceivable things, and notices what laws link them together, and in what order, what comes first as a cause and what follows as an effect. And for that reason we say that the moving body is the cause of motion in another body, or that it impresses motion on it, that it pulls it or pushes it. That is the sense in which secondary corporeal causes should be understood, without taking any account of the true seat of forces or of active powers or the real cause in which they inhere. Besides, in addition to body, shape, and motion, the primary axioms of mechanical philosophy may be said to be mechanical principles or causes, insofar as they are viewed as causes of the consequences.

72   Causes that are truly active can be known to some extent only by reflection and reasoning, and can be brought to light from the darkness in which they are immersed. The discussion of these causes, however, is reserved to first philosophy or metaphysics. If each science is given the scope that properly belongs to it and its limits are assigned, and if the principles and objects that belong to each one are carefully distinguished, it will be possible to treat each one with greater facility and clarity.

# Alciphron: or, the Minute Philosopher

In Seven Dialogues, Containing an Apology for the Christian Religion, against those who are called free-thinkers.

3rd edition 1752

[Excerpts from Dialogues IV and VII]

## The Fourth Dialogue

1  Early the next morning, as I looked out of my window, I saw Alciphron walking in the garden with all the signs of a man in deep thought. Upon which I went down to him.

Alciphron, said I, this early and profound meditation puts me in no small fright. How so? Because I should be sorry to be convinced there was no God. The thought of anarchy in nature is to me more shocking than in civil life, inasmuch as natural concerns are more important than civil and the basis of all others.

I grant, replied Alciphron, that some inconvenience may possibly follow from disproving a God; but as to what you say of fright and shocking, all that is nothing but prejudice, mere prejudice. Men frame an idea or chimera in their own minds, and then fall down and worship it. Notions govern mankind; but of all notions, that of God's governing the world has taken the deepest root and spread the farthest. It is therefore in philosophy an heroical achievement to dispossess this imaginary

269

monarch of his government, and banish all those fears and spectres which the light of reason alone can dispel:

> *Non radii solis, non lucida tela diei*
> *Discutiunt, sed naturae species ratioque.*[a]

My part, said I, shall be to stand by, as I have hitherto done, and take notes of all that passes during this memorable event, while a minute philosopher, not six foot high, attempts to dethrone the monarch of the universe.

Alas! replied Alciphron, arguments are not to be measured by feet and inches. One man may see more than a million; and a short argument, managed by a free-thinker, may be sufficient to overthrow the most gigantic chimera.

As we were engaged in this discourse, Crito and Euphranor joined us.

I find you have been beforehand with us today, said Crito to Alciphron, and taken the advantage of solitude and early hours, while Euphranor and I were asleep in our beds. We may, therefore, expect to see atheism placed in the best light, and supported by the strongest arguments.

2 *Alciphron.* The being of a God is a subject upon which there has been a world of commonplace, which it is needless to repeat. Give me leave therefore to lay down certain rules and limitations, in order to shorten our present conference. For, as the end of debating is to persuade, all those things which are foreign to this end should be left out of our debate.

First then, let me tell you I am not to be persuaded by metaphysical arguments; such, for instance, as are drawn from the idea of an all-perfect being, or the absurdity of an infinite progression of causes. This sort of arguments I have always found dry and jejune; and, as they are not suited to my way of thinking, they may perhaps puzzle but never will convince me. Secondly, I am not to be persuaded by the authority either of past or present ages, of mankind in general, or of particular wise men, all which passes for little or nothing with a man of sound argument and free thought. Thirdly, all proofs drawn from utility or convenience are foreign to the purpose. They may prove indeed the usefulness of the notion, but not the existence of the thing. Whatever legislators or

---

[a] Lucretius [*The Nature of Things*, vi, 40: 'They are dispelled, not by the sun's rays or the bright shafts of day, but by the phenomena of nature and their explanation'].

statesmen may think, truth and convenience are very different things to the rigorous eyes of a philosopher.

And now, that I may not seem partial, I will limit myself also not to object, in the first place, from anything that may seem irregular or unaccountable in the works of nature, against a cause of infinite power and wisdom; because I already know the answer you would make, to wit, that no one can judge of the symmetry and use of the parts of an infinite machine, which are all relative to each other and to the whole, without being able to comprehend the entire machine or the whole universe. And, in the second place, I shall engage myself not to object against the justice and providence of a supreme Being from the evil that befalls good men, and the prosperity which is often the portion of wicked men in this life; because I know that, instead of admitting this to be an objection against a Deity, you would make it an argument for a future state, in which there shall be such a retribution of rewards and punishments as may vindicate the Divine attributes and set all things right in the end. Now these answers, though they should be admitted for good ones, are in truth no proofs of the being of God, but only solutions of certain difficulties which might be objected, supposing it already proved by proper arguments. Thus much I thought fit to premise, in order to save time and trouble both to you and myself.

*Crito.* I think that, as the proper end of our conference ought to be supposed the discovery and defence of truth, so truth may be justified, not only by persuading its adversaries but, where that cannot be done, by showing them to be unreasonable. Arguments, therefore, which carry light have their effect, even against an opponent who shuts his eyes, because they show him to be obstinate and prejudiced. Besides, this distinction, between arguments that puzzle and that convince, is least of all observed by minute philosophers and need not therefore be observed by others in their favour. But, perhaps, Euphranor may be willing to encounter you on your own terms, in which case I have nothing further to say.

3 *Euphranor.* Alciphron acts like a skilful general, who is bent upon gaining the advantage of the ground and alluring the enemy out of their trenches. We who believe a God are entrenched within tradition, custom, authority, and law. And nevertheless, instead of attempting to force us, he proposes that we should voluntarily abandon these entrenchments and

make the attack, when we may act on the defensive with much security and ease, leaving him the trouble to dispossess us of what we need not resign. Those reasons (continued he, addressing himself to Alciphron) which you have mustered up in this morning's meditation, if they do not weaken, must establish our belief of a God; for the utmost is to be expected from so great a master in his profession, when he sets his strength to a point.

*Alc.*   I hold the confused notion of a Deity, or some invisible power, to be of all prejudices the most unconquerable. When half a dozen ingenious men are got together over a glass of wine, by a cheerful fire, in a room well lighted, we banish with ease all the spectres of fancy or education and are very clear in our decisions. But, as I was taking a solitary walk before it was broad daylight in yonder grove, methought the point was not quite so clear; nor could I readily recollect the force of those arguments which used to appear so conclusive at other times. I had I know not what awe upon my mind, and seemed haunted by a sort of panic, which I cannot otherwise account for than by supposing it the effect of prejudice. For you must know that I, like the rest of the world, was once upon a time catechized and tutored into the belief of a God or Spirit. There is no surer mark of prejudice than the believing a thing without reason. What necessity then can there be that I should set myself the difficult task of proving a negative, when it is sufficient to observe that there is no proof of the affirmative, and that the admitting it without proof is unreasonable? Prove therefore your opinion; or, if you cannot, you may indeed remain in possession of it, but you will only be possessed of a prejudice.

*Euph.*   O Alciphron! to content you we must prove, it seems, and we must prove upon your own terms. But, in the first place, let us see what sort of proof you expect.

*Alc.*   Perhaps I may not expect it, but I will tell you what sort of proof I would have. And that is, in short, such proof as every man of sense requires of a matter of fact, or the existence of any other particular thing. For instance, should a man ask why I believe there is a king of Great Britain? I might answer: because I had seen him. Or a king of Spain? Because I had seen those who saw him. But as for this King of kings, I neither saw Him myself nor anyone else that ever did see Him. Surely, if there be such a thing as God, it is very strange that He should leave Himself without a witness; that men should still dispute

His being; and that there should be no one evident, sensible, plain proof of it, without recourse to philosophy or metaphysics. A matter of fact is not to be proved by notions, but by facts. This is clear and full to the point. You see what I would be at. Upon these principles I defy superstition.

*Euph.* You believe then as far as you can see.

*Alc.* That is my rule of faith.

*Euph.* How! will you not believe the existence of things which you hear, unless you also see them?

*Alc.* I will not say so neither. When I insist on seeing, I would be understood to mean perceiving in general. Outward objects make very different impressions upon the animal spirits, all which are comprised under the common name of sense. And whatever we can perceive by any sense we may be sure of.

4 *Euph.* What! do you believe then that there are such things as animal spirits?

*Alc.* Doubtless.

*Euph.* By what sense do you perceive them?

*Alc.* I do not perceive them immediately by any of my senses. I am nevertheless persuaded of their existence, because I can collect it from their effects and operations. They are the messengers which, running to and fro in the nerves, preserve a communication between the soul and outward objects.

*Euph.* You admit then the being of a soul?

*Alc.* Provided I do not admit an immaterial substance, I see no inconvenience in admitting there may be such a thing as a soul. And this may be no more than a thin fine texture of subtle parts or spirits residing in the brain.

*Euph.* I do not ask about its nature. I only ask whether you admit that there is a principle of thought and action, and whether it be perceivable by sense.

*Alc.* I grant that there is such a principle, and that it is not the object of sense itself but inferred from appearances which are perceived by sense.

*Euph.* If I understand you rightly, from animal functions and motions you infer the existence of animal spirits, and from reasonable acts you infer the existence of a reasonable soul. Is it not so?

*Alc.* It is.

*Euph.* It should seem, therefore, that the being of things imperceptible to sense may be collected from effects and signs, or sensible tokens.

*Alc.* It may.

*Euph.* Tell me, Alciphron, is not the soul that which makes the principal distinction between a real person and a shadow, a living man and a carcass?

*Alc.* I grant it is.

*Euph.* I cannot, therefore, know that you, for instance, are a distinct thinking individual or a living real man, by surer or other signs than those from which it can be inferred that you have a soul?

*Alc.* You cannot.

*Euph.* Pray tell me, are not all acts immediately and properly perceived by sense reducible to motion?

*Alc.* They are.

*Euph.* From motions, therefore, you infer a mover or cause; and from reasonable motions (or such as appear calculated for a reasonable end) a rational cause, soul or spirit?

*Alc.* Even so.

5 *Euph.* The soul of man actuates but a small body, an insignificant particle, in respect of the great masses of nature, the elements and heavenly bodies, and system of the world. And the wisdom that appears in those motions, which are the effect of human reason, is incomparably less than that which discovers itself in the structure and use of organized natural bodies, animal or vegetable. A man with his hand can make no machine so admirable as the hand itself. Nor can any of those motions by which we trace out human reason approach the skill and contrivance of those wonderful motions of the heart, and brain, and other vital parts, which do not depend on the will of man.

*Alc.* All this is true.

*Euph.* Does it not follow, then, that from natural motions, independent of man's will, may be inferred both power and wisdom incomparably greater than that of the human soul?

*Alc.* It should seem so.

*Euph.* Further, is there not in natural productions and effects a visible unity of counsel and design? Are not the rules fixed and immoveable? Do not the same laws of motion obtain throughout?

The same in China and here, the same two thousand years ago and at this day?

*Alc.*  All this I do not deny.

*Euph.*  Is there not also a connexion or relation between animals and vegetables, between both and the elements, between the elements and heavenly bodies; so that, from their mutual respects, influences, subordinations, and uses, they may be collected to be parts of one whole, conspiring to one and the same end and fulfilling the same design?

*Alc.*  Supposing all this to be true.

*Euph.*  Will it not then follow that this vastly great or infinite power and wisdom must be supposed in one and the same Agent, Spirit, or Mind; and that we have at least as clear, full and immediate certainty of the being of this infinitely wise and powerful Spirit, as of any one human soul whatsoever besides our own?

*Alc.*  Let me consider; I suspect we proceed too hastily. What! Do you pretend you can have the same assurance of the being of a God that you can have of mine, whom you actually see stand before you and talk to you?

*Euph.*  The very same, if not greater.

*Alc.*  How do you make this appear?

*Euph.*  By the person 'Alciphron' is meant an individual thinking thing, and not the hair, skin, or visible surface, or any part of the outward form, colour, or shape of Alciphron.

*Alc.*  This I grant.

*Euph.*  And in granting this, you grant that, in a strict sense, I do not see Alciphron, *i.e.* that individual thinking thing, but only such visible signs and tokens as suggest and infer the being of that invisible thinking principle or soul. Even so, in the self-same manner it seems to me that, though I cannot with eyes of flesh behold the invisible God, yet I do in the strictest sense behold and perceive by all my senses such signs and tokens, such effects and operations, as suggest, indicate, and demonstrate an invisible God as certainly, and with the same evidence, at least, as any other signs, perceived by sense, do suggest to me the existence of your soul, spirit, or thinking principle; which I am convinced of only by a few signs or effects, and the motions of one small organized body, whereas I do at all times and in all places perceive sensible signs which evince the being of God. The point, therefore, doubted or denied by you at the beginning, now seems manifestly to follow from the premises. Throughout this whole inquiry, have we not considered every step with care, and made not the least advance without clear evidence? You and I examined and assented singly to each foregoing proposition; what shall we do then with the conclusion? For my part, if you do not help me out, I find myself under an absolute necessity of admitting it for true. You must therefore be content henceforward to bear the blame, if I live and die in the belief of a God.

6   *Alc.* It must be confessed, I do not readily find an answer. There seems to be some foundation for what you say. But, on the other hand, if the point was so clear as you pretend, I cannot conceive how so many sagacious men of our sect should be so much in the dark as not to know or believe one syllable of it.

*Euph.*   O Alciphron, it is not our present business to account for the oversights, or vindicate the honour, of those great men the free-thinkers, when their very existence is in danger of being called in question.

*Alc.*   How so?

*Euph.*   Be pleased to recollect the concessions you have made and then show me, if the arguments for a Deity be not conclusive, by what better arguments you can prove the existence of that thinking thing which in strictness constitutes the free-thinker.

As soon as Euphanor had uttered these words, Alciphron stopped short and stood in a posture of meditation, while the rest of us continued our walk and took two or three turns, after which he joined us again with a smiling countenance, like one who had made some discovery.

I have found, said he, what may clear up the point in dispute and give Euphranor entire satisfaction; I would say an argument which will prove the existence of a free-thinker, the like whereof cannot be applied to prove the existence of God. You must know then that your notion of our perceiving the existence of God, as certainly and immediately as we do that of a human person, I could by no means digest, though I must own it puzzled me, till I had considered the matter. At first methought a particular structure, shape, or motion was the most certain proof of a thinking reasonable soul. But a little attention satisfied me that these things have no necessary connexion with reason, knowledge, and wisdom. And that, allowing them to be certain proofs of a living soul, they cannot be so of a thinking and reasonable one. Upon second thoughts, therefore, and a minute examination of this point, I have found that nothing so much convinces me of the existence of another person as his speaking to me. It is my hearing you talk that, in strict and philosophical truth, is to me the best argument for your being. And this is a peculiar argument, inapplicable to your purpose. For you will not, I suppose, pretend that God speaks to man in the same clear and sensible manner as one man does to another?

7  *Euph.* How! is then the impression of sound so much more evident than that of other senses? Or, if it be, is the voice of man louder than that of thunder?

*Alc.* Alas! You mistake the point. What I mean is not the sound of speech merely as such, but the arbitrary use of sensible signs, which have no similitude or necessary connexion with the things signified, so as by the apposite management of them to suggest and exhibit to my mind an endless variety of things, differing in nature, time, and place; thereby informing me, entertaining me, and directing me how to act, not only with regard to things near and present, but also with regard to things distant and future. No matter whether these signs are pronounced or written, whether they enter by the eye or the ear, they have the same use and are equally proofs of an intelligent, thinking, designing cause.

*Euph.* But what if it should appear that God really speaks to man; should this content you?

*Alc.* I am for admitting no inward speech, no holy instincts or suggestions of light or spirit. All that, you must know, passes with men of sense for nothing. If you do not make it plain to me that God speaks to men by outward sensible signs, of such sort and in such manner as I have defined, you do nothing.

*Euph.* But if it shall appear plainly that God speaks to men by the intervention and use of arbitrary, outward, sensible signs, having no resemblance or necessary connexion with the things they stand for and suggest; if it shall appear that, by innumerable combinations of these signs, an endless variety of things is discovered and made known to us, and that we are thereby instructed or informed in their different natures; that we are taught and admonished what to shun, and what to pursue, and are directed how to regulate our motions, and how to act with respect to things distant from us, as well in time as place, will this content you?

*Alc.* It is the very thing I would have you make out; for therein consist the force and use and nature of language.

**8**  *Euph.*   Look, Alciphron, do you not see the castle upon yonder hill?
*Alc.*   I do.
*Euph.*   Is it not at a great distance from you?
*Alc.*   It is.
*Euph.*   Tell me, Alciphron, is not distance a line turned end-wise to the eye?[1]
*Alc.*   Doubtless.
*Euph.*   And can a line, in that situation, project more than one single point on the bottom of the eye?
*Alc.*   It cannot.
*Euph.*   Therefore the appearance of a long and of a short distance is of the same magnitude, or rather of no magnitude at all, being in all cases one single point.
*Alc.*   It seems so.
*Euph.*   Should it not follow from hence that distance is not immediately perceived by the eye?
*Alc.*   It should.
*Euph.*   Must it not then be perceived by the mediation of some other thing?
*Alc.*   It must.
*Euph.*   To discover what this is, let us examine what alteration there may be in the appearance of the same object placed at different distances from the eye. Now, I find by experience that when an object is removed still farther and farther off in a direct line from the eye, its visible appearance still grows lesser and fainter. And this change of appearance, being proportional and universal, seems to me to be that by which we apprehend the various degrees of distance.
*Alc.*   I have nothing to object to this.
*Euph.*   But littleness or faintness, in their own nature, seem to have no necessary connexion with greater length of distance?
*Alc.*   I admit this to be true.
*Euph.*   Will it not follow then that they could never suggest it but from experience?
*Alc.*   It will.
*Euph.*   That is to say, we perceive distance, not immediately, but by mediation of a sign, which has no likeness to it or necessary connexion with it, but only suggests it from repeated experience, as words do things.

---

[1] Berkeley repeats the argument first used in *NTV*, 2.

*Alc.* Hold, Euphranor. Now I think of it, the writers in optics tell us of an angle made by the two optic axes, where they meet in the visible point or object; which angle, the obtuser it is the nearer it shows the object to be, and by how much the acuter, by so much the farther off; and this from a necessary demonstrable connexion.[2]

*Euph.* The mind then finds out the distance of things by geometry?

*Alc.* It does.

*Euph.* Should it not follow, therefore, that nobody could see but those who had learned geometry, and knew something of lines and angles?

*Alc.* There is a sort of natural geometry which is got without learning.

*Euph.* Pray inform me, Alciphron, in order to frame a proof of any kind or deduce one point from another, is it not necessary that I perceive the connexion of the terms in the premises, and the connexion of the premises with the conclusion; and, in general, to know one thing by means of another, must I not first know that other thing? When I perceive your meaning by your words, must I not first perceive the words themselves, and must I not know the premises before I infer the conclusion?

*Alc.* All this is true.

*Euph.* Whoever, therefore, collects a nearer distance from a wider angle, or a farther distance from an acuter angle, must first perceive the angles themselves. And he who does not perceive those angles can infer nothing from them, is it so or not?

*Alc.* It is as you say.

*Euph.* Ask now the first man you meet whether he perceives or knows anything of those optic angles? Or whether he ever thinks about them or makes any inferences from them, either by natural or artificial geometry? What answer do you think he would make?

*Alc.* To speak the truth, I believe his answer would be that he knew nothing of those matters.

*Euph.* It cannot therefore be that men judge of distance by angles; nor, consequently, can there be any force in the argument you drew from thence, to prove that distance is perceived by means of something which has a necessary connexion with it.

*Alc.* I agree with you.

---

[2] This Cartesian theory is examined in *NTV*, 4.

9. *Euph.* To me it seems that a man may know whether he perceives a thing or no; and, if he perceives it, whether it be immediately or mediately: and, if mediately, whether by means of something like or unlike, necessarily or arbitrarily connected with it.

*Alc.* It seems so.

*Euph.* And is it not certain that distance is perceived only by experience, if it be neither perceived immediately by itself, nor by means of any image, nor of any lines and angles which are like it or have a necessary connexion with it?

*Alc.* It is.

*Euph.* Does it not seem to follow from what has been said and allowed by you that, before all experience, a man would not imagine the things he saw were at any distance from him?

*Alc.* How! let me see.

*Euph.* The littleness or faintness of appearance, or any other idea or sensation not necessarily connected with or resembling distance, can no more suggest different degrees of distance or any distance at all, to the mind which has not experienced a connexion of the things signifying and signified, than words can suggest notions before a man has learned the language.

*Alc.* I allow this to be true.

*Euph.* Will it not thence follow that a man born blind and made to see, would, upon first receiving his sight, take the things he saw not to be at any distance from him, but in his eye, or rather in his mind?

*Alc.* I must own it seems so. And yet, on the other hand, I can hardly persuade myself that, if I were in such a state, I should think those objects which I now see at so great a distance to be at no distance at all.

*Euph.* It seems, then, that you now think the objects of sight are at a distance from you.

*Alc.* Doubtless I do. Can any one question but yonder castle is at a great distance?

*Euph.* Tell me, Alciphron, can you discern the doors, windows, and battlements of that same castle?

*Alc.* I cannot. At this distance it seems only a small round tower.

*Euph.* But I, who have been at it, know that it is no small round tower, but a large square building with battlements and turrets, which it seems you do not see.

*Alc.* What will you infer from thence?

*Euph.* I would infer that the very object which you strictly and properly perceive by sight is not that thing which is several miles distant.

*Alc.* Why so?

*Euph.* Because a little round object is one thing, and a great square object is another. Is it not?

*Alc.* I cannot deny it.

*Euph.* Tell me, is not the visible appearance alone the proper object of sight?

*Alc.* It is.

What think you now (said Euphranor, pointing towards the heavens) of the visible appearance of yonder planet? Is it not a round luminous flat, no bigger than a sixpence?

*Alc.* What then?

*Euph.* Tell me, then, what you think of the planet itself. Do you not conceive it to be a vast opaque globe, with several unequal risings and valleys?

*Alc.* I do.

*Euph.* How can you therefore conclude that the proper object of your sight exists at a distance?

*Alc.* I confess I know not.

*Euph.* For your farther conviction, do but consider that crimson cloud. Think you that, if you were in the very place where it is, you would perceive anything like what you now see?

*Alc.* By no means. I should perceive only a dark mist.

*Euph.* Is it not plain, therefore, that neither the castle, the planet, nor the cloud, which you see here, are those real ones which you suppose exist at a distance?

10  *Alc.* What am I to think then? Do we see anything at all, or is it altogether fancy and illusion?

*Euph.* Upon the whole, it seems the proper objects of sight are light and colours, with their several shades and degrees. All which, being infinitely diversified and combined, form a language wonderfully adapted to suggest and exhibit to us the distances, figures, situations, dimensions, and various qualities of tangible objects: not by similitude, nor yet by inference of necessary connexion, but by the arbitrary imposition of Providence, just as words suggest the things signified by them.

*Alc.* How! Do we not, strictly speaking, perceive by sight such things as trees, houses, men, rivers, and the like?

*Euph.* We do, indeed, perceive or apprehend those things by the faculty of sight. But, will it follow from thence that they are the proper and immediate objects of sight, any more than that all those things are the proper and immediate objects of hearing which are signified by the help of words or sounds?

*Alc.* You would have us think, then, that light, shades, and colours, variously combined, answer to the several articulations of sounds in language; and that, by means thereof, all sorts of objects are suggested to the mind through the eye, in the same manner as they are suggested by words or sounds through the ear: that is, neither from necessary deduction to the judgment, nor from similitude to the fancy, but purely and solely from experience, custom, and habit.

*Euph.* I would not have you think anything more than the nature of things obliges you to think, nor submit in the least to my judgment, but only to the force of truth, which is an imposition that I suppose the freest thinkers will not pretend to be exempt from.

*Alc.* You have led me, it seems, step by step, till I am got I know not where. But I shall try to get out again, if not by the way I came, yet by some other of my own finding.

Here Alciphron, having made a short pause, proceeded as follows.

11  Answer me, Euphranor, should it not follow from these principles that a man born blind, and made to see, would at first sight not only not perceive their distance, but also not so much as know the very things themselves which he saw, for instance, men or trees? which surely to suppose must be absurd.[3]

*Euph.* I grant, in consequence of those principles, which both you and I have admitted, that such a one would never think of men, trees, or any other objects that he had been accustomed to perceive by touch, upon having his mind filled with new sensations of light and colours, whose various combinations he does not yet understand or know the meaning of; no more than a Chinese, upon first hearing the words 'man' and 'tree', would think of the things signified by them. In both cases, there must be time and experience, by repeated acts, to acquire a habit of knowing the

---

[3] Refers to the Molyneux problem, first discussed by Berkeley in *NTV*, 132.

connexion between the signs and things signified; that is to say, of understanding the language, whether of the eyes or of the ears. And I conceive no absurdity in all this.

*Alc.*   I see, therefore, in strict philosophical truth, that rock only in the same sense that I may be said to hear it when the word 'rock' is pronounced.

*Euph.*   In the very same.

*Alc.*   How comes it to pass then that everyone shall say he sees, for instance, a rock or a house, when those things are before his eyes; but nobody will say he hears a rock or a house, but only the words or sounds themselves by which those things are said to be signified or suggested, but not heard? Besides, if vision be only a language speaking to the eyes, it may be asked: when did men learn this language? To acquire the knowledge of so many signs, as go to the making up a language, is a work of some difficulty. But, will any man say he has spent time, or been at pains, to learn this language of vision?

*Euph.*   No wonder, we cannot assign a time beyond our remotest memory. If we have been all practising this language, ever since our first entrance into the world; if the Author of nature constantly speaks to the eyes of all mankind, even in their earliest infancy, whenever the eyes are open in the light, whether alone or in company; it does not seem to me at all strange that men should not be aware they had ever learned a language begun so early, and practised so constantly, as this of vision. And, if we also consider that it is the same throughout the whole world and not, like other languages, differing in different places, it will not seem unaccountable that men should mistake the connexion between the proper objects of sight and the things signified by them to be founded in necessary relation or likeness, or that they should even take them for the same things. Hence it seems easy to conceive why men, who do not think, should confound in this language of vision the signs with the things signified, otherwise than they are wont to do in the various particular languages formed by the several nations of men.

12   It may be also worth while to observe that signs, being little considered in themselves or for their own sake, but only in their relative capacity and for the sake of those things whereof they are signs, it comes to pass that the mind overlooks them, so as to carry its attention immediately on to the things signified. Thus, for example in reading, we run over the

characters with the slightest regard and pass on to the meaning. Hence it is frequent for men to say, they see words, and notions, and things, in reading of a book; whereas in strictness they see only the characters which suggest words, notions, and things. And, by parity of reason, may we not suppose that men, not resting in, but overlooking the immediate and proper objects of sight, as in their own nature of small moment, carry their attention onward to the very things signified and talk as if they saw the secondary objects which, in truth and strictness, are not seen, but only suggested and apprehended by means of the proper objects of sight, which alone are seen?

*Alc.* To speak my mind freely, this dissertation grows tedious, and runs into points too dry and minute for a gentleman's attention.

I thought, said Crito, we had been told that minute philosophers loved to consider things closely and minutely.

*Alc.* That is true, but in so polite an age who would be a mere philosopher? There is a certain scholastic accuracy which ill suits the freedom and ease of a well-bred man. But, to cut short this chicane, I propound it fairly to your own conscience, whether you really think that God Himself speaks every day and in every place to the eyes of all men?

*Euph.* That is really and in truth my opinion; and it should be yours too, if you are consistent with yourself and abide by your own definition of language. Since you cannot deny that the great Mover and Author of nature constantly explains Himself to the eyes of men by the sensible intervention of arbitrary signs, which have no similitude or connexion with the things signified; so as, by compounding and disposing them, to suggest and exhibit an endless variety of objects, differing in nature, time, and place; thereby informing and directing men how to act with respect to things distant and future, as well as near and present. In consequence, I say, of your own sentiments and concessions, you have as much reason to think the Universal Agent or God speaks to your eyes as you can have for thinking any particular person speaks to your ears.

*Alc.* I cannot help thinking that some fallacy runs through this whole ratiocination, though perhaps I may not readily point it out. [It seems to me that every other sense may as well be deemed a language as that of vision. Smells and tastes, for instance, are signs that inform us of other qualities to which they have neither likeness nor necessary connexion.

*Euph.* That they are signs is certain, as also that language and all other signs agree in the general nature of sign, or so far forth as signs. But it is as certain that all signs are not language; not even all significant sounds, such as the natural cries of animals, or the inarticulate sounds and interjections of men. It is the articulation, combination, variety, copiousness, extensive and general use and easy application of signs (all which are commonly found in vision) that constitute the true nature of language. Other senses may indeed furnish signs; and yet those signs have no more right than inarticulate sounds to be thought a language.

*Alc.*]⁴ Hold! let me see. In language the signs are arbitrary, are they not?

*Euph.* They are.

*Alc.* And consequently, they do not always suggest real matters of fact. Whereas this natural language, as you call it, or these visible signs, do always suggest things in the same uniform way, and have the same constant regular connexion with matters of fact. Whence it should seem the connexion was necessary and, therefore, according to the definition premised, it can be no language. How do you solve this objection?

*Euph.* You may solve it yourself by the help of a picture or looking-glass.

*Alc.* You are in the right. I see there is nothing in it. I know not what else to say to this opinion more, than that it is so odd and contrary to my way of thinking that I shall never assent to it.

**13** *Euph.* Be pleased to recollect your own lectures upon prejudice, and apply them in the present case. Perhaps they may help you to follow where reason leads, and to suspect notions which are strongly riveted without having been ever examined.

*Alc.* I disdain the suspicion of prejudice. And I do not speak only for myself. I know a club of most ingenious men, the freest from prejudice of any men alive, who abhor the notion of a God, and I doubt not would be very able to untie this knot.

Upon which words of Alciphron, I, who had acted the part of an indifferent stander-by, observed to him: That it misbecame his character and repeated professions to own an attachment to the judgment, or build upon the presumed abilities of other men, how ingenious soever; and that this proceeding might encourage his adversaries to have recourse to authority, in which perhaps they would find their account more than he.

---

⁴ The material in parentheses was added in the 1752 edition.

Oh! said Crito, I have often observed the conduct of minute philosophers. When one of them has got a ring of disciples round him, his method is to exclaim against prejudice and recommend thinking and reasoning, giving to understand that himself is a man of deep researches and close argument, one who examines impartially and concludes warily. The same man, in other company, if he chance to be pressed with reason, shall laugh at logic and assume the lazy supine airs of a fine gentleman, a wit, a railleur, to avoid the dryness of a regular and exact inquiry. This double face of the minute philosopher is of no small use to propagate and maintain his notions. Though to me it seems a plain case that, if a fine gentleman will shake off authority and appeal from religion to reason, unto reason he must go. And, if he cannot go without leading-strings, surely he had better be led by the authority of the public than by that of any knot of minute philosophers.

*Alc.* Gentlemen, this discourse is very irksome and needless. For my part, I am a friend to inquiry. I am willing reason should have its full and free scope. I build on no man's authority. For my part, I have no interest in denying a God. Any man may believe or not believe a God, as he pleases, for me. But, after all, Euphranor must allow me to stare a little at his conclusions.

*Euph.* The conclusions are yours as much as mine, for you were led to them by your own concessions.

**14** You, it seems, stare to find that God is not far from every one of us; and that in Him we live, and move, and have our being.[5] You who, in the beginning of this morning's conference, thought it strange that God should leave Himself without a witness, do now think it strange the witness should be so full and clear.

*Alc.* I must own I do. I was aware, indeed, of a certain metaphysical hypothesis of our seeing all things in God by the union of the human soul with the intelligible substance of the Deity, which neither I nor anyone else could make sense of.[6] But I never imagined it could be pretended that we saw God with our fleshly eyes as plain as we see any human person whatsoever, and that He daily speaks to our senses in a manifest and clear dialect.

*Cri.* [As for that metaphysical hypothesis, I can make no more of it than you. But I think it plain,] this [optic][7] language has a necessary

---

[5] Berkeley often quotes Acts 17: 28.    [6] An oblique reference to Malebranche's theory.
[7] The material in parentheses was added in the second edition (1732) and subsequent editions.

connexion with knowledge, wisdom, and goodness. It is equivalent to a constant creation, betokening an immediate act of power and providence. It cannot be accounted for by mechanical principles, by atoms, attractions, or effluvia. This instantaneous production and reproduction of so many signs, combined, dissolved, transposed, diversified, and adapted to such an endless variety of purposes, ever shifting with the occasions and suited to them, being utterly inexplicable and unaccountable by the laws of motion, by chance, by fate, or the like blind principles, sets forth and testifies the immediate operation of spirit or thinking being; and not merely of a spirit, which every motion or gravitation may possibly infer, but of one wise, good, and provident Spirit, which directs, and rules, and governs the world. Some philosophers, being convinced of the wisdom and power of the Creator from the make and contrivance of organized bodies and orderly system of the world, did nevertheless imagine that he left this system with all its parts and contents well adjusted and put in motion, as an artist leaves a clock, to go thenceforward of itself for a certain period. But this visual language proves, not a Creator merely, but a provident Governor, actually and intimately present, and attentive to all our interests and motions, who watches over our conduct and takes care of our minutest actions and designs throughout the whole course of our lives, informing, admonishing, and directing incessantly in a most evident and sensible manner. This is truly wonderful.

*Euph.* And is it not so, that men should be encompassed by such a wonder, without reflecting on it?

**15** Something there is of divine and admirable in this language, addressed to our eyes, that may well awaken the mind, and deserves its utmost attention. It is learned with so little pains; it expresses the differences of things so clearly and aptly; it instructs with such facility and despatch, by one glance of the eye conveying a greater variety of advices, and a more distinct knowledge of things, than would be got by a discourse of several hours. And, while it informs, it amuses and entertains the mind with such singular pleasure and delight. It is of such excellent use in giving a stability and permanency to human discourse, in recording sounds and bestowing life on dead languages, enabling us to converse with men of remote ages and countries. And it answers so apposite to the uses and necessities of mankind, informing us more distinctly of those objects whose nearness and magnitude qualify them to be of greatest detriment or benefit to our bodies, and less exactly in proportion as their littleness or distance make them of less concern to us.

*Alc.* And yet these strange things affect men but little.

*Euph.* But they are not strange; they are familiar, and that makes them to be overlooked. Things which rarely happen strike, whereas frequency lessens the admiration of things, though in themselves ever so admirable. Hence a common man, who is not used to think and make reflexions, would probably be more convinced of the being of a God by one single sentence heard once in his life from the sky than by all the experience he has had of this visual language, contrived with such exquisite skill, so constantly addressed to his eyes, and so plainly declaring the nearness, wisdom, and providence of Him with whom we have to do.

*Alc.* After all, I cannot satisfy myself how men should be so little surprised or amazed about this visive faculty, if it was really of a nature so surprising and amazing.

*Euph.* But let us suppose a nation of men born blind from their infancy, among whom a stranger arrives, the only man who can see in all the country. Let us suppose this stranger travelling with some of the natives, and that one while he foretells to them that, in case they walk straight forward, in half an hour they shall meet men, or cattle, or come to a house; that, if they turn to the right and proceed, they shall in a few minutes be in danger of falling down a precipice; that, shaping their course to the left, they will in such a time arrive at a river, a wood, or a mountain. What think you? Must they not be infinitely surprised that one who had never been in their country before should know it so much better than themselves? And would not those predictions seem to them as unaccountable and incredible as prophecy to a minute philosopher?

*Alc.* I cannot deny it.

*Euph.* But it seems to require intense thought to be able to unravel a prejudice that has been so long forming, to get over the vulgar error of ideas common to both senses and so to distinguish between the objects of sight and touch,[b] which have grown (if I may so say), blended together in

---

[b] See the annexed Treatise, wherein this point and the whole theory of vision are more fully explained: the paradoxes of which theory, though at first received with great ridicule by those who think ridicule the test of truth, were many years after surprisingly confirmed, by a case of a person made to see who had been blind from his birth. See *Philosophical Transactions*, No. 402. [Vol. 35 (1727–8), 447–50. This note was added, in two stages, in the 1732 editions of *Alciphron*, to which the *Essay towards a New Theory of Vision* was appended. It was omitted from the 1752 edition, from which the *New Theory of Vision* was also omitted.]

our fancy, as to be able to suppose ourselves exactly in the state that one of those men would be in, if he were made to see. And yet this I believe is possible, and might seem worth the pains of a little thinking, especially to those men whose proper employment and profession it is to think, and unravel prejudices and confute mistakes. I frankly own I cannot find my way out of this maze, and should gladly be set right by those who see better than myself.

*Cri.*    The pursuing this subject in their own thoughts would possibly open a new scene to those speculative gentlemen of the minute philosophy. It puts me in mind of a passage in the Psalmist, where he represents God to be covered with light as with a garment, and would methinks be no ill comment on that ancient notion of some eastern sages – that God had light for His body, and truth for His soul.

This conversation lasted till a servant came to tell us the tea was ready; upon which we walked in, and found Lysicles at the tea-table.

16    As soon as we sat down, I am glad, said Alciphron, that I have here found my second, a fresh man to maintain our common cause, which, I doubt, Lysicles will think has suffered by his absence.

*Lysicles.*    Why so?

*Alc.*    I have been drawn into some concessions you won't like.

*Lys.*    Let me know what they are.

*Alc.*    Why, that there is such a thing as a God and that his existence is very certain.

*Lys.*    Bless me! How came you to entertain so wild a notion?

*Alc.*    You know we profess to follow reason wherever it leads. And in short I have been reasoned into it.

*Lys.*    Reasoned! You should say amused with words, bewildered with sophistry.

*Euph.*    Have you a mind to hear the same reasoning that led Alciphron and me, step by step, that we may examine whether it be sophistry or no?

*Lys.*    As to that I am very easy. I guess all that can be said on that head. It shall be my business to help my friend out, whatever arguments drew him in.

*Euph.*    Will you admit the premises and deny the conclusions?

*Lys.*    What if I admit the conclusion?

*Euph.*    How! will you grant there is a God?

*Lys.*    Perhaps I may.

*Euph.*   Then we are agreed.

*Lys.*   Perhaps not.

*Euph.*   O Lysicles, you are a subtle adversary. I know not what you would be at.

*Lys.*   You must know then that at bottom the being of God is a point in itself of small consequence, and a man may make this concession without yielding much. The great point is what sense the word 'God' is to be taken in. The very Epicureans allowed the being of gods; but then they were indolent gods, unconcerned with human affairs. Hobbes allowed a corporeal God, and Spinoza held the universe to be God. And yet nobody doubts they were staunch free-thinkers. I could wish indeed the word 'God' were quite omitted, because in most minds it is coupled with a sort of superstitious awe, the very root of all religion. I shall not, nevertheless, be much disturbed though the name be retained and the being of God allowed in any sense but in that of a Mind, which knows all things and beholds human actions, like some judge or magistrate, with infinite observation and intelligence. The belief of a God in this sense fills a man's mind with scruples, lays him under constraints and embitters his very being; but in another sense it may be attended with no great ill consequence. This I know was the opinion of our great Diagoras, who told me he would never have been at the pains to find out a demonstration that there was no God, if the received notion of God had been the same with that of some Fathers and Schoolmen.

*Euph.*   Pray what was that?

17   *Lys.* You must know, Diagoras, a man of much reading and inquiry, had discovered that once upon a time the most profound and speculative divines, finding it impossible to reconcile the attributes of God, taken in the common sense or in any known sense, with human reason and the appearances of things, taught that the words 'knowledge', 'wisdom', 'goodness', and such like, when spoken of the Deity, must be understood in a quite different sense from what they signify in the vulgar acceptation, or from anything that we can form a notion of or conceive.[8] Hence, whatever objections might be made against the attributes of God, they easily solved by denying those attributes belonged to God, in this, or that, or any known

---

[8]   An oblique reference to two of Berkeley's fellow bishops in the Church of Ireland, William King and Peter Browne, who defended the theory that words such as 'wise' etc. are not applied literally to God and man in the same sense.

particular sense or notion; which was the same thing as to deny they belonged to Him at all. And thus denying the attributes of God, they in effect denied His being, though perhaps they were not aware of it.

Suppose, for instance, a man should object that future contingencies were inconsistent with the foreknowledge of God, because it is repugnant that certain knowledge should be of an uncertain thing. It was a ready and an easy answer to say that this may be true with respect to knowledge taken in the common sense, or in any sense that we can possibly form any notion of; but that there would not appear the same inconsistency between the contingent nature of things and Divine foreknowledge, taken to signify somewhat that we know nothing of, which in God supplies the place of what we understand by knowledge; from which it differs not in quantity or degree of perfection, but altogether and in kind, as light does from sound; and even more, since these agree in that they are both sensations; whereas knowledge in God has no sort of resemblance or agreement with any notion that man can frame of knowledge. The like may be said of all the other attributes, which indeed may by this means be equally reconciled with everything or with nothing. But all men who think must needs see, this is cutting knots and not untying them. For, how are things reconciled with the Divine attributes when these attributes themselves are in every intelligible sense denied, and consequently the very notion of God taken away and nothing left but the name without any meaning annexed to it? In short, the belief that there is an unknown subject of attributes absolutely unknown is a very innocent doctrine; which the acute Diagoras well saw and was therefore wonderfully delighted with this system.

18 For, said he, if this could once make its way and obtain in the world, there would be an end of all natural or rational religion, which is the basis both of the Jewish and the Christian. For he who comes to God, or enters himself in the church of God, must first believe that there is a God in some intelligible sense; and not only that there is something in general, without any proper notion, though never so inadequate, of any of its qualities or attributes; for this may be fate, or chaos, or plastic nature, or anything else as well as God. Nor will it avail to say there is something in this unknown being analogous to knowledge and goodness; that is to say, which produces those effects which we could not conceive to be produced by men, in any degree, without knowledge and goodness. For this is in fact to give up the point in dispute between theists and atheists,

the question having always been, not whether there was a principle (which point was allowed by all philosophers, as well before as since Anaxagoras), but whether this principle was a νούς, a thinking intelligent being: that is to say, whether that order and beauty and use, visible in natural effects, could be produced by anything but a Mind or Intelligence, in the proper sense of the word? And whether there must not be true, real, and proper knowledge in the First Cause? We will, therefore, acknowledge that all those natural effects, which are vulgarly ascribed to knowledge and wisdom, proceed from a being in which there is, properly speaking, no knowledge or wisdom at all but only something else, which in reality is the cause of those things which men, for want of knowing better, ascribe to what they call knowledge and wisdom and understanding. You wonder perhaps to hear a man of pleasure, who diverts himself as I do, philosophize at this rate. But you should consider that much is to be got by conversing with ingenious men, which is a short way to knowledge, that saves a man the drudgery of reading and thinking.

And, now we have granted to you that there is a God in this indefinite sense, I would fain see what use you can make of this concession. You cannot argue from unknown attributes or, which is the same thing, from attributes in an unknown sense. You cannot prove that God is to be loved for His goodness, or feared for His justice, or respected for His knowledge: all which consequences, we own, would follow from those attributes admitted in an intelligible sense. But we deny that those or any other consequences can be drawn from attributes admitted in no particular sense, or in a sense which none of us understand. Since, therefore, nothing can be inferred from such an account of God about conscience, or worship, or religion, you may even make the best of it. And, not to be singular, we will use the name too, and so at once there is an end of atheism.

*Euph.* This account of a Deity is new to me. I do not like it, and therefore shall leave it to be maintained by those who do.

[Sections 19 –25 are omitted]


## The Seventh Dialogue

1 The philosophers having resolved to set out for London next morning, we assembled at break of day in the library. Alciphron began with a declaration of his sincerity, assuring us he had very maturely and with a

most unbiased mind considered all that had been said the day before. He added that upon the whole he could not deny several probable reasons were produced for embracing the Christian faith. But, said he, those reasons being only probable, can never prevail against absolute certainty and demonstration. If, therefore, I can demonstrate your religion to be a thing altogether absurd and inconsistent, your probable arguments in its defence do from that moment lose their force, and with it all right to be answered or considered. The concurring testimony of sincere and able witnesses has without question great weight in human affairs. I will even grant that things odd and unaccountable to human judgment or experience may sometimes claim our assent on that sole motive. And I will also grant it possible for a tradition to be conveyed with moral evidence through many centuries. But at the same time you will grant to me that a thing demonstrably and palpably false is not to be admitted on any testimony whatever, which at best can never amount to demonstration. To be plain, no testimony can make nonsense sense; no moral evidence can make contradictions consistent.

Know, then, that as the strength of our cause does not depend upon, so neither is it to be decided by, any critical points of history, chronology, or languages. You are not to wonder if the same sort of tradition and moral proof, which governs our assent with respect to facts in civil or natural history, is not admitted as a sufficient voucher for metaphysical absurdities and absolute impossibilities. Things obscure and unaccountable in human affairs or the operations of nature may yet be possible and, if well attested, may be assented unto; but religious assent or faith can be evidently shown in its own nature to be impracticable, impossible, and absurd. This is the primary motive to infidelity. This is our citadel and fortress, which may indeed be graced with outworks of various erudition but, if those are demolished, remains in itself and of its own proper strength impregnable.

*Euph.* This, it must be owned, reduces our inquiry within a narrow compass. Do but make out this, and I shall have nothing more to say.

*Alc.* Know, then, that the shallow mind of the vulgar, as it dwells only on the outward surface of things and considers them in the gross, may be easily imposed on. Hence a blind reverence for religious faith and mystery. But when an acute philosopher comes to dissect and analyse these points, the imposture plainly appears; and as he has no blindness, so he has no reverence for empty notions or, to speak more properly, for mere forms of speech, which mean nothing and are of no use to mankind.

2   Words are signs; they do or should stand for ideas, which so far as they suggest they are significant. But words that suggest no ideas are insignificant. He who annexes a clear idea to every word he makes use of speaks sense; but where such ideas are wanting, the speaker utters nonsense. In order therefore to know whether any man's speech be senseless and insignificant, we have nothing to do but lay aside the words and consider the ideas suggested by them. Men, not being able immediately to communicate their ideas one to another, are obliged to make use of sensible signs or words, the use of which is to raise those ideas in the hearer which are in the mind of the speaker; and if they fail of this end they serve to no purpose. He who really thinks has a train of ideas succeeding each other and connected in his mind; and when he expresses himself by discourse, each word suggests a distinct idea to the hearer or reader; who by that means has the same train of ideas in his, which was in the mind of the speaker or writer. As far as this effect is produced, so far the discourse is intelligible, has sense and meaning. Hence it follows that whoever can be supposed to understand what he reads or hears must have a train of ideas raised in his mind, correspondent to the train of words read or heard. These plain truths, to which men readily assent in theory, are but little attended to in practice, and therefore deserve to be enlarged on and inculcated, however obvious and undeniable. Mankind are generally averse from thinking, though apt enough to entertain discourse either in themselves or others; the effect whereof is that their minds are rather stored with names than ideas, the husk of science rather than the thing. And yet these words without meaning do often make distinctions of parties, the subject matter of their disputes and the object of their zeal. This is the most general cause of error, which does not influence ordinary minds alone, but even those who pass for acute and learned philosophers are often employed about names instead of things or ideas, and are supposed to know when they only pronounce hard words without a meaning.

3   Though it is evident that, as knowledge is the perception of the connexion or disagreement between ideas,[9] he who does not distinctly

---

[9] Cf. Locke, *Essay*, IV, I, 2: 'Knowledge then seems to me to be nothing but the perception of the connexion and agreement, or disagreement and repugnancy of any of our Ideas.'

perceive the ideas marked by the terms, so as to form a mental proposition answering to the verbal, cannot possibly have knowledge. No more can he be said to have opinion or faith, which imply a weaker assent, but still it must be to a proposition, the terms of which are understood as clearly, although the agreement or disagreement of the ideas may not be so evident as in the case of knowledge. I say, all degrees of assent, whether founded on reason or authority, more or less cogent, are internal acts of the mind which alike terminate in ideas as their proper object; without which there can be really no such thing as knowledge, faith, or opinion. We may perhaps raise a dust and dispute about tenets purely verbal; but what is this at bottom more than mere trifling? All which will be easily admitted with respect to human learning and science; wherein it is an allowed method to expose any doctrine or tenet by stripping them of the words, and examining what ideas are underneath or whether any ideas at all?[10] This is often found the shortest way to end disputes, which might otherwise grow and multiply without end, the litigants neither understanding one another nor themselves. It were needless to illustrate what shines by its own light and is admitted by all thinking men. My endeavour shall be only to apply it in the present case. I suppose I need not be at any pains to prove that the same rules of reason and good sense, which obtain in all other subjects, ought to take place in religion. As for those who consider faith and reason as two distinct provinces, and would have us think good sense has nothing to do where it is most concerned, I am resolved never to argue with such men but leave them in quiet possession of their prejudices.

And now, for the particular application of what I have said, I shall not single out any nice disputed points of school divinity, or those that relate to the nature and essence of God, which, being allowed infinite, you might pretend to screen them under the general notion of difficulties attending the nature of infinity.

4  Grace is the main point in the Christian dispensation. Nothing is oftener mentioned or more considered throughout the New Testament, wherein it is represented as somewhat of a very particular kind, distinct from anything revealed to the Jews or known by the light of nature. This same grace is spoken of as a gift of God, as coming by Jesus Christ, as reigning, as abounding, as operating. Men are said to speak through

[10] Cf. *DM*, 53, where this method is applied to absolute space.

grace, to believe through grace. Mention is made of the glory of grace, the riches of grace, the stewards of grace. Christians are said to be heirs of grace, to receive grace, grow in grace, be strong in grace, to stand in grace, and to fall from grace. And lastly, grace is said to justify and to save them. Hence Christianity is styled the covenant or dispensation of grace.

And it is well known that no point has created more controversy in the church than this doctrine of grace. What disputes about its nature, extent, and effects, about universal, efficacious, sufficient, preventing, irresistible grace, have employed the pens of Protestant as well as Popish divines, of Jansenists and Molinists, of Lutherans, Calvinists, and Arminians, as I have not the least curiosity to know, so I need not say. It suffices to observe that there have been, and are still subsisting, great contests upon these points.[11]

Only one thing I should desire to be informed of, to wit: What is the clear and distinct idea marked by the word 'grace'? I presume a man may know the bare meaning of a term, without going into the depth of all those learned inquiries. This surely is an easy matter, provided there is an idea annexed to such term. And if there is not, it can be neither the subject of a rational dispute, nor the object of real faith. Men may indeed impose upon themselves or others, and pretend to argue and believe, when at bottom there is no argument or belief further than mere verbal trifling. Grace taken in the vulgar sense, either for beauty or favour, I can easily understand. But when it denotes an active, vital, ruling principle, influencing and operating on the mind of man, distinct from every natural power or motive, I profess myself altogether unable to understand it or frame any distinct idea of it. And therefore I cannot assent to any proposition concerning it, nor consequently have any faith about it; and it is a self-evident truth, that God obliges no man to impossibilities. At the request of a philosophical friend, I did cast an eye on the writings he showed me of some divines, and talked with others on this subject; but after all I had read or heard could make nothing of it, having always found, whenever I laid aside the word 'grace' and looked into my own mind, a perfect vacuity or privation of all ideas. And, as I am apt to think men's

---

[11] Berkeley alludes to some of the controversies about grace that occurred during the seventeenth century. One of the main issues, disputed by Jansenists and Molinists among Roman Catholic theologians, and by Arminians and Gomarists within the Calvinist church, was whether grace was sufficiently efficacious that, once granted, it guaranteed the salvation of individuals. This dispute raised problems about free will, and about the predestination (to salvation or perdition) of those to whom such sufficient grace was given or denied.

minds and faculties are made much alike, I suspect that other men, if they examine what they call grace with the same exactness and indifference, would agree with me that there was nothing in it but an empty name.

This is not the only instance where a word often heard and pronounced is believed intelligible, for no other reason but because it is familiar. Of the same kind are many other points reputed necessary articles of faith. That which in the present case imposes upon mankind I take to be partly this. Men speak of this holy principle as of something that acts, moves, and determines, taking their ideas from corporeal things, from motion and the force or 'momentum' of bodies, which, being of an obvious and sensible nature, they substitute in place of a thing spiritual and incomprehensible, which is a manifest delusion. For, though the idea of corporeal force be ever so clear and intelligible, it will not therefore follow that the idea of grace, a thing perfectly incorporeal, must be so too. And though we may reason distinctly, perceive, assent, and form opinions about the one, it will by no means follow that we can do so of the other. Thus, it comes to pass that a clear sensible idea of what is real produces, or rather is made a pretence for, an imaginary spiritual faith that terminates in no object; a thing impossible! For there can be no assent where there are no ideas, and where there is no assent there can be no faith; and what cannot be, that no man is obliged to. This is as clear as anything in Euclid![12]

5   *Euph.* Be the use of words or names what it will, I can never think it is to do things impossible. Let us then inquire what it is, and see if we can make sense of our daily practice. Words, it is agreed, are signs; it may not therefore be amiss to examine the use of other signs, in order to know that of words. Counters, for instance, at a card-table are used, not for their own sake but only as signs substituted for money, as words are for ideas. Say now, Alciphron, is it necessary every time these counters are used throughout the progress of a game, to frame an idea of the distinct sum or value that each represents?

*Alc.*   By no means. It is sufficient the players at first agree on their respective values, and at last substitute those values in their stead.

*Euph.*   And in casting up a sum, where the figures stand for pounds, shillings, and pence, do you think it necessary, throughout the whole

---

[12] Three sections numbered 5, 6, and 7, which were published in the 1732 edition, were omitted in 1752, and are likewise omitted here. Berkeley renumbered the subsequent sections accordingly.

progress of the operation, in each step to form ideas of pounds, shillings, and pence?

*Alc.*  I do not; it will suffice if, in the conclusion, those figures direct our actions with respect to things.

*Euph.*  From hence it seems to follow that words may not be insignificant, although they should not, every time they are used, excite the ideas they signify in our minds; it being sufficient that we have it in our power to substitute things or ideas for their signs when there is occasion. It seems also to follow, that there may be another use of words besides that of marking and suggesting distinct ideas, to wit, the influencing our conduct and actions; which may be done either by forming rules for us to act by, or by raising certain passions, dispositions, and emotions in our minds. A discourse, therefore, that directs how to act or excites to the doing or forbearance of an action may, it seems, be useful and significant, although the words whereof it is composed should not bring each a distinct idea into our minds.

*Alc.*  It seems so.

*Euph.*  Pray tell me, Alciphron, is not an idea altogether inactive?

*Alc.*  It is.

*Euph.*  An agent therefore, an active mind or spirit, cannot be an idea or like an idea. Whence it should seem to follow that those words which denote an active principle, soul, or spirit do not, in a strict and proper sense, stand for ideas. And yet they are not insignificant neither; since I understand what is signified by the term 'I', or 'myself', or know what it means, although it be no idea nor like an idea, but that which thinks, and wills, and apprehends ideas, and operates about them. [Certainly it must be allowed that we have some notion, that we understand or know what is meant by, the terms 'myself', 'will', 'memory', 'love', 'hate' and so forth; although to speak exactly these words do not suggest so many distinct ideas.][13]

*Alc.*  What would you infer from this?

*Euph.*  What has been inferred already – that words may be significant, although they do not stand for ideas.[c] The contrary whereof, having been presumed, seems to have produced the doctrine of abstract ideas.

*Alc.*  Will you not allow then that the mind can abstract?

[c] See the *Principles of Human Knowledge*, section 135, and the Introduction, section 20.

[13] The sentence in parentheses was added in the 1752 edition.

*Euph.* I do not deny it may abstract in a certain sense, inasmuch as those things that can really exist, or be really perceived asunder, may be conceived asunder or abstracted one from the other; for instance, a man's head from his body, colour from motion, figure from weight. But it will not thence follow that the mind can frame abstract general ideas, which appear to be impossible.

*Alc.* And yet it is a current opinion that every substantive name marks out and exhibits to the mind one distinct idea separate from all others.

*Euph.* Pray, Alciphron, is not the word 'number' such a substantive name?

*Alc.* It is.

*Euph.* Do but try now whether you can frame an idea of number in abstract, exclusive of all signs, words, and things numbered. I profess for my own part I cannot.

*Alc.* Can it be so hard a matter to form a simple idea of number, the object of a most evident demonstrable science? Hold, let me see if I cannot abstract the idea of number from the numeral names and characters, and all particular numerable things.

Upon which Alciphron paused awhile, and then said: To confess the truth, I do not find that I can.

*Euph.* But, though it seems neither you nor I can form distinct simple ideas of number, we can nevertheless make a very proper and significant use of numeral names. They direct us in the disposition and management of our affairs, and are of such necessary use that we should not know how to do without them. And yet, if other men's faculties may be judged of by mine, to obtain a precise simple abstract idea of number is as difficult as to comprehend any mystery in religion.

6 But to come to your own instance, let us examine what idea we can frame of force abstracted from body, motion, and outward sensible effects. For myself I do not find that I have or can have any such idea.

*Alc.* Surely everyone knows what is meant by 'force'.

*Euph.* And yet I question whether everyone can form a distinct idea of force. Let me entreat you, Alciphron, be not amused by terms; lay aside the word 'force' and exclude every other thing from your thoughts, and then see what precise idea you have of force.

*Alc.* Force is that in bodies which produces motion and other sensible effects.

*Euph.* It is then something distinct from those effects?

*Alc.* It is.

*Euph.* Be pleased now to exclude the consideration of its subject and effects, and contemplate force itself in its own precise idea.

*Alc.* I profess I find it no such easy matter.

*Euph.* Take your own advice, and shut your eyes to assist your meditation.

Upon this, Alciphron, having closed his eyes and mused a few minutes, declared he could make nothing of it.

And that, replied Euphranor, which it seems neither you nor I can frame an idea of, by your own remark of men's minds and faculties being made much alike, we may suppose others have no more an idea of than we.

*Alc.* We may.

*Euph.* But, notwithstanding all this, it is certain there are many speculations, reasonings, and disputes, refined subtleties and nice distinctions about this same force. And to explain its nature, and to distinguish the several notions or kinds of it, the terms 'gravity', 'reaction', '*vis inertiae*', '*vis insita*', '*vis impressa*', '*vis mortua*', '*vis viva*', 'impetus', 'momentum', '*solicitatio*', '*conatus*', and divers other such-like expressions have been used by learned men; and no small controversies have arisen about the notions or definitions of these terms. It has puzzled men to know whether force is spiritual or corporeal; whether it remains after action; how it is transferred from one body to another. Strange paradoxes have been framed about its nature, properties, and proportions: for instance, that contrary forces may at once subsist in the same quiescent body; that the force of percussion in a small particle is infinite. For which, and other curiosities of the same sort, you may consult Borellus *De Vi Percussionis*, the *Lezioni Academiche* of Torricelli, the Exercitations of Hermanus, and other writers.[14] It is well known to the learned world

---

[14] Berkeley repeats comments made and cites references already used in the *Essay on Motion*, 9, 16, 67. 'Hermanus' refers to Jacques Hermann or Jacob Hermannus (1678–1733), author of *Phoronomia, sive de viribus et motibus corporum solidorum et fluidorum libri duo* (Amsterdam, 1716). 'Exercitations' refers to his frequent contributions to the *Acta Eruditorum*, in which he defended views about force similar to those of Leibniz, and which were the likely source of Berkeley's knowledge of him.

what a controversy has been carried on between mathematicians, particularly Monsieur Leibniz and Monsieur Papin,[15] in the Leipzig *Acta Eruditorum*, about the proportion of forces: whether they be each to other in a proportion compounded of the simple proportions of the bodies and the celerities, or in one compounded of the simple proportion of the bodies and the duplicate proportion of the celerities? A point, it seems, not yet agreed, as indeed the reality of the thing itself is made a question.

Leibniz distinguishes between the *nisus elementaris* and the *impetus*, which is formed by a repetition of the *nisus elementaris*, and seems to think they do not exist in nature, but are made only by an abstraction of the mind. The same author, treating of original active force, to illustrate his subject has recourse to the substantial forms and *entelecheia* of Aristotle. And the ingenious Torricelli says of force and impetus that they are subtle abstracts and spiritual quintessences; and concerning the *momentum* and the velocity of heavy bodies falling, he says they are *un certo che*, and *un non so che*;[16] that is, in plain English, he knows not what to make of them. Upon the whole, therefore, may we not pronounce that – excluding body, time, space, motion, and all its sensible measures and effects – we shall find it as difficult to form an idea of force as of grace?

*Alc.* I do not know what to think of it.

7 *Euph.* And yet, I presume, you allow there are very evident propositions or theorems relating to force, which contain useful truths: for instance, that a body with conjunct forces describes the diagonal of a parallelogram, in the same time that it would the sides with separate [forces]. Is not this a principle of very extensive use? Does not the doctrine of the composition and resolution of forces depend upon it and, in consequence thereof, numberless rules and theorems directing men how to act, and explaining phenomena throughout the mechanics and mathematical philosophy? And if, by considering this doctrine of force, men arrive at the knowledge of many inventions in mechanics and are taught to frame engines, by means of which things difficult and otherwise impossible may be performed; and if the same doctrine, which is so beneficial here below, serves also as a key to discover the nature of the celestial motions, shall we deny that it is of use, either in practice or speculation, because we have no distinct idea of force? Or

[15] Denis Papin (1647–1712?), exchanged letters with Leibniz on the subject; see *Leibnizens und Huygens Briefwechsel mit Papin* (Berlin, 1881).
[16] 'A certain something', and 'an I know not what'.

that which we admit with regard to force, upon what pretence can we deny concerning grace? If there are queries, disputes, perplexities, diversity of notions and opinions about the one, so there are about the other also; if we can form no precise distinct idea of the one, so neither can we of the other.

Ought we not, therefore, by a parity of reason to conclude there may be divers true and useful propositions concerning the one as well as the other? And that grace may, for aught you know, be an object of our faith and influence our life and actions, as a principle destructive of evil habits and productive of good ones, although we cannot attain a distinct idea of it, separate or abstracted from God the author, from man the subject, and from virtue and piety its effects?

8   Shall we not admit the same method of arguing, the same rules of logic, reason, and good sense, to obtain in things spiritual and things corporeal, in faith and science? And shall we not use the same candour, and make the same allowances, in examining the revelations of God and the inventions of men? For aught I see, that philosopher cannot be free from bias and prejudice, or be said to weigh things in an equal balance, who shall maintain the doctrine of force and reject that of grace, who shall admit the abstract idea of a triangle and at the same time ridicule the Holy Trinity. But, however partial or prejudiced other minute philosophers might be, you have laid it down for a maxim that the same logic which obtains in other matters must be admitted in religion.

*Lys.*   I think, Alciphron, it would be more prudent to abide by the way of wit and humour than thus to try religion by the dry test of reason and logic.

*Alc.*   Fear not: by all the rules of right reason, it is absolutely impossible that any mystery, and least of all the Trinity, should really be the object of man's faith.

*Euph.*   I do not wonder you thought so, as long as you maintained that no man could assent to a proposition without perceiving or framing in his mind distinct ideas marked by the terms of it. But, although terms are signs, yet having granted that those signs may be significant, though they should not suggest ideas represented by them, provided they serve to regulate and influence our wills, passions, or conduct, you have consequently granted that the mind of man may assent to propositions containing such terms, when it is so directed or affected by them, notwithstanding it should not perceive distinct ideas marked by those terms. Whence it seems to follow that a man may believe the doctrine of the Trinity, if he finds it revealed in Holy Scripture that the Father, the Son, and the Holy Ghost are God, and that there is but one God, although he does not frame in his mind any abstract or distinct ideas of Trinity, substance, or personality; provided that this doctrine of a Creator, Redeemer, and Sanctifier makes proper impressions on his mind, producing therein love, hope, gratitude, and obedience, and thereby becomes a lively operative principle, influencing his life and actions, agreeably to that notion of saving faith which is required in a Christian. This, I say, whether right or wrong, seems to follow from your own principles and concessions.

But for further satisfaction, it may not be amiss to inquire whether there be anything parallel to this Christian faith in the minute philosophy. Suppose a fine gentleman or lady of fashion, who are too much employed to think for themselves, and are only free-thinkers at second-hand, have the advantage of being betimes initiated in the principles of your sect by conversing with men of depth and genius, who have often declared it to be their opinion, the world is governed either by fate or by chance, it matters not which; will you deny it possible for such persons to yield their assent to either of these propositions?

*Alc.*   I will not.

*Euph.*   And may not such their assent be properly called 'faith'?

*Alc.*   It may.

*Euph.*   And yet it is possible those disciples of the minute philosophy may not dive so deep as to be able to frame any abstract, or precise, or any determinate idea whatsoever, either of fate or of chance?

*Alc.*   This too I grant.

*Euph.*   So that, according to you, this same gentleman or lady may be said to believe or have faith where they have not ideas?

*Alc.*   They may.

*Euph.*   And may not this faith or persuasion produce real effects, and show itself in the conduct and tenor of their lives, freeing them from the fears of superstition, and giving them a true relish of the world, with a noble indolence or indifference about what comes after?

*Alc.*   It may.

*Euph.* And may not Christians, with equal reason, be allowed to believe the Divinity of our Saviour, or that in him God and man make one Person, and be verily persuaded thereof, so far as for such faith or belief to become a real principle of life and conduct: inasmuch as, by virtue of such persuasion, they submit to His government, believe His doctrine, and practise His precepts, although they frame no abstract idea of the union between the Divine and human nature, nor may be able to clear up the notion of person to the contentment of a minute philosopher? To me it seems evident that if none but those who had nicely examined, and could themselves explain, the principle of individuation in man or untie the knots and answer the objections which may be raised even about human personal identity, would require of us to explain the Divine mysteries, we should not be often called upon for a clear and distinct idea of person in relation to the Trinity, nor would the difficulties on that head be often objected to our faith.

*Alc.* Methinks, there is no such mystery in personal identity.

*Euph.* Pray, in what do you take it to consist?

*Alc.* In consciousness.

*Euph.* Whatever is possible may be supposed?

*Alc.* It may.

*Euph.* We will suppose now (which is possible in the nature of things, and reported to be fact) that a person, through some violent accident or distemper, should fall into such a total oblivion as to lose all consciousness of his past life and former ideas. I ask, is he not still the same person?

*Alc.* He is the same man, but not the same person. Indeed you ought not to suppose that a person loses its former consciousness; for this is impossible, though a man perhaps may; but then he becomes another person. In the same person, it must be owned, some old ideas may be lost, and some new ones got; but a total change is inconsistent with identity of person.

*Euph.* Let us then suppose that a person has ideas and is conscious during a certain space of time, which we will divide into three equal parts, whereof the later terms are marked by the letters *A*, *B*, *C*. In the first part of time, the person gets a certain number of ideas, which are retained in *A*. During the second part of time, he retains one half of his old ideas, and loses the other half, in place of which he acquires as many new ones; so that in *B* his ideas are half old and half new. And in the third part, we suppose him to lose the remainder of the ideas acquired in the first and to get new ones in their stead, which are retained in *C*, together with those acquired in the second part of time. Is this a possible fair supposition?

*Alc.* It is.

*Euph.* Upon these premises, I am tempted to think, one may demonstrate that personal identity does not consist in consciousness.

*Alc.* As how?

*Euph.* You shall judge; but thus it seems to me. The persons in *A* and *B* are the same, being conscious of common ideas by supposition. The person in *B* is (for the same reason) one and the same with the person in *C*. Therefore, the person in *A* is the same with the person in *C*, by that undoubted axiom: *Quae conveniunt uni tertio conveniunt inter se.*[17] But the person in *C* has no idea in common with the person in *A*. Therefore personal identity does not consist in consciousness. What do you think, Alciphron, is not this a plain inference?

*Alc.* I tell you what I think: you will never assist my faith by puzzling my knowledge.

9  *Euph.* There is, if I mistake not, a practical faith or assent, which shows itself in the will and actions of a man, although his understanding may not be furnished with those abstract, precise, distinct ideas, which, whatever a philosopher may pretend, are acknowledged to be above the talents of common men. Among whom, nevertheless, may be found, even according to your own concession, many instances of such practical faith in other matters which do not concern religion. What should hinder, therefore, but that doctrines relating to heavenly mysteries might be taught, in this saving sense, to vulgar minds, which you may well think incapable of all teaching and faith in the sense you suppose?

Which mistaken sense, said Crito, has given occasion to much profane and misapplied raillery. But all this may very justly be retorted on the minute philosophers themselves, who confound Scholasticism with Christianity, and impute to other men those perplexities, chimeras, and inconsistent ideas which are often the workmanship of their own brains, and proceed from their own wrong way of thinking. Who does not see that such an ideal abstracted faith is never thought of by the bulk of Christians – husbandmen, for instance, artisans, or servants? Or what footsteps are there in the Holy Scripture to make us think that the wiredrawing of abstract ideas was a task enjoined either Jews or

---

[17] 'Things that equal a third thing are equal to each other.'

Christians? Is there anything in the law or the prophets, the evangelists or apostles, that looks like it? Everyone whose understanding is not perverted by science falsely so-called may see the saving faith of Christians is quite of another kind, a vital operative principle, productive of charity and obedience.

*Alc.* What are we to think then of the disputes and decisions of the famous Council of Nice, and so many subsequent Councils? What was the intention of those venerable Fathers – the *homoousians* and the *homoiousians*? Why did they disturb themselves and the world with hard words and subtle controversies?[18]

*Cri.* Whatever their intention was, it could not be to beget nice abstracted ideas of mysteries in the minds of common Christians, this being evidently impossible. Nor does it appear that the bulk of Christian men did in those days think it any part of their duty to lay aside the words, shut their eyes, and frame those abstract ideas; any more than men now do of force, time, number, or several other things, about which they nevertheless believe, know, argue, and dispute. To me it seems that, whatever was the source of those controversies, and howsoever they were managed, wherein human infirmity must be supposed to have had its share, the main end was not, on either side, to convey precise positive ideas to the minds of men by the use of those contested terms, but rather a negative sense, tending to exclude Polytheism on the one hand, and Sabellianism[19] on the other.[d]

*Alc.* But what shall we say to so many learned and ingenious divines, who from time to time have obliged the world with new explications of mysteries, who, having themselves professedly laboured to acquire accurate ideas, would recommend their discoveries and speculations to others for articles of faith?

*Cri.* To all such innovators in religion I would say with Jerome: 'Why after so many centuries do you pretend to teach us what was

---

[d] *Vide* Sozomen, lib. ii, cap. 8 [Hermias Sozomen, *The Ecclesiatical History of Sozomen*, trans. E. Walford (London: Bohn, 1899); Berkeley's reference is incorrect, and should refer in general to Book I].

[18] The Council of Nicea, a general council of the Church, was held in 325; one of the issues discussed was whether the persons of the Trinity are only similar in substance (*homoiousion*) (a view defended by semi-Arians), or whether the Son of God is substantially identical with the Father (i.e. *homoousion*). The council adopted the latter view, which then became orthodox Trinitarian doctrine.

[19] Berkeley argues that the Council of Nicea was concerned to teach that there is only one God rather than many (polytheism), and that one should not interpret the Scriptures (as Sabellius did) as if the Father, Son and Holy Spirit were merely different manifestations of a single person.

untaught before? Why explain what neither Peter nor Paul thought necessary to be explained?'[e] And it must be owned that the explication of mysteries in divinity, allowing the attempt as fruitless as the pursuit of the philosopher's stone in chemistry or the perpetual motion in mechanics, is no more than they chargeable on the profession itself, but only on the wrongheaded professors of it.

10   It seems that what has been now said may be applied to other mysteries of our religion. Original sin, for instance: a man may find it impossible to form an idea of in abstract or of the manner of its transmission,[20] and yet the belief thereof may produce in his mind a salutary sense of his own unworthiness, and the goodness of his Redeemer; from whence may follow good habits, and from them good actions, the genuine effects of faith; which, considered in its true light, is a thing neither repugnant nor incomprehensible, as some men would persuade us, but suited even to vulgar capacities, placed in the will and affections rather than in the understanding, and producing holy lives rather than subtle theories.

Faith, I say, is not an indolent perception, but an operative persuasion of mind, which ever works some suitable action, disposition, or emotion in those who have it, as it were easy to prove and illustrate by innumerable instances taken from human affairs. And, indeed, while the Christian religion is considered an institution fitted to ordinary minds rather than to the nicer talent, whether improved or puzzled, of speculative men; and our notions about faith are accordingly taken from the commerce of the world and practice of mankind, rather than from the peculiar systems of refiners; it will, I think, be no difficult matter to conceive and justify the meaning and use of our belief of mysteries, against the most confident assertions and objections of the minute philosophers, who are easily to be caught in those very snares which they have spun and spread for others. And that humour of controversy, the mother and nurse of heresies, would doubtless very much abate, if it was considered that things are to be rated, not by colour, shape, or stamp, so truly as by the weight. If the moment of

---

[e]  Hieronymus, *Ad Pammachium et Oceanum de Erroribus Origenis* [St. Jerome, 'Letter to Pammachius and Oceanus concerning the Errors of Origin'; Letter 65 in Saint Jerome, *Opera Omnia*, 11 vols. (Frankfurt, C. Genschius, 1684), II, 129–32, on p. 131, col. A–D. This letter is elsewhere identified as Letter 84; see J.-P. Migne, ed., *Patrologiae Cursus Completus*; Series Prima (Paris, 1845), vol. 22, 743–52].

[20]  Refers to the Christian teaching that all human beings share, in some sense, the sin committed by Adam in the Garden of Eden and that they inherit the effects of that sin.

opinions had been by some litigious divines made the measure of their zeal, it might have spared much trouble both to themselves and others. Certainly one that takes his notions of faith, opinion, and assent from common sense and common use, and has maturely weighed the nature of signs and language, will not be so apt to controvert the wording of a mystery, or to break the peace of the church, for the sake of retaining or rejecting a term.[21]

11   *Alc.* It seems, Euphranor, and you would persuade me into an opinion, that there is nothing so singularly absurd as we are apt to think in the belief of mysteries, and that a man need not renounce his reason to maintain his religion. But, if this were true, how comes it to pass that, in proportion as men abound in knowledge, they dwindle in faith?

*Euph.*   O Alciphron, I have learned from you that there is nothing like going to the bottom of things, and analysing them into their first principles. I shall therefore make an essay of this method for clearing up the nature of faith; with what success I shall leave you to determine, for I dare not pronounce myself on my own judgment, whether it be right or wrong. But thus is seems to me. The objections made to faith are by no means an effect of knowledge, but proceed rather from an ignorance of what knowledge is; which ignorance may possibly be found even in those who pass for masters of this or that particular branch of knowledge. Science and faith agree in this, that they both imply an assent of the mind and, as the nature of the first is most clear and evident, it should be first considered in order to cast a light on the other. To trace things from their original, it seems that the human mind, naturally furnished with the ideas of things particular and concrete, and being designed, not for the bare intuition of ideas, but for action and operation about them, and pursuing her own happiness therein, stands in need of certain general rules or theorems to direct her operations in this pursuit; the supplying which want is the true, original, reasonable end of studying the arts and sciences.

Now, these rules being general, it follows that they are not to be obtained by the mere consideration of the original ideas, or particular things, but by the means of marks and signs, which, being so far forth universal, become the immediate instruments and materials of science. It is not, therefore, by mere contemplation of particular things and much

---

[21]   I omit a paragraph inserted here in the second (1732) and subsequent editions.

less of their abstract general ideas, that the mind makes her progress, but by an apposite choice and skilful management of signs. For instance, force and number, taken in concrete with their adjuncts, subjects, and signs, are what everyone knows; and considered in abstract, so as making precise ideas of themselves, they are what nobody can comprehend. That their abstract nature, therefore, is not the foundation of science is plain; and that barely considering their ideas in concrete is not the method to advance in the respective sciences, is what everyone that reflects may see; nothing being more evident than that one who can neither write nor read, in common use understands the meaning of numeral words as well as the best philosopher or mathematician.

12 But here lies the difference: the one who understands the notation of numbers, by means thereof is able to express briefly and distinctly all the variety and degrees of number, and to perform with ease and despatch several arithmetical operations by the help of general rules. Of all which operations, as the use in human life is very evident, so it is no less evident that the performing them depends on the aptness of the notation. If we suppose rude mankind without the use of language, it may be presumed they would be ignorant of arithmetic. But the use of names, by the repetition whereof in a certain order they might express endless degrees of number, would be the first step towards that science. The next step would be, to devise proper marks of a permanent nature, and visible to the eye, the kind and order whereof must be chosen with judgment and accommodated to the names. Which marking or notation would, in proportion as it was apt and regular, facilitate the invention and application of general rules to assist the mind in reasoning and judging, in extending, recording, and communicating its knowledge about numbers: in which theory and operations, the mind is immediately occupied about the signs and notes, by mediation of which it is directed to act about things, or number in concrete (as the logicians call it) without ever considering the simple, abstract, intellectual, general idea of number. [The signs, indeed, do in their use imply relations or proportions of things; but these relations are not abstract general ideas, being founded in particular things, and not making of themselves distinct ideas to the mind exclusive of the particular ideas and the signs.][22] I imagine one need not think much to be convinced that the

---

[22] The sentence in parentheses was added in the 1752 edition.

science of arithmetic in its rise, operations, rules, and theorems, is altogether conversant about the artificial use of signs, names, and characters. These names and characters are universal, inasmuch as they are signs. The names are referred to things, and the characters to names, and both to operation. The names being few, and proceeding by a certain analogy, the characters will be more useful, the simpler they are and the more aptly they express this analogy. Hence the old notation by letters was more useful than words written at length. And the modern notation by figures, expressing the progression or analogy of the names by their simple places, is much preferable to that, for ease and expedition, as the invention of algebraical symbols is to this for extensive and general use. As arithmetic and algebra are sciences of great clearness, certainty, and extent, which are immediately conversant about signs, upon the skilful use and management whereof they entirely depend, so a little attention to them may possibly help us to judge of the progress of the mind in other sciences, which, though differing in nature, design, and object, may yet agree in the general methods of proof and inquiry.

13    If I mistake not, all sciences, so far as they are universal and demonstrable by human reason, will be found conversant about signs as their immediate object, though these in the application are referred to things. The reason whereof is not difficult to conceive. For, as the mind is better acquainted with some sort of objects, which are earlier offered to it, strike it more sensibly, or are more easily comprehended than others, it seems naturally led to substitute those objects for such as are more subtle, fleeting, or difficult to conceive. Nothing, I say, is more natural than to make the things we know a step towards those we do not know, and to explain and represent things less familiar by others which are more so. Now, it is certain we imagine before we reflect, and we perceive by sense before we imagine; and of all our senses the sight is the most clear, distinct, various, agreeable, and comprehensive. Hence it is natural to assist intellect by imagination, imagination by sense, and other senses by sight. Hence figures, metaphors, and types. We illustrate spiritual things by corporeal; we substitute sounds for thoughts, and written letters for sounds; emblems, symbols, and hieroglyphics, for things too obscure to strike, and too various or too fleeting to be retained. We substitute things imaginable for things intelligible, sensible things for imaginable, smaller things for those that are too great to be comprehended easily and greater things for such as are too small to be discerned distinctly, present things

for absent, permanent for perishing, and visible for invisible. Hence the use of models and diagrams. Hence right lines are substituted for time, velocity, and other things of very different natures. Hence we speak of spirits in a figurative style, expressing the operations of the mind by allusions and terms borrowed from sensible things, such as 'apprehend', 'conceive', 'reflect', 'discourse', and such-like; and hence those allegories which illustrate things intellectual by visions exhibited to the fancy.

Plato, for instance, represents the mind presiding in her vehicle by the driver of a winged chariot, which sometimes moults and droops and is drawn by two horses, the one good and of a good race, the other of a contrary kind; symbolically expressing the tendency of the mind towards the Divinity, as she soars or is borne aloft by two instincts like wings, the one in the intellect towards truth, the other in the will towards excellence, which instincts moult or are weakened by sensual inclinations, expressing also her alternate elevations and depressions, the struggles between reason and appetite, like horses that go an unequal pace, or draw different ways, embarrassing the soul in her progress to perfection. I am inclined to think the doctrine of signs a point of great importance and general extent, which, if duly considered, would cast no small light upon things and afford a just and genuine solution of many difficulties.

14   Thus much, upon the whole, may be said of all signs: that they do not always suggest ideas signified to the mind; that when they suggest ideas, they are not general abstract ideas; that they have other uses besides barely standing for and exhibiting ideas, such as raising proper emotions, producing certain dispositions or habits of mind, and directing our actions in pursuit of that happiness, which is the ultimate end and design, the primary spring and motive, that sets rational agents at work: [that signs may imply or suggest the relations of things; which relations, habitudes or proportions, as they cannot be by us understood but by the help of signs, so being thereby expressed and confuted, they direct and enable us to act with regard to things:][23] that the true end of speech, reason, science, faith, assent, in all its different degrees, is not merely, or principally, or always the imparting or acquiring of ideas, but rather something of an active operative nature, tending to a conceived good; which may sometimes be obtained, not only although the ideas marked are not offered to the mind, but even although there should be no

---

[23] The phrase in parentheses was added in the 1752 edition.

possibility of offering or exhibiting any such idea to the mind: for instance, the algebraic mark, which denotes the root of a negative square, has its use in logistic operations, although it be impossible to form an idea of any such quantity.[24] And what is true of algebraic signs is also true of words or language, modern algebra being in fact a more short, apposite, and artificial sort of language, and it being possible to express by words at length, though less conveniently, all the steps of an algebraical process. And it must be confessed that even the mathematical sciences them-selves, which above all others are reckoned the most clear and certain, if they are considered, not as instruments to direct our practice, but as speculations to employ our curiosity, will be found to fall short in many instances of those clear and distinct ideas, which, it seems, the minute philosophers of this age, whether knowingly or ignorantly, expect and insist upon in the mysteries of religion.

**15** Be the science or subject what it will, whensoever men quit particulars for generalities, things concrete for abstractions, when they forsake practical views and the useful purposes of knowledge for barren speculation, considering means and instruments as ultimate ends and labouring to attain precise ideas which they suppose indiscriminately annexed to all terms, they will be sure to embarrass themselves with difficulties and disputes. Such are those which have sprung up in geometry about the nature of the angle of contact, the doctrine of proportions, of indivisibles, infinitesimals, and divers other points; notwithstanding all which, that science is very rightly esteemed an excellent and useful one, and is really found to be so in many occasions of human life, wherein it governs and directs the actions of men, so that by the aid or influence thereof those operations become just and accurate which would other-wise be faulty and uncertain. And from a parity of reason, we should not conclude any other doctrines which govern, influence, or direct the mind of man to be, any more than that, the less true or excellent, because they afford matter of controversy and useless speculation to curious and licentious wits, particularly those articles of our Christian faith, which, in proportion as they are believed, persuade, and, as they persuade, influence the lives and actions of men. As to the perplexity of contra-dictions and abstracted notions, in all parts whether of human science or

[24] Refers to the use in mathematics of symbols such as $\sqrt{-1}$, despite the fact that no quantity can be squared and produce a result of $-1$.

divine faith, cavillers may equally object, and unwary persons incur, while the judicious avoid it. There is no need to depart from the received rules of reasoning to justify the belief of Christians. And if any pious men think otherwise, it may be supposed an effect, not of religion or of reason, but only of human weakness. If this age be singularly productive of infidels, I shall not therefore conclude it to be more knowing, but only more presuming, than former ages; and their conceit, I doubt, is not the effect of consideration. To me it seems that the more thoroughly and extensively any man shall consider and scan the principles, objects, and methods of proceeding in arts and sciences, the more he will be convinced there is no weight in those plausible objections that are made against the mysteries of faith; which it will be no difficult matter for him to maintain or justify in the received method of arguing, on the common principles of logic, and by numberless avowed parallel cases, throughout the several branches of human knowledge, in all which the supposition of abstract ideas creates the same difficulties.

*Alc.* According to this doctrine, all points may be alike maintained. There will be nothing absurd in Popery, not even transubstantiation.

*Cri.* Pardon me. This doctrine justifies no article of faith which is not contained in Scripture, or which is repugnant to human reason, which implies a contradiction, or which leads to idolatry or wickedness of any kind – all which is very different from our not having a distinct or an abstract idea of a point.

[Sections 16–34 are omitted]

# Siris: A Chain of Philosophical Reflexions and Inquiries Concerning the Virtues of Tar-Water, and divers other subjects connected together and arising one from another

## New edition 1747

### [excerpts]

For introduction to the following piece, I assure the reader that nothing could, in my present situation, have induced me to be at the pains of writing it but a firm belief that it would prove a valuable present to the public. What entertainment soever the reasoning or notional part may afford the mind, I will venture to say the other part seems so surely calculated to do good to the body that both must be gainers. For if the lute be not well tuned, the musician fails in his harmony. And, in our present state, the operations of the mind so far depend on the right tone or good condition of its instrument that anything which greatly contributes to preserve or recover the health of the body is well worth the attention of the mind. These considerations have moved me to communicate to the public the salutary virtues of tar-water; to which I thought myself indispensably obliged by the duty every man owes to mankind. And, as effects are linked with their causes, my thought on this low but useful theme led to farther inquiries, and those on to others, remote perhaps and speculative, but, I hope, not altogether useless or unentertaining.

1    In certain parts of America, tar-water is made by putting a quart of cold water to a quart of tar, and stirring them well together in a vessel, which is left standing till the tar sinks to the bottom. A glass of clear

water, being poured off for a draught, is replaced by the same quantity of fresh water, the vessel being shaken and left to stand as before. And this is repeated for every glass, so long as the tar continues to impregnate the water sufficiently, which will appear by the smell and taste . . .

32   A body, therefore, either animal or vegetable, may be considered as an organized system of tubes and vessels, containing several sorts of fluids. And as fluids are moved through the vessels of animal bodies by the systole and diastole of the heart, the alternate expansion and condensation of the air, and the oscillations in the membranes and tunics of the vessels, even so, by means of air expanded and contracted in the tracheae or vessels made up of elastic fibres, the sap is propelled through the arterial tubes of a plant, and the vegetable juices, as they are rarefied by heat or condensed by cold, will either ascend and evaporate into air or descend in the form of a gross liquor.

51   It is a great maxim for health that the juices of the body be kept fluid in a due proportion. Therefore, the acid volatile spirit in tar-water, at once attenuating and cooling in a moderate degree, must greatly conduce to health, as a mild salutary deobstruent, quickening the circulation of the fluids without wounding the solids, thereby gently removing or preventing those obstructions which are the great and general cause of most chronical diseases; . . .

68   It is I think allowed that the origin of the gout lies in a faulty digestion. And it is remarked by the ablest physicians that the gout is so difficult to cure because heating medicines aggravate its immediate, and cooling its remote cause. But tar-water, although it contain active principles that strengthen the digestion beyond anything I know, and consequently must be highly useful, either to prevent or lessen the following fit, or by invigorating the blood to cast it upon the extremities, yet it is not of so heating a nature as to do harm even in the fit. Nothing is more difficult or disagreeable than to argue men out of their prejudices; I shall not therefore enter into controversies on this subject but, if men dispute and object, shall leave the decision to time and trial.

74   It is certain tar-water warms, and therefore some may perhaps still think it cannot cool. The more effectually to remove this prejudice, let it

be farther considered that as, on the one hand, opposite causes do some-times produce the same effect – for instance, heat by rarefaction and cold by condensation, do both increase the air's elasticity – so, on the other hand, the same cause shall sometime produce opposite effects: heat for instance thins, and again heat coagulates the blood. It is not therefore strange that tar-water should warm one habit and cool another, have one good effect on a cold constitution and another good effect on an inflamed one; nor, if this be so, that it should cure opposite disorders. All which justifies to reason what I have found true in fact. The salts, the spirits, the heat of tar-water are of a temperature congenial to the constitution of a man, which receives from it a kindly warmth but no inflaming heat. It was remarkable that two children in my neighbourhood, being in a course of tar-water, upon an intermission of it never failed to have their issues inflamed by a humour much more hot and sharp than at other times. But its great use in the small-pox, pleurisies, and fevers is a sufficient proof that tar-water is not of an inflaming nature.

76 The best physicians make the idea of a fever to consist in a too great velocity of the heart's motion, and too great a resistance at the capillaries. Tar-water, as it softens and gently stimulates those nice vessels, helps to propel their contents, and so contributes to remove the latter part of the disorder. And for the former, the irritating acrimony which accelerates the motion of the heart is diluted by watery, corrected by acid, and softened by balsamic remedies, all which intentions are answered by this aqueous, acid, balsamic medicine. Besides, the viscid juices coagulated by the febrile heat are resolved by tar-water as soap, and not too far resolved, as it is a gentle acid soap; to which we may add that the peccant humours and salts are carried off by its diaphoretic and diuretic qualities.

77 I found all this confirmed by my own experience in the late sickly season of the year one thousand seven hundred and forty-one, having had twenty-five fevers in my own family cured by this medicinal water, drunk copiously.[1] The same method was practised on several of my poor neighbours with equal success. It suddenly calmed the feverish anxieties, and seemed every glass to refresh and infuse life and spirit into the patient. At first some of those patients had been vomited, but afterwards I found that, without vomiting, bleeding, blistering, or any

---

[1] There was a famine in County Cork (where Berkeley's diocese was located) and the neighbouring counties in 1739.

other evacuation or medicine whatever, very bad fevers could be cured by the sole drinking of tar-water, milk-warm and in good quantity, perhaps a large glass every hour or oftener, taken in bed. And it was remarkable that such as were cured by this comfortable cordial recovered health and spirits at once, while those who had been cured by evacuations often languished long, even after the fever had left them, before they could recover of their medicines and regain their strength.

**86**  As the body is said to clothe the soul, so the nerves may be said to constitute her inner garment. And as the soul animates the whole, what nearly touches the soul relates to all. Therefore the asperity of tartarous salts, and the fiery acrimony of alkaline salts, irritating and wounding the nerves, produce nascent passions and anxieties in the soul; which both aggravate distempers and render men's lives restless and wretched, even when they are afflicted with no apparent distemper. This is the latent spring of much woe, spleen, and *taedium vitae*.[2] Small imperceptible irritations of the minutest fibres or filaments, caused by the pungent salts of wines and sauces, do so shake and disturb the microcosms of high livers as often to raise tempests in courts and senates; whereas the gentle vibrations that are raised in the nerves by a fine subtle acid sheathed in a smooth volatile oil, softly stimulating and bracing the nervous vessels and fibres, promotes a due circulation and secretion of the animal juices, and creates a calm satisfied sense of health. And, accordingly, I have often known tar-water procure sleep and compose the spirits in cruel vigils occasioned either by sickness or by too intense application of mind.

**87**  In diseases sometimes accidents happen from without by misman-agement, sometimes latent causes operate within, jointly with the specific taint or peculiar cause of the malady. The causes of distempers are often complicated, and there may be something in the idiosyncrasy of the patient that puzzles the physician. It may therefore be presumed that no medicine is infallible, not even in any one disorder. But as tar-water possesses the virtues of fortifying the stomach, as well as purifying and invigorating the blood, beyond any medicine that I know, it may be presumed of great and general efficacy in all those numerous illnesses which take their rise from foul or vapid blood, or from a bad digestion. The animal spirits are elaborated from the blood. Such therefore as the blood is, such will be

---

[2] Weariness, listlessness.

the animal spirit, more or less, weaker or stronger. This shows the usefulness of tar-water in all hysteric and hypochondriac cases, which, together
with the maladies from indigestion, comprise almost the whole tribe of
chronical diseases.

88   The scurvy may be reckoned in these climates a universal malady,
as people in general are subject to it, and as it mixes more or less in almost
all diseases. Whether this proceeds from want of elasticity in our air,
upon which the tone of the vessels depends, and upon that the several
secretions; or whether it proceeds from the moisture of our climate, or
the grossness of our food, or the salts in our atmosphere, or from all these
together – thus much at least seems not absurd to suppose, that as
physicians in Spain and Italy are apt to suspect the venereal taint to be
a latent principle and bear a part in every illness, so for as good reason
the scurvy should be considered by our physicians as having some share
in most disorders and constitutions that fall in their way. It is certain
our perspiration is not so free as in clearer air and warmer climates.
Perspirable humours not discharged will stagnate and putrefy. A diet
of animal food will be apt to render the juices of our bodies alkalescent.
Hence ichorous and corrosive humours and many disorders. Moist air
makes viscid blood, and saline air inflames this viscid blood. Hence
broken capillaries, extravasated blood, spots, and ulcers, and other scorbutic symptoms. The body of a man attracts and imbibes the moisture and
salts of the air and whatever floats in the atmosphere, which as it is
common to all, so it affects all more or less.

97   In the cure of the scurvy the principal aim is to subdue the acrimony
of the blood and juices. But as this acrimony proceeds from different
causes, or even opposite, as acid and alkaline, what is good in one sort of
scurvy proves dangerous and even mortal in another ... Hence fatal
blunders are committed by unwary practitioners who, not distinguishing
the nature of the disease, do frequently aggravate instead of curing it. If
I may trust what trials I have been able to make, this water is good in the
several kinds of scurvy, acid, alkaline, and muriatic, and I believe it the
only medicine that cures them all without doing hurt in any.

101   Many hysteric and scorbutic ailments, many taints contracted by
themselves or inherited from their ancestors, afflict the people of condition in these islands, often rendering them, upon the whole, much

more unhappy than those whom poverty and labour have ranked in the lowest lot of life; which ailments might be safely removed or relieved by the sole use of tar-water, and those lives which seem hardly worth living for bad appetite, low spirits, restless nights, wasting pains and anxieties, be rendered easy and comfortable.

**102** As the nerves are instruments of sensation, it follows that spasms in the nerves may produce all symptoms, and therefore a disorder in the nervous system shall imitate all distempers and occasion, in appearance, an asthma for instance, a pleurisy, or a fit of the stone. Now, whatever is good for the nerves in general is good against all such symptoms. But tar-water, as it includes in an eminent degree the virtues of warm gums and resins, is of great use for comforting and strengthening the nerves,[a] curing twitches in the nervous fibres, cramps also, and numbness in the limbs, removing anxieties, and promoting sleep; in all which cases I have known it very successful.

**103** This safe and cheap medicine suits all circumstances and all constitutions, operating easily, curing without disturbing, raising the spirits without depressing them, a circumstance that deserves repeated attention, especially in these climates, where strong liquors so fatally and so frequently produce those very distresses they are designed to remedy; and, if I am not misinformed, even among the ladies themselves, who are truly much to be pitied. Their condition of life makes them a prey to imaginary woes, which never fail to grow up in minds unexercised and unemployed. To get rid of these, it is said, there are [those] who betake themselves to distilled spirits. And it is not improbable they are led gradually to the use of those poisons by a certain complaisant pharmacy, too much used in the modern practice, palsy drops, poppy cordial, plague water, and such like which being in truth nothing but drams disguised, yet, coming from the apothecaries, are considered only as medicines.

**104** The soul of man was supposed by many ancient sages to be thrust into the human body as into a prison, for punishment of past offences. But the worst prison is the body of an indolent epicure, whose blood is inflamed by fermented liquors and high sauces, or rendered putrid, sharp, and corrosive by a stagnation of the animal juices through sloth and indolence; whose membranes are irritated by pungent salts; whose mind is agitated by painful oscillations of the nervous system;[b] and

[a] Section 86.   [b] Section 86.

whose nerves are mutually affected by the irregular passions of his mind. This ferment in the animal economy darkens and confounds the intellect. It produces vain terrors and vain conceits, and stimulates the soul with mad desires, which, not being natural, nothing in nature can satisfy. No wonder, therefore, there are so many fine persons of both sexes, shining themselves and shone on by fortune, who are inwardly miserable and sick of life.

**153** The animal spirit in man is the instrumental or physical cause both of sense and motion. To suppose sense in the world would be gross and unwarranted. But locomotive faculties are evident in all its parts. The Pythagoreans, Platonists, and Stoics held the world to be an animal, though some of them have chosen to consider it as a vegetable. However, the phenomena and effects do plainly show there is a spirit that moves, and a Mind or Providence that presides. This Providence, Plutarch says, was thought to be in regard to the world what the soul is in regard to man.

**154** The order and course of things, and the experiments we daily make, show there is a Mind that governs and actuates this mundane system, as the proper real agent and cause; and that the inferior instrumental cause is pure ether, fire, or the substance of light, which is applied and determined by an Infinite Mind in the macrocosm or universe, with unlimited power, and according to stated rules, as it is in the microcosm with limited power and skill by the human mind. We have no proof, either from experiment or reason, of any other agent or efficient cause than mind or spirit. When, therefore, we speak of corporeal agents or corporeal causes, this is to be understood in a different, subordinate, and improper sense.

**155** The principles whereof a thing is compounded, the instrument used in its production, and the end for which it was intended, are all in vulgar use termed causes, though none of them be, strictly speaking, agent or efficient. There is not any proof that an extended corporeal or mechanical cause does really and properly act, even motion itself being in truth a passion. Therefore though we speak of this fiery substance as acting, yet it is to be understood only as a mean or instrument, which indeed is the case of all mechanical causes whatsoever. They are, nevertheless, sometimes termed agents and causes, although they are by no means active in a strict and proper signification. When therefore force, power, virtue, or action are mentioned as subsisting in an extended and corporeal or mechanical being, this is not to be taken in a true, genuine and real, but only in a gross and popular sense, which sticks in appearances and does not analyse things to their first principles. In compliance with established language and the use of the world, we must employ the popular current phrase. But then in regard to truth we ought to distinguish its meaning. It may suffice to have made this declaration once for all, in order to avoid mistakes.

**156** The *calidum innatum*,[3] the vital flame or animal spirit in man, is supposed the cause of all motions in the several parts of his body, whether voluntary or natural. That is, it is the instrument by means whereof the mind exerts and manifests herself in the motions of the body. In the same sense, may not fire be said to have force, to operate and agitate the whole system of the world, which is held together and informed by one presiding mind, and animated throughout by one and the same fiery substance, as an instrumental and mechanical agent, not as a primary real efficient?

**157** This pure spirit or invisible fire is ever ready to exert and show itself in its effects, cherishing, heating, fermenting, dissolving, shining, and operating in various manners, where a subject offers to employ or determine its force. It is present in all parts of the earth and firmament, though perhaps latent and unobserved, till some accident produces it into act and renders it visible in its effects.

**158** There is no effect in nature great, marvellous, or terrible but proceeds from fire, that diffused and active principle which, at the same time that it shakes the earth and heavens, will enter, divide, and dissolve the smallest, closest, and most compacted bodies. In remote cavities of the earth it remains quiet, till perhaps an accidental spark, from the collision of one stone against another, kindles an exhalation that gives birth to an earthquake or tempest which splits mountains or overturns cities. This same fire stands unseen in the focus of a burning glass, till subjects for it to act upon come in its way, when it is found to melt, calcine, or vitrify the hardest bodies.

**159** No eye could ever hitherto discern, and no sense perceive, the animal spirit in a human body, otherwise than from its effects. The same may be said of pure fire or the spirit of the universe, which is perceived only by means of some other bodies on which it operates or with which it

---

[3] Innate heat.

is joined. What the chemists say of pure acids being never found alone might as well be said of pure fire.

**160** The mind of man acts by an instrument necessarily. The τό ἡγεμονικόν, or Mind presiding in the world, acts by an instrument freely. Without instrumental and second causes, there could be no regular course of nature. And without a regular course, nature could never be understood; mankind must always be at a loss, not knowing what to expect or how to govern themselves, or direct their actions for the obtaining of any end. Therefore in the government of the world physical agents, improperly so called, or mechanical, or second causes, or natural causes, or instruments, are necessary to assist, not the Governor, but the governed.

**161** In the human body the mind orders and moves the limbs, but the animal spirit is supposed the immediate physical cause of their motion. So likewise, in the mundane system, a mind presides; but the immediate, mechanical, or instrumental cause that moves or animates all its parts is the pure elementary fire or spirit of the world. The more fine and subtle part or spirit is supposed to receive the impressions of the First Mover, and communicate them to the grosser sensible parts of this world. Motion, though in metaphysical rigour and truth a passion or mere effect, yet in physics passes for an action; and by this action all effects are supposed to be produced. Hence the various communications, determinations, accelerations of motions, constitute the laws of nature.

**162** The pure ether or invisible fire contains parts of different kinds that are impressed with different forces, or subjected to different laws of motion, attraction, repulsion, and expansion, and endued with divers distinct habitudes towards other bodies. These seem to constitute the many various qualities, virtues, flavours, odours, and colours which distinguish natural productions. The different modes of cohesion, attraction, repulsion, and motion appear to be the source from whence the specific properties are derived, rather than different shapes or figures. This, as has been already observed, seems confirmed by the experiment of fixed salts operating one way, notwithstanding the difference of their angles. The original particles productive of odours, flavours, and other properties, as well of colours, are, one may suspect, all contained and blended together in that universal and original seminary of pure elementary fire; from which they are diversely separated and attracted by the various subjects of the animal, vegetable, and mineral kingdoms, which thereby become classed into kinds and endued with those distinct properties which continue till their several forms, or specific proportions of fire, return into the common mass.

**207**  But it is now well known that light moves; that its motion is not instantaneous; that it is capable of condensation, rarefaction, and collision; that it can be mixed with other bodies, enter their composition, and increase their weight. All which seems sufficiently to overthrow those arguments of Ficinus,[4] and show light to be corporeal. There appears indeed some difficulty at first sight about the non-resistance of rays or particles of light occurring one to another, in all possible directions or from all points. Particularly if we suppose the hollow surface of a large sphere studded with eyes looking inwards one at another, it may perhaps seem hard to conceive how distinct rays from every eye should arrive at every other eye without jostling, repelling, and confounding each other.

**208**  But these difficulties may be got over by considering, in the first place, that visible points are not mathematical points, and consequently that we are not to suppose every point of space a radiating point. Secondly, by granting that many rays do resist and intercept each other, notwithstanding which the act of vision may be performed. Since as every point of the object is not seen, so it is not necessary that rays from every such point arrive at the eye. We often see an object, though more dimly, when many rays are intercepted by a gross medium.

**209**  Besides, we may suppose that particles of light to be indefinitely small, that is, as small as we please, and their aggregate to bear as small a proportion to the void as we please, there being nothing in this that contradicts the phenomena. And there needs nothing more in order to conceive the possibility of rays passing from and to all visible points, although they be not incorporeal. Suppose a hundred ports placed round a circular sea, and ships sailing from each port to every other; the larger the sea, and the smaller the vessels are supposed, the less danger will there be of their striking against each other. But as there is by hypothesis no limited proportion between the sea and the ships, the void and solid particles of light, so there is no difficulty that can oblige us to conclude the sun's light incorporeal from its free passage, especially when there are so many clear proofs to the contrary. As for the difficulty, therefore,

---

[4]  Marsilio Ficino (1433–99): *De Sole & lumine libri duo* (Venice: B. Venetum, 1503), Chapters II and XIII.

attending the supposition of a sphere studded with eyes looking at each other, this is removed only by supposing the particles of light exceeding small relatively to the empty spaces.

**231**  The laws of attraction and repulsion are to be regarded as laws of motion; and these only as rules or methods observed in the productions of natural effects, the efficient and final causes whereof are not of mechanical consideration. Certainly, if the explaining a phenomenon be to assign its proper efficient and final cause,[c] it should seem the mechanical philosophers never explained anything; their province being only to discover the laws of nature, that is, the general rules and methods of motion, and to account for particular phenomena by reducing them under, or showing their conformity to, such general rules.

**232**  Some corpuscularian philosophers of the last age have indeed attempted to explain the formation of this world and its phenomena by a few simple laws of mechanism. But if we consider the various productions of nature, in the mineral, vegetable, and animal parts of the creation, I believe we shall see cause to affirm that not any one of them has hitherto been, or can be, accounted for on principles merely mechanical; and that nothing could be more vain and imaginary than to suppose with Descartes that, merely from a circular motion's being impressed by the supreme Agent on the particles of extended substance, the whole world, with all its several parts, appurtenances, and phenomena, might be produced by a necessary consequence from the laws of motion.[5]

**233**  Others suppose that God did more at the beginning, having then made the seeds of all vegetables and animals, containing their solid organical parts in miniature, the gradual filling and evolution of which, by the influx of proper juices, constitutes the generation and growth of a living body.[6] So that the artificial structure of plants and animals daily generated required no present exercise of art to produce it, having been already framed at the origin of the world ...

**234**  Mechanical laws of nature or motion direct us how to act, and teach us what to expect. Where intellect presides there will be method and order, and therefore rules, which if not stated and constant would

---

[c]  Sections 154, 155, 160.

[5]  The development of all natural phenomena from matter in motion is discussed by Descartes in the *Principles of Philosophy*, Parts II–IV (*Oeuvres*, VIII-1, 40–329).

[6]  This preformation theory was supported by Nicolas Malebranche.

cease to be rules. There is therefore a constancy in things, which is styled the course of nature.[d] All the phenomena in nature are produced by motion. There appears a uniform working in things great and small, by attracting and repelling forces. But the particular laws of attraction and repulsion are various. Nor are we concerned at all about the forces, neither can we know or measure them otherwise than by their effects, that is to say, the motions; which motions only, and not the forces, are indeed in the bodies.[e] Bodies are moved to or from each other, and this is performed according to different laws. The natural or mechanic philosopher endeavours to discover those laws by experiment and reasoning. But what is said of forces residing in bodies, whether attracting or repelling, is to be regarded only as mathematical hypotheses, and not as anything really existing in nature.

**235** We are not therefore seriously to suppose, with certain mechanic philosophers, that the minute particles of bodies have real forces or powers by which they act on each other to produce the various phenomena in nature. The minute corpuscles are impelled and directed, that is to say moved to and from each other, according to various rules or laws of motion. The laws of gravity, magnetism, and electricity are diverse. And it is not known what other different rules or laws of motion might be established by the Author of nature. Some bodies approach together, others fly asunder, and perhaps some others do neither. When salt of tartar flows *per deliquium*,[7] it is visible that the particles of water floating in the air are moved towards the particles of salt and joined with them. And when we behold vulgar salt not to flow *per deliquium*, may we not conclude that the same law of nature and motion does not obtain between its particles and those of the floating vapours? A drop of water assumes a round figure, because its parts are moved towards each other. But the particles of oil and vinegar have no such disposition to unite. And when flies walk in water without wetting their feet, it is attributed to a repelling force or faculty in the fly's feet. But this is obscure, though the phenomenon be plain.

---

[d] Section 160.   [e] Section 155.

[7] i.e. by absorbing water from the atmosphere. In the second edition of the *Opticks* (1717), Newton added 'Questions' at the conclusion of Book III, Part I. This discussion is borrowed by Berkeley from Question 31 (Dover edn. 376–7).

**236**  It is not improbable, and seems not unsupported by experiments, that as in algebra, where positive quantities cease there negative begin, even so in mechanics, where attracting forces cease there repelling forces begin; or (to express it more properly) where bodies cease to be moved towards, they begin to be moved from each other. This Sir Isaac Newton infers from the production of air and vapours, whose particles fly asunder with such vehement force.[8] We behold iron move towards the loadstone, straws towards amber, heavy bodies towards the earth. The laws of these motions are various. And when it is said that all the motions and changes in the great world arise from attraction – the elasticity of the air, the motion of water, the descent of heavy and the ascent of light bodies, being all ascribed to the same principle; when from insensible attractions of most minute particles at the smallest distance are derived cohesion, dissolution, coagulation, animal secretion, fermentation, and all chemical operations; and when it is said that without such principles there never would have been any motion in the world, and without the continuance thereof all motion would cease; in all this we know or understand no more than that bodies are moved according to a certain order, and that they do not move themselves.

**249**  The mechanical philosopher, as has been already observed, inquires properly concerning the rules and modes of operation alone, and not concerning the cause; forasmuch as nothing mechanical is or really can be a cause.[f] And although a mechanical or mathematical philosopher may speak of absolute space, absolute motion, or of force as existing in bodies, causing such motion and proportional thereto; yet what these forces are, which are supposed to be lodged in bodies, to be impressed on bodies, to be multiplied, divided, and communicated from one body to another, and which seem to animal bodies like abstract spirits or souls, has been found very difficult, not to say impossible, for thinking men to conceive and explain; as may be seen by consulting Borelli, *De vi percussionis*, and Torricelli in his *Lezioni Academiche*, among other authors.[9]

---

[f]  Sections 236, 247 [the latter omitted in this edition].

[8]  Berkeley borrows from the *Opticks*, Question 31: 'And as in Algebra, where affirmative Quantities vanish and cease, there negative ones begin; so in Mechanicks, where Attraction ceases, there a repulsive Virtue ought to succeed' (Dover edn. 393).

[9]  This argument is reproduced from the *Essay on Motion* (*passim*).

**250**  Nor, if we consider the proclivity of mankind to realize their notions, will it seem strange that mechanic philosophers and geometricians should, like other men, be misled by prejudice, and take mathematical hypotheses for real beings existing in bodies so far as even to make it the very aim and end of their science to compute or measure those phantoms; whereas it is very certain that nothing in truth can be measured or computed beside the very effects of motions themselves. Sir Isaac Newton asks: Have not the minute particles of bodies certain forces or powers by which they act on one another, as well as on the particles of light, for producing most of the phenomena in nature?[10] But, in reality, those minute particles are only agitated according to certain laws of nature, by some other agent, wherein the force exists and not in them, which have only the motion; which motion, in the body moved, the Peripatetics rightly judge to be a mere passion, but in the mover to be ἐνέργεια or act.

**251**  It passes with many, I know not how, that mechanical principles give a clear solution of the phenomena. The Democritic hypothesis, says Dr. Cudworth, does much more handsomely and intelligibly solve the phenomena than that of Aristotle and Plato.[11] But, things rightly considered, perhaps it will be found not to solve any phenomenon at all. For all phenomena are, to speak truly, appearances in the soul or mind; and it has never been explained, nor can it be explained, how external bodies, figures, and motions should produce an appearance in the mind. Those principles, therefore, do not solve, if by 'solving' is meant assigning the real, either efficient or final, cause of appearances, but only reduce them to general rules.

**252**  There is a certain analogy, constancy, and uniformity in the phenomena or appearances of nature, which are a foundation for general rules; and these are a grammar for the understanding of nature, or that series of effects in the visible world whereby we are enabled to foresee what will come to pass in the natural course of things. Plotinus observes, in his third *Ennead*, that the art of presaging is in some sort the reading of natural letters denoting order, and that so far forth as analogy obtains in

[10] *Opticks*, Query 31: 'Have not the small particles of bodies certain powers, virtues, or forces, by which they act at a distance, not only upon the rays of light for reflecting, refracting, and inflecting them, but also upon one another for producing a great part of the phenomena of nature?' (Dover edn. 375–6).

[11] Ralph Cudworth, *The True Intellectual System of the Universe*, 2 vols. (London, 1678), Vol. I: I, 45 (p. 53).

the universe, there may be vaticination.[12] And in reality, he that foretells the motions of the planets, or the effects of medicines, or the result of chemical or mechanical experiments, may be said to do it by natural vaticination.

**253** We know a thing when we understand it; and we understand it when we can interpret or tell what it signifies. Strictly, the sense knows nothing. We perceive indeed sounds by hearing, and characters by sight; but we are not therefore said to understand them. After the same manner, the phenomena of nature are alike visible to all; but all have not alike learned the connexion of natural things, or understand what they signify, or know how to vaticinate by them. There is no question, says Socrates in the *Theaetetus*, concerning that which is agreeable to each person, but concerning what will in time to come be agreeable, of which all men are not equally judges. He who foreknows what will be in every kind is the wisest. According to Socrates, you and the cook may judge of a dish on the table equally well; but while the dish is making, the cook can better foretell what will ensue from this or that manner of composing it.[13] Nor is this manner of reasoning confined only to morals or politics, but extends also to natural science.

**257** It must be owned, we are not conscious of the systole and diastole of the heart, or the motion of the diaphragm. It may not nevertheless be thence inferred that unknowing nature can act regularly, as well as ourselves. The true inference is that the self-thinking individual, or human person, is not the real author of those natural motions. And, in fact, no man blames himself if they are wrong, or values himself if they are right. The same may be said of the fingers of a musician, which some object to be moved by habit which understands not, it being evident that what is done by rule must proceed from something that understands the rule; therefore, if not from the musician himself, from some other active intelligence, the same perhaps which governs bees and spiders, and moves the limbs of those who walk in their sleep.

**258** Instruments, occasions, and signs[g] occur in, or rather make up, the whole visible course of nature. These, being no agents themselves, are

g Section 160.

[12] *Enneads*, III, iii, 6 (*Enneads*, trans. A. H. Armstrong, Loeb Classical Library, vol. III, p. 133).
[13] *Theaetetus*, 178 D–E.

under the direction of one Agent concerting all for one end, the supreme good. All those motions, whether in animal bodies or in other parts of the system of nature, which are not effects of particular wills, seem to spring from the same general cause with the vegetation of plants – an ethereal spirit actuated by a Mind.

**261**    As in the microcosm, the constant regular tenor of the motions of the viscera and contained juices does not hinder particular voluntary motions to be impressed by the mind on the animal spirit; even so, in the mundane system, the steady observance of certain laws of nature, in the grosser masses and more conspicuous motions, does not hinder but a voluntary agent may sometimes communicate particular impressions to the fine ethereal medium, which in the world answers the animal spirit in man. Which two (if they are two), although invisible and inconceivably small, yet seem the real latent springs whereby all the parts of this visible world are moved – albeit they are not to be regarded as a true cause, but only an instrument of motion, and the instrument not as a help to the Creator, but only as a sign to the creature.

**290**    Body is the opposite to spirit or mind. We have a notion of spirit from thought and action. We have a notion of body from resistance. So far forth as there is real power, there is spirit. So far forth as there is resistance, there is inability or want of power; that is, there is a negation of spirit. We are embodied, that is, we are clogged by weight and hindered by resistance. But in respect of a perfect spirit, there is nothing hard or impenetrable. There is no resistance to the Deity; nor has he any body; nor is the supreme Being united to the world as the soul of an animal is to its body, which necessarily implies defect, both as an instrument and as a constant weight and impediment.

**291**    Thus much it consists with piety to say, that a divine Agent does by His virtue permeate and govern the elementary fire or light,[h] which serves as an animal spirit to enliven and actuate the whole mass, and all the members of this visible world. Nor is this doctrine less philosophical than pious. We see all nature alive or in motion. We see water turned into air, and air rarefied and made elastic by the attraction of another medium, more pure indeed, more subtle, and more volatile, than air. But still, as

[h] Sections 157, 172 [the latter omitted here].

this is a moveable, extended, and consequently a corporeal being,[i] it cannot be itself the principle of motion, but leads us naturally and necessarily to an incorporeal spirit or agent. We are conscious that a spirit can begin, alter, or determine motion; but nothing of this appears in body. Nay, the contrary is evident, both to experiment and reflection.

**292** Natural phenomena are only natural appearances. They are, therefore, such as we see and perceive them. Their real and objective natures are, therefore, the same – passive without anything active, fluent and changing without anything permanent in them. However, as these make the first impressions, and the mind takes her first flight and spring, as it were, by resting her foot on these objects, they are not only first considered by all men, but most considered by most men. They and the phantoms that result from those appearances, the children of imagination grafted upon sense – such, for example, as pure space – are thought by many the very first in existence and stability, and to embrace and comprehend all other beings.

---

[i] Section 207.

# Glossary

| | |
|---|---|
| *acrimony*: | pungent, acrid, sharp to the taste |
| *alkalescent*: | tending to become alkaline |
| *ambage*: | roundabout or indirect way of speaking |
| *archetype*: | a prototype, or of such a nature that other things are copied from it |
| *asperity*: | sharpness, tartness |
| *asymptote*: | a line which gradually approaches a curve without ever meeting it within a finite distance |
| *axifugal*: | centrifugal, tendency to move from the axis of rotation |
| *to banter*: | to trick or delude |
| *to bate*: | to omit, to leave out of account, to except |
| *to burlesque*: | to ridicule or mock |
| *to calcine*: | to reduce to quick-lime or something similar by burning, to desiccate by burning |
| *celerity*: | speed |
| *chicane*: | quibbling, the use of subterfuge or trickery in argument |
| *circumjacent*: | surrounding, situated in the immediate environment of |
| *compages*: | a structure composed of parts |
| *complection*: | combination |
| *congeries*: | a collection of things merely heaped together |
| *consecution*: | an inference or train of reasoning |

| | |
|---|---|
| *decussation*: | a crossing of lines or rays in the figure X, an intersection |
| *deobstruent*: | something that removes obstructions by opening natural pores or passages in the body |
| *diaphoretic*: | having the ability to cause or promote perspiration |
| *to dilate*: | to expand on, to discuss at length |
| *dioptrics*: | part of the science of optics that deals with the refraction of light, especially through lenses |
| *distempered*: | disturbed or abnormal, diseased |
| *ectypal*: | of such a nature that it is a copy of something else, in contrast with archetypal |
| *to embrangle*: | to entangle, confuse or perplex |
| *endued*: | endowed |
| *equicrural*: | having sides of equal length, or isosceles |
| *exercitation*: | an exercise, essay or discourse |
| *to extravasate*: | to let or force out a liquid, especially blood, from its appropriate vessel |
| *febrile*: | feverish, affected by or associated with fever |
| *fund*: | bottom; retina (of the eye) |
| *to gravel*: | to puzzle, confound |
| *hylarchic*: | ruling over matter |
| *hysteric*: | pertaining to the womb or a remedy for hysteria |
| *ichorous*: | a blood-like fluid in the veins |
| *index*: | the hour hand of a clock |
| *indiscerpible*: | incapable of being divided into parts or being destroyed by such a division |
| *to intromit*: | to cause or allow to enter |
| *jejune*: | lacking in solidity, naïve, unsupported |
| *let*: | an obstruction, impediment |
| *to moult*: | (literally) to shed feathers or an outer skin |
| *muriatic*: | pertaining to brine, salty water |
| *nisus*: | effort, endeavour |
| *outness*: | the quality or condition of being external to the mind |
| *obliquangular*: | at an angle other than a right angle |

| | |
|---|---|
| *parts*: | talents, gifts (in limited contexts, such as PHK, *Introd.* 17) |
| *peccant*: | unhealthy, inducing disease |
| *phrensy*: | frenzy, an agitated state or mental disorder |
| *praenotion*: | an idea or notion of something before having experience of it |
| *to presage*: | to foreshadow, to indicate in advance |
| *to prescind*: | to detach or abstract |
| *propension*: | tendency, propensity |
| *radious*: | forming rays of light |
| *raillery*: | good-humoured ridicule, banter |
| *railleur*: | one who practises raillery |
| *to retund*: | to weaken or diminish |
| *sapid*: | having a taste, or a pleasant taste |
| *scalenon*: | a triangle having three unequal sides |
| *scorbutic*: | pertaining to scurvy |
| *seminary*: | a place of origin or development, a seed-plot |
| *surplusage*: | a surplus or excess |
| *sustentation*: | sustenance, support or maintenance in existence |
| *taints*: | an infection, or a disease in a latent state |
| *terraqueous*: | composed of earth and water |
| *throughly*: | thoroughly |
| *vapid*: | weak, devoid of strength |
| *to vaticinate*: | to foretell events, to speak as a prophet |
| *viscid*: | viscous, sticky |
| *visive (faculty)*: | faculty of sight, ability to see |
| *to wiredraw*: | to stretch or strain by subtle argument |
| *without*: | (in some contexts only) outside, external to |

# Index

active 178, 198
  and volition 220
analogy 291
Anaxagoras 252, 253, 292
animal spirits 273, 318, 321, 322
archetypes 187, 188
Aristotle 248, 251, 252, 253, 257, 258
atheism 120, 195
attraction
  *see* force

Bacon, Francis xxxii, 102
Barrow, Isaac 12–15, 18, 19
blind perceiver *see* perception
bodies
  animal 316
  external 23, 24, 29, 44, 115, 121, 144
Borelli, Giovanni Alfonso 246, 248, 249,
  265, 300, 327
Boyle, Robert xxiv
brain 190
Browne, Peter xii, xxvii, xxix, xxx, 290

causes
  corporeal 103, 106, 108–9, 126–31, 198,
    217, 321–3
  finite (spiritual) 218
  God's causality 146, 197, 321
  not perceived immediately 157, 185

occasional 110–12, 113, 201–2, 329
  secondary 145, 198, 237, 251, 267, 323
certainty xvii–xix
colour 166–70
common sense 68, 72, 155, 156, 166
Copernicanism 219
creation 100, 230–6
Cudworth, Ralph 249, 328

Democritus 261
Descartes, René xiv, xvi, xxiv, xxviii,
  xxxiii, 34, 325
Diagoras (i.e. Anthony Collins) 290
dreams 216

empiricism xiii–xiv, xxxvi
Epicureans 120
essence 123
  unknowable 68, 123, 152, 208–10
evil (natural) 146–8
existence
  absolute 193, 216
  of perceivable things 84–5, 92, 96, 101
  of spirits 142
explanation xxiii–xxvii, xxxiv, 9, 30, 102,
  126–31, 254, 255, 266,
  325, 327
  *see* instrumentalism, laws of nature,
    natural philosophy

335

Cambridge Texts in the History of Philosophy

*Titles published in the series thus far*

Kant *Groundwork of the Metaphysics of Morals* (edited by Mary Gregor with an introduction by Christine M. Korsgaard)

Kant *Metaphysical Foundations of Natural Science* (edited by Michael Friedman)

Kant *The Metaphysics of Morals* (edited by Mary Gregor with an introduction by Roger Sullivan)

Kant *Prolegomena to any Future Metaphysics* (edited by Gary Hatfield)

Kant *Religion within the Boundaries of Mere Reason and Other Writings* (edited by Allen Wood and George di Giovanni with an introduction by Robert Merrihew Adams)

Kierkegaard *Fear and Trembling* (edited by C. Stephen Evans and Sylvia Walsh)

La Mettrie *Machine Man and Other Writings* (edited by Ann Thomson)

Leibniz *New Essays on Human Understanding* (edited by Peter Remnant and Jonathan Bennett)

Lessing *Philosophical and Theological Writings* (edited by H. B. Nisbet)

Malebranche *Dialogues on Metaphysics and on Religion* (edited by Nicholas Jolley and David Scott)

Malebranche *The Search after Truth* (edited by Thomas M. Lennon and Paul J. Olscamp)

*Medieval Islamic Philosophical Writings* (edited by Muhammad Ali Khalidi)

*Medieval Jewish Philosophical Writings* (edited by Charles Manekin)

Melanchthon *Orations on Philosophy and Education* (edited by Sachiko Kusukawa, translated by Christine Salazar)

Mendelssohn *Philosophical Writings* (edited by Daniel O. Dahlstrom)

Newton *Philosophical Writings* (edited by Andrew Janiak)

Nietzsche *The Antichrist, Ecce Homo, Twilight of the Idols and Other Writings* (edited by Aaron Ridley and Judith Norman)

Nietzsche *Beyond Good and Evil* (edited by Rolf-Peter Horstmann and Judith Norman)

Nietzsche *The Birth of Tragedy and Other Writings* (edited by Raymond Geuss and Ronald Speirs)

Nietzsche *Daybreak* (edited by Maudemarie Clark and Brian Leiter, translated by R. J. Hollingdale)

Nietzsche *The Gay Science* (edited by Bernard Williams, translated by Josefine Nauckhoff)

Nietzsche *Human, All Too Human* (translated by R. J. Hollingdale with an introduction by Richard Schacht)

Nietzsche *Thus Spoke Zarathustra* (edited by Adrian Del Caro and Robert B. Pippin)

Nietzsche *Untimely Meditations* (edited by Daniel Breazeale, translated by R. J. Hollingdale)

Nietzsche *Writings from the Late Notebooks* (edited by Rüdiger Bittner, translated by Kate Sturge)

Novalis *Fichte Studies* (edited by Jane Kneller)

Plato *The Symposium* (edited by M. C. Howatson and Frisbee C. C. Sheffield)

Reinhold *Letters on the Kantian Philosophy* (edited by Karl Ameriks, translated by James Hebbeler)

Schleiermacher *Hermeneutics and Criticism* (edited by Andrew Bowie)

Schleiermacher *Lectures on Philosophical Ethics* (edited by Robert Louden, translated by Louise Adey Huish)
Schleiermacher *On Religion: Speeches to its Cultured Despisers* (edited by Richard Crouter)
Schopenhauer *Prize Essay on the Freedom of the Will* (edited by Günter Zöller)
Sextus Empiricus *Against the Logicians* (edited by Richard Bett)
Sextus Empiricus *Outlines of Scepticism* (edited by Julia Annas and Jonathan Barnes)
Shaftesbury *Characteristics of Men, Manners, Opinions, Times* (edited by Lawrence Klein)
Adam Smith *The Theory of Moral Sentiments* (edited by Knud Haakonssen)
Spinoza *Theological-Political Treatise* (edited by Jonathan Israel, translated by Michael Silverthorne and Jonathan Israel)
Voltaire *Treatise on Tolerance and Other Writings* (edited by Simon Harvey)

Made in the USA
Las Vegas, NV
03 April 2023

70109878R00214